D0016399

THE EXOTIC IN WESTERN MUSIC

NORTHEASTERN UNIVERSITY 1898–1998

Music Advisor to Northeastern University Press

GUNTHER SCHULLER

780
E96w

$54.00
1575

The Exotic in Western Music

 EDITED BY *Jonathan Bellman*

Christian Heritage
College Library
2100 Greenfield Dr.
El Cajon, CA 92019

Northeastern University Press
BOSTON

78439

Northeastern University Press

Copyright 1998 by Jonathan Bellman

All rights reserved. Except for the quotation of short passages for the purposes of criticism and review, no part of this book may be reproduced in any form or by any means, electronic or mechanical, including photocopying, recording, or any information storage and retrieval system now known or to be invented, without written permission of the publisher.

Library of Congress Cataloging-in-Publication Data

The exotic in western music / edited by Jonathan Bellman.
p. cm.
Includes bibliographical references and index.
ISBN 1–55553–320–5 (cloth : alk. paper). — ISBN 1–55553–319–1 (pbk. : alk. paper)
1. Music—History and criticism. 2. Exoticism in music.
I. Bellman, Jonathan, 1957– .
ML55.E9 1998
780—dc21 97–16407

Designed by Ann Twombly

Composed in Minion by G&S Typesetters, Inc., in Austin, Texas.
Printed and bound by Thomson-Shore, Inc., in Dexter, Michigan.
The paper is Glatfelter Supple Opaque Recycled, an acid-free sheet.

MANUFACTURED IN THE UNITED STATES OF AMERICA
02 01 00 99 98 5 4 3 2 1

 CONTENTS

ACKNOWLEDGMENTS

THIS BOOK BEGAN, improbably, as a series of electronic mail brainstorming exchanges between myself and Ralph Locke. In addition to reading drafts of my essays, Prof. Locke has provided counsel, encouragement, and friendship throughout the project, from solicitation of essays to indexing, for which I am deeply grateful. James Parakilas also generously looked over my own writing with a cool editor's eye when it was most needed. William A. Frohlich and Gunther Schuller of Northeastern University Press have been most supportive and helpful to the project. I and all the authors would like to give copyeditor Larry Hamberlin a standing ovation for his superb, meticulous work. And my wife, Deborah Kauffman, has my undying gratitude, not only for encouragement and support, but more particularly for the computer processing of all the musical examples. They are artful, and this project and I are very much in her debt.

Introduction

JONATHAN BELLMAN

ON ONE LEVEL, the idea of "musical exoticism" is almost self-explanatory: it may be defined as the borrowing or use of musical materials that evoke distant locales or alien frames of reference. The essays in this volume address Western repertories that seek to remind us either of foreign lands (such as the Arab countries, Bali and Java, India, Spain) or various discrete groups within the home society who were regarded as exotic (Romani Gypsies, Native Americans, African Americans, even women). In each of these cases, characteristic and easily recognized musical gestures from the alien culture are assimilated into a more familiar style, giving it an exotic color and suggestiveness. On this nuts-and-bolts level, musical exoticism is a matter of compositional craft, of making the notes do something different from what they usually do.

The parallels between exoticism and musical folklorism—the use of folk materials from the home culture to evoke a national sound or sensibility—have been observed before, but there are crucial differences as well. Both folklorism and exoticism use musical gestures derived from folk, indigenous, or popular musics to flavor an artwork and to evoke a particular geographical and cultural frame of reference. But a Balakirev symphony, for example, which to American concertgoers sounds boundlessly exotic and suggestive of Ancient Mother Russia (truncated phrasing, modal melodic and harmonic vocabulary, low sonorities characteristic of Russian Orthodox Church music, high string writing suggestive of bleak, snow-covered landscapes), was intended more as a work of Russian nationalism, that is, Russian music for Russians. Conversely, the Gershwinesque inflections of Jim Parker's *A Londoner in New York* for brass ensemble might sound familiar to most Americans, but in reality have an exotic tint because they were penned by an English composer and project a bemused but excited visitor's unspoiled reactions to a new place and pace of life. For all the unmistakable musical codes, therefore, much depends on who is doing the composing and who the listening.

Scholarly interest in exoticism has seen a recent increase; to the four book-length studies cited by Miriam K. Whaples at the beginning of her essay (those by Griffel, Betzwieser, Schmitt, and Gradenwitz) should be added three more recent books on specific exotic "flavors": Roger Fiske's *Scotland in Music: A European Enthusiasm* (Cambridge University Press, 1983); the editor's own study of the Hungarian Gypsy style, *The* Style Hongrois *in the Music of Western Europe* (Northeastern University Press, 1993); and Mervyn Cooke's *Britten and the Far East,* Aldeburgh Studies in Music no. 4 (Boydell and Breyer, 1996), as well as articles, many written by our contributing authors, which are cited throughout this book. Another important recent contribution is Susan McClary's Cambridge Opera Handbook, *Georges Bizet: Carmen* (Cambridge University Press, 1992), which devotes a good deal of attention to contemporary French views of other cultures and classes, and to the various degrees of musical Spanishness, Gypsydom, and so on that play throughout the opera. A recent and extremely important resource is the article "Exotismus," by Thomas Betzwieser and Michael Stegemann, in the most recent edition of the German musical encyclopedia *Die Musik in Geschichte und Gegenwart* (3: 226–43). The article contains the most extensive exoticism bibliography in existence, to my knowledge, although it stops at 1993, does not always follow its own chronological divisions, and has the occasional odd omission (e.g., Anke Schmitt's dissertation). Also, such "exotics within" as the Hungarian Gypsy and the Native American, and the musics that grew up to evoke them, seem to be outside the article's purview. Other recent chapter-length studies include Lawrence Kramer's "Consuming the Exotic" (on Ravel's *Daphnis and Chloe)* in his *Classical Music and Postmodern Knowledge* (University of California Press, 1995), the chapter on Orientalism and music in John M. MacKenzie's *Orientalism: History, Theory, and the Arts* (Manchester University Press, 1995), and the chapter on Ravel and exoticism in Stephen Zank's Ph.D. dissertation, "*L'arrière pensée* in Music of Maurice Ravel: Sound, Style, and Virtuosity" (Duke University, 1996). And a great deal of attention has been shown in recent decades in disciplines outside music to discourses of Colonialist versus Colonized and Hegemonist versus Minority. Many of these nonmusical studies are cited in these pages. Unquestionably, much more work in both musical and nonmusical areas will follow in the coming years.

The groundwork for many such Self-and-Other inquiries was laid by Edward Said's *Orientalism* (1978). Said's study is a masterful and meticulous deconstruction of "Orientalism," which to that point was usually the standard name for the broad field of scholarly study of the Middle East (including biblical archaeology, travelers' reports, and studies in Arabic literature), but could include the study of Asian peoples and cultures as well. With constant use of primary sources to support his arguments, Said laid bare many of Orientalism's subtexts, including colonialism and racial and ethnic condescension, in what came to be a canonic text in the area of Cultural Criticism.[1] For all the weight of scholarly proof and righteous indignation that Said brings to the issue, though, his perspective is not crudely reductivist: he consistently acknowledges the complexities of the multifaceted West-East equation, the tendencies of the West to "read" the East not as itself but rather as an idealized object of desire, focus of evil, focus of good, bastion of purity, bastion of decay, or any of myriad other interpretations. Indeed, as he acknowledges in a later book (*Culture and Imperialism,* 1993), the Orientalist discourse is only one of many present in the East-West encounter.[2] There is, in short, a bewildering number of simultaneous conversations intrinsic to this cultural and geographic exchange.

Musical writers, however, have too often viewed the exoticism equation in more polarized terms. Whereas Kramer's aforementioned treatment of Ravel's *Daphnis* is a complex appreciation of the work, Joseph Kerman, in *Opera and Drama,* used a rather broad brush in castigating virtually all evocations of the exotic: Meyerbeer and Verdi in *L'Africaine* and *Aida,* Richard Strauss in *Salome,* and Puccini in *Turandot,* from the way "Calaf's vitality is exhausted in *chinoiserie*" to "the bogus orientalism lacquered over every page of the score."[3] Susan McClary (oddly, in light of the multifaceted treatment of musical languages in her *Carmen* book) takes the process one step further when, in her review of Charles Rosen's *The Romantic Generation,* she implies that his reasons for disliking certain musical works are wanting: "[Rosen] does not take issue with [operas of Bellini and Meyerbeer] because he finds in them something ideologically pernicious, such as anti-Semitism, orientalism, or misogyny; rather he grounds his criticism in old-fashioned hierarchies of taste."[4] She finds Rosen's privileging of what music sounds like over what it polemically may be taken to represent "old-fashioned" and therefore extraordinary, and in her list of the features that she and the reader, presumably, might find politically objectionable (if found in artworks that they admire) she equates orientalism with anti-Semitism and misogyny, freeze-drying Said's complex matrix of cultural dissonances into a crude, unidirectional hatred. Ralph P. Locke's ironic phrase about the critical response to musical exotica rings true here:

regardless of craft, inspiration, or even popularity, as long as the local color is not assimilated almost past recognition, the music is still somehow considered too politically charged to be "clean enough to praise."

But is exoticism simply exotic? At this point the picture grows cloudier. Exotic does not mean merely distant (indeed, distance is not even a necessary prerequisite). The suggestion of strangeness is the overriding factor: not only does the music *sound* different from "our" music, but it also suggests a specifically alien culture or ethos. To the fertile imagination, a different culture or distant place suggests far more than the sum of its external musical indicators—indicators such as new uses of percussion, an increased use of drones, or perhaps a modal scale. Such aural signifiers suggest the different mores, goals, circumstances, and practices of the exotic culture. In turn, the very acknowledgment of difference carries within it an implicit comparison and judgment; that is, the idea that "they are different from us" cannot help becoming "they are happier, sadder, more serious, more pleasure-loving, purer, more corrupt." For example, we in the West tend to associate alien cultures with a range of forbidden and desirable sexualities; indeed, well over half the musical exoticisms discussed in this volume have a specific and amply demonstrated sexual component. But whether or not we imagine an alien culture to be more sexual, violent, haughty, ancient, pure, or noble than our own, music with that particular tint of exoticism reminds us not merely of a geographic locale or ethnic group but more powerfully of an elemental sexuality, violence, haughtiness, and so on, be such qualities desirable, undesirable, or some measure of both. The exotic equation, therefore, goes well beyond familiar versus unfamiliar, and it is in large part the attendant cultural connections, tensions, and suggestions that make such stylistic blends as compelling, alluring, and ultimately troubling as they are.

Musical exoticism above all seeks to state the otherwise unstatable. The shock of a foreign phrase deployed in a native language is a twofold acknowledgment: first, that the hearer, though perhaps not a fluent speaker of the foreign tongue, will understand the phrase, and second, that no native phrase would have made the point in the same way—in other words, that the native language falls short. One speaks less convincingly of the strange and shocking, after all, in the language of the everyday. Inherent in the compositional choice to use a foreign language, musically, is the desire to evoke something titillatingly out of the ordinary. Nonetheless, musical exoticism is not equivalent to ethnomusicological verisimilitude, to the foreign music in its true form. The exotic equation is a balance of familiar and unfamiliar: just enough "there" to spice the "here" but remain comprehensible in making the point. Exoticism is not about the earnest study of foreign cultures; it is about drama, effect, and evocation. The listener is intrigued, hears something new and savory, but is not aurally destabilized enough to feel uncomfortable.

There are many common threads between the exoticisms discussed herein. In every case, we must come to terms with the relationship of exotic-sounding music to our impressions of the exotic people (both our impressions today and those of the culture from which the music emanated), our fantasies of forbidden pleasures and undreamed-of freedoms, or our fears and judgments. For all the commonalities, though, it will be seen that each exotic language is, in sound, use, and significance, unique. Each is shaped by specific cultural circumstances, the relative proximity of the people or culture in question, and the purpose for which composers choose to use it. It seems prudent, therefore, to avoid reducing the exoticizing process to a template; we seek to view each variety of musical exoticism on its own terms, rather than as another in a series of oppressive colonialisms, righteously judged according to the critical sensitivities of our own time. When Lawrence Kramer states, "The unsuspecting *Daphnis and Chloe* is not about to be charged with blatant Eurocentrism, colonialism, imperialism, sexism, capitalism, racism, or any other -ism,"[5] he implicitly acknowledges that the trap is hard to avoid when we confidently interrogate decades- or centuries-old pieces using modern critical apparatus.

The greatest danger inherent in approaching musical exoticism from a rigorously postcolonial perspective, then, is the breezy facility with which it may be judged and subsequently dismissed. No one denies the popularity and attractiveness of musical exotica, but it seems almost invariably to be castigated as artistically or culturally objectionable, as resulting in artworks that are somehow not as authentic as those free of exotic stimuli, as either imperialistic or at least a poor imitation of the real music of a particular foreign land or alien culture, and—following from all of these objections—as inhabiting a lower plane than other varieties of music.

But music that has proven as consistently captivating, resilient, and ultimately as powerful as much of this repertoire deserves more careful analysis, regardless of whether the conclusions reached are positive or negative, admiring or excoriating, or perhaps all of the above in shifting proportions. It is in this spirit that we put forth this volume.

THE EXOTIC IN WESTERN MUSIC

Early Exoticism Revisited

MIRIAM K. WHAPLES

READING ABOUT the exotic stage works of the fifteenth and sixteenth centuries, reading through those of the seventeenth and eighteenth, one is eventually struck by the degree to which, for most Europeans, the entire non-European world was seen as no more than theater, an endless Arabian Nights entertainment. Nothing of any lasting import could happen there; its people—so long as they were not actually fighting one's armies or besieging one's cities—were imaginary creatures whose deeds and words could be edifying or farcical, as one chose. Their principal occupation was to inhabit unusual landscapes and architecture and to wear astonishing costumes. Often they would dance. To modern eyes it is all very self-satisfied and naïve and irresponsible.

They order this matter better in literary criticism, which for at least a quarter century has been taking a close look at appropriations and representations of various Others and has exposed again and again the chauvinist/hegemonic/imperialist subtexts that they betray. Musicology, following a few years behind, has fixed on gender and sexuality as its designated arena of difference and discovered its own subtexts.[1] If we look at the musicology of exoticism, however, the outlook does not appear to have changed much over the last century. Although four books and numerous articles have appeared in the past twenty years, the subject has scarcely been affected by (as one writer delicately puts it) "the Western anthropologist's slow realization of some ethical complexities involved in representing non-European peoples."[2]

The term "Turkish opera" (*Türkenoper*) is a case in point. In the musical depiction of exotic characters and situations, seventeenth- and eighteenth-century composers almost entirely ignored what was known in Europe about authentic non-European musics. There was no interest in quoting or imitating the few published examples. Moreover, composers made virtually no musical distinctions among inhabitants of quite separate Eastern cultures: Turkish, Arab, Persian, Tartar, even Indian and Chinese. The eighteenth-century term *Türkenoper*—opera on any Oriental subject—is a problematic legacy of this indifference.

The term entered the twentieth century in Walter Preibisch's seminal study of the background of W. A. Mozart's *Entführung aus dem Serail,* where he writes it without quotation marks, that is, without distancing himself from it.[3] (To be sure, Mozart's opera is literally "Turkish"—i.e., it takes place in Turkey and not elsewhere in the Orient—and so are most of its sources.) Acceptance of the term has been continued in recent years, notably in the titles and texts of Margaret Griffel's 1975 dissertation and Thomas Betzwieser's 1989 one (published in 1993).[4] Anke Schmitt, in her dissertation, *Der Exotismus in der deutschen Oper zwischen Mozart und Spohr,* published in 1988, attempts to discredit the term—"which even in the most recent literature we find all too often"—and prefers "opera of Oriental color" (*Oper orientalischen Kolorits*).[5] Betzwieser rejects this formulation on the questionable ground that "Oriental color" or *couleur locale* should imply authenticity; he has no problem with *Türkenoper* and regards quotation marks as "essentially secondary" (*im Grunde sekundär*).[6] My own 1958 dissertation he faults for "the striving for differentiation among the various exoticisms"; it "suffers, above all as concerns the reception aspect, from the constant opposition of authentic to 'exotic' music."[7] Since the stated point of my study was to investigate the influence, if any, of descriptions and quotations of all non-European musics in the available travel literature on composers of exotic stage works before 1800, Betzwieser seems to be criticizing it for not begging its own primary question.

The fourth book, Peter Gradenwitz's *Musik zwischen Orient und Okzident* (1977), covers much of the same ground as mine, in that travelers' descriptions of non-European music are treated side by side with "exotic" European music. But Gradenwitz, who brings his study up to the late twentieth century and offers it as "a contribution to one of the many necessary points of departure for a universal history of music," directs it toward a multicultural breaking down of musical barriers.[8] (His book ends with an inspirational afterword by Yehudi Menuhin, who, one will recall, was then giving joint recitals with the Indian sitar virtuoso Ravi Shankar.) If Gradenwitz has a political agenda, then, it is one in which intercultural contacts are viewed as benign rather than suspect. Thus he can join the other writers in taking the exotic entertainment essentially at face value.

To do otherwise with any rigor would be to belabor the obvious. One comes up constantly against the sturdy naïveté of the "exotic" material. It partakes in every case of the common opinion of its age. Its deplorable subtexts lie cheerfully on the surface. It is of course Eurocentric. (How could it be otherwise?) Ethnologically it is obtuse or sentimental or both—but I belabor the obvious.

The Representation of Exotic Characters

Much about the early history of the exotic entertainment is obscure or ambiguous. What is incontrovertible is its antiquity. The earliest such activities clearly predate the first written descriptions, to say nothing of the earliest preserved music for them. It is furthermore likely that in the first stages, exotic entertainments were less aesthetic performances than violent games, as for instance in exhibition tourneys where knights jousted against others representing "Saracens" or "Moors." Details of the elaborate exotic costuming of men and horses in these and in the later *caroussels* (equestrian ballets in which these combats were stylized) survive in contemporaneous accounts, which extend well into the seventeenth century.[9]

A different kind of violence seems to have been the rationale of the earliest recorded exotic entertainment, the disastrous charivari devised under strenuous secrecy by the young King Charles VI of France and five of his courtiers in January 1393. Sewn from head to foot into linen costumes to which shaggy hempen "hair" was glued with pitch, and effectively disguised by masks, the six broke into the ballroom where the court was celebrating the third marriage of a favorite lady-in-waiting of the queen (a marriage that the king himself had sponsored). Howling like wolves and gesturing obscenely, they capered about unrecognized until the king's brother, who was not in on the secret, came incautiously close with a torch and set fire to one of the highly inflammable costumes. As the flames spread, four of the six were burned to death. Charles himself was spared, saved (reports Froissart) by his fifteen-year-old aunt, the Duchesse de Berry, who covered him with her skirts.[10]

We have three more-or-less contemporary descriptions of the accident, none by an eyewitness and each with its particular details. The monk of Saint-Denys who chronicled the reign of Charles is unrelentingly censorious, not only about the lewd behavior of the six but about the prejudice against remarriage of widows—a prejudice held in many parts of the realm by "certain foolish people"—that he believes prompted it. It is possible, then, that in the minds of its authors the escapade was suggested by low local custom and had little or no conscious exotic content. It is the chroniclers who make that content explicit—independently, and from different directions. Thus the monk of Saint-Denys reports: "Even more hideous than their cries were the Saracen dances [*choreas sarracenicas*] they took up, stamping their feet in, as I firmly believe, a frenzy of the Devil's prompting."[11] Froissart, who says nothing of prejudice or obscenity and regards the performance as no more than an "amusement to give pleasure to the king and to the ladies in attendance," says that the six were disguised in their shaggy costumes as "hommes sauvages."[12] In 1393 this term need have had no specific geographical reference. There were always barbarians without the gates; or it might relate to the largely imaginary ethnology that had been passed down faithfully for many centuries, from Pliny to Sir John Mandeville.[13]

Citing the royal sumptuousness of the wedding feast ("nothing was neglected that could increase the gaiety of the company"), the monk of Saint-Denys mentions that musical instruments played for dancing until the middle of the night;[14] but we know nothing about what instructions, if any, the musicians had for accompanying the ill-fated masquerade. In fact, we have almost no music for French court entertainments with exotic content until Jean-Baptiste Lully, although librettos for ballets began to be printed in the sixteenth century.[15] One of the earliest of these on an exotic theme, in a set of "Stanzas written hastily for the Ballet of the Princes of China" in 1600 or 1601, sets a topos (and a standard of fatuity) from which such verses were rarely to deviate. "From the mountains of China," where these princes never know liberty, they are enabled by Love to fly on invisible wings to France, where they may find "de plus douces prisons":

> Allez-vous en France, et là soyent vos geolieres,
> Ces beautez dont la fleur regne en toutes saisons;
> Ces beautez qui, naguere au monde retournées,
> Y tiennent des plus grands les âmes enchaisnées.[16]
>
> (Go to France, and there shall be your jailers,
> those beauties whose flowering reigns in all seasons;
> those beauties who, lately returned to earth,
> hold there the souls of the greatest men enchained.)

In court ballets for years to come, figures from the far reaches of the world—Turks, Persians, Ethiopians, Moors, (South) Americans, or "masques assez hideux et sauvages"[17]—drawn by the fame of the *beautez* of the French court, would arrive to recite verses in their praise. Turkish warriors, whose feats of love were as proverbial as their martial ones, laid down their arms and their hearts in tribute. The famous *Grand bal de la Douairière de Billebahaut,* a Carnival ballet of 1626 in which Louis XIII himself took part, deliberately carried this topos to a level of grotesquerie that could never be surpassed. Here the aged but still game Douairière (the "Dowager of Disorder," a distant descendant perhaps of the Lord of Disorder of the medieval carnival), accompanied by her fiancé, Fanfan de Sotte-Ville ("the darling of Boobytown"), receives extravagant amorous homage from Turks, Persians, Africans, Tartars, and "People of the North," who include both Greenlanders and Frisians and in one *récit* express themselves in an invented, vaguely Spanish-Catalan gibberish that, unlike the Italian lingua franca that appears in later exotic pieces, is not meant to be intelligible:

> Toupan mepchico doulon
> Tartanilla Norveguén laton,
> El bino fortan nil gonfongo
> Gan tourpin noubla rabon torbengo.
>
> Pinfa zapaly noncan,
> Britanu gogita moüescan
> Vallaguino nordamidon
> Golgon midarman ninbolbodidon.[18]

AMERICANS

Elsewhere in the *Douairière* some particularly egregious inanities are put into the mouth of "Atabalipa" (Atahualpa, the Peruvian king murdered by Pizarro in 1533). In one set of verses he is presented (by the official poet, Bordier), like any Eastern potentate, as a monster of vainglory ("and the sun does not shine in the heavens but to guide the messengers of my renown") subdued by the same adoration that has brought all the others to France. In another poem he describes himself as possessing an outsized head ("for I put into it all the cares of the world") and sitting on a perch.[19]

The representation of American natives, of which this may be the first on a European stage, continued to be marked by a peculiar awkwardness. Turks, familiar old enemies (and nominal allies) as they were, posed no such problem to the French. Librettists of all nations, in fact, agreed in depicting them in their various stereotypes: cruel barbarians, magnanimous tyrants, keepers of harems, clowns. Other Asians were far less well known, but they had always been there; they did not disturb the world. Essentially neutral and unproblematic, they could be imagined at will or mined for the splendor of their costumes alone. The Chinese Man and Woman in the final masque of *The Fairy Queen* (an adaptation of *A Midsummer Night's Dream* with added musical numbers) are presented in an elaborately arranged garden but sing as innocent primitives:

> Thus Happy and Free,
> Thus treated are we
> With Nature's chiefest Delights. . . .
> Thus wildly we live,
> Thus freely we give,
> What Heaven as freely bestows.
> We were not made
> For Labour and Trade,
> Which Fools on each other impose.[20]

(Their scene is immediately followed by a dance of six monkeys.) The characters of Metastasio's *Le cinesi* and of his *L'eroe cinese,* far from being constructions of an Other, might be so many cultivated Europeans.

But the Americans did disturb the world, and the confusion of their representation onstage only reflects the more fundamental consternation in Europe at large. The discovery of the New World had created an anthropological crisis: How did these hitherto unknown peoples fit into the same postdiluvian dispersion as the inhabitants of the relatively compact Afro-Eurasian world and thus into the monogenetic family of man? Or must their existence be seen as evidence of a separate creation?[21] More important was the long-standing debate about "savagery." On one side, and centuries before the Enlightenment vogue of the "Noble Savage," were those who saw the Americans as simple, innocent denizens of the natural world, close to their Edenic origins and representatives of a contemporary Golden Age. The other side, primarily but by no means exclusively men of the church, considered the nakedness of the "savages," the poverty of their material culture, and their presumed lack of government, laws, and organized religion to be outward signs of a debased and vicious state.[22] The controversy, with a family of related ambivalences, is echoed by virtually every representation of Native Americans on the musical stage.

Three decades before the *Douairière,* during Henri IV's wars against Philip II for the French throne, the Spaniards were demonized for, among other sins, their treatment of American natives. But captive Americans had been paraded through the streets of Troyes (1564) and Bordeaux (1565) before Charles IX, with all the ignominy of a Roman triumph, and some fifty Tupinambá had been displayed in a "native habitat" setting in Rouen (1550) to entertain Henri II—and to convince him of the desirability of establishing French colonies in Brazil.[23]

William Davenant's two English "operas" on American themes—*The Cru-*

elty of the Spaniards in Peru (1658) and *The History of Sir Francis Drake* (1659)—are arrant anti-Spanish propaganda. The first of these purports to be a history of the Peruvians, as presented by the Priest of the Sun; it is in six "entries," of which the fifth, beginning with "a doleful pavin," bears the weight of the title. The (painted) scene shows "a dark prison at great distance . . . racks, and other engines of torment, with which the Spaniards are tormenting the Natives and English mariners." On the stage, "Two Spaniards are likewise discovered . . . the one turning a spit, whilst the other is basting an Indian Prince, which is roasted at an artificial fire." Later in the same entry, to a "mournful air," three Peruvians enter, "limping in silver fetters. They are driven into the wood by an insulting Spaniard, with a truncheon." Reentering heavily laden with Spanish plunder, they collapse but are "raised by the blows of the Spaniard and fall into a halting dance, till the Spaniard reviving their weariness with his truncheon, drives them again into the wood." In the sixth entry English troops arrive to help the natives defeat the Spanish and drive them out. "These imaginary English forces may seem improper," Davenant acknowledges, but "in poetical representations of this nature, it may pass as a vision discern'd by the Priest of the Sun."[24]

The History of Sir Francis Drake (loosely based on the published account of his voyage of 1572–73) alternates between Peru and Panama, establishes its hero's amicable and benign relations with the natives, and culminates in his successful capture of a Spanish mule train laden with "wedges of silver and ingots of gold."

By the eighteenth century Indians have become *philosophes,* spokesmen for nature and rationality. In Frederick the Great's libretto for Carl Heinrich Graun's "tragedia in musica" *Montezuma* (Berlin, 1755), Cortez and his men are still broadly drawn villains, while both the Mexican ruler (like Cortez, a castrato role) and his betrothed, Eupaforice, are heroic and articulate. In other eighteenth-century *opere serie* on the Montezuma story, the two antagonists are on more equal moral ground; and by 1809 Gaspare Spontini's *Fernand Cortez,* under the influence of Napoleon, glorifies the conquistador as a noble hero pitted against the evil fanaticism of the Aztec priests.

The treatment of North American natives is even more problematic. Betzwieser claims that in André Grétry's *opéra comique Le Huron* (1768, after Voltaire's story "L'ingénu" of the previous year), for the first time "a central theme of the French Enlightenment was made the subject matter of an independent piece [i.e., rather than merely an *entrée* in a ballet]: the figure of the 'noble savage' was finally acquired for the opera stage."[25] But it is not at all certain what has been acquired. As with fairy tales in which the noble heart, however lowly, is revealed to be of noble birth, the title character—who has come to

France, he explains, because he had nothing else to do and it was "convenient"—turns out to be no savage at all but a Frenchman who was captured as an infant by Hurons and grew up believing himself to be one of them. ("Quel bonheur! Je suis François!" he rejoices upon discovering his identity.) The opera is a comedy of manners, as the woodland hero has his rough edges smoothed to make him fit to marry a wellborn French girl, all the while delivering himself of the enlightened opinions of his author. Thus several problematic themes are skirted here, among them miscegenation.

Not that this provocative matter was altogether avoided. The various operas on the Mexican and Peruvian conquests routinely include liaisons between Spaniards and native maidens. In 1657 Richard Ligon published the story of Yarico, a slave in his house on Barbados. A young British sailor in a scouting party on the South American mainland was rescued from an Indian ambush by the Indian maid Yarico, who fell in love with him and kept him alive in a cave until it was safe for them both to regain his ship. Upon reaching Barbados, he "forgot the kindness of the poor maid, that had ventured her life for his safety, and sold her for a slave, who was born as free as he: and so poor *Yarico* for her love, lost her liberty."[26]

Samuel Arnold's 1787 musical version turns tragedy to comedy. The sailor, Thomas Inkle, reforms and remains true to Yarico, while his man Trudge woos and marries Yarico's maid Wowski, who is apparently also an Indian but is black.[27] This second pairing is treated as vulgar farce: "A white Othello I, can trust / a dingy Desdemona," sings the well-contented Trudge. British public opinion is represented—and thus forestalled—by a character named Patty, who seems to be there for no other purpose, and who is entrusted with the last word:

> Sure men are grown absurd
> Thus taking black for white.
> To hug and kiss a dingy miss
> Will hardly suit an age like this,
> Unless here
> Some friends appear
> Who like this wedding night.

Clearly there were some who did. In the same composer's *New Spain, or Love in Mexico* (1790), Fabio, who has been in love simultaneously with a white woman and a native one and lost them both, sings, "I sobb'd by day and by night, / with a kind of pye-ball'd passion."

The touchier subject of a white woman romantically paired with a Native American, though rare, is not absent from the musical stage and seems to have occasioned no outcry.[28] *Polly,* John Gay's sequel to his *Beggar's Opera,* was written in the same year, 1728. Although the Lord Chamberlain prohibited its appearance on the stage, this seems to have been the settling of an old political score. In any case, nothing in the play was cited as injurious, and there was no bar to its publication. Like many another banned piece, it sold briskly.

Polly reached the stage in 1777 (forty-five years after Gay's death) and was revived in 1782 and 1813; and though its inspiration—and some say its tunes—are far inferior to those of *The Beggar's Opera,*[29] it would not be incautious to suppose that the continued currency of the piece over some eighty-five years owed much to a plot as piquant in its own way as that of its predecessor. *Polly* takes place in the West Indies. Only three characters from *The Beggar's Opera* reappear, among them Macheath, transported for his crimes and disguised in blackface throughout as the pirate chief Morano. But his author has lost interest in him: he is a mere villain, without a trace of the style or élan that in his earlier incarnation had won him two devoted wives and a perennial audience. Indeed, after an opening scene that shows some of the old verve—in which the bawd Diana Trapes proposes to sell Polly, newly arrived and unsuspecting, to the depraved planter Ducat (a scene that resonates with the opening one of *The Beggar's Opera,* where Mr. and Mrs. Peachum plan which of their gang of thieves to denounce to the law for the forty-pound bounty)—Gay has little use for any of his characters except as mouthpieces. Virtue, only implied in *The Beggar's Opera* by its opposite, in the sequel finds its insistent voice in the heroine (disguised for most of the opera as a young man) and the local Indians. Polly, ever the adoring and persistent wife, who has come to the islands to find Macheath—although she fails to penetrate Morano's disguise—learns his true identity a moment after the Indians have put him to death. Her comrade, the noble Indian prince Cawwawkee, learning *her* identity as a woman and fortuitously a widow, loses no time in proposing marriage; she accepts him without any show of passion, only pleading, like Donna Anna, a suitable delay for mourning.

LE BOURGEOIS GENTILHOMME

The centerpiece, and raison d'être, of Molière and Lully's 1670 comedy-ballet is an elaborate hoax. The title character, the gullible arriviste Jourdain, intent on mastering the niceties and prerogatives of his new station in life, has rejected his daughter Lucile's suitor, Cléonte, because he has higher social ambitions for her. Cléonte, therefore, prompted at every turn by his valet Covielle, has little difficulty in convincing Jourdain that the son of the Grand Turk wishes to marry Lucile. But because the young prince (who will be played, of course, by Cléonte himself) cannot wed a commoner, his future father-in-law must be raised to a suitable rank of Turkish nobility.

The subsequent "Turkish" scene, in which Jourdain is elevated to the rank of "Mamamouchi," demands separate consideration here as an exceptional case. For one thing, although as bizarre as anything in *La Douairière de Billebahaut,* it is both pointed and subtle. For another, although it has more authentically exotic elements than any other musical entertainment of its century (or the following one), it does not depict a single non-European character—only, significantly, French characters who pretend to be Turks. And third, although the scene has been much studied, and its sources in both dervish and less exotic ceremonial are generally recognized, one other essential source has so far escaped analysis in the musicological literature: a serious diplomatic episode involving French-Turkish political relations that was conducted by Louis XIV along the lines of an exotic entertainment, demonstrating the extent to which court ballet could pervade court life.

The affair in question is the visit late in 1669 of an envoy to France from the sultan of Turkey.[30] Earlier that year Louis had withdrawn his ambassador from Constantinople. The subsequent announcement that a Turkish diplomat, one Soliman Aga, was on his way to Paris with a letter from the Grand Turk raised extraordinary excitement and consternation in the French court. What was the import of his title, *Mutefaraca*?[31] Was this at last an ambassador with a letter of accreditation? (The sultan exchanged ambassadors with no European monarch except the emperor.) Or was he simply an envoy, little more than a courier? The prestige of France hung upon the issue of too much or too little ceremony.

The story, in great detail, occupies some sixty pages in the *Mémoires* of the Chevalier Laurent d'Arvieux, a young adventurer of good family (although he arrived at court as a mere Monsieur Arvieu) who had spent a number of years in Oriental travel. His knowledge of the East and his fluency in Turkish and Arabic made him indispensable and secured his fortune at court, for the king, after—and perhaps in spite of—due consultation with his ministers, made his decision: France would receive the visitor with *more* than usual ambassadorial pomp. Nothing would do but to duplicate Turkish diplomatic ceremonial itself, with authentic details to be supplied by d'Arvieux.

Viewed in the light of the court ballet, with its long tradition of royal performers, this decision seems to have been governed almost entirely by the king's sense of theater. Here would be a real-life Turkish spectacle—with genuine Turks alongside French ones—to put all previous "Turkish" ballets in the shade. It did little good for d'Arvieux to argue that such affectation would be seen as an acknowledgment of Turkish cultural superiority.[32] Prodigies of sumptuous exotic costumery and decoration had to be prepared and M. de Lionne, the secretary of state for foreign affairs, to be coached in his role of grand vizier, in which, reclining upon a divan, he would give audience to the distinguished visitor and receive his letter for transmission to the king.

In the end the French were humiliated. In two such elaborate audiences with the secretary, Soliman Aga firmly refused to deliver the letter to any hands but those of the "emperor of France," who, as a mark of respect to the sultan, must rise to receive it. This was too much. Nevertheless, and though still in ignorance of the envoy's rank, Louis could not resist the temptation to put on an even more magnificent Turkish pageant than the first two—one, moreover, in which he himself could play the starring role. After much planning and preparation he granted the royal audience, wearing a robe of gold brocade covered with diamonds ("so that he seemed enveloped in light," said d'Arvieux and other witnesses). But he remained seated, and the letter, which Soliman Aga was obliged to place on his knees, was after all handed to him by M. de Lionne. A quick perusal on the spot by d'Arvieux established that the crucial word *eltchy* (ambassador) did not appear; the audience was cut short and Soliman Aga, with his entourage, dismissed. The sultan's letter, as it turned out, was a peremptory demand that the recalled French ambassador be replaced without delay.

In the months that passed before his departure at the end of May 1770, Soliman Aga scandalized the court by grumbling in public over the disrespect with which he, and by implication his master, had been treated. It was in the aftermath of this debacle that the king ordered Molière and Lully to create a comedy in which the intolerable presumption of the courier would be satirized—again with authentic details to be supplied by d'Arvieux in "all that pertained to the dress and manners of the Turks." The *Mémoires* are disappointing here. D'Arvieux, most of whose writing evidently comes from precisely dated journal entries written while memory was fresh, describes his part in creating *Le bourgeois gentilhomme* absent-mindedly, with factual errors and without apparent interest in anything but his own brilliant success.[33] In later years a belief grew up that he was responsible for the actual composition of the Turkish scene.[34] But given his obvious disinclination to false modesty, there is no reason to think that his participation went any farther than the advisory capacity that he claimed for himself.

It is hard to find in *Le bourgeois gentilhomme* any parody that could be turned against Soliman Aga. If the subtext of the comedy-ballet—and not merely of the "Turkish" scene—was, as some think, a parody of the king's part in the episode, he may have been too engrossed to notice; in any case, the piece was repeated two days after its premiere and twice more within the week.[35] The following month it began a long run in Paris.

There was, of course, not the slightest reason within the logic of the story why the Mamamouchi scene, a practical joke masterminded by a Parisian valet, should have any authentic Turkish details at all. That they are so copious supports d'Arvieux's claim that Louis had indeed required them. The authentic basis of the scene has long been recognized to be a ritual of the Mevlevi dervishes that d'Arvieux had witnessed and describes in volume 2 of the *Mémoires.*[36] But there is nothing there about the reception of novices. Jourdain's initiation, with its lingua franca catechism ("Como chamara? . . . Star bon Turca? . . . Non star furfanta?") and echo of the Crusades ("Voler far un Paladina . . . Per deffender Palestina"), comes from a very different experience of d'Arvieux's.

Two centuries after his death Molière was suddenly accused of blasphemy; a number of French scholars had "discovered" in the Mamamouchi scene a satire on the ordination ceremony of Roman Catholic bishops. It was to put this late canard to rest that Pierre Martino found, again in the *Mémoires,* a more likely source.[37] The initiation was most likely based on the reception of knights into the order of Hospitaliers de Saint-Lazare de Jérusalem et de Notre-Dame du Mont Carmel, which the king was reviving and d'Arvieux was shortly to enter. The requirements for entry and the form of the ceremony had been published, and d'Arvieux, as socially ambitious as any Jourdain, was certain to have studied them. (They are eventually described in volume 5 of the *Mémoires.*)

Given this extraneous matter and the bizarre mixture of authentic Arabic and Turkish exclamations with passages in an equally "authentic" Mediterranean lingua franca,[38] it is strange to read that in 1704 (seventeen years after Lully's death) another Turkish envoy, one Hajji Mustapha, saw the scene and could find fault with only two ceremonial particulars, one of them being that a mufti would not behave in such a undignified way. The part of the mufti, who presides somewhat manically over the ceremony, was created by Lully himself in the Chambord performances; without his presence onstage in Paris, the role, and the "Turkish" scene altogether, had been considerably curtailed by the time of Hajji Mustapha's visit.

The Music of the Exotic Theater

> In Turkey there are also several sorts of instruments, with which they play most often in a confused way, without the use of consonances, except those that come by accident, and they are pleased only to hear a great confused noise.[39]

> If you will credit [the Chinese] they are the first who invented Musick, and they boast of having formerly brought it to the highest perfection: If what they say is true they must be greatly degenerated, for it is at present so imperfect that it hardly deserves the Name.[40]

> They [Iroquois prisoners in Québec] all began to sing, in order to show that they were not at all afraid of death, however cruel it might be. Their singing seemed to me very disagreeable; the cadence always ended with reiterated aspirations, "oh! oh! oh! ah! ah! ah! hem! hem! hem!" etc.[41]

> My father asked [Omai] very much to favour us with a song of his own country. . . . Nothing can be more *curious* or less *pleasing* than his singing voice; he seems to have none; and *tune* or *air* hardly seems to be aimed at; so queer, wild, strange a *rumbling of sounds* never did I before hear; and very contentedly can I go to the grave, if I never do again. His *song* is the only thing that is *savage* belonging to him.[42]

> Music, even in the most terrible situations, must never offend the ear, but must please the hearer, or in other words must never cease to be *music.*[43]

The foregoing quotations are of course outrageously tendentious. It would be just as easy to find favorable pronouncements on non-European musics, and Mozart's "terrible situations"—although the proximate subject is Osmin's rage aria—refers only to extremes of passion. Nevertheless, the quotations give a rapid précis of a rationale for avoiding authentic exoticisms.

Instead, for two centuries beginning around 1600, composers invented or adopted a number of musical codes for exotic characters and situations that appear consistently enough to be categorized. They include: (1) dances, (2) exotic instruments, especially when played by characters onstage, and (3) several miscellaneous stylistic effects, including what I have identified elsewhere as an "exotic" style of ceremonial march,[44] as well as unusual textures (especially in bass arias) and some conspicuous "primitivisms."

DANCES

Exotic dances are of two kinds in the seventeenth century. On the one hand are the dances of genuinely non-European provenance or connotation: the Moresca, Canaries, sarabande, chaconne, forlana. On the other are dances, frequently called merely "dance" or "air," rendered exotic in context by the identity of the characters performing them. Occasionally the two coincide, as in Lully's 1658 ballet *Alcidiane,* where a Princess of Mauritania dances "a Chaconne, of which the Moors were the first inventors." (Actually, it was originally imported to Spain from America—most likely Peru—around the turn of the seventeenth century.)[45] In the 1626 *Grand bal de la Douairière de Billebahaut,* "Grenadins"—described as the vagabond descendants of Moors expelled from Spain—include guitar players and "dancers of sarabandes, whose suppleness of body and fleetness of foot astonish all who see them."[46] (Notice the indication that at this early date in its European history the sarabande was still a quick dance.)

But there is no necessary correspondence between exotic dance and exotic character. For example, an earlier—if not the earliest—appearance of the sarabande is at the end of the 1608 *Ballet des dieux marins,* a court ballet without other exotic content;[47] and after the middle of the century Lully made the chaconne, now tamed and domesticated, the conventional dance with which to close any French or French-influenced opera. (Thus Henry Purcell ends *The Fairy Queen* with a "Chaconne for the Chinese Man and Woman.") On the other hand, in 1735 the Persians and Incas of Rameau's *Les Indes galantes* danced, among other things, gavottes (named as such in the score), as did the Turks of Rebel and Francoeur's *Scanderbe[r]g,* along with minuets.

An important occasion for exotic dances was the *ballet des nations,* a genre that was called into existence (a good many years before it was named) to celebrate the spectacle of national diversity. Quite possibly the first of these was a "grand ballet des Etrangers," performed before Henri IV in 1598, which included dances and *récits* by Turks, Persians, and "Indiens." The redoubtable Douairière, as we have seen, presided over another—certainly the most comprehensive of the genre. In the *balli* of Venetian opera the genre is represented by the "four corners of the earth"—Europe, Africa, Asia, and America—and other more miscellaneous mixtures of nations.[48] The *ballet des nations* retained its popularity throughout the seventeenth century: *Le bourgeois gentilhomme* ends with one (of Europeans only), and André Campra's *L'Europe galante* of 1697 includes Turkey among the European nations.

Les Indes galantes (1735) is the last high point of the genre. With it we are in a new world of exoticism, a world that encompasses both philosophical rationalism and Noble Savage sentimentality. Although all four *entrées* take place in the "Indies"[49]—the first three are Turkish, Peruvian (with a combined earthquake and volcanic eruption), and Persian—it is the fourth, "Les sauvages," added to the work in March 1736, that attracted the most attention in its own time and in ours.[50] Most of the attention centers on its big set piece, a peace pipe ceremony with music of particular suavity and elegance (example 1.1). By 1736 this music was already well known; it had first appeared almost a decade earlier as a harpsichord piece, also called “Les sauvages.” And while the original version lacks the polyphonic complexity of the later one, we are no less bemused to read that in it Rameau had (in his own words) “characterized the singing and the dance” that he had seen performed in public by two North American Indians in Paris in 1725.[51]

Ex. 1.1. Jean-Philippe Rameau, *Les Indes galantes,* fourth *entrée,* Peace pipe dance.

We cannot linger here over the widespread European idealization of the “savage” of which this is only one of the more remarkable examples. But we can be fairly certain that Rameau was characterizing not the actual Indian performance that he had seen so much as a real or imagined nobility of bearing, a natural dignity, a quality of soul. Suffice it to say that the piece caught the prevailing winds. Howard Brofsky cites no fewer than twelve subsequent borrowings of Rameau's melody, eleven of them for variations, suites, improvisations, and a "concerto comique" (by Michel Corrette).[52] The twelfth appearance is in the overture to Nicolas Dalayrac's 1787 opera *Azémia, ou Les sauvages,* where it is not only quoted extensively but actually danced to. Since *Azémia,* exceptionally for its period, takes an altogether dim view of savages, one may wonder what Dalayrac intended to characterize there with Rameau's melody.

INSTRUMENTS

At the end of the ceremonial scene of *Le bourgeois gentilhomme,* we read that "all the Turks, leaping, dancing, and singing around the Mufti, withdraw to the sound of several instruments *à la turque.*"[53] While stage directions at the beginning of the scene specify that these are to be played on the stage by "les Turcs musiciens, et autres joueurs d'instrumens," they are neither identified nor notated in the score.

What would have been recognized as Turkish instruments in France a century before the "Turkish" style of Gluck and Mozart? D'Arvieux had witnessed dervish ceremonies and could have informed Lully that they had been accompanied only by flutes and kettledrums,[54] but it is doubtful that, given the participation of Lully's normal orchestra, a meticulous attention to authentic onstage instruments would have been an important consideration. We can be confident, however, that they included *nacaires,* small paired kettledrums that had been known since the Crusades and had never lost their exotic connotations.[55] It is just possible that a flute also appeared onstage in the Mamamouchi scene, since one of the "dervishes," Philbert, is identified as an onstage flutist in the score of *Monsieur de Pourceaugnac* (1669). Since the rest of the performers impersonating "Turks" are identified in other scores only as dancers and singers, the only additional Turkish instruments likely would be tambourines.[56]

Lully began to include notated timpani parts in his opera orchestra five years later (*Thésée,* 1675), and there are other sporadic appearances of notated parts in the seventeenth century before they became associated with trumpets as a normal part of the baroque and classical orchestra.[57] Meanwhile, impromptu onstage percussion disappeared for most of the eighteenth century, showing up again shortly before its end. A march in the third act of François-

Adrien Boieldieu's *Zoraïme et Zulnar* (1798) is accompanied by a direction in the score: "Cette Marche doit être accompagnée de triangles [et] de tambours à l'usage du pays où se passe la scène" (this March is to be accompanied by triangles and by drums according to the custom of the country where the scene takes place). Is this a joke? The country of the action is never named, nor the *usage* specified. If not, might it be the only time that a European composer made any reference, however cryptic, to actual Oriental percussion playing?—i.e., the repeated rhythmic patterns (Turkish *usul*) on two differently pitched drums that many travelers' reports had described, yet which is never imitated in the "Turkish" music of either the seventeenth or the eighteenth century.

Two years later, Boieldieu's opera *Le calife de Bagdad* not only begins and ends with a fully notated "Turkish" battery, including two sizes of triangle, but also contains a mirror image of exoticism—a divertissement in which Kézie, the companion of the lovesick Zetulbé, attempts to distract her with a succession of songs in various *European* styles.[58]

In two late cases, named esoteric instruments are played onstage by dancers. John O'Keefe's 1785 pantomime *Omai, or A Trip Round the World,* a very free adaptation of the published accounts of Captain James Cook's three great voyages, has a choral scene in the Friendly Islands (Tonga) accompanied by "Drums, Naffas, Pagges, &c &c."[59] Spontini, in one dance of *Fernand Cortez,* introduces "l'instrument appellé *Ajacatzily,* que le danseur frappera ad libitum." Since the instrument in question is a gourd or pottery rattle,[60] we may wonder why it was to be struck; but efforts at authenticity could go only so far. In the first decade of the nineteenth century Spontini was still writing generic "Turkish" opera: the Mexican scenes are scored with the usual janissary percussion, and in addition to the rattle the dancers play (unscored) tambourines and cymbals.

OTHER "EXOTIC" EFFECTS

The "March of the Priests" that opens Act 2 of *The Magic Flute* (example 1.2) is often cited as one of the purest examples of Mozart's pellucid *Zauberflöte* or "Masonic" style. Despite the "Egyptian" locale (and its associations for Freemasonry) and the "magnificent Japanese hunting costume" in which Tamino makes his first entrance, this style has no apparent connection with exoticism. Nevertheless the march is coded. Its obvious model is the chorus of priestesses, "Chaste fille de Latone," in Act 4 of Gluck's *Iphigénie en Tauride* (example 1.3), but the tradition goes back at least to Lully. Example 1.4 gives the beginning of the "Marche pour la cérémonie des Turcs" that begins the Mamamouchi ritual in *Le bourgeois gentilhomme*.

Ex. 1.2. W. A. Mozart, *Die Zauberflöte,* Act 2, March of the Priests, opening.

Ex. 1.3. C. W. Gluck, *Iphigénie en Tauride,* Act 4, Chorus of Priestesses, opening.

Ex. 1.4. Jean-Baptiste Lully, *Le bourgeois gentilhomme,* "Marche pour la cérémonie des Turcs," opening.

Similar instances are found in the "Air des Américains" in André-Cardinal Destouches's "pastorale héroique" *Issé* (1699)—this air, the only example not associated with a ritual, is paired with a minuet in a *ballet des nations*—and in the "Air des Incas pour la devotion du soleil" in *Les Indes galantes.* Of the three marches in *Idomeneo,* only the procession to the temple in Act 3 is based on the same pattern. (Like the *Zauberflöte* march, it is in F major.) The common feature of all these movements is the rhythm of the first four measures; in addition, Gluck's chorus and both of Mozart's F major marches, as well as Lully's (the only example in a minor key), begin with a I(i)–V–vi(VI) progression.

Another arbitrarily "exotic" device is the bass aria in which the vocal part doubles the continuo (sometimes heterophonically). This texture also appears routinely in normal contexts (in Handel, for instance), but there the voice part remains "vocal" in character; frequently a differentiation is made in the voicing between a disjunct instrumental bass and a more conjunct part for the singer. (For an example, taken at random, see Achilla's aria "Tu sei il cor di questo core" in Act 1 of Handel's *Giulio Cesare.*) In the "exotic" adaptation, on the other hand, the voice part is "instrumental," usually ungainly, and primitive in effect. Osmin's "Das ist des Bassa Selim Haus . . . Ich bin in seinem Diensten, Freund!"—on bare 1–4–5–1 cadences—is the minimalist end product of the tradition.[61]

The beginning is again Lully, and the mufti is an ancestor of Osmin.[62] But the first appearance of this device came three years earlier in "Le sicilien, ou L'amour peintre" (part of the *Ballet des muses*), where we also find Lully's and Molière's first use of the Mediterranean lingua franca (example 1.5).

Ex. 1.5. Lully, *Ballet des muses,* "Le Sicilien, ou L'amour peintre," scene 8.

Ex. 1.5. (*continued*)

Other exotic inventions are too miscellaneous to enumerate here, but our next two examples of eighteenth-century "savage" music, by Rameau and Dalayrac, are similar in being unusually "realistic." Early in the fourth *entrée* of *Les Indes galantes* there is a characterization of Indian dance very different from the peace pipe dance (example 1.6). Here the absence of harmony and the repetitions of single notes approach a kind of stylized "primitivism" that would become cliché at a much later date. Dalayrac too, in the course of *Azémia,* presents *danse sauvage* in an unidealized way (and one that may even owe something to travelers' reports), in a scene where threatening natives dance about a Spanish prisoner, singing the words "Yak mala," first to a single repeated tone, then to a two-note melody (example 1.7).

Ex. 1.6. Rameau, *Les Indes galantes,* fourth *entrée,* Indian Dance.

Ex. 1.7. Nicolas Dalayrac, *Azémia,* Act III, Natives' Dance.

Our final entertainment is presented in the spirit of a quodlibet, combining strains of exoticism from two centuries and several countries in an unexpected counterpoint. In 1790 Dr. Samuel Arnold, Organist and Composer to His Majesty King George III, editor of Handel's works, and composer of the much admired oratorio *The Prodigal Son* as well as of the operas *Turk and No Turk* and *Inkle and Yarico,* presented a new opera entitled *New Spain, or Love in Mexico* (from which we have already quoted). The two principal American characters are the hostile chief Zempoalla (the name was, a century earlier, that of Dryden's and Purcell's Indian Queen) and the noble Cherokee Alknomook (also spelled "Alckmonack," "Alkmonook," and "Almonoak" in the score), who expresses himself in such language as the following:

> Thou that liv'st in ev'ry part,
> in the busy pulse doth beat,
> Panting in the faithful heart,
> glowing with the Vital heat,
> Canst thou mingle thus with Life,
> even cease to warm the breast?
> Never, till this mortal strife
> ending gives the Soul to rest.

In addition, he sings a Death Song (no. 17), which is the sole raison d'être of his presence in an opera about Mexico and of which more in a moment.

In the inevitable scene of Indian warfare and threatened torture, Zempoalla sings the lines excerpted in example 1.8, whereupon the proleptic spirit of Gilbert and Sullivan is met by that of Lewis Carroll:

> Zempoalla: This is war [trumpet fanfare], advance, advance!
> Chorus: Join the Warrior's glorious dance!

Ex. 1.8. Samuel Arnold, *New Spain, or Love in Mexico,* no. 18.

Although the music of the opera was advertised as "Entirely New Composed," the words and music of no. 17 had been in print, anonymously, for about a decade. This was the by then famous "Death Song of the Cherokee Indians" (example 1.9),[63] which is found in over fifty sources from its first appearance to 1854, both printed and manuscript, and from both sides of the Atlantic.[64] It was adopted into two American stage pieces before 1800, Royall Tyler's play *The Contrast* (New York, 1787) and the opera *Tammany* by Julia Hatton (New York, 1794); introduced *in extenso* into Maria Edgeworth's 1821 story "Rosamond"; and transformed by mid-nineteenth century into an American shape-note hymn called "Morality."

Ex. 1.9. Anne Hunter (?), "The Death Song of the Cherokee Indians."

The earliest prints of the song state that it was "An original AIR, brought from America by a Gentleman long conversant with the Indian Tribes, and particularly with the Nation of the CHEROKEES. / The words adapted to the Air by a LADY." Of the Gentleman nothing is known; a letter to an Edinburgh newspaper in 1791 names him Turner, and our first instinct is to cast him as the Covielle of this comedy. Here is Mrs. Hunter's own account of the poem's genesis: "The idea of the ballad was suggested . . . by hearing a gentleman, who had resided many years in America, among the tribe called the Cherokees, sing a wild air, which he assured me it was customary for these people to chaunt with a barbarous jargon, implying contempt for their enemies in the moment of torture and death."[65]

In the extensive literature on the song in the eighteenth and nineteenth centuries, its authenticity is not questioned. The nearest thing to an expression of doubt occurs in a diary entry of Hester Thrale. Under date of 18 April 1782 she writes: "Mr. Seward has picked up the original music—or *thinks* he has, of the Song the Indians sing while their Tormentors are preparing and inflicting various Tortures upon them: it is well known that the North American Tribes do make their Prisoners endure the most bitter Agonies before Death. . . . Mrs. John Hunter, Wife to the famous Anatomist has made a Base to the Tune; & set these words to it; I had no Notion She could write so well."[66] Mrs. Thrale, while proud of her literary accomplishments, evinces no interest in either music or ethnology; so it is more likely that here she is expressing her learned friend's slight uncertainty than any opinion of her own.

Anne Hunter, who had composed and published music to her own poetry, was certainly capable of composing a bass to a given tune. But John Koegel has taken conjecture a step further and proposed her as the actual composer of the melody, acting in a spirit of sympathetic interpretation: "Her statement might be interpreted to mean that she had encountered 'a gentleman' . . . who had inspired her to cast her thoughts westward to the subject of torture and death among the Indians, with her famous song being the end result of such poetic and musical ruminations."[67]

Since covert authorship tended to become an open secret in London's high social circles,[68] Mrs. Thrale's matter-of-fact association of Anne Hunter with both words and music of the "Death Song" quite possibly leads in the right direction. But given the stated provenance of the song, Koegel's suggestion still implies an imposture, and nothing we know about Mrs. Hunter suggests that she would publish a deliberate misrepresentation.[69] If the music did originate with her, it is more likely that it was a naïve attempt at a transcription of the gentleman's performance—but a "transcription" instinctively modified to recommend the musical character of the noble savage to European sympathies no less than his poetic character, since a faithful reproduction (supposing either her informant or her capable of one) would certainly have alienated any conceivable audience.

Mrs. Hunter is of course best known as a collaborator of Haydn, who set nine of her lyrics as canzonettas. We would love to know what he made of the Cherokee Death Song, but that is not on record.

"Forreine Conceites and Wandring Devises": The Exotic, the Erotic, and the Feminine

LINDA PHYLLIS AUSTERN

> [Music] carrieth away the eare with the sweetnesse of the melodie, and bewitcheth the minde, with a *Syrenes* sounde, pulling it from that delite, wherein of duetie it ought to dwell, unto harmonicall fantasies, and withdrawing it from the best meditations and most vertuous thoughtes to forreine conceites and wandring devises.
>
> —RICHARD MULCASTER, *Positions wherein those primitive circumstances be examined, which are necessary for the training up of children* (London: Thomas Vautrollier for Thomas Chare, 1581), 38

FROM THE TRAVELS of Odysseus to the voyages of the starship *Enterprise,* the Western mind has been called to vicarious adventure in distant lands of pleasure and danger through the voice of an exotic woman. We are first brought to the hero of Homer's *Odyssey* by way of Calypso's preternaturally seductive song, while an invisible space-siren wordlessly invites us "to boldly go where no man has gone before" as the male narrative voice fades out and images of a universe filled with unearthly dreams pass before us. The Western imagination has long considered music a phantasmic language through which the unspeakably alien may be evoked, and through which the exotic and the feminized erotic have the capacity to unite in forbidden and dangerous desire. Some of the most basic and powerful myths of Western culture present unfathomable female singers who would destroy the manly heroes who pass through their distant domains.[1] Moving across the centuries, as Catherine Clément and Susan McClary point out, many of the greatest operatic heroines remain foreign objects of sexual magnetism whose very Otherness and capacity to inspire obsessive love leads to tragedy and death.[2] And as any modern moviegoer knows, the tonal languages of exoticism and magnetic femininity are strikingly similar, relying on chromatic harmony, pulsating and often syncopated rhythms, irregular metrical accents, a deemphasis of the violin family (the backbone of Classical and Romantic art music), and sometimes scales or melodic patterns blatantly borrowed from specific foreign cultures—in short, on an aesthetically intriguing violation of Western High Art auditory norms.

Long before Western art music dichotomized Selves and Others by ethnicity, it did so through gender. The utterly stereotypical musical connection between the exotic and the feminine traces its roots at least as far back as the emergence of the tonal system and early modern discourses of music theory at the end of the Renaissance. The strident dualities and inherent hierarchies of pitch and harmony associated with tonality loaned themselves especially well to stock Western intellectual conceptions of dominant versus submissive, masculine versus feminine, and familiar versus strange, from the very beginning. The cusp between the Renaissance and modernity was at once marked by the first major wave of European imperialist expansion, increasing travel on the European continent, fascination with ethnographic description, and an absolute obsession with the place of women in society, each of which influenced musical style or ideas about music. Late sixteenth- and early seventeenth-century England in particular demonstrated an insalubrious and often schizophrenic fixation on distant lands and on womanhood and developed a musical theoretical language in which the feminine became foreign in a way not dissimilar from later geographically-inspired differentiations.

As the cultural critic Edward Said has pointed out, all peoples are ultimately involved in each other and none remains pure, homogeneous, or monolithic.[3] However, perhaps because the absolute differences between the secret cultures of men and women, or one nation and another, are not as distant as our desires would have us believe, we devise ways of emphasizing difference above similarity. The basic human tendency to bifurcate the world, its peoples, and their accoutrements into the familiar and the foreign, or the Self and the Other, is an internal process that only appears to take place in an external world of objective truth, for the division itself is merely an illusion born of mental process.[4] Human societies seem to possess a deep-seated psychological need to create the crude mental representations known as stereotypes, which in turn have generated, in the words of Sander Gilman, "a fantastic variety of images of the Other, some of them quite remote from observable fact but all of them at one time or another solemnly accepted as veritable truth."[5] As Bill Nichols reminds us in his perceptive study of modern visual ethnography, when one culture confronts another, especially in terms of specifically sensory representation, the resultant product will say as much about desire and the unconscious as about reason, science, or quantifiable reality. It is too easy to record and interpret what is experienced without recognizing one's own cultural values, prevalent mythologies of travel, and the valorization of certain forms of knowledge above others:

> From this perspective, the location of anthropology's Other may reside less in another culture than in the anthropological unconscious, as it were. Among other things, the anthropological unconscious might contain whiteness and maleness, and consequently the body of the observer; the experiential; the narrative conventions and forms of other cultures; the canonical conventions of Western narrative; the full indexical particularity of the image and its emotional impact; the erotics of the gaze; textual theory and interpretation; [and] the actual workings of the institutional procedures that determine what counts as anthropological knowledge.[6]

Although Nichols speaks of the arts of vision rather than of hearing, and of an era in which the scientific study of peoples and their cultures is a clear and recognized branch of human inquiry with its own methodology and boundaries, what he says applies equally well to a time when European sailing men committed alien tunes to Western musical notation and described such semi-mythical and associatively musical marvels as mermaids in the same canny language as all other creatures.[7] As Said reminds us, "Throughout the exchange between Europeans and their 'others' that began systematically half a millennium ago, the one idea that has scarcely varied is that there is an 'us' and a 'them,' each quite settled, clear, and unassailably self-evident."[8] To reinscribe alien wonders in familiar words or notes, or to bind or embed them within safely familiar frames, was, of course, to reinterpret, to control, and to take away some of their frightening distance and incomprehensible power. As Stephen Greenblatt explains in his study of the European conquest of the Americas, it is perhaps less important to distinguish between true and false representations of Westward Wonders than to recognize that European images of the New World tell us something vital about the sixteenth- and seventeenth-century European practice of representation.[9] Likewise, European narrative journeys to the supposedly more ancient East have always emphasized those qualities that "exiled it into an irretrievable state of 'otherness,'" and revealed more than anything the hidden longings and proclivities of those who literally re-presented this unfamiliar world, shrouded in their own dreams and desires.[10]

As the sixteenth century gave way to the seventeenth, England's fantasies of distant lands were pulled in two directions even as her hardened adventurers traveled east or west to seek that which was missing at home. Throughout the sixteenth century, England's practical interest in foreign countries and its awareness of cultural differences had increased enormously. The rapid growth of formal diplomacy, coupled with domestic prosperity and the political and cultural effects of the Reformation, led to increased travel through formerly alien European lands and to the inevitable exchange of cultural information.[11] English culture effectively remained violent and hierarchical, however, overwhelmingly dominated by local pieties, local tradition, local knowledge, and local prejudices against "foreigners" from even so far away as other English towns.[12] Stereotyped sets of characteristics ascribed by English thinkers to other European nationals extend back at least as far as the Middle Ages and had become quite important in a wide variety of literature by the early seventeenth century.[13]

The second half of the sixteenth century particularly witnessed an increasing xenophobia and patriotism as England redefined her political position in a changing world. Meanwhile, just beyond Britain, its domestic problems with foreign residents, and its paradoxically increasing taste in Continental music, art, and literature, lay not just the relatively familiar, if somewhat despicable, cultures of Europe, but also the gates to more alien lands further to the south and east. As we shall see, it was particularly Italy, with its warmer climate, its decadent mixture of the taints of Classical paganism and Catholic idolatry, and its open ports to the heathen East, that most caught the English imagination. In the opposite direction shimmered the Americas, the metaphysical contrary to the ancient Mediterranean lands onto which England had long projected fantasies of Otherness, creating paired cultural and discursive emblems of distance and desire. As the literary critic Peter Hulme explains, America became a new magnetic pole compelling a reorientation of the traditional axes of contrast between East and West by serving as a third variable, "an 'other' so radically different that you can no longer bring yourself to its threat by offering it your daughter, no matter how much it wants you to."[14]

It is hardly coincidental that the theatrical and narrative fictions of the Elizabethans and Jacobeans present the greatest lawlessness, magic, and passion in the distant lands to the east and to the west, perhaps best represented by Shakespeare's *Tempest,* in which both extremes join together. But undoubtedly the most revealing fictions of geography, conquest, and desire are to be found in those works that literally embody foreign locales as exotic, sexually available women; as Uzoma Esonwanne has remarked, discourses of colonialism and racialism have long transformed Woman quite literally into foreign territory.[15] And as Simone de Beauvoir once observed in the classic work that inspired subsequent generations of feminist theorists and cultural critics, Woman's very ambiguity and inescapable alterity at all points in Western thought have rendered her into the Other that encompasses all other Others in their position of inferiority and malleability.[16] For the later Renaissance, in one metageographical direction, the more distant shores of the Mediterranean had always proffered fantastic dreams of lascivious delight, embodied in willing, wanton flesh, for European travelers of all sexual proclivities.[17] In the opposite direction, as the literary critic Louis Montrose has pointed out, by the 1570s allegorical personifications of America as a nude woman whose unbound, flowing hair is crowned in feathers began to appear in engravings and paintings, on maps and title pages, throughout western Europe. In subsequent years such images worked their way into the cultural consciousness and effectively rendered the New World into an exotic, unbridled woman whose body could be explored, mastered, and bent by the most virile of heroes.[18]

Both of these geographical extremes are given flesh in John Donne's famous Elegies 18 and 19, in which the willing body of his mistress becomes a map of distant, exotic lands for his perusal and pleasure. In the first of these poems, "Loves Progress," the narrator sails downward from the native forest of her hair through more exotic Mediterranean sites, past "Syren's songs" and "wise *Delphick* Oracles," through the Hellespont, between "the Sestos and Abydos of her breasts," until he finally arrives at the most inexplicably foreign but inwardly feminine port on a woman's body: "her *India.*"[19] In the latter elegy, "Going to Bed," the poet urges his mistress to undress, each phase of the lengthy operation reminding him of some distant, semimythical destination:

> Off with that girdle, like heaven's Zone glittering,
> But a far fairer world incompassing.
> Unpin that spangled breast-plate, which you wear,
> That th'eyes of busie fooles may be stopt there,
> Unlace your self, for that harmonious chyme,
> Tells me from you, that now it is bed time.
> Off with that happy busk, which I envie,
> That still can be, and still can stand so nigh.
> Your gown going off. Such beauteous state reveals,
> As when from flow'ry meads th'hills shadow steales.
> Off with that wyerie Coronet, and shew
> The hairy Diademe, which on your head doth grow:
> Now off with those shooes, and then safely tread
> In this Love's hallow'd temple, this soft bed.
> In such white robes, heaven's Angels us'd to be
> Reveal'd by men; Thou Angel bringst with thee
> A heaven like *Mahomet's* Paradise. . . .

. . .
License my roving hands, and let them go,
Before, behind, between, above, below.
O my America! my *Newfoundland!*
My Kingdom, safest when with one man man'd
My Myne of precious stones: My Emperie,
How blest am I in thus discovering thee![20]

In both of these elegies we see the strong conjoinment of the pliant female body and the equally passive foreign lands to which an Englishman of Donne's era could travel and find eager, if not mystically ecstatic, reception of his superior skills. Donne's mistress becomes, like Beauvoir's primal Eve, "the absolute Other, without reciprocity . . . nature elevated to transparency of consciousness . . . a conscious being, but naturally submissive."[21] In these paired poetic fantasies, Woman is unequivocally united with the distant, the pagan, the unearthly, and the unexplored, primal realm of Nature. She becomes every remotely imagined region of physical space, and even suggests the portal into the mystical regions of eternity. As Esonwanne observes of similar textual topoi in the more modern world, "Tropes of otherness are so nomadic, so extraterritorial, that, prospectively or retrospectively, we would come to witness the emergence of a singular transcendental theoretical paradigm or methodology for the critical analysis of the technologies of othering and strategies of power."[22] What has too often gone unnoticed in Donne's highly erotic elegies of exoticism and conquest is the evocation of the distant "Syren's songs" and the magical, melodious chime of the unlaced bodice as the narrator begins his journey, again linking travel and the promise of sexual conquest to primal auditory arousal beyond the level of familiar mundane music.

The strong connection between the physically unfamiliar, the sensually arousing, and the raw primacy of unconquered Nature that we see in Donne and others of his contemporaries is also as old as the West, and ultimately unites femininity, music, and the distant places of the Earth into one of the most deeply entrenched of several widespread metaphors connecting Woman with the primeval. As Genevieve Lloyd remarks in her study of the Western understanding of "maleness" and "femaleness," "From the beginnings of [Western] philosophical thought, femaleness was symbolically associated with what Reason left behind—the dark powers of the earth goddesses, immersion in unknown forces associated with mysterious female powers."[23] The same innate categorical system of binary opposition that divides all Selves from Others, all approbatory familiar things from their inferior foreign equivalents, has often made orderly human artifice a wonderful, manly thing. And it has classified the simple, unrefined state of nature as a feminine one for Man to mold to his liking and thus bring to its full potential. Donne's contemporary Francis Bacon, often stereotypically if somewhat erroneously regarded as the father of modern scientific inquiry, endowed Nature with feminine form even as the New World was so embodied by the mapmakers and poets of his time and place. Bacon presents the proper task of Science as the control and domination of this rather eroticized Nature through the nuptial union that would help to set aside her disorderly aspect and allow her to become properly known through manly rationality.[24] As Beauvoir similarly observed centuries later,

> Once the subject seeks to assert himself, the Other, who limits and denies him, is none the less a necessity to him: he attains himself only through that reality which he is not, which is something other than himself. That is why man's life is never abundance and quietude; it is dearth and activity, it is struggle. Before him man encounters Nature; he has some hold upon her, he endeavors to mold her to his desire. But she cannot fill his needs. Either she appears simply as a purely impersonal opposition, she is an obstacle and remains a stranger; or she submits passively to man's will and permits assimilation, so that he takes possession of her only through consuming her—that is, through destroying her.[25]

The implications for the "modern" categorization of "native" peoples and their musics from Bacon's day through Beauvoir's and our own is clear and startling: in our film sound tracks and images, and often through the packaging and marketing of non-Western musics for urban Euro-American audiences, we have tended to project some sort of earthy "authenticity" and closeness to uncorrupted nature in diametric contrast to the high artifice of our "classical" forms.

Music, of course, is the most overtly sensual of the arts in Western thought, bypassing our dominant sense of vision, and going directly to the ear and the imagination. In fact, as John Shepherd reminds us in *Music as Social Text,* the silent, inert pathway of vision, which, more than the other sense, allows a distancing of the self from any object of study or interest, is the one through which male hegemony and dominance is most strongly established. In contrast, he explains, music, with its implicit qualities of social interaction, has long been considered more feminine and thus in need of control.[26] This same dichotomy between the relative physical distance of objects and the concomitant value assigned to their sensory apprehension was clearly recognized by the end of the Renaissance.[27] Even in terms of the auditory and visual components of language, as Michel Foucault reminds us as if referring to a premodern ancestress of Star Trek's space-siren, the men of Donne's and Bacon's era considered vocality "merely the female part of language," stripped of the intellectual power of the written word and the proper masculine key to esoteric discourse.[28] As an anonymous English music theoretical treatise, *The Praise of Musicke* of 1586, informs its readers, music becomes fully sublime only when it moves beyond nature to art—or, in the conceptual framework of the time, progresses beyond the fleetingly unstable feminine to the fully-ordered masculine.[29] Along with its original geographical fantasy of newfound lands, the late Renaissance resurrected an ancient embodiment of Music as a pliant woman, her body open to any fantasy from the sadistic to the nurturing. Donne and Bacon's more musical contemporary, the composer, music theorist, and former chorister Thomas Ravenscroft, borrows from Plutarch an image that would be equally at home in some of the poetic or scientific literature of his day: "*Musicke* in forme and habite of a Woman, her body pitteously scourged and mangled" by those who abuse her through barbaric compositional techniques and devices.[30] The author lingers almost lovingly on her battered body before suggesting "a medicine to *Her Maladies,*" at which point she quickly metamorphoses from an abused love-object into the hallowed mother he defends.[31] Through this sort of image, shared by the musician, the poet, the natural philosopher, and the mapmaker of the early modern world, metaphors of art meet those of science. As Gilman says,

> Unlike fictions of "high art," the fictions of psychology, biology, anthropology, sociology, genetics, and medicine relate, directly or tangentially, to perceived realities. Their point of departure is not the assumptions of a closed world of fiction, but the nature of humanity. But the very act of perception is of course colored by our mental representations of the world. Science creates fictions to explain facts, and an important criterion for endorsing these fictions is their ideological acceptability. Science, in spite of its privileged status in the West as an arbiter of reality, is in this respect a blood relation to art.[32]

In fact, such combined early modern fictions of music, science, geography, biology, and anthropology as these also cross into the bounds of pornography, which, in the words of Helen Haste, "trades on the male voyeur having privileged and gratuitous power over the object of his gaze."[33]

This presentation of Music as an alien Other in need of the same firm, manly control as distant lands and their inhabitants ultimately opened the art to the same set of stereotypes applied to such other distant, vanquishable, and potentially dangerous entities as foreigners and women.[34] Suzanne Cusick's recent reexamination of the famous Artusi-Monteverdi controversy reveals that Italian musical-intellectual circles at the turn of the seventeenth century were equally obsessed with descriptive ideas of feminine inferiority and submission versus proper manly mastery, suggesting a pan-European musical topos in which the weak and vanquishable was identified as feminine and the vigorously stable as masculine.[35] Such anthropomorphic gendering of intellectual entities from art and science relates strongly to early modern ideas concerning the notions of sexuality and social power.[36] In the words of Thomas Laqueur, "It is a sign of modernity to ask for a single, consistent biology as the source and foundation of masculinity and femininity."[37] Further, as Robert Padgug explains,

> The sexual sphere is seen as the realm of psychology, while the public sphere is seen as the realm of politics and economics. . . . Sexuality tends to be identified most closely with the female and the homosexual, while the public sphere is conceived of as male and heterosexual.
>
> The intertwined dualities are not absolute, for those who believe in them are certain that although sexuality properly belongs to an identifiable private sphere, it slips over, legitimately or, more usually, illegitimately, into other spheres as well, spheres which otherwise would be definitely desexualized.[38]

At no time has this been more clear than those years during which the Renaissance faded into seventeenth-century modernity, and during which revolutionary changes affected notions of the arts, the sciences, human social interactions, and conceptions of the world. What Michel Foucault says of sexuality—the interior realm associated with the woman, the homosexual, and other dangerous entities—clearly resonates with what has already been shown for music and for distant cultures: "The seventeenth century, then, was the beginning of an age of repression. . . . As if in order to gain mastery over [sex] in reality, it had first been necessary to subjugate it at the level of language, control its free circulation in speech, expunge it from the things that were said, and extinguish the words that rendered it too visibly present."[39] As Gilman points out, the cultural fantasies that incorporate ideas of gender and ethnicity into a web of analogical anxiety also rely strongly on ideas of sexuality, for "human sexuality is a wellspring for much of our fantasy life," positive or negative.[40]

The same ideas of maleness and femaleness, and of sexuality, that influenced the discourses of music and global conquest during the late sixteenth and early seventeenth centuries were based on centuries of accumulated wisdom that human beings were basically one sex, which, in its undeveloped form, remained pliant and female, and which, upon fulfilling its potential, became male. Sex was completely inseparable from power, for it was a world in which all things public and perfect were manly, and in which the standard of human representation was masculine, regardless of individual differences that rendered some men inferior and some women superior to others. It was "a world where at least two genders correspond to but one sex, where the boundaries between male and female are all of degree and not of kind, and where the reproductive organs are but one sign among many of the body's place in a cosmic and cultural order that transcends biology."[41]

Instead of perceiving the clear, enduring genetic distinctions between the sexes that inform our own attitudes, thinkers on the border between the Renaissance and modern worlds thus considered the female an incomplete, imperfect male, lacking only the heat at conception that could transform her into the superior sex.[42] Within the fluid framework of oppositions founded on this potentially metamorphic model, Woman, the "femall of the man," remained a weak, pliant vessel, and all possible paired contrarieties played off a single flesh until mind and body, like male and female, were so closely linked that conception might be likened to having an idea, and Man came to embody Mind as Woman embodied Sensation.[43] God Himself, the heavenly Father of All, was proof that abstract ideas were superior to sensory perception, for not only was He the God who could not be seen, but began as the eternal Word that would make itself flesh.[44] Thus purely sensual pleasures became the province of the weakly effeminate, while more manly beings, closer to the divine, reveled in the realm of abstract thought, guided by sensory signs to higher action. Even music itself can be divided into the appropriately manly and the softly effeminate by its purpose, either as an incidental aspect of some higher calling or duty, or as pure entertainment for the senses. Such a division represents the very one between the sexes, for men are creatures of public action where women are creatures of, or for, private pleasure. "Is it not strange that men should be so foolish to dote on women, who differ so farre in nature from men?" asks one English misogynist. "For a man delights in arms, & in hearing the rattling drums, but a woman loves to heare sweet musick on the Lute, Cittern, or Bandora: A man rejoyceth to march among the murthered carkesses, but a woman to dance on a silken carpet: a man loves to heare the threatnings of his Princes enemies, but a woman weepes when she heares of wars."[45]

Such a world that perceived absolute maleness and femaleness as qualitative rather than strictly biological oppositions had few firm rules about erotic dotage on male or female partners. To be a woman was to not be a man, to belong to an inconsistent category with no ontological foundation, to be "a mirror of inconstancy, idle fantastick, desirous of novelties, disdainfull, changeable . . .

and every way irregular."[46] To be a woman was to be sexualized rather than humanized, to remain strange, foreign, pliant, tractable in any encounter, as we have seen, and to prove physically procreative rather than intellectually creative in interaction with God's earthly image in Man. However, at the same time,

> There is, for example, no inherent gendering of desire and hence of coupling. It was in no way thought unnatural for mature men to be sexually attracted to boys. The male body, indeed, seemed equally capable of responding to the sight of women as to attractive young men. . . .
>
> But where honor and status are at stake, desire for the same sex is regarded as perverse, diseased, and wholly disgusting. A great deal more was written about same-sex love between men than between women because the immediate social and political consequences of sex between men was potentially so much greater. . . . whether between men or between women, the issue is not the identity of sex but the difference in status between partners and precisely what was done to whom. The active male, the one who penetrates in anal intercourse, or the passive female, the one who is rubbed against, did not threaten the social order. It was the weak, womanly partner, who was deeply flawed, medically and morally. His very countenance proclaimed his nature . . . *mollis,* the passive, effeminate one . . . the victim of a wicked imagination as well as excess and misdirection of semen. The actions of the mollis and the tribade [the woman playing the active role of the man] were thus unnatural not because they violated natural heterosexuality but because they played out—literally embodied—radical, culturally unacceptable reversals of power and prestige.[47]

The social hierarchies of late sixteenth- and early seventeenth-century England were full of sexual exchanges between men, and of literature and drama catering to those with homosexual taste.[48] On the other hand, the rather nonspecific sodomy laws governing the country at the time, punishing with death those who engaged in the rather nebulously "detestable and abhomynable vice of buggery commyttid with mankynde or beaste," seem to have represented not so much a set of forbidden acts of homosexuality or bestiality but the performance of such acts by those who threatened the social order—heretics, spies, traitors, or Catholics. The lure of such indefinite but thoroughly illegal, traitorous, and unpatriotic acts, whether in the negative or as a fashionable vice that one simply must try, was strongly linked to the thoroughly alien cultures of the Mediterannean and the newfound Americas, once again the malleable regions of fantasy, desire, and all that is not the Self.[49] As in Padgug's theoretical apparatus and Gilman's insight into the human condition, all fearsome Others seem to come together into the same region of the psyche that especially delimits private thought, private fear, and private pleasure, the irrational realm in which thought is obliterated by sensuality and bestial instinct.

As suggested above, the alien land that most caught the early modern English imagination, and from which England imported the largest number of cultural products, including music, was Italy. When one thinks of the Golden Age of English Culture, one quickly recalls, on the one hand, theaters brought to life with Italian characters and their fiery passions of vengeance, family loyalty, and erotic fury, and on the other, the sound of the madrigal, brought north from the land below the Alps, made respectably English through deft textual translation and native composers' reinterpretations of the relevant styles. If one were to believe the plays, prose fiction, and travelers' accounts, Italy was a land of pagan superstition masquerading as the damnable vice of Catholicism, of brilliant color, beautiful boys, and wildly wanton women. English travelers, following routes opened by increased diplomacy, returned with stunning tales of forbidden sensual pleasure, of whoring, poisoning, sodomy, atheism, epicureanism, and papal idolatry. According to the burgeoning science of geography, climate exerted specific effects on native peoples, and the Mediterranean man of Italy was quick and crafty, prone to vivid, fantastical dress and all manner of curious vice.[50] Roger Ascham, former tutor to the princess who later became Elizabeth I, a sober intellectual who professed to love Italian literature and culture, warns readers of his 1570 educational philosophy that, should a young, impressionable Englishman travel to that region without a suitably cautious chaperon, he will chart a moral course for himself as dangerous as Odysseus's fabled voyage:

> For he shall not alwayes in his absence out of England, light upon a jentle *Alcynous,* and walke in his faire gardens full of all harmlesse pleasures: but he shall sometimes fall, either into the handes of some cruell *Cyclops,* or into the lappe of some wanton and dalying Dame *Calipso:* and to suffer the danger of many a deadly Denne, not so full of perils to destroy the body, as full of vayne pleasures, to poyson the mynde. Some *Siren* shall sing him a song, sweete in tune, but sounding in the ende, to his utter destruction. . . . some *Circes* shall make him, of a plaine Englash man, a right *Italian*—And at length to hell, or some hellish place, is he likely to go.[51]

Even the native English reader must be warned against so much as the translations of Italian literature that clogged good London bookshops, for they were merely a plot to convert sober Anglicans to the vices of Catholicism. For, as Ascham explains, "mo[re] Papists be made, by your merry bookes of Italie, than by your earnest bookes of Louvain." If this sober warning is not enough, he adds that

> If some yet do not wel understand, what is an English man Italianated, I will plainlie tell him. He, that by living, & traveling in Italie, bringeth home into Engla[n]d out of Italie, the Religion, the learning, the policie, the experience, the maners of Italie, that is to say, for Religion, Papistrie, or worse: for learning, lesse commonly than they caried out with them: for policie, a factious hart, a discoursing head, a mind to medle in all mens matters: for experience, plentie of new mischieves never knowen in England before: for maners, varietie of vanities, and chaunge of filthie living. These be the inchantmentes of *Circes,* brought out of Italie, to marre mens manners in England: much, by example of ill life, but more by preceptes of fonde bookes, of late translated out of Italian into Englishe, solde in every shop in London.[52]

In a eulogistic anthology whose title almost prefigures the much later New World apothegm "the only good Injun is a dead Injun," *An Italians dead bodie, stucke with English Flowers,* a good English poet immortalizes the deceased Sir Oratio Pallavicino by exclaiming

> An English man Italionate
> Becomes a divell incarnate:
> But an Italian Anglyfide,
> Becomes a Saint Angelifide.[53]

The title of the collection, which was dedicated to the grieving widow, juxtaposes a grotesque image of necrophilic sexual perversion with the suggestion of a strangely metamorphic resurrection as the deceased feeds native flora, rendering the Italian into an utterly alien object of fear and fantasy.

But the most compelling fantasies of Italy borrowed, as Ascham's evocation of Circe and the Sirens suggests, the ancient and powerful topos of the seductive singing woman. To begin with, Italian music itself was perceived by the most sober intellectuals as pure sensory pleasure of the basest, most earthly sort; as Ascham's horror of papal piety suggests, even in the houses of worship "vaine soundes, to please the eare, do quite thrust out of the Churches all service of God in spirite and truth."[54] But there were even less ostensibly godly venues for musicmaking. As a Jacobean traveler to Venice, Thomas Coryat, describes one of the learned courtesans for which the city was famous, and who seem to have served as legendary tourist attractions for such disapproving visitors from the north, she is compellingly beautiful, trained in courtly arts, and clothed from head to toe in enticingly vivid and undeniably exotic jewels and garments. She shines in red, sparkles in gold and crystal, and smells enticingly of rare perfume. Even as Coryat condemns this despicably alien creature, an intense, erotic fascination stains his pedagogical voice, perhaps subconsciously meant to arouse such naïve young men as those discussed by Ascham nearly half a century earlier. Of all the sensual weapons available to this exotic being, described almost as if she was one of the unholy idols her people worship, the most dangerous, and perhaps unnatural, is her music. "Moreover shee will endeavour to enchaunt thee partly with her melodious notes that shee warbles out upon her lute," exclaims Coryat midway through his description, "which shee fingers with as laudable a stroake as many men that are excellent professors in the noble science of Musicke; and partly with the heart-tempting harmony of her voice."[55] Nothing about this Italian siren is remotely resistible or natural; the fact that her music combines the power of enchantment with the technical excellence of a male professional inverts the normal hierarchy of dominance and places him at her mercy, rendering him her sexual plaything even as she has become, unwittingly in his narrative of disapproval, the foreign idol of his worship. He therefore becomes blameless in any erotic encounter with this utterly un-English creature, a modern Circe to distract the modern moral traveler from his approved goal. More musical Englishmen, at least in the popular imagination, met more fearsome fates at the hands of even more sexually exotic Italians; Thomas Dekker and John Webster, for example, present a fictitious musician who has lost his sanity through the love of an "Italian dwarf," presumably of his own sex.[56]

Although Coryat left no indication of the music his exotic courtesan performed for him, a glance at English theoretical literature about music gives us an idea of what would have been suitable for a woman whose profession involves an emphasis on feminine sexuality, or even perhaps what might entice an imaginary Italian dwarf to an implicitly effeminate English musician. What John Shepherd says of stereotypically feminine music in the modern world—that it is equated with sex—was clearly recognized by Coryat's contemporaries.[57] The same Ravenscroft who so lingered on the imagined body of his beloved Music explains in the same treatise, published three years after Coryat's travelogue, that "*Enamoring* [is] a *Passion* as (more or lesse) possessing and affecting all, so truely expresst by none, but *Musicke* . . . inasmuch as *Passionate Tunes* make *Amorous Poems* both willinglier heard, and better remembred. I have heard it said, that *Love* teaches a man *Musick*, who ne're before knew what pertayned thereto."[58]

Love music was undeniably feminine music. As the radical Puritan preacher William Prynne explains disparagingly, amorous poems, like those mentioned by Ravenscroft, are invariably set to "effeminate, delicate, lust-provoking Musicke," which is the diametric opposite of the more godly, chaste, sober, and evidently masculine music to which psalm texts are set.[59] In less disapproving prose, the music theorist Charles Butler, elsewhere an admirer of the "feminine monarchy" of the bee kingdom, defines his unique "*Ionik* mode"—not to be confused with the more familiar Renaissance mode of the same name—as "an effeminate and delicate kinde of Musik set unto the pleasant songs and sonnets of loov, and such like fancies for honest mirth and delight, chiefly in feasting and other merriments."[60] Here Butler hints at the same sort of overriding sensuality that surrounds Coryat's exotic courtesan, bringing together auditory, gustatory, tactile, and other nebulous pleasures in musical style and its inseparable social occasion.

As the definition of "effeminate music" becomes more specific, we begin to see a unity of all of the sorts of Otherness associated through the Western psychohistorical web delineating the familiar and the foreign. What Thomas Wright refers to in his *Passions of the Minde in Generall* as "a certain kind of tickling symphonie [which] maketh men effeminat and delicat," and later as "a manifest loose effeminateness" of musical style, renders Music's metaphysical body female through a compositional style that is dominated by artifice, ornamentation, rhetorical excess, and a teasing, sensory delight that pleases the ear above the mind.[61] Both Butler and the earlier but far more famous Thomas Morley, whose name is perhaps most strongly associated with the "Anglyfication" of the native Italian madrigal in the early years of its English popularity, consider this import an effeminate genre. Morley and Butler both particularly cite the varied delicacy of madrigalian music, the mastery of compositional artifice required of the successful madrigal writer, and the frequent delights of love described in madrigal texts and illustrated through their music as the specific features that render madrigals feminine rather than masculine—all features shared by other contemporary anthropomorphizations into the incomplete or inferior gender. When Morley explains how to compose madrigals in his *Plaine and Easie Introduction to Practicall Musicke,* he uses language that suggests the caprices of a flirtation designed to gain attention, but that promises to remain pleasingly passive should the object be captured and won: "If therefore you will compose in this kind you must possesse your self with an amorous humor . . . so that you must in your musicke be wavering like the wind, sometime wanton, sometime drooping, sometime grave and staide, otherwhile effeminat, you must maintaine points and revert them, use triplaes, and shew the verie uttermost of your varietie, and the more varietie you shew the better shall you please."[62]

To this image of constant change of meter and direction, with its implicit addition of ornament and unexpected harmonic shift, Butler later adds that chromaticism, another standard aspect of madrigal composition, is in itself effeminate "becaus as pictures ar beautifyed with trim lively coollors, to pleaz the wanton ey; so this kinde is as it were coollored with delicate lively sounds to pleaz the wanton ear." In addition to this synaesthetic link between the more feminine sense of hearing and masculine sense of vision, Butler continues to tell us that "woords of effeminate lamentations, sorrowful passions, and complaints ar fitly exprest by the inordinate half-notes (such as the smal keys of the Virginals) which change the direct order of the Scale, flattening the Notes naturally sharp, and sharpening them which are naturally flat: and those in longer time; with slow Bindings and discording Cadences."[63]

Here one recognizes the chromatic alterations and modulations that later tended to signify exotic elements. William Prynne takes this idea to the next logical step, conjuring images that blend Pallavicino's blossom-bound body with Coryat's enticing lutenist as he presents an exotic, erotic musical language full of controlled ornament and wildly changing harmony, and which he clearly finds as disturbingly arousing as any wanton woman: "Modest and chaste harmonies are to be admitted by removing as farre as may be all soft effeminate musicke from our strong and valiant cogitation, which using a dishonest art of warbling the voice, do lead to a delicate and slothful kinde of life. Therefore, Chromaticall harmonies are to be left to impudent malapertnesse, to whorish musicke crowned with flowers."[64]

Auditory femininity is the enemy of strength, of thought, of honesty, and leads to a lazy life of ease—all terms equally applicable to the hated denizens of distant lands, who represent the inversion of Our values in music and in life. As if this were not bad enough, within the conceptual framework of the early modern era, in which like spoke to like and the metamorphosis from sex to sex was a frighteningly real possibility, music, the essence of effeminacy, could call one's son from the dutiful life and *turn him into a woman!* As the Elizabethan Puritan Philip Stubbes warns any good man who would read his words, "If you would have your sonne softe, wommanishe, uncleane, smothe mouthed, affected to *baudrie, scurrilitie, filthy Rimes,* & unsemely talkying: briefly, if you would have hym, as it were[,] transnatured into a Woman, or worse, and inclined to all kinde of Whoredome and abhomination, sett hym . . . to learne Musicke, and then shall you not faile your purpose."[65]

Not only is this description strikingly similar to some of Stubbes's countrymen's predictions of a good young Englishman's fate should he travel alone to the alien shores of Italy, but it also recalls virtually all fears of unseemly foreign influence. Music herself, Ravenscroft's sensual mother and the beautiful virgin "fitte to wedde mens eares and heartes unto her" of an earlier English music theorist,[66] embodies all elements of seductive, yet passive, sexuality. She is theorized as the alien Other, singing songs that call the listener to adventure in unfamiliar auditory territory, strikingly similar to the ideas of geographically distant musics that caught the imaginations of Europeans of succeeding generations.

The Alla Turca *Style in the Late Eighteenth Century: Race and Gender in the Symphony and the Seraglio*

MARY HUNTER

OF ALL THE "exotic" cultures that inhabited popular consciousness during the eighteenth century, that of the Ottoman Empire was one of the few of which a significant number of Western Europeans could have had some direct (albeit limited) experience. There had been occasional Ottoman envoys and embassies in various cities in Europe since the sixteenth century, but after the final military defeat of the Ottomans, reified in the Treaty of Passarowitz in 1718, Ottoman envoys and ambassadors were regularly sent (along with enormous retinues) to establish political alliances, cultural exchanges, and technological understandings with the West.[1] Although travelers' descriptions of Turkish music begin long before 1700, they continue in profusion during the eighteenth century, and the many musical treatises of the time also routinely mention Turkish musical devices or practices.[2] Janissary (i.e., Turkish military) bands were among the principal agents of cultural exchange; they played quite frequently in Europe from the early eighteenth century on and were found in a number of European courts after the Polish and Russian monarchs had ordered them in the 1720s. European imitations of these bands were commonplace by the second half of the century, and the *alla turca* style or topos, as it is normally understood, is based principally on janissary music.[3]

The *alla turca* style, however, as several commentators have noted, represents only one of several possible versions of Turkishness, and I take for granted that the version chosen has more to do with European interests than with anything intrinsic to the Turks or Turkish music.[4] Thus in describing examples of this style I am as interested in the musical *principles* underlying *alla turca* as in the particular Turkish devices employed; particular ways of deforming classic-period syntax turn out to be as important in this style as imitation, for example. Eurocentric concerns are as evident on the more general social and semantic levels of *turquerie* as they are on the level of musical syntax. For example, the Muslim authority figure in "Turkish" stories, plays, and operas was shown—not coincidentally, in a period of European history in which the nature of power was a pervasive interest—as either barbarously and irrationally cruel, as in many of the *Arabian Nights* stories, or as enervated and directionless, living only for ephemeral pleasures, as in Charles-Simon Favart's *Les trois sultanes* (1761).[5] Such portraits of power abused or squandered served European audiences both as thinly disguised warnings and as self-congratulatory comparisons; they encouraged notions of Western superiority and thus eventually justified the nineteenth-century political and economic domination of the East.[6] Similarly, at a time when the relation of women to an emerging public sphere was a frequent subject of discussion, the twin stereotypes of the wanton Oriental mistress and the submissive Eastern slave functioned as both warning and fantasy.[7]

Power and gender are not separate topics in late eighteenth-century versions of the Orient, however. Although in instrumental music the connotation of the *alla turca* topos is always hypermasculine saber-rattling barbarism, in opera the venue for *turquerie* is almost always a seraglio—ruled and guarded by men identified as Muslim and marked by janissary music, but inhabited by and centered on women. These women have a variety of ethnic origins and are typically identified by no obviously "exotic" musical topics. They do, however, still embody to one degree or another the Orientalist fantasies about seraglio women. A variety of obvious and subtle musical exoticisms paint a complex picture of the attractions and repulsions of male and female, dominant and submissive, compliant and resistant Others.

The Janissary Topos in Instrumental Music

DOMESTICATION AND EXOTICIZATION

Two distinct categories of janissary imitation can be found in late eighteenth-century instrumental music, often in conjunction, but sometimes separately; they have rather different stories, but both represent the tensions between assimilating and distancing musically exotic phenomena in this period. The first janissary effect was instrumentation, especially the use of such colorful percussion instruments as the cymbals (invented in Turkey and introduced to Western music through the janissary bands), bass drum, tambourine, and Turkish crescent, all of which were to be found in the authentic Turkish *mehter* (janissary band), as well as the triangle, which seems to have been a Western addition.[8] Although the *batterie turque* (the collection of "Turkish" percussion) started out as a marker of exoticism, it rapidly became assimilated into military or military-style music with few obviously exotic implications. Indeed, "Turkish" marches for band quite rapidly became indistinguishable from regular military band marches in the late eighteenth and early nineteenth centuries. The (now largely defunct) British custom of dressing marching-band drummers in leopard skin aprons and having them perform tricks with their sticks, even when the music is completely without exotic association, is a remnant of the profoundly Orientalist practice of hiring men of African descent to play the "Turkish" percussion, and hence an echo of the exoticism of the janissary bands.[9]

The meaning of the *batterie turque* is entirely clear in exotic program music or instrumental sections of operas such as the overtures to Christoph Willibald Gluck's *La rencontre imprévue* or Mozart's *Die Entführung aus dem Serail,* or the "Dance of the Scythians" in Gluck's *Iphigénie en Tauride.* However, particularly in conjunction with the military domestication of Turkish percussion, the extent to which, say, the *alla marcia* section of the last movement of Beethoven's Ninth Symphony, or the second and last movements of Haydn's "Military" Symphony, No. 100, connote the exotic is not clear. These symphonic examples of janissary instrumentation do not completely lose an association with an exotic topic—indeed, one reading of both these instances is that they enfold the barbarian in a Eurocentric universalism,[10] but their equally strong connections with local military music weaken the sense that their sole purpose is to reiterate the current caricature of Islam.

If the use of janissary timbres in military-style music became quickly domesticated, losing on occasion its explicit association with "Turkish" music, piano music with no *alla turca* associations could by the late eighteenth century handily be "Turkified" by the application of the "Turkish" or "janissary" stop on pianos so equipped. This stop provided "bass drum," "cymbal," and "triangle" effects.[11] Timbre, in this instance, could be used as the only indicator of exoticism.

The second category of janissary effect includes melodic, rhythmic, harmonic, and phraseological devices with no particular timbral associations. These musical characteristics beyond the use of Turkish percussion, well described by Miriam Whaples and Jonathan Bellman,[12] remained exotic throughout the latter part of the century. Indeed, as Bellman has pointed out, they persisted, barely modified, in the "Gypsy music" traditions (*alla turca* turned to *all'ongherese*) of the nineteenth century. Melodic "*turca*-isms" include repeated "hopping" thirds, turn figures, and frequent or repeated neighbor-note patterns like those found in the overture to Haydn's *L'incontro improvviso* (see example 3.1). (Mozart's well-known Rondo "alla turca" also includes all these.) In addition, the melodic characteristics of the topos may include an abundance of acciaccaturas or other "jangling" before-the-beat ornaments, as in Gluck's overture to *La rencontre imprévue* (example 3.2, and also the Mozart excerpt seen below in example 3.3c). With respect to rhythm, music in the *alla turca* style is almost always in duple meter; the first beat is often heavily accented and precedes one or more lighter beats, possibly imitating the janissary technique of "[marking] the larger rhythmic beats [on the bass drum] with a large drumstick in [the] right hand, while keeping up a smaller running figure with a light switch in [the] left hand."[13] Harmonically, *alla turca* music is often quite static, retaining the same chords for several measures at a time and moving quite abruptly from one chord (or even one single-harmony-phrase) to another. (Examples 3.1 and 3.2 exhibit these rhythmic and harmonic characteristics.) Alternatively, harmony is eschewed altogether in favor of unison writing, as in the opening measures of Gluck's aria "Les hommes pieusement," later treated by Mozart as variations (on "Unser dummer Pöbel meint")—which not only begin in unison but also retain prominent parallel octaves even when the texture is not unison (example 3.3).

Ex. 3.1. Franz Joseph Haydn, *L'incontro improvviso,* overture, mm. 20–25.

Ex. 3.2. C. W. Gluck, *La rencontre imprévue,* overture, mm. 12–20.

Ex. 3.3a. W. A. Mozart, Variations on "Unser dummer Pöbel meint," K. 455; theme, mm. 1–2.

Ex. 3.3b. Mozart, Variations on "Unser dummer Pöbel meint"; variation 1, mm. 1–2.

Ex. 3.3c. Mozart, Variations on "Unser dummer Pöbel meint"; variation 2, mm. 1–2.

ALLA TURCA IN PRACTICE AND PRINCIPLE: IMITATION AND TRANSLATION

If the *alla turca* style is considered primarily as an imitation of an original, the obvious and primary question for the scholar is the accuracy of the imitation. Answers to this question tend to focus on relatively small segments of the music.[14] If the *alla turca* topos is considered as a translation of a perception of Turkish music, however, then the primary question for the scholar becomes not the particularities of individual figures or devices, but the underlying principles of translation and the nature of the perceptions on which the translation is based. With this question in mind it becomes possible to consider larger spans of music. Both approaches are necessary, though the former is more common in the literature than the latter.

It is difficult to say which particular features of the *alla turca* topos—repeated thirds, ornaments, repetitive duple rhythms, and so on—most faithfully transmitted the salient characteristics of janissary music, since so little of that was notated. It is clear, however, that no European imitation matched the timbres or volume of the real thing. Johann Adam Hiller, for example, describes the "janissary band" at the Russian court in 1739, which was peopled by German court musicians, as "immer noch zu melodiös, und nicht genung [*sic*] irregulär oder türkisch."[15] Even given Hiller's overt desire to represent the janissary music as irreduceably savage and different, other commentaries confirm that the quality of the janissary sound was unreproduceable with European instruments. Not only that, but (in line with Hiller's comments) there was clearly a sense that it was not desirable that European music go beyond the acceptable norms, even in depicting a barbarian in a state of rage. Mozart's famous letter about Osmin's rage in his "Drum beim Barte des Propheten" illustrates exactly that point: "Passions, whether violent or not, must never be expressed to the point of exciting disgust, and . . . music, even in the most terrible situations, must never offend the ear."[16] This aesthetic would, of course, apply equally to the rage of a European character, but it was particularly important to state it with respect to a Muslim, where "crude" and "primitive" musical devices were perhaps all too easily at hand.

Miriam Whaples trenchantly points out that despite the individual features of Turkish music adopted more or less faithfully by European composers, the most striking aspect of the European version of Turkish music was its general avoidance of the *usul,* the repeated rhythmic pattern that structures the flow of the music. And even when a simple *usul* (like half note–half note/quarter–quarter–half) appears in European music (as in Mozart's Rondo "alla turca") it is not the invariable fundament of the piece, but rather a more or less coloristic device deployed intermittently. The *usul* was mentioned in many theoretical writings about Turkish music, and it was, as Whaples notes, by no means inaudible.[17] The reasons for the omission of a literal reproduction of the *usul* from European Turkish-style music are not clear. However, the *usul* has no obvious analogue in European music of that period, whereas the other surface features associated with the "Turkish" style were either relatively easily transferrable (the percussion instruments, for example, or the repeated thirds), or were reproduceable within the practices of eighteenth-century style in ways that the "isorhythmic" aspects of the *usul* were not.[18] At the same time, the *principle* of repetitiveness is quite characteristic of the *alla turca* style, as Thomas Betzwieser implies in his discussion of the "Marche des janissaires" included in Sébastien Brossard's unpublished *Collection de partitions de sonates.*[19]

Indeed, to think of *alla turca* as a set of principles of translation as much as (or more than) a set of imitative devices highlights the orientalizing mindset of the topos and suggests instances of exoticism that may not make obvious use of its timbres or melodic turns. And one need look no further than the comments of contemporary observers to find the relevant principles. Even travel and treatise writers who showed interest in Turkish or other Islamic music and described its instruments and repertory with some sympathy could not avoid partial negative judgments. These negative judgments fall into two large categories: deficiency, and incoherence or irrationality. Although Whaples's term "wrong-note style" also invokes the principle of deforming the familiar to evoke the exotic, it also suggests a level of dissonance that I have found to be relatively rare in the late eighteenth-century *alla turca,* and it also suggests a focus on tonal expectations that minimizes the importance of rhythm and form in this version of the exotic. At the same time it is important to recognize that in the absence of specific signs of "Turkishness," "deficiency" and "incoherence" must take particular forms to function as markers of exoticism.

Seventeenth- and eighteenth-century accounts of Middle Eastern music most often articulated the principle of deficiency with respect to its lack of polyphony or harmony. Even Charles Fonton, who made heroic efforts at cultural relativism in his *Essai sur la musique orientale comparée a la musique européenne* of 1751, reproached Oriental musicians for their lack of knowledge of proportion and harmony, calling the European reliance on harmony "the only advantage that European music has over Oriental":

> But what one can reproach them with is that, ignoring the rules of proportion in the choice [*assortiment*] of notes, they have no idea of music in many parts, nor of the sound [*ton*] divided into root, third, fifth, and octave, which forms the base

and fundament of our music and of everything that one calls simple or figured counterpoint. As a result, in a concert of Oriental music one hears neither bass, nor treble, nor alto, nor tenor, etc. All the instruments play exactly the same thing in unison, and cannot make but a single instrument, while in European music, the division of the sound into four furnishes, with [added] octaves, eight different parts, of which each is played by an instrument and which, nevertheless, united together and by means of the rapport and similarity among them, form a concordant and harmonious whole.[20]

Franz Joseph Sulzer's discussion of the *usul* demonstrates wonderfully how a principle of incoherence could emerge even from a reasoned and detailed discussion of Middle Eastern music. After describing the actual sound of the janissary band with words like "turmoil" (*Wirbel*), "clatter" (*Klappern*), and "noisy caterwauling" (*lärmendes Katzengeschrey*), he moves on to a description of the principles of the *mehterhane* as he imagines it "properly performed" (*gut aufgeführet*). Among the principles, of course, are the different "Taktarten" (*usuls*), of which he describes three. Of the third (a thirty-one-beat pattern) he remarks, "Not until now is the first bar over! But who can make sense of it?" (*Wer kann sich darein finden?*).[21] Even dissection and explication do not erase or even minimize the music's fundamental incoherence. For other observers, the lack of notation in Turkish music was further evidence of irrationality. Charles de Blainville, for example, noted that "the Turks have no rational system of music; they hardly [even] notate their songs."[22]

The Scythian choruses and dances from Gluck's *Iphigénie en Tauride* exemplify these principles quite well, both intrinsically and in context. Deficiency is more marked than incoherence (indeed, in places the music is all too coherent), but there are moments of awkwardness that could be read as representing a sort of irrationality. The opening chorus displays the *batterie turque*, the repetitive rhythms, and the frequent turn figures characteristic of this style. Although the texture is not unison, the largely parallel movement between bass and treble in measures 4–7 (example 3.4) suggests a contrapuntal inadequacy fully commensurate with Fonton's complaints about Turkish music. Unison itself arrives in measures 22–24 (example 3.5), as the seemingly inevitable movement to the tonic is deflected to a half cadence with a unison scale from the third to the fifth. This half cadence is answered by another four-measure phrase, whose expected four-measure conclusion is extended to six measures by a series of melodic non sequiturs. Although the mere fact of extension to six measures is utterly unremarkable, it is rendered striking not only by the ironclad adherence to four-measure phrases in the rest of the chorus but by the awkwardness of the motivic construction.[23] The final dance movement also breaks into irregularity at the end (mm. 89ff); measure 112 functions both as the end of a two-measure unit, following the pattern established throughout the movement, and as the beginning of a five(!)-measure phrase in which either measure 113 or 114 seems to be "extra," and the expected dominant chord in measure 115 is delayed half a measure (example 3.6). In fact, the final six measures would not disturb a dance pattern based on the six-measure phrases of the rest of the movement, but they give the impression of awkwardness or phraseological incoherence, especially at the end of an aggressively regular movement. This movement, more obviously than the opening chorus, exemplifies the principle of deficiency: there is more unison; the vast majority of the harmonies are in root position and involve nothing more complicated than a vii⁶/V; every motivic idea is repeated several times, either immediately or later; and the inclusion of either a rest or a half note at the end of almost every two-measure unit (except mm. 101–6) suggests not only a rather motoric repertory of gestures but also a certain deficiency of musical invention. Gluck then emphasizes the rudimentary character of his Scythian music by beginning the intersticial recitatives (both initiated by Iphigenia) with harmonies in exquisitely chromatic relation to the tonality of the Scythian movements.[24]

Ex. 3.4. Gluck, *Iphigénie en Tauride,* Act 1, scene 3, Scythian chorus, mm. 1–8.

The *alla turca* style in relation to actual janissary music, then, represents Turkish music as a deficient or messy version of European music rather than as a phenomenon with its own terms of explication and reference. The representation of the Other in terms defined completely by the presumed norm of the familiar is a colonialist and patriarchal strategy described by many writers;

Ex. 3.5. Gluck, *Iphigénie en Tauride,* Scythian chorus, mm. 21–34.

Ex. 3.6. Gluck, *Iphigénie en Tauride,* Act 1, scene 4, ballet 4, mm. 109–16.

alla turca style is yet another instance of the way larger social and political ideologies can be encoded in the music "itself."

TURKS AND OTHER OTHERS

Not only does the musical content of the *alla turca* style represent a straightforwardly "Orientalist" attitude to Turkish music, but the way this topos was used also exemplifies a classically Orientalizing blurring of boundaries among different sorts of Others. The transmutation of *alla turca* into *all'ongherese* has already been mentioned. Commensurate with this ethnic indeterminacy, several of the features of the *alla turca* style were used to signify general barbarity rather than Turkishness per se. The music of Haydn's overbearing Rodomonte in *Orlando paladino,* for example, is full of *turca*-isms, from saber-rattling measured trills, to a whole aria whose chief musical subject is a positively virtuosic lack of invention. This aria, "Mille lampi d'accese faville," reinforces its structural "Turkishness" with surface *turca*-isms (example 3.7). The use of the *alla turca* mode to represent general barbarity carries over into instrumental music of the period, which is full of moments that suggest barbarity or difference without identifying themselves through the use of percussion, or by extra-

Ex. 3.7. Haydn, *Orlando paladino,* no. 26: Rodomonte, "Mille lampi d'accese faville," mm. 11–17. (Trans.: "This war sword will hurl a thousand lightning bolts with burning sparks.")

musical indications, as "Turkish." For example, while the last phrase of the exposition of the last movement of Haydn's Symphony No. 104 clearly adds a sort of barbarity to the already-established peasant topos of the movement, the barbarians have no clear ethnic identity (example 3.8). The same might be said of measures 27–34 and its later repetition (mm. 262–69) in the last movement of Beethoven's String Quartet in F, op. 18, no. 1 (example 3.9), and of countless other moments that suddenly resort to a unison texture, repeated ornaments, unusual motivic repetitiveness, or a surprise minor mode, or that use some other exoticizing musical device that discards or diminishes a "normal" feature of the style. The social/political implication of such moments may be that there is a certain safety or comfort in exoticization; once "the Turk" (and his equivalents) can be contained by means of a caricature, that caricature becomes a normalized or domesticated part of "civilized" discourse.

Ex. 3.8. Haydn, Symphony No. 104 in D, "London," last movement, mm. 108–16.

Ex. 3.9. Ludwig van Beethoven, String Quartet in F, op. 18, no. 1, last movement, mm. 27–34.

Gender Alla Turca

The jangling simplicity of the *alla turca* style in late eighteenth-century instrumental music is so striking, so clear, and so exclusive as a marker of exoticism that it is surprising to read contemporary descriptions that conjure up quite different—even contradictory—images of this music. Such anecdotal and theoretical writings describe the janissary bands, of course, but they also often note both the religious music of the dervishes and a more domestic or "chamber" style chiefly distinguished by "pathetic and touching . . . soft and languorous" qualities.[25] J.-B. de La Borde's evaluative comment after pages of more analytic or "scientific" description exemplifies this: "The music of the Turks is not as lively as that of the Bedouins: there is a melancholy and gloomy aspect to everything they do."[26]

Lady Mary Wortley Montagu's 1718 description of music and dancing in the apartments of Fatima, the wife of the Kabya in Constantinople, also suggests an aspect of Turkish music quite different from the janissary bands:

> Four [female slaves] immediately begun [*sic*] to play some soft airs on instruments, between a lute and a guitar, which they accompanied with their voices, while the others danced by turns. . . . Nothing could be more artful or more proper to raise certain ideas; the tunes so soft, the motions so languishing, accompanied with pauses and dying eyes, half falling back and then recovering themselves in so artful a manner that I am very positive the coldest and most rigid prude on earth could not have looked upon them without thinking of something not to be spoke of. . . . I can assure you the music is extremely pathetic.[27]

Particularly striking in comparison to the usual connotations of the *alla turca* style are the pervasively "feminine" adjectives and settings of these descriptions and others like them, which fall squarely into the notion of the Orient *tout court* as feminine. It is almost a truism of current considerations of Orientalism that "the Orient," "the Other," and "the feminine" are inextricably tied up with each other, and that the Orient itself plays the feminine role of the to-be-penetrated object to the Occident's masculine role of the exploring and subduing subject. In studies of primarily nineteenth-century Orientalist artworks and discourses, the figure of the voluptuous Oriental woman, or her multiplication in the seraglio (for example, Ingres's *Turkish Bath*) is said to encapsulate and (literally) embody the Orient's mystery, allure, and political, sexual, and commercial availability.[28] The roots of the nineteenth-century feminization of the Orient go deep into the preceding centuries, as Wortley Montagu's and La Borde's comments suggest,[29] but the pervasiveness of feminine and feminizing imagery about the Orient raises a question about why the only clear musical way of representing the Islamic world in the eighteenth century was the excessive masculinity of the janissary topos. The standard explanations for the use of janissary sounds for this purpose have to do with the ready availability of janissary bands—composers had something specific to imitate—and with the perception of the Ottoman Empire as a primarily military threat.[30] These explanations are perfectly plausible, but they neither take account of the larger analytical context of Orientalism, nor—more importantly in this context—make sense of that most gendered of all Oriental settings, the seraglio.

In the eighteenth century, as in other times, the seraglio functioned as a paradigm of the Orient, with respect to the extremes of domination and submission, of irrational power, capricious cruelty, and sexual abandon it seemed to allow, as well as the unbridled eroticism—both homo- and heterosexual—it was thought to encourage. The seraglio represented both political and sexual relations; indeed, it was an exotic version of absolutism rendered both appealing and repellent by the gendered clarity of its social divisions, and there is scarcely a "Turkish" story or opera in the eighteenth century that does not include it or its equivalent. Despite the clarity of its social divisions, however, the music of seraglio operas tells a more complex story, particularly with respect to the intersections of gender and ethnicity.

THE SERAGLIO AND OPERA

By far the most famous opera on a Turkish theme is Mozart's *Die Entführung aus dem Serail,* whose well-known story involves the rescue of a European princess from a harem whose ruler has nefarious designs upon her. Her rescuer is her true love, a European prince. Their escape is thwarted, and all looks lost until the Pasha (himself a renegade European), discovering that Belmonte is the son of his worst enemy, gives him a reprieve as a demonstration of greater magnanimity than his enemy would have shown; he then relinquishes his own interest in the princess, bestowing both mercy and a blessing on the fortunate couple. The comedy is provided primarily by the lower-class characters, chief among whom is Osmin, the Pasha's principal servant, overseer of his estate. This story of true love and rescue, of mercy and nobility, and also of comic ineptitude and hypocrisy, uses both a general plot archetype and a series of character types common to many Turkish operas during this period.[31] Gluck's and Louis Hurtaut Dancourt's *opéra comique La rencontre imprévue* (1764) and

Haydn's and Karl Frieberth's *L'incontro improvviso* (Eszterháza, 1775)—actually a reworking of Dancourt's libretto and, to a lesser extent, Gluck's music—are, after Mozart's canonic opera, the best-known examples.[32] Niccolò Jommelli's *La schiava liberata* (Ludwigsburg, 1768, libretto by Gaetano Martinelli)[33] and Mozart's unfinished *Zaide* (1779–80, libretto by Johann Andreas Schachtner) are two other operas on this theme that remain on the edges of the repertory today. Antonio Salieri's *Tarare* (Paris, 1787) and its Italian adaptation *Axur* (Vienna, 1788) refer to this plot structure, as do Giovanni Paisiello's *L'arabo cortese* (Naples, 1769) and the second act of Pasquale Anfossi's *Isabella e Rodrigo* (Venice 1776). André Grétry's *La caravane du Caire* (Paris, 1783) was perhaps the single most successful opera on this theme during this period, receiving 506 performances, which extended well into the nineteenth century. In addition to these and many other late eighteenth-century operatic versions of this story, this theme is found in innumerable intersticial ballets in the second half of the century, and in spoken form at least as early as the 1720s in the *théâtre de la foire* repertory, as Thomas Betzwieser has shown; in addition, as W. Daniel Wilson has suggested, it was comparably popular on the German stage.[34]

The seraglio is also central to operatic works that do not replay the captivity, rescue, and dispensation theme. To take only two well-known examples, Favart's and Paul-César Gibert's immensely popular *Les trois sultanes,* which involves the amorous subduing of a bored and aimless sultan by the wily French slave Roxelane, is also about the politics of the seraglio; and even Beauty's (Zémire's) isolation in a foreign land and imprisonment by a monstrous Beast (Azor) in Jean-François Marmontel's and André Grétry's *Zémire et Azor* (1771) might be considered related to the seraglio stories current at the time.

Despite the eighteenth-century reliance on the seraglio as the location for Turkish stories, however, the eighteenth-century versions of the Orient that I have examined differ from the later literary representations discussed by Lisa Lowe and others, as well as from the later operatic repertory, in that they typically do not fold the primary markers of Otherness into the single image of the voluptuous Oriental woman, but rather distribute them among a variety of character types, divided by class and by gender.[35]

MEN *ALLA TURCA:* TWO SIDES OF AN ORIENTAL COIN

We have already noted that the *alla turca* style in eighteenth-century opera is associated with extreme masculinity (bravado, fierceness, an obsessive interest in domination); these highly gendered qualities are then mapped, in a classically Orientalizing manner, onto clear markers of ethnic difference. Despite the referential clarity of the *alla turca* style, however, the operatic men marked by this musical topos are not a monolithic group, and the "Oriental" qualities they display are variously and multivalently attached to familiar operatic stereotypes. W. Daniel Wilson points out that the qualities of "Turkishness" or of the male Islamic character that the eighteenth century chose to represent were complicated and often ambivalent.[36] From the earliest days of the Crusades, the Muslim was marked as simultaneously cruel and sensual, barbaric and sybaritic, swashbuckling and indolent; by the mid-eighteenth century, and particularly during the Russo-Turkish war of 1768–74, when the Ottoman Empire's weakness was publicly demonstrated, and (not coincidentally) when the majority of "Turkish" operas were written,[37] the dualities of the old stereotype were modified and complicated by a desire to represent the Turk (or one version of the Turk) as almost Christian, or at least as enlightened. Wilson describes how these potentially incompatible notions of Turkishness were divided between the enlightened Pashas and the fleshly, out-of-control "Osmin equivalents (my term, not Wilson's)." The former tend toward Enlightenment despite a propensity for irrational cruelty; their "nobility" is recognizable as such by virtue of its resemblance to dispensations of mercy and justice by such characters as Mozart's and Caterino Mazzolà's Emperor Titus,[38] or to the orderly transfer of power to the next generation, as represented in Mozart's and Giambattista Varesco's *Idomeneo.* The latter are hopelessly enmeshed in barbarity and superstition; lower-class Turks (seraglio guards and dervishes) represent the anti-ideal, their undesirable "Oriental" characteristics reinforced by qualities comparable to those of comic opera buffoons (e.g., Leporello or Papageno). These characters lose control rather than exercising restraint (witness Mozart's Osmin's gleeful description of the multiple tortures due Pedrillo), they have no interests beyond their own, as opposed to having a larger principle or a greater good in mind, they are hypocritical, unlike the Pashas, who at least are clear about their desires and motives, and they do not know their own limits, either in appetite or in virtue.[39]

Although the Pashas of these seraglio operas are marked in one way or another by *alla turca* music (see below), the most flamboyant and pervasive uses of the topos occur in connection with the low-Turk characters. These involve not only not only the melodic, harmonic, and rhythmic devices noted above but also the use of faux-Turkish (e.g., the Kalender's "illah illah, ha ha" in *La rencontre imprévue*) and lingua franca (a pidgin language combining various romance-language elements, used by sailors around the Mediterranean). As with the *alla turca* style in instrumental music, however, the compositional principles used in connection with these low characters are at least as important as the more local melodic, rhythmic, and harmonic devices. Deficiency and incoherence as compositional strategies characterize to varying degrees the exigencies of the dramatic situation and the specific nature of the low-Turk role. Mozart's deployment of these characteristics in the portrayal of Osmin differs interestingly from Haydn's use of the same characteristics to represent the Kalender (dervish) in *L'incontro improvviso.* A comparison of the two suggests how the principles of *alla turca* composition could be deployed for dramatic effect.

Both of these characters remind us of the foreignness of the setting, but their dramatic functions, which derive in part from their occupations, are quite different. Osmin the seraglio guard is positively dangerous, representing the barbaric cruelty of the stereotypical Turk; the Kalender, a mendicant dervish with no power over the principal characters, has a much less direct role in the intrigue and functions more as a splash of exotic local color.[40] Osmin's "O, wie will ich triumphieren" vividly demonstrates the principle of incoherence with its sudden changes of topos, from patter to menacing half notes, to mock-heroic octave leaps, to triplet coloratura, each one illustrating a particular point in the text, but none growing inevitably or predictably out of another, and all of them invoking different sets of social and musical resonances. Topical eclecticism of this sort (though usually not of this degree) is characteristic of *buffo* arias sung by characters with no Oriental associations. The explicit references to Osmin's ethnicity as well as his class, however, lend the topical "incoherence" of Osmin's aria exotic as well as comic resonances. In addition, the impression of capriciousness conveyed by the aria's incoherence reinforces the possibility that Osmin could suddenly engage in "Orientally" excessive and unmotivated violence.

The Kalender's aria "Noi pariamo Santarelli," in which he explains to Osmin the truth behind the façade of mendicant virtue also demonstrates the principle of incoherence, though in a different manner. The sudden and phraseologically odd changes in dynamics and orchestration in the ritornello suggest jerky, even grotesque, gestures (especially the one-beat *forte* in m. 4) and set up the expectation of peculiarity (example 3.10). Motivically and topically this aria is much less various than Osmin's "O, wie will ich triumphieren"; even so, the three different motives making up the move to the dominant (mm. 18–24), with pauses in between, give the impression of improvisatory list-making with only the thinnest of connecting rhetorical threads (example 3.11). The overall form is the strongest conveyor of incoherence. Like Osmin's aria, it has multiple repetitions of the opening text, and in that respect suggests a rondo form. Unlike Osmin's aria, however, it does not have contrasting episodes (the material from the exposition suffices for the whole aria); nor does the central iteration of the text (mm. 35–57) really function as a development section, even though the opening section functions quite clearly as an exposition. This mixture of sonata, rondo, and strophic elements is not particularly unusual among Haydn's *buffo* arias, though again, as with the topical variety of Osmin's aria, the particular circumstances lend specific meanings to general devices; in this instance formal "confusion" or "garrulousness"—a normal comic characteristic—is identified with the Kalender's Turkishness. This character shows himself to be more than merely garrulous at the end, however, with the final repetition of the opening text to a considerably varied version of the opening theme—in the minor (example 3.12). Haydn uses neither the tonic minor nor flat mediant earlier in the aria to anticipate this sudden turn; it cannot be justified on "purely musical" grounds. Rather, it functions as confirmation of our growing suspicion that this character has no sense of proportion and no instinct for formal "propriety."

Ex. 3.10. Haydn, *L'incontro improvviso,* no. 8: Calandro, "Noi pariamo Santarelli," mm. 1–6.

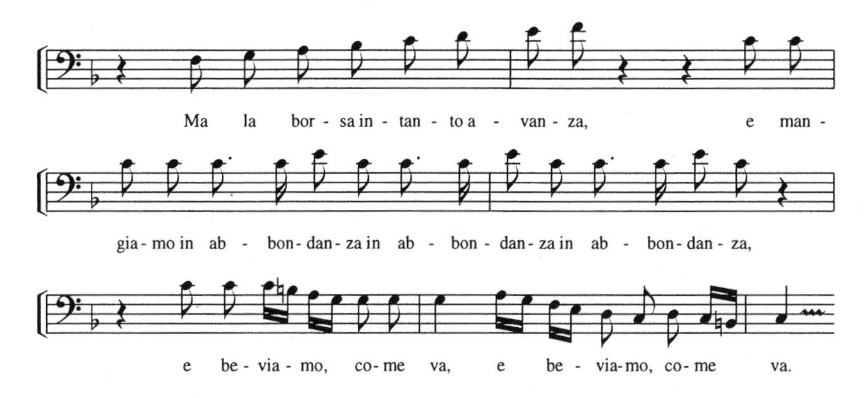

Ex. 3.11. Haydn, "Noi pariamo Santarelli," mm. 18–23. (Trans.: "But meanwhile the purse comes out, and we eat abundantly and drink likewise.")

Ex. 3.12. Haydn, "Noi pariamo Santarelli," mm. 88–92. (Trans.: "We appear holier than thou, and deceive everyone.")

If Osmin is more virtuosically incoherent than the Kalender, his incoherence adding to the threat he represents, then Haydn's dervish is more strikingly deficient in rhetorical and musical competence. His deficiencies undermine any putative authority conferred by his religious calling and reinforce his status as a figure to be ridiculed. His almost monomotivic "Castagno, castagna" exemplifies this throughout, with its almost exclusive reliance on repeated-note motives, its immediate repetition of every motivic unit, and the harmonic stasis of every phrase. Harmonically, the Kalender's "Castagno, castagna" also exhibits striking deficiencies; not only are the phrases remarkably static, but the voice leading is often "wrong" (e.g., the seventh leap in the bass from m. 2 to m. 3 and the parallel voice leading in mm. 29–36, as seen in example 3.13). Mozart's music for Osmin is not without its intentional deficiencies, but they

Ex. 3.13a. Haydn, *L'incontro improvviso,* no. 6: Calandro, "Castagno, castagna," mm. 1–4.

Ex. 3.13b. Haydn, "Castagno, castagna," mm. 29–36.

are typically combined with other characteristics, so that the overall impression of the character is not merely a ridiculous emptiness, but emptiness made frightening or threatening. For example, the *envoi* of Osmin's "Solche hergelauf'ne Laffen" ("Erst geköpft, dann gehangen"), with its extraordinary repetitions of anacrustic Es and its reliance on eighth-eighth-quarter note rhythms, as well as the minimal content of the text and the exclusive use of tonic and dominant harmonies, all project the idea of a man not only "overcome with anger" but also stuck on a single (singularly uninventive) idea and with only one way of expressing it (example 3.14). And the opening twelve-and-a-half measures of tonic pedal in Osmin's "O, wie will ich triumphieren" and the fourfold repetition of this rudimentary opening material in the course of the aria (each occasion coming after a pause, as if it were the only thing Osmin could come up with) also suggest poverty of invention in the service of a representation of uncontrollable and capricious rage.[41]

Ex. 3.14. Mozart, *Die Entführung aus dem Serail,* no. 3: Osmin, "Solche hergelauf'ne Laffen," mm. 147–58. (Trans.: "First beheaded, then hanged, then impaled on hot stakes, then burned, then bound, and immersed, and finally flayed.")

The Pasha characters do not exhibit the flamboyant incoherence or linguistic differences of the low-Turk characters. Indeed, in the three most closely related operas considered here (*La rencontre imprévue, L'incontro improvviso,* and *Die Entführung*), the Pashas hardly sing at all.[42] This could be considered a deficiency; indeed, there is no other character type of comparable importance in opera of this period who is so routinely voiceless. Alain Grosrichard offers one explanation for this. He analyzes the structure of the seraglio (or at least of the seraglio fantasy), with its complicated assemblage of eunuchs black and white, deaf mutes, children, and women, as glorifying the power of the ruler by the way it sets out in negative all the characteristics supposedly possessed by the ruler (potency, sensory capability, adulthood, and masculinity).[43] The ruler's characteristic absence from most seraglio scenes functions, according to Grosrichard, as yet another way of enhancing the impression of his despotic power. The viewer's imagination (already stimulated by looking voyeuristically into a secret realm) is fueled by the exaggerated sense of possibilities suggested in reverse, so to speak, by the seraglio's assemblage of negativities. The Orientalizing strategy of these "voiceless" operatic representations of the Pasha, then, may suggest the immensity of his power by excusing him from the aesthetic rules of the genre and by presenting a set of other characters who all oppose or negatively mirror his qualities. At the same time, these operas also represent his power as irrational by denying it an operatic character's normal means of expression, namely, the persuasive power of musical rhetoric. In other words, if the audience cannot experience the rhetorical and expressive capabilities of the Pasha, his evident power has no rational means of comprehension and can only be understood as capricious and unjust.

In the little music attached to the figure of the Pasha in operas other than the three mentioned above, there is typically a combination of more or less neutral noble material and some of the *alla turca* characteristics also associated with the low Turk. Thus the sultan's aria in Mozart's *Zaide* includes not only typically noble dotted rhythms and triadic melodies but also the typically *alla turca* devices of the written-out trill (see example 3.15a) and slightly decorated unison passages (3.15b). This is the point where he describes his fury (the saber rattling of the stereotypical Muslim). In Grétry's *La caravane du Caire* the Pasha sings an air praising France and the French; when he gets to the admirable warlikeness of the Frenchman, Grétry uses the same *alla turca* device of a decorated unison texture (example 3.16).[44] The first appearance of the sultan in this opera is marked by an instrumental march including the *batterie turque.* In *L'incontro improvviso* the only appearance of the sultan is preceded by an intermezzo using *alla turca* percussion, and the final chorus (the only time he sings) also includes these instruments. The *batterie turque* also occurs in overtures to "set the scene"—the place where only the Pasha and the low Turk truly belong (the one rules, and the other has a job; everyone else is either enslaved or visiting). Unlike the low Turk, then, the Pasha is a distinctly ambivalent character, marked as Turkish by the ceremonial music surrounding him and by certain moments in his own music, represented as European by his act of

Ex. 3.15a. Mozart, *Zaide,* no. 9: Sultan Soliman, "Der stolze Löw lässt sich nicht zähmen," mm. 110–14. (Trans.: ". . . he roars with a fearful voice . . .")

mercy, and rendered both deficient and all-powerful by his small or nonexistent singing role.

Whether fixed or ambivalent, terrifying or laughable, inept or (partly) admirable, the low Turk and the Pasha are united with respect to both race and gender by means of *alla turca* musical devices. In addition, these characters are connected by the relative clarity of their origins and function, despite the Pashas' or sultans' characteristic wavering between "Oriental" despotism and "European" notions of justice.[45]

WOMEN *ALLA TURCA?*

The women of seraglio operas are ethnically, musically, and dramatically distinct from their captors. They do, however, share one characteristic with them,

Ex. 3.15b. Mozart, "Der stolze Löw lässt sich nicht zähmen," mm. 119–25. (Trans.: ". . . chains in fragments on the ground . . .")

Ex. 3.16. André Grétry, *La caravane du Caire,* Act 2: "Air du Pacha," mm. 158–62. (Trans.: " . . . burning to fly into combat . . .")

namely, a clear division into classes. The highest level usually involves a princess or other nobly born woman to whom the Pasha is in some sense a social equal; the next level comprises a group of women less desirable to the Pasha and often connected as servants to or followers of the captive heroine. These women may be European, as in Mozart's *Die Entführung* and its direct and indirect sources, but they can also be of indeterminate, often Oriental, origin. Among the heroines, Princess Rezia in Gluck's *La rencontre imprévue* and Haydn's *L'incontro improvviso* is Persian, and her rescuer, Prince Ali, is Prince of Balsora (Basra, now in southern Iraq). Grétry's Zélime in *La caravane du Caire* is the "daughter of a Nabob," thus Indian; her beloved, Saint Phar, is, unlike Rezia's Ali, uncomplicatedly French. Mozart's Zaide is of indeterminate origin in the opera and (if the broader tradition of operas is considered) can be read as nonindigenous. Voltaire's original, however, reveals her as the daughter of the Sultan's minister Allazim, thus as Muslim. Her beloved, Gomatz, is also ethnically unidentified in the opera, though Voltaire's original has him as Zaide's brother.

The female slaves are even more indeterminate in origin than the heroines, though their names often suggest other-than-European origins. Balkis, for example (in the Gluck and the Haydn) seems to refer to Balqis of Yemen, "the Arab beauty to whom King Solomon addresses his most passionate words," and Dardane (Haydn, Gluck) may refer either to the descendents of the Trojans (the Dardanidai) or to one of the several rulers from Asia Minor called Dardanos.[46] Other slave names (e.g., Almaïde in *La caravane du Caire,* Scerifa in Anfossi's *Isabella e Rodrigo*) may have less specific referents, but still sound Oriental. In addition to the heroines and servants there may be slaves who sing in chorus or dance, and whose only function is to communicate the ambience of the seraglio.

Even the women with exotic names and apparently Oriental or at least non-European origins are rarely depicted as musically exotic; in particular, the *alla turca* topos is almost never deployed as a means of expression for these women. Even Almaïde, Grétry's jealous Sultana, is completely without musical *turca*-isms. What is more, the sort of sinuous chromaticism associated with exotic women in the nineteenth century is also generally absent from these eighteenth-century depictions of Oriental womanhood.[47]

Two related but distinguishable effects result from this. The first is that the distance between the seraglio masters and their captives remains clear and unambiguous. The *alla turca* style, as we have seen, manipulated elements of the prevailing European musical vocabulary to represent threat and inadequacy, barbarism and crudity, splendor and emptiness. Everything about the *alla turca* topos proclaims a reversal or undermining of European aesthetic (and by extension political) values. At the same time, despite the fairly broad implications of the *alla turca* topos with respect to late eighteenth-century musical style, the topos itself had a rather limited lexicon and (especially in opera) relatively clear boundaries. This combination of clarity and negativity works to objectify and alienate the characters defined by the topos. The second effect is that the seraglio women remain part of "our" expressive world, and thus call on a range and depth of associations unavailable for the Turks. Even the women not evidently desperate to leave the seraglio do not exhibit obviously exotic musical characteristics. Rana Kabbani points out that in nineteenth-century Orientalist paintings, the harem keepers and guards are often dark skinned and fearsome, while the female inhabitants of the seraglio are almost always light skinned (they are often identified as Circassian) and indistinguishable from paintings of European women.[48] The stylistic distinctions in eighteenth-century operatic seraglios, then, mirror this visual distinction, with the *alla turca* topos standing in for (and no doubt sometimes complementing) the visual difference of the harem masters.[49]

The "domestic" quality of the musical topoi used for the women in these operas is reinforced by their resemblances to character types in nonseraglio operas. The captive princesses, for example, all to one degree or another resemble the noble lovers in other subgenres of opera. They all have at least one heroic aria in which defiance of the Pasha and constancy to their lover are mixed, and they typically also have a more sentimental aria by means of which the sympathies of the audience can be activated. (In *Die Entführung*, sympathy and admiration touch one another, as "Martern aller Arten" follows directly on "Traurigkeit.") Thus, although the proclaimed ethnicities of the captive heroines are not all actually European, the heroines are at least in their crucial solo utterances "semiotically" European.[50] Rezia's heroic C major aria "Or vicina a te mio bene," in Haydn's *L'incontro improvviso*, for example, bears both musical and textual comparison with Konstanze's famous C major "Martern aller Arten"; both arias rely on the *opera seria* stereotype of the high-flown eloquence of the noble heroine.[51] Gluck's "Ah! qu'il est doux de se revoir" for his Rezia uses the same musical style without the topic of defiance. And Zélime's touching "Ah! sur moi vengez-vouz" in *La caravane du Caire* uses some of the same Italianate figures as Rezia's prayer for liberation: "S'egli è vero, che dagli astri" in *L'incontro improvviso* (no. 41).

The secondary women in these operas fill a number of functions. Blonde in

Die Entführung and *Belmont und Constanze,* and Balkis and Dardane in *L'incontro improvviso,* and the same two plus Amine in *La rencontre imprévue,* are all followers of the captive princesses, as is the "esclave française" in *La caravane du Caire.* The strongly asserted European allegiance of Mozart's Blonde is unique among these characters; even Bretzner's Blonde is not English. (We can presume that she is Spanish, like Konstanze, but her origins are as unclear as those of most of the other secondary women.) The evidently non-Western followers and servants in the Gluck, Haydn, and Grétry works fulfill the dual (and in some ways contradictory) functions of both aiding the princess in her attempt to escape and of conveying the languorous ambience of the seraglio, and their music reinforces this double-edged message. While avoiding (with one exception) obvious Orientalism, it still manages to communicate some of the current Orientalist notions of the seraglio.[52]

One of these notions of the seraglio is that it contained a multiplicity of equally available women, or embodied an infinitely replicable quality of femaleness, suggested first and most powerfully by its institutionalized polygamy. Grosrichard comments generally about representations of the seraglio, "The distinction between man and woman is genuine, whereas between women there are only numerical distinctions."[53] Lady Mary Wortley Montagu's description of the dance in the chambers of the Kabya's wife, quoted above, suggests the same thing; one and a half centuries later, Ingres's painting *The Turkish Bath,* with its tangle of more or less indistinguishable female bodies lounging by a tiled pool, communicates unmistakably the same message of female interchangeability. As Rana Kabbani observes: "The women in the painting all appear to be cloned from one model, as if depictions of one woman in an endless variety of poses."[54] Operatic versions of the seraglio could not, for practical reasons, present innumerable indistinguishable women, but they do in various ways suggest the replicability of the seraglio female. For example, in *La caravane du Caire,* when the jealous wife Almaïde decides to charm the Pasha back into loving her in her aria "Du Pacha qu'on révère" (Act 2, scene 3), she enlists a female chorus to back up and multiply her efforts, suggesting that the spectacle of many seductive women will be at least as likely to work as Almaïde's own charms. Gluck and Dancourt have not one but three women play at seducing Prince Ali "on behalf of" his true love Rezia, whom he has not yet seen. Haydn's librettist reduces the followers to two, but they also play the same repeatable game with Ali. Grétry's opera has no repeated seductions, but the second-act series of airs by three unnamed female slaves all describing their reactions to slavery, the two latter ones in gentle parodies of the non-French styles (the Italian aria concertolike, and the German one quasi-folklike), repeatedly and redundantly hide any suggestion of individual identity behind the assertions of ethnic allegiance.

Apart from this musical divertissement on national styles, and apart from Amine's angry aria in *La rencontre imprévue,* which mixes low comic style with *alla turca* elements, the solo music for the subsidiary women typically occupies a middle stylistic and expressive range, neither virtuosically or heartrendingly eloquent nor coarsely comic. Both within and between the operas, the subsidiary women's music is sufficiently differentiated that it does not literally suggest replication or interchangeability. At the same time, none of these women (with the exception of Grétry's Almaïde, who is in any case an antagonist rather than a follower) has a particularly striking musical profile; they sing in ways adapted to the moment rather than to their personalities. If not exactly interchangeable, then, they are also not individually memorable. This is not true of the heroines of these operas; equally importantly, it is not strongly true of subsidiary female roles in other eighteenth-century opera. Many serving girls in *opera buffa,* for example, have strong and consistent (if not very interesting) personae; these more sharply etched profiles are, of course, reinforced by being attached to single individuals rather than to twin or triplet seraglio inmates.

One of the persistent fantasies about the seraglio was the frisson of lesbianism that it could provide for the Western (male) voyeur.[55] Montesquieu's *Lettres persanes* suggest that some of the untoward goings-on in the seraglio "back home" involved affairs between the women, and Jean Chardin stated quite baldly in his 1686 account of his travels that harem inmates were often "Tribades." The lesbian subplot in seraglio fantasies is part of their projection of the "absolute limitlessness of pleasure" described by Malek Alloula, and connects to the equally pervasive notion of seraglio inmates (slaves and wives alike) as wanton and sexually abandoned, living only for pleasure, achieving that pleasure however and whenever possible.[56]

It goes without saying that what could be read (and even painted) could not be literally reenacted onstage. Nevertheless, opera did not completely avoid suggesting that the seraglio was a place of female sexual initiative, and of general, all-pervading, sensual pleasure. All the non-European subsidiary women in these operas attempt to seduce (or win back by seducing) either the captive princess's beloved (*La rencontre imprévue* and *L'incontro improvviso*) or the Pasha himself (*La caravane du Caire*); openly seductive behavior of this sort is unusual in representations of European operatic women, even servants, who may hint that they need a husband but do not flatter and cajole like these (temporary) denizens of the seraglio. As far as sensuality is concerned, the harp accompaniment for the French slave's divertissement aria in *La caravane du Caire* and the gorgeous cor anglais accompaniment to Dardané's "J'ai fait un rêve plus doux" in *La rencontre imprévue* both suggest sensual delights by means of the sheer beauty of musical sound.[57] But the music that most strikingly encapsulates the Orientalist fantasy of timeless pleasure, female replicability, and homoeroticism while still containing that fantasy within a domesticated dramatic and musical framework is the trio "Mi sembra un sogno" sung by Rezia, Balkis, and Dardane in Haydn's *L'incontro improvviso.*[58]

The women sing this trio after realizing that Prince Ali is in the vicinity and before deciding to test his fidelity with the series of false seductions mentioned above. The six-line text merely indicates their surprise at this unexpected turn of events.[59] Haydn extends this brief text into a ten-minute, 242-measure web of sound. All-female trios are extremely unusual in this repertory; the personnel, the orchestration (two English horns plus horn and strings), and the length of this slow ensemble are unique in Haydn's operatic output.[60] This ensemble also has no precedent in the Gluck. Dardané's "J'ai fait un rêve plus doux," in which she imagines Ali in love with her, uses the dream topos and the English horn; however, both as a solo and as a speech addressed directly to an interlocutor, this number is crucially different from Haydn's work. Everything about Haydn's piece plays out the seraglio dream suggested in the first line of text. It is in a fairly straightforward sonata form, but the languorous repetitiveness of the musical material vitiates any sense of direction or drive normally associated with this form. The combination of the leisurely tempo and the repetitions and lack of contrast in the thematic material convey a sense of frozen time, of the immovable sameness of the Orient. The extraordinary color of the three female voices in close harmony conveys a purely sensual pleasure unique in this opera and unusual in Haydn's operas in general, and the indistinguishable intertwining of the three voices, touching on exquisite dissonances and taking turns on top, can easily be heard as a simulacrum of female homoerotic pleasure, engaged in by three representatives of the sex rather than by three distinct individuals (example 3.17). This is, in fact, one of the few instances where we find (however briefly) the "sinuous chromaticism" associated with nineteenth-century exotic women. The absence of other characters onstage and the indeterminacy of their address encourage in the audience a voyeuristic stance perfectly commensurate with other representations of the seraglio, both before and after the late eighteenth century.

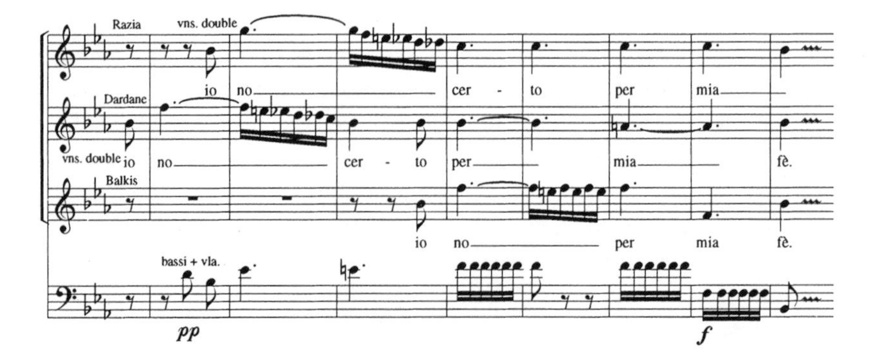

Ex. 3.17. Haydn, *L'incontro improvviso,* no. 12: Rezia, Dardane, Balkis, "Mi sembra un sogno," mm. 111–19. (Trans.: ". . . not me, indeed . . .")

It should be remembered that, unlike the *alla turca* topos, which strongly denotes or distantly evokes the barbaric-exotic more or less regardless of context, in both instrumental and vocal music, the features I have identified in the Haydn trio—stillness, exceptional color, intertwining parts of similar ranges, and so on—are not intrinsically exotic. The many moments of comparable heart-stopping beauty in the slow movements of Mozart's string quintets, for example, do not evoke Oriental sensuality. The point of this moment in *L'incontro improvviso* and of other late eighteenth-century operatic portraits of femininity in purdah is precisely that the combination of textual, visual, and musical elements allows the Orientalist representation of forbidden pleasures to be connected to a conditioned sympathetic response to nonexotic beautiful music. As captives, the women deserve sympathy; that is why the basic musical means used are not "Oriental." In addition, since all these operas end happily, the women's achievements of their desires have to be justified; palpable indolence or lust could not be rewarded in any eighteenth-century comedy. Nevertheless, as non-Europeans in a setting imagined as the site of limitless pleasure, the denizens of the seraglio suggest delights unavailable from European operatic women.[61] I believe it was exactly the need for multivalent representations of captive womanhood that prevented the development of a feminine *alla turca* style in late eighteenth-century opera. As we have seen, the clarity of the topos works effectively to objectify and caricature the uncouth and barbarous low Turk; the more complex figures of the Pashas either avoid the issue by singing as little as possible or use *alla turca* devices to indicate the nature of their domain rather than the content of their characters. Lacking the authority or autonomy to turn Oriental barbarity into mercy, sympathetic exotic women in male-authored seraglio operas were compelled to convey a soft appeal completely at odds with any intrinsically exoticizing musical gesture.

The late eighteenth-century musical exotic, then, is irreduceably gendered. Whereas the masculine exotic is clearly defined and musically unambiguous, the feminine exotic in this period is hard to discern and dependent on nonmusical clues. Both sorts of exoticism objectify the characters to whom they are attached, however; the *alla turca* style fits every Islamic man explicitly or implicitly into the same caricature of swashbuckling barbarity, whereas the less clearly defined devices of replication and sensuality deny female seraglio inmates any particular individuality. Perhaps more importantly, both genders of exoticism in this period activate a dizzying array of binary oppositions, both within and between characters: some of the most obvious pairs are attraction and repulsion, sympathy and ridicule, baseness and nobility, simplicity and complexity, and sensuality and propriety. All of these binaries are unequally balanced; one side of the opposition is always better, or more familiar, than the other. Edward Said remarks that one of the defining features of Orientalism is the positing of the basic dichotomy of "us" and "them."[62] Perhaps the most profound way in which both genders of eighteenth-century exoticism are Orientalist, however, is that both rely on the familiar to define otherness; the male *alla turca* topos achieves this by reversing or negativizing "normal" musical processes and expectations and the late eighteenth-century feminine exotic suggests otherness by using familiarizing and distancing techniques in ambivalent simultaneity.

The Hungarian Gypsies and the Poetics of Exclusion

JONATHAN BELLMAN

I

> [The Gypsy orchestra] began playing some violins, and viola and bass, with a zither. It swept me off my feet; for it was not music; it was an expression of a directness too naïve, too naked and living to be music. It is something I shall never forget, and I left Budapest early for I did not wish to hear it again.
>
> —SAMUEL BARBER (1928)[1]

THE REMOTE but alluring Gypsy musician, dark of skin and eye, venting nameless griefs and frenzied exultations with diabolical virtuosity, is a cultural commonplace of long standing. The inability of the eighteen-year-old and impressionable Samuel Barber, destined to be one of America's most celebrated composers, to withstand the raw power of a Gypsy performance echoes the story of the child Liszt bursting into tears after hearing a piano sonata, and validates the Gypsies' meta-musician stereotype. We, possibly stronger but certainly duller, might have been entertained, or moved even, but to one such as Barber, flight was the only possible response.

Musicianship, independence, and above all a legacy of grief and suffering—and those in almost fatally strong measure—are still the unquestioned cultural associations of the central and eastern European Romani Gypsies. By comparison, the once-prevalent stereotypes of most other ethnic groups are unthinkable without an immediate, reactive awareness of how they evolved, how unfair they are, and the kind of potential dangers they represent. Today, in a time of raised ethnic consciousness and political activism, it is peculiar that the Romani Gypsies still stand, in folklore and as a cultural stereotype, alone. This is a position they have occupied for centuries, one that has long informed the way they were perceived and depicted.

II

> The gypsies [play] the true national compositions of Hungary, which breathe a peculiar spirit, and are distinguished by certain original turns and phrases, which I never remember to have heard anywhere else. . . . I could easily understand the partiality manifested by the people generally for this music, for there is something in its character so wild and impassioned—it has tones of such deep melancholy, such heart-piercing grief, and wild despair, that one is involuntarily carried away by it; and although, on the whole, the performance of the gypsies is rude and wild, many of them manifest so much of musical inspiration, as may well make amends for their deficiencies in scientific culture.
>
> —JOHANN GEORG KOHL, traveling in Austria and Hungary (about 1840).[2]

"Deep melancholy, heart-piercing grief, and wild despair." There are myriad historical reasons for this particular Romani inheritance. European cultures have rarely proven hospitable to the stateless, particularly when their mores differed markedly from those of the surrounding country and people. In the case of the Roma, who had already been traveling for centuries when they moved west into Europe during the Renaissance, they could hardly have been more different. They were dark-skinned and spoke a foreign tongue, the Indic roots of which went unrecognized until the second half of the eighteenth century. Their predisposition to a mobile lifestyle would have seemed perverse to a Europe that associated personhood, for most of society, with the locality of one's birth. (This is not to say that no Gypsies wanted or managed to settle, simply that many either preferred or had to keep traveling.) Finally, the fact that they not only were non-Christian but also did not make public proclamations about their religious beliefs made them completely suspect to Europeans. As was already illustrated by Europe's Jewish population, the suspect, non-Christian Stranger was both unwelcome and a vulnerable target.

The Jews provide an apt point of comparison here because the similarity of their situation to that of the Roma is striking. Both groups migrated (throughout much of their history, at least), were considered stateless and potentially threatening, and were above all non-Christian. Settlement, when desired, was problematic. But the differences between the two groups were critical. The Jews had ample role in the scriptures Christendom recognized as holy, and from this role resulted blame, accusations of blood libel and so on, and religiously sanctioned (indeed, mandated) persecutions. The Roma looked, as far as one can surmise, even more "alien" than the Jews,[3] and they had no ready-made place in Christian history, culture, or consciousness. In European thought of the time, this was impossible: each caste of the societal hierarchy, from nobility to peasantry, occupied its particular place for a reason, to fulfil a particular mission. As the ancient resentments against the Jews served as excuse for the treatment they received, so a similar mythology was needed for the Roma, both to explain their wretchedness, migrations, and apparently accursed state, and to serve as justification for abuse they would receive.

The belief therefore grew up that the Roma were descended from the surviving remanents of Pharaoh's army after Moses parted the Red Sea.[4] (Hence "Gypsy," from "Egyptian.") But this parabiblical origin, while highly uncomplimentary, was still insufficient cause for the "divine retribution" represented by their apparent status and circumstances; their societal condition required greater historical blood guilt.

Folkloric reflections of such requisite ancient crimes may be found in later Romantic literature. One of the premises of Ludwig Achim von Arnim's 1812 novella *Isabella von Ägypten* is the widely accepted belief that the Gypsies' peculiar Original Sin had been the unwillingness to shelter Mary and the baby Jesus during the flight into Egypt.[5] Isabella, in this story, is basically a positive character, but Arnim nonetheless makes her blood guilt explicit: "She also knew the old crime of her people, that they would not give the Holy Mother Mary shelter on her flight to Egypt when she entered with her beatific son in the strong rain; then [the child] lifted his hand in a circle, and over them stood a rainbow, that no drop could fall on them. 'Has our guilt not yet been expiated!' sighed Bella."[6]

Clemens Brentano, Arnim's friend and collaborator on *Des Knaben Wunderhorn,* told the Gypsy story another way, in his incomplete *Die Romanzen vom Rosenkreuz,* an epic poem detailing a whole laundry list of horrors—adultery, incest, theft, violence, the obligatory curse from the Virgin Mary—centering on the descendants of an illicit union between a Crusader and a Gypsy girl.[7] The setting was postbiblical, but the original sacrilege was apparently no less grievous: to the nascent Romantic imagination, no symbol could be purer or less blemished than the Crusading Knight.

Reality, for Roma living in the wake of such folklore, was far darker: accused of every possible crime and treachery, they were openly punished and persecuted on the basis of obvious calumnies.[8] Depending on locale and period, they could be openly and legally hunted, enslaved, or simply subjected to far more common forms of persecution: banishment, harassment, and general abuse and contempt. As non-Christians with no economic power, they occupied the lowest conceivable place in European society, to which all known contemporary sources bear witness. This from an Englishman, writing in 1673 about a recent visit to Ottoman Hungary:

> Nor were we without fear also of *Gypsies,* who are stout and bold, and some of them have been noted Robbers. There are many of them in Hungaria, Servia [*sic*], Bulgaria, and Macedonia; and some I saw at Larissa and other parts of Thessaly . . . many of them conceived to be spies unto the *Turk.* A little before I came to *Leopoldstadt,* by *Freystadt,* a great drove of them appeared in those parts; which the people suspected to be Spies of the *Visier* of *Buda,* to take notice of the state of those parts, and how that Fort proceeded.[9]

But their threat did not stem only from their supposed confederacy with the Heathen; it was apparent in their essential nature and occupations. A German encyclopedia of 1841 cites "a love for indolence and freedom, which, with propensity to cheating and thievery, is above all inherent in their character."[10] Even more to the point, another encyclopedia (1749) states:

> They were at the very least liars, who try to get by with all kinds of falsehoods about their own circumstances. . . . They were insolent beggars, who got through craft or force what they could not get through goodness of heart; thus they were well set up, through all kinds of schemes and cheating, to rob people of their money.[11]

The root cause of such behaviors had to be their lack of solid religious foundation:

> Their religious practices conform for the most part to those that prevail in the country in which they stay; and as they are Mohammedans in Turkey, so they are outwardly Christians in Siebenbürgen, Hungary, and Spain, but without caring anything about the conception or study of spiritual things. Not infrequently, it happens that they have their children baptized repeatedly in various places, in order to receive gifts from godparents several times.[12]

And according to the English seminarian Robert Walsh, in 1828:

> They acknowledge no particular religion as their own, but generally profess the Greek rites, of which they have but a crude and debased conception. They baptize their children; but it is generally done by themselves in a public-house, with a profaine [*sic*] mixture of ribaldry and folly. They have no notion of a resurrection, independent of the same body being again brought to life before it decays, which they say is impossible. One of their children died at school in this place, and the parents requested he might be buried with his school-fellows. On being asked if they expected to meet him in a future state, they said they knew he could never live again; and showing a skinned horse, asked whether it was possible that it could be ever restored to life.[13]

Obviously, human living circumstances were out of the question:

> The children are seldom provided with clothing before their tenth year. This is true primarily for the wandering Gypsies. . . . Every kind of meat is good to them, and dogs, cats, rats, mice, and even fallen livestock are consumed by them. What is more, in the previous century in Hungary, Gypsies were even accused of having eaten human flesh and were severely punished for that reason, although no one was able to prove it.[14]

> When inclined to a settled life, several families herd together, with pigs and other animals, in a small enclosure, which is rendered exceedingly offensive by their total disregard of cleanliness.
>
> They are in temper irascible, even to frenzy, and live in a state of constant discord with each other, which is greatly increased by a propensity to intoxication. Notwithstanding their debased and despised situation in society, they are proud and consequential, exceedingly loquacious and vainglorious, with no regard to truth. . . . Notwithstanding their general depravity, there are grades of infamy, and many are so vile that they are rejected by the rest; of these some are made executioners, who set about the task with delight, prepare extraordinary instruments of torture, and take a savage pleasure in telling the victim the punishment he is to undergo, and the pain he is to suffer.[15]

As the Gypsies were perceived, so would they be treated. Since they enjoyed the protection of neither church nor state, they were completely vulnerable to whatever version of the law was being enforced in a particular locality at any particular time. To a Europe already prepared to torture and kill its Jews, witches, accused heretics, and so on (when they were not merely banished, imprisoned, or their goods seized and children baptized), this was a dire prospect indeed. It is the German encyclopedia of 1749 that gives perhaps the clearest, most concise picture of the cultural reception of Roma (and, I underscore, this is an encyclopedia, not a tract):

> Certainly Gypsies have been godless, evil people for all time, and are persecuted for good reason. . . . now since this Gypsy folk is in the habit of causing much mischief, as it is now reported, thus it is certainly a fair and just punishment for this people that they are searched out with force of arms in all places (be it in cities, boroughs, villages, bushes, and woods) and expelled out of the country by force, as it is ordered almost everywhere in Germany; it is permitted to shoot and kill them on the spot for perceived resistance, and to arrest and inflict bodily and capital punishment upon them without any mercy or investigation, and without any further process, simply and solely on account of their forbidden moral conduct and manifest insubordination; however, the women and children [are] condemned for life in penitentiaries and workhouses.[16]

It is no wonder, then, that the public psychology of the European Gypsy did not reflect the merry, carefree life celebrated in nineteenth- and twentieth-century operetta:

> On the brow of a [male] Gypsy, surrounded by long, black hair, one can usually read deep melancholy; the black eyes look gloomily out from under dark eyelashes, and there is no feature in the countenance that does not indicate sadness and gloomy brooding. Not their children, not their wives arouse their compassion; the entire weight of the sad fate of this outcast people seems to press upon their souls, and their aspect is suited to inspire the deepest sympathy. These wanderers are treated everywhere with scorn and contempt, and even the rough Wallachians (full of physical and moral defects) look down on the Gypsies with disdain.[17]

The Gypsy sympathizer and champion Franz Liszt would put it more simply: "Who could even sound the depths of that profound abyss of suffering endured by Gipsies through many generations—outcasts; all born to misfortune, degradation, hazard, and want?"[18]

III

> In the very act of passing the bow across the violin-strings a natural inspiration suggested itself; and, without any search for them, there came rhythms, cadences, modulations, melodies and tonal discourses. . . . In his music [the Gypsy] revealed that golden ray of interior light proper to himself, which otherwise the world would never have known or suspected. He made it dance and glitter in the fascination of a wild harmony, fantastic and full of discords; and thus, by a mixture of unexpected outline, glaring colour, sudden change and quick transformation, endowed it with its many seductive features.
>
> —FRANZ LISZT (1859)[19]

In direct contradiction to the pervasive image of criminal subhumanity, there existed another, equally prevalent Romani stereotype: the Gypsies as musicians of sublime, God-given talent. For example, in 1837 the Austrian National Encyclopedia observed: "Now, they are the most excellent musicians in Hungary, and unsurpassable in Hungarian performance. . . . They are not only masters in the making and handling of instruments but also imaginative composers and poets, even if they never write down a note, or ever even know a note.[20]

Invariably, Gypsy musical ability is something of which the writer has direct experience, while the horror stories regarding Romani origins, occupations, hygiene, and so on seem to come instead from the common and unquestioned pool of folklore and legend. Robert Walsh, whom we have already seen to be willing to repeat the most sordid and sensationalized accusations, wraps up his discussion of the Gypsies with these comments:

> They have naturally very acute and delicate perceptions of sounds, and hence they are greatly disposed to and delighted with music: this talent is much cultivated; and they form usually the musicians of these countries, particularly on wind instruments. I have often heard them play, and always with pleasure. . . . by the delicacy of the sense of hearing, they readily catch the melody, and take their parts in the harmony of a concert; but I was informed they could not be taught to read a note of music, and all their knowledge was by their ear.[21]

And again, later:

> We entered the inn to get pipes and coffee. In one room were two Hungarians . . . and in another were two Bohemians [i.e., Gypsies] playing a duet on two clarionets. The Bohemians . . . resembled our [English] gipseys; their complexions were very dark, with black hair and eyes, and drooping noses; rather silent and gentle in their manners. They played duets in good time and tune; and, in fact, are the musicians of Hungary.[22]

The open acknowledgment of musical accomplishment and ability makes an odd counterpoint to the fear and revulsion with which Roma normally seem to have been treated, but these images are in one way complementary. It will be noticed that not only the Barber, Kohl, and Liszt quotations but also the comments of Robert Walsh characterize Romani musicianship as *natural,* untaught, as if given to them (in their presumably savage state) by nature. The power of their music seems to stem from a physical need to express their "animal" sorrows and joys; the ability for any higher musical learning is clearly felt to be beyond them, as is implied by Kohl and stated explicitly by Walsh. Even while paying tribute to what seemed to be a superior skill, in other words, the praise was couched in subtly dehumanizing terms.

An immediate similarity is seen here to the various popular African American musics (Ragtime, Blues, Jazz, etc.). Both Roma and African Americans know the dichotomy between mistreatment and revulsion and, paradoxically, the admiration and envy caused by their supposedly God-given musical skills (i.e., skills for which they can claim no credit). And the African American parallel serves to remind us of two more aspects of the Gypsy stereotype. Roma were believed to be possessed of both unbridled sexuality and a more general disregard of normative social codes such as "respectability" and economic responsibility. These are perhaps the most feared and desired of forbidden freedoms. The Romani self-liberation and mobile life, then, engendered a cultural image of proud, independent people who follow their own (primitive and intuitive) whims and desires in open defiance of accepted standards, of which the sexual component is perhaps most familiar. (The "Gypsy Davy" family of folksongs is one of many testaments to the power that Gypsy men—invariably swarthy, smouldering-eyed lotharios—supposedly had over women.) For the women, it is not as if the unfaithful Gypsy girl in Pushkin's *The Gypsies* comes solely from the poet's imagination: a German source states that Gypsy women are "often of a very charming appearance in their younger years, yet are also, as a rule, wanton and cunning paramours."[23] The familiar and ugly nineteenth- and early twentieth-century stereotypes of African Americans are similar, therefore, to those of the Hungarian Gypsies in nineteenth-century European society, or for that matter the Jews in pre–World War II Germany: the Stranger Among You is (1) not fully human, (2) lazy and parasitical, but (3) still has boundless energy for evil—particularly that involving sexual activity and perversion, which threatens the entire fabric of family and society. While this Stranger has obvious (and dangerous) talents, they were not acquired honestly by study and labor. They are natural, no sooner inherited than abused, becoming the potential instrument of Your undoing.

Romani musicianship actually has a complicated origin; while the beginnings of their ongoing migration are far from clear, their name suggests a musical root: "Romany *romani,* plural of *romano,* gypsy, from *rom,* man, husband, gypsy man, from Sanskrit *domba, doma,* man of a low caste of musicians, from Dravidian, akin to Telegu *tamatama,* drum."[24] The Romani presence in Hungarian music was less a product of God-given genius (taking nothing away from individual musicians, of course)[25] than it was of historical circumstances. As with any group, if options for professional activity are severely limited, many will show marked success in whatever areas are open to them; this is simple survival. In post-Counter-Reformation Hungary, one area most prominently available to Romani people was music and entertainment.

IV

> In our country, we do not know of any music which bears the character of the gypsy people.
>
> —GÁBOR MÁTRAY, Hungarian musicologist, composer, and teacher, mid-nineteenth century[26]

One of the common leitmotifs seen in contemporary documents is the Gypsies' widely understood and accepted role as Hungary's musical caste. In the straitened climate of Catholic Hungary following the Counter-Reformation, music was felt to be immoral and was certainly not trusted as an occupation.[27] Thereafter, many talented composers belonged to the middle classes or even the petty nobility; for them to have been professional composers or performing musicians would have amounted to social suicide.[28] Because mere entertainment occupations guaranteed neither stable income nor respectability, they were best left for society's untouchables, whose unsettled mode of living readily accomodated musicians' peculiar needs and circumstances.[29] The result was that Gypsies came to be the prime disseminators of Hungarian music, in fact virtually synonymous with it. The rural Hungarian folk music that showed no apparent Gypsy musical influence would remain largely unexamined until Bartók's time.

Eventually, this dependence became a sore spot for many Hungarians, who resented that their own music was definitively played by non-Hungarians. Gábor Mátray, a pioneering figure in Hungarian musicology, admitted in 1854,

> Unfortunately earlier the more cultured Hungarians did not generally practice the national music, and entrusted its preservation and spreading only to gypsies; on account of which it must not be a matter of surprise if foreign musicians begin to doubt the true Hungarian character of the national music customarily performed by our gypsies, and if they regard this as being Indian gypsy music rather than Hungarian music.[30]

The Temesvár periodical *Delejtü* (Compass) could likewise admit, "the music is Hungarian whereas its principal guardian is the gypsy," but it added in the same breath, "although this is not always to its advantage."[31] Things became particularly ugly when, in his 1859 book about the Gypsies and their place in Hungarian music, Liszt got it exactly wrong: he felt that the music was Gypsy in origin, while it was nurtured and preserved by Hungarians. Even though Liszt was raised as a German-speaking Hungarian and had some affinity even as a child for Gypsy performances, this kind of glaring error by a Hungarian was still regarded as almost treasonous, and Liszt was somewhat bloodied by the ensuing journalistic conflagration.[32]

The issue is further complicated by Hungary's peculiar history. The Gypsies had entered Hungary from the Turkish lands to the east. But major parts of Hungary itself had long been under Turkish domination, and allegiances remained divided. Indeed, when the Hapsburg forces were besieged in Vienna during the last great Turkish attempt at imperial expansion, in 1681, the Hungarian nationalist leader and hero Imre Thököly was allied with the Turks, although he actually withheld the decisive help that would have defeated the Hapsburg forces.[33] Living conditions for a great mass of Hungarians had been equally bad under Hapsburg and Turkish domination, so the supposedly heathen Turk was less feared in the Hungarian lands than in western Europe. Hungary was thus culturally as well as geographically peripheral to the standard European outlook, and its own heritage showed strong influences from lands east. Turkish influence in traditional Hungarian music, furthermore, is unquestionable; the prominence of the Turkish oboe, or *zurla,* is one example, the profusion of small, jangling ornaments another. Other musical characteristics that seem to have come to Hungary with the Gypsies, such as wildly fanciful ornamentation, the prevalence of the augmented second interval, or microtonal inflections in performance, could well have been brought by the Gypsies from the Turkish lands.

The centerpiece of the Gypsies' repertory was *verbunkos,* a traditional Hungarian dance music used for recruiting purposes (*verbunkos* is taken from the German *Werbung,* recruitment), that is, convincing or conning Hungarian village boys to join the army. Because the Gypsies usually played this music, it came to be closely identified with them.[34] Many of the most salient and familiar features of Hungarian Gypsy playing come directly from *verbunkos.*

The *csárdás,* now well known as a Hungarian national dance, is probably just a later development of *verbunkos.* This dance generally has two sections: *lassu* or *lassan* (slow) and *friska* (from the German *frisch,* fresh or fast). The slow sections could vary from a slow, proud, heavy march to a much more rhapsodic style, in which there was no regular pulse, but rather wild ornamental flourishes (provided by fiddle, clarinet, or cimbalom soloist) between phrases or even individual notes of a melody. This style, called *hallgató* ("to be listened to," as opposed to music for dancing),[35] evolved from Gypsy performances of *nóta* ("melody") songs. *Nóta* songs were a kind of Hungarian middlebrow art song that began to be written in the mid-nineteenth century, as a kind of response to German art songs (although precursors date from as early as the end of the eighteenth century), and flourished into the twentieth.[36] Liszt offered this evocative description of the Gypsy approach to a preexistent melody:

> The true Bohemian master never accepts a song or dance motive except either as the text of his discourse, or as the epigraph of a poem. This idea is one of which he never loses sight and upon which he is prepared to expatiate simply without end. The master most to be admired is he who enriches his theme with such a profusion of traits (appoggiaturas, tremolos, scales, arpeggios and diatonic or chromatic

> passages) that under this luxuriant embroidery the primitive thought appears no more prominently than the fabric of his garment appears upon his sleeve, peeping through the lacework which artistically hides it by its closeness of design.[37]

The *friska,* on the other hand, is dance music of great speed and abandon, in the so-called *cifra* ("flashy" is probably closest) style. So, what came to be understood as "Gypsy music" was Hungarian music, characteristically ornamented in both slow and fast styles, and given the indelible stamp of the Gypsy performers. When this style was imitated by art music composers such as Schubert, Liszt, and Brahms, it became known as the *style hongrois,* the Hungarian style, which was inseparable from the Gypsies who played it.

One crucial point about this "Gypsy" peformance style, grafted onto Hungarian music, is that it has nothing to do with authentic Romani folk music, of which there are many varieties worldwide. The songs upon which Romani musicians made their improvisational exegeses had Hungarian, not Romani, texts, and there is no apparent relation between the *style hongrois* and, say, the music played by Spanish or Greek Romani musicians.[38] It is therefore less a "Gypsy" style than a *Hungarian-Gypsy* product.

An even more important aspect is that the motivations in the development of this style have been overpoweringly commercial. Gypsy musicians (and later, others who imitated their style) did and continue to do this for a living. Solos are specifically demanded and paid for, songs requested, and even extramusical "entertainments," such as allowing the customer to become involved in the performance, can be bought. This is entertainment, which is ideally enjoyed in a rollicking, alcohol-lubricated atmosphere; it is not music to be politely and decorously "appreciated."[39] Many musical decisions are made on the spur of the moment, depending on the musician's "read" of the customer. The Hungarian musicologist Bálint Sárosi describes the relationship between bandleader and customer this way:

> In his playing each determines the proportion between the expressive means of the style himself—with particular regard for the "customer" and his desires. In the nineteenth century, for example, they were much more liberal in spicing their playing with augmented seconds than today—and they were reprimanded for it, too, although it was obvious that they were trying to please their audience with it; and the average public certainly did want it this way. . . . It happened with one of our folklorists that when he was collecting from a village gypsy musician, the gypsy came to realize that it was mainly the melodies with a *Phrygian* cadence which pleased the collector. . . . From then onwards, whenever it was at all possible, he brought even the commonest melody to an end with a Phrygian cadence—while

his companion obligingly observed the effect on the face of the listener: "Just as the customer likes it—I can do it *kuruc* style, too."[40]

From all of these fasts and slows, intervalic alterations, and other expressive means, many derived ultimately from *verbunkos,* there evolved a relatively codified style.[41] Obviously, when a style has a certain number of elements peculiar to it, it becomes immediately and unmistakably recognizable. The *style hongrois* could thus be reproduced and imitated by non-Gypsies and non-Hungarians without necessarily even using the original instruments, simply by using these musical formulas in a familiar and compelling way. Such formulas, when they appeared in music of the Viennese orbit, immediately suggested not only Hungary but more specifically the Gypsies: their musicianship, their rootlessness, their life circumstances.

V

> But Mamusia's music was the true Magyar Gypsy strain, lamenting, mourning, yowling, and suddenly modulating into frenzied high spirits, the fingers sliding up the fingerboard in *glissandi* that seemed to be primitive screams of some sort of ecstasy. . . . The Gypsy scale—minor third, augmented fourth, minor sixth, and major seventh—fretted my nerves. . . . I had to fight this music; its primitivism and sentimentality grated on everything the University meant to me.
>
> —ROBERTSON DAVIES, *The Rebel Angels*[42]

Example 4.1 gives the first two sections of the intermezzo from Ruggero Leoncavallo's opera *Zincari* ("The Gypsies") of 1912. This episode is an essay in the *style hongrois,* artfully executed by the Italian opera composer, and as such is a veritable catalogue of Hungarian Gypsy formulas.[43] Two of the most obvious, and most frequently described with regard to this style, are apparent from the first bar: the so-called Gypsy scale, a harmonic minor scale with a raised fourth degree (as described by Robertson Davies's character Maria Theotoky), and the wild ornamentation, both in the glissando-like ornaments in the opening section and the flute solo beginning in measure 29. It is one of the wonderful aspects of the *style hongrois* that its component gestures are not value-neutral; all have accrued some kind of rhetorical import. Thus the double suggestion of the ornamental style is both a kind of eastern ("Oriental") exotic profusion and the artist's self-abandonment to inspiration, unfettered by metric restric-

Ex. 4.1. Ruggiero Leoncavallo, Intermezzo from *Zincari,* mm. 1–40.

tions (note the "tempo rubato" performance indication). This alien/exotic sense is heightened by the prominence of the augmented seconds within the scale—a scale that is, in fact, only illegitimately eastern and probably results from liberal insertions of augmented seconds by performers. The scale itself seems to have no basis in either Hungarian or earlier Gypsy music.[44]

Ex. 4.1. (*continued*)

Two more gestures function virtually as *style hongrois* calling cards, marking any musical discourse as undeniably Hungarian. The first of these is the so-called *kuruc*-fourth, a trumpet-call figure that rebounds between the fifth scale degree and upper prime.[45] Example 4.2 gives a famous example, taken from the *hallgató* section of Franz Liszt's Hungarian Fantasia for piano and orchestra (this section is based on the *Rákóczi Song*, an early ancestor of the much more famous *Rákóczi March*). This device may also be seen in measures 34–35 and 38 of example 4.1.

Ex. 4.2. Franz Liszt, Hungarian Fantasia, *hallgató* section, opening.

The so-called *bókazó* rhythm, or *bókazó* cadence, also has roots deep in Hungarian folk consciousness. This figure, which is given in example 4.3 (and another variant of which appears in mm. 13 and 16 of example 4.1), symbolizes the clicking of spurs (*bókazó* means "capering"), a staple gesture in traditional Hungarian dance. In hearkening back to the equestrian roots of the Magyar tribes, this figure functions in the same way as does the *kuruc*-fourth; it evokes the deepest kind of folk memories in Hungarian listeners and becomes a kind of Hungarian musical essence.

Several *style hongrois* gestures consist of imitations of characteristic instruments. For example, Liszt made much of his decision to transcribe cimbalom effects on the piano.

Ex. 4.3a. The *bókazó* rhythm: Franz Schubert, *Divertissement à l'hongroise,* first movement, m. 21.

Ex. 4.3b. The *bókazó* rhythm: Liszt, Hungarian Rhapsody No. 3, m. 12.

> The cymbalo is known by its special traits of indiscipline to be totally unfit for the aristocratic society of our orchestras. [Perhaps Liszt refers to the clumsy sustaining pedal, the clattering sound, and a tendency to be out-of-tune.] The piano, on the other hand, which might be used for it (though unable to replace its incisive sonority) possesses certain features which might permit it to simulate the orchestra of the nomads; at all events less unfavourably than any other. It lends itself to the most luxuriant orchestration and is capable of delivering its rhythm simultaneously. It is also able to support the latter with a fair richness of harmony and a sufficiently massive sonority to give shadow where required and ensure the desired contrast between situations of opposite character. It can also in the meantime sing its melody with liberty; the more so as the intervals and other features of Bohemian music lend themselves perfectly to its effects and give not the slightest trouble. . . . This instrument, in fact, seemed better calculated than our orchestra to render the stranger features of this music; more capable of giving the reproduction as a whole of the abnormal passions which the Gipsy has therein infused.[46]

Example 4.4 gives two examples of pianistic evocations of the cimbalom: 4.4a demonstrates the declamatory and background-strum styles, and 4.4b shows the virtuoso approach. (Note that the hands are alternated in a percussive fashion that approximates the cimbalom player's use of the mallets.) Within the *style hongrois,* tremolando background passages, such as that which introduces the final movement of Schubert's Octet, can be taken to evoke the cimbalom.

The Hungarian bagpipe is another instrument that is frequently imitated. The situation is different here, since the bagpipe, originally used solo or as part of a bagpipe-fiddle duo, declined in use in many areas from the mid-nineteenth century on and had no place in the traditional Gypsy band. Nonetheless, open fifths, particularly in the bass, are frequently found in this style, as if audiences were less willing to let the instrument go than the musicians themselves. One writer, speaking of the 1920s and 1930s, said that "in tavern

Ex. 4.4a. Liszt, Hungarian Rhapsody No. 12, opening.

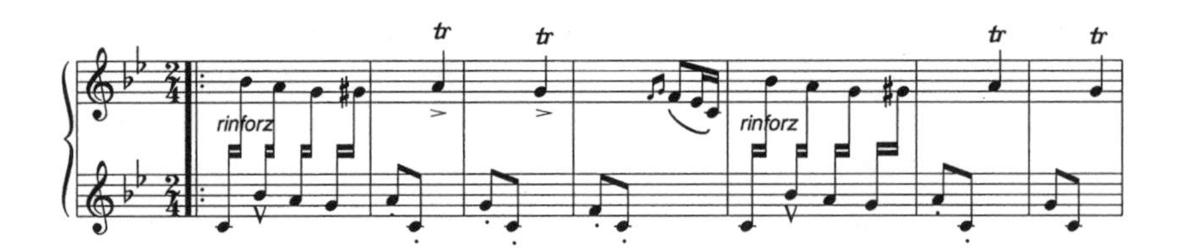

Ex. 4.4b. Liszt, Hungarian Fantasia, *vivace* section.

revelries in the villages of Nógrád County elderly Palóc people not infrequently compelled the Gypsy band to imitate the vanished bagpipes in their playing."[47] Example 4.5 gives two Schubertian examples of this gesture.

In addition to cimbalom, bagpipes, and of course the ubiquitous fiddle, solo woodwinds and woodwind-type writing are prominent in the *style hongrois.* The shrill *tárogató,* a shawmlike wind instrument that is probably related to the Turkish *zurla,* may be evoked by either the clarinet or the oboe. The Brahms passage in example 4.6a gives a splendid example of *hallgató* clarinet playing

Ex. 4.5a. Bagpipe imitations: Schubert, *Divertissement à l'hongroise,* first movement, mm. 70–71.

Ex. 4.5b. Schubert, String Quintet in C Major, D. 956, third movement, trio.

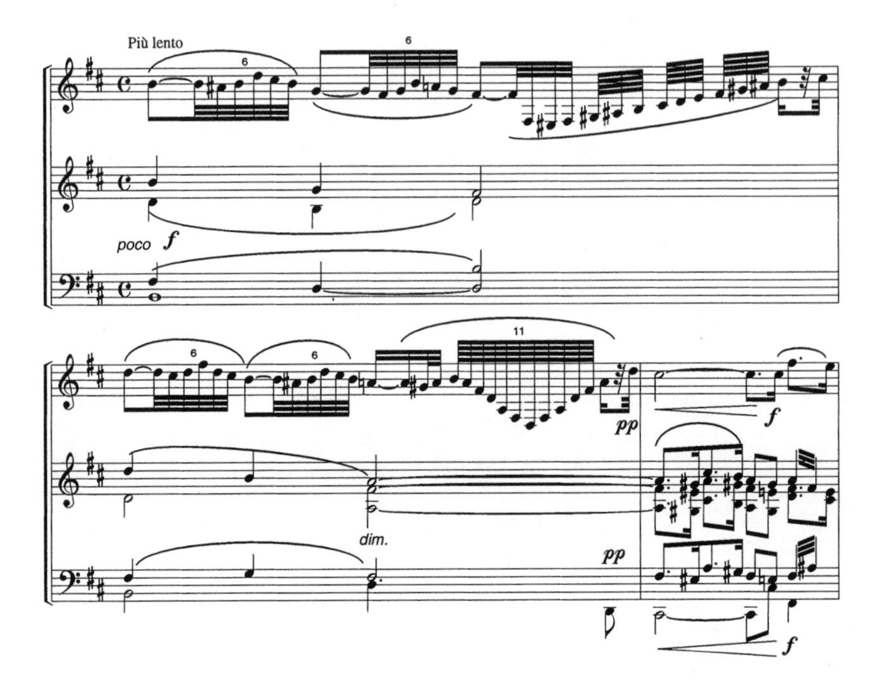

Ex. 4.6a. Woodwind deployments: Johannes Brahms, Clarinet Quintet, op. 115, second movement, middle section.

(answered by crying thirds and sixths in the strings, which in turn suggest an eastern European vocal backdrop), while the Schubert passage in example 4.6b gives the solo oboe an accompanying *bókazó* figure in the trumpet, horn, and first violins.

Another subcategory of *style hongrois* formulas are rhythmic figures. In 1860 Sámuel Brassai could dismiss the much-celebrated Gypsy rhythm this way: "to be truthful its variety is no greater than the degree to which a *spondeus* may be varied."[48] The spondee, a metric foot consisting of two longs, does indeed hold a primary place: for example, we see it unadorned in measure 162 of example 4.6b. It is used a great deal not only in Schubert's *style hongrois* pieces but also in Bartók's "real" Hungarian music. Its effect, to the typical Western ear, is one of caprice, of arbitrary stopping or truncating a line, and as such it feeds the expectation, so to speak, for the unexpected. Common ornamentations of the spondee include the *bókazó* rhythm and the Hungarian choriambus, a long-short-short-long metric foot that has an accent on the second short. The choriambus is seen in measures 18–19 and 23–24 of example 4.1.

Ex. 4.6b. Woodwind deployments: Schubert, "Great" Symphony in C Major, D. 944, second movement, mm. 160–66.

Another common Hungarian Gypsy rhythm is the dotted rhythm, which was particularly common in *verbunkos* (we see this in examples 4.1, 4.5b, and 4.6b). The reverse dotted rhythm, a splendidly brusque and percussive gesture that is also typical, we see in example 4.1 (e.g., mm. 4, 7). The syncopated *alla zoppa* rhythm, short-long-short, we see in example 4.1 (used melodically in mm. 2 and 10, for example) and in example 4.7, where Schubert makes it the basis of a *friska* in one of the prototypes of the nineteenth-century Gypsy rondo-finale. In general, all of these rhythms have their bases either in dance figures or in the Hungarian language, which as text originally helped to shape the rhythms of the songs the Gypsies played.

Ex. 4.7. Schubert, String Quintet in C Major, D. 956, last movement, opening.

The harmonic vocabulary is one of the most remarkable aspects of the *style hongrois.* It has long been debated whether its origin was Gypsy genius or Gypsy ignorance of conventional harmonic practice,[49] but ultimately that does not really matter. It suffices for us to know that one of the most salient aspects of the *style hongrois* was a kind of triadic but nontonal harmonic use that made free use of modal juxtapositions, and that the surprising and unexpected chord progressions possessed a wild beauty beloved of nineteenth-century listeners. We have seen examples of this already: the sudden, accented, "Neapolitan" F triads in the key of E in example 4.1 (mm. 2 and 10), and a commanding example is 4.5b, where, after the A section of the third movement of Schubert's String Quintet has ended in C major, he departs from the parallel minor and takes exactly six measures to modulate to D-flat major, through its subdominant of G-flat, a gesture echoed a few bars later with the subdominant in minor. This is more elegant than many such modulations, but the effect is still surprising to the ear that expects even a semiconventional tonal syntax. Like the rhythmic vocabulary of the *style hongrois,* the harmonic use stymies expectation.

This is what is most striking about the style as a whole. Its gestures are immediately recognizable, whether because of specific Hungarian content or because they essentially contradict European musical conventions of the late eighteenth and nineteenth centuries. What this means is that, for a competent composer, the style was relatively easy to use: its "words," its component gestures, could be readily deployed and comprehended. As late as the Gypsy operettas of the late nineteenth and early twentieth centuries (e.g., those of Johann Strauss and Franz Léhar), it enjoyed great popularity and was used by master composer and mediocrity alike. The key question is *why*—why composers, particularly composers of the greatest artistry, repeatedly found it necessary to use this particular foreign musical language, long associated with the Gypsies themselves and the café milieu in which they most frequently appeared. To this end, let us examine two individual cases—two of the most accomplished "speakers" of this musical dialect, in the nineteenth century or any other time.

VI

> The pleasure of transferring to our instrument the . . . reveries, effusions and exaltations of this wild muse seemed to become more and more seductive . . . to include the quintessence of their most remarkable qualities, and form a compendium of their most striking beauties.
>
> Such a compendium . . . might fairly be regarded as a national Epic—Bohemian Epic—and the strange tongue in which its strains would be delivered would be no stranger than everything else done by the people from whom it emanated.
>
> —FRANZ LISZT (1859)[50]

One of the most interesting cases in the entire history of the *style hongrois* is that of Franz Schubert. As a born-and-bred Viennese, he unquestionably would have had substantial exposure to the style from a very early point. The *style hongrois* had been emerging as a popular form since the last third of the eighteenth century, also appearing occasionally, in the form of a stylized *ongherese*, in the music of, among others, Haydn and Mozart. Not only were *verbunkos* arrangements first published for amateur use in Vienna in 1784, thirteen years before Schubert's birth, but there is even evidence that, at age seventeen or so, he arranged a "zingara" movement of a guitar trio by the composer Wenzel Matiegka that used an actual *verbunkos* melody.[51] His later uses of the *style hongrois*, such as the *Divertissement à l'hongroise* for piano, four hands, the String Quintet in C Major, D. 956, and the "Great" C Major Symphony, D. 944 (but there are many others, of varying concentrations), are as eloquent as any music in this style. Given this background, it would not be surprising to find that Schubert used this style throughout his compositional life.

But such is not at all the case. While a good deal of documentary evidence surrounding Schubert's life survives, testimony on this subject is markedly lacking. His friend Anselm Hüttenbrenner remembered Schubert's comment that Gypsy music interested him a great deal,[52] and other friends spoke admiringly of the Hungarian *Divertissement,* one of the themes for which Schubert had supposedly noted down from the the singing of a kitchen maid he overheard when staying at the Esterházy palace in 1824. The assumption has generally been that Schubert discovered Hungarian Gypsy music at Esterháza, in the Hungarian countryside.

This assumption has two rather glaring inconsistencies. The first of these is that he had visited Esterháza for an extended period before, in 1818, but no *style hongrois* music seems to have resulted at all. This fact, as well as the prevalence of Hungarian Gypsy music in Vienna well before this time, casts doubt on the idea that Schubert had to visit Hungary to be exposed to, or begin composing in, the style. The second point is that there is a cluster of *style hongrois* works dating from the twelve or so months preceding his second Hungarian visit: the F minor *Moment musical* (D. 780/op. 94, no. 3), the final movements of the A Minor String Quartet (D. 804), the Octet (D. 803), and the four-hand Sonata in C Major ("Grand Duo"), D. 812. Between his adolescent Matiegka arrangement and this group, a period of some nine years, there had been almost no Hungarian flavor in his music. An exception, the finale of his G Minor String Quartet (D. 173/op. posth. 1815) is an ongherese clearly based on earlier models, particularly Haydn (for example, the finale of the D major keyboard concerto) and Mozart (for example, the Rondo "alla turca," particularly the F-sharp minor *verbunkos* strain). This movement is completely different from any of Schubert's later Hungarian Gypsy works. What had changed radically after this period was not his location, but rather his health and psyche.

Schubert contracted syphilis in late 1822, and his recovery from the initial phase of the illness does not seem to have been completed until late 1824. By that time, the pre-Hungarian-visit cluster of works had been written, and he had been to Hungary and returned. But his correspondence from this period suggests that his previous good spirits had turned dark and that he fought a profound and lengthy depression. He described himself as "the most unhappy, wretched creature in the world," "a miserable, unhappy being," and gives the impression of dire emotional circumstances.[53] The outlook here corresponds directly to that of Schubert's final year, autumn 1827–autumn 1828, when his health was also poor, he was also depressed, and he also produced a group of works utilizing the *style hongrois:* the Fantasies in F minor for piano, four hands (D. 940) and C major for violin and piano (D. 934), the aforementioned String Quintet in C, and the E-flat (D. 899, no. 2/op. 90, no. 2) and F minor (D. 935, no. 4/op. 142, no. 4) Impromptus for piano.

Two isolated years were thus responsible for almost all of Schubert's *style hongrois* output. The only real exception is the second movement of the "Great" C Major Symphony, which came after a period of ill health and during a relatively happy and carefree musical tour with his friend Johann Michael Vogl in the summer of 1825. (According to a recent article by Maria Domokos, the *Divertissement à l'hongroise* may belong in this time period as well.)[54] Whether the ill health was still present in his mind, or the musicians-enjoying-the-life-of-the-road idea brought up the Gypsy inspiration again, it seems clear that a specific psychological state led him to use this particular musical style, a style—it cannot be coincidental—that was associated with the most down-trodden group known to the Viennese at the time, the group whose music was felt to express the deepest conceivable despair. Moreover, these associations are not something from our own time that we are reading into nineteenth-century consciousness: the motivations for Schubert's use of the *style hongrois* that we find implicit in his biography, compositional chronology, and correspondence were stated outright by Liszt when he wrote about Schubert's and Beethoven's use of this style.

Liszt was the first *style hongrois* composer to make an aesthetic and polemical issue out of using it. He not only composed the Hungarian Rhapsodies (actually, the culmination of more than a decade's effort in this area) and other Hungarian-inflected works, but he also wrote an explanatory book describing Gypsy music and what it all meant to him. This was *Des bohémiens et de leur musique en Hongrie* (1859); it was later expanded, and the expanded version translated into English by Edwin Evans as *The Gipsy in Music.*[55] Liszt saw himself as advocate for both Gypsies and Hungarians (despite his aforementioned problems in sorting out the relationship between the two), as publicist and disseminator of this musical style, and he registered pleasure when one Gypsy he met in the street referred to him as "half-Gypsy, half-Franciscan."[56] His book gives ample evidence of both an outrageously romanticized view of the Gypsies and some awareness of the sufferings they had undergone. But it is in his efforts at transcribing Hungarian Gypsy music for the piano—to produce a so-called national epic—that his commitment to the idiom is most apparent. The Hungarian Rhapsodies are still, after all these years, standard repertoire for pianists, long after the extramusical significance of the *style hongrois* has been largely forgotten. (Sadly, it has been forgotten by pianists in particular, with a resulting flattening of the expressive contours of these works in most performances.)

Liszt's problem, unfortunately, was that not only was he no scholar, but he also looked upon the *style hongrois* as his exclusive turf. True, he was of Hungarian birth, and he had heard the legendary Gypsy bandleader and fiddler

János Bihary as a child in 1823.[57] But his connections with Hungarian culture were tenuous; he moved to Paris when very young and never knew more than a few words of Hungarian. Moreover, the issue is further complicated in that one always gets the sense, with Liszt, of a *wunderkind* who felt he had something to prove, someone to *be*. In this light, his strenuous advocacy of the *style hongrois* begins to appear rather like one of a series of fairly public projects or interests that followed his retirement from virtuoso life in the late 1840s. His conducting position at Weimar was one such project, and the advocacy of new music by other composers (such as Wagner) was another. More focused attention to composing music of a very progressive kind was a third (his importance to the "futurist" compositional school is uncontested), and the composition of church music a fourth. But the only areas in which he had ever been widely accepted and well received were pianistic, both as performer and teacher. He was never regarded as a major figure in conducting, Wagner got far more notice as a composer than he did, and despite a meeting with the pope, his sacred music was not widely sung with church sponsorship. In his correspondence, particularly that from the end of his life, there is a sense of profound disappointment and bitterness.

Sad to say, in certain areas Liszt was a dilettante. The accuracy problems with his Gypsy book were only part of that story; with that work there was also in fact a serious authorship problem, particularly with the second, expanded edition (his companion, the Princess Sayn-Wittgenstein, had a huge role here).[58] His writings were often short on substance and long on verbiage, and authorship problems abound with most, including his early travel commentaries to French newspapers (Marie d'Agoult, the mother of his children, being the likely co-author here) and his dreadful biography of Chopin. The Gypsy book, an attempt at a serious work, is not only full of misinformation regarding the Gypsies, but it is also full of its co-author's anti-Semitism, which caused further critical backlash. (The pretext was a lengthy introductory comparison between the two stateless, migrating peoples, the Jews and the Gypsies, in which the Gypsies are repeatedly shown to be more noble, more honest, etc.)[59] Liszt was sufficiently chivalrous (or naïve) that, rather than point a finger of blame, he himself took the deserved pounding the book got, but none of this contributed to his relationship with the musical and educated public.

All of this is to illustrate that while Liszt was loved and lionized by the public at large, on a certain level he was not taken seriously, and he felt increasingly frustrated and marginalized in the musical world in which he had previously had such success. The Gypsy book bears a kind of odd testimony to this; the *style hongrois* had been used in art music since the late eighteenth century, but in the book Liszt does his utmost to imply that he was the real groundbreaker in this area. Beethoven and Schubert, composers whose music he had previously championed, performed, and arranged, are here marginalized. "It is easy," he says, "to convince oneself to what an imperfect degree 'civilised' musicians have penetrated the characteristics of Bohemian art on the few occasions of their occupying themselves with it when we see such masters as Beethoven and Schubert failing to produce features essential to its form, and evidently not realising that those features constitute its very essence."[60]

Certainly, Beethoven's *style hongrois* efforts, such as the *King Stephen* Overture, the C Minor String Quartet (op. 18, no. 4), and the spuriously titled "Rage over a Lost Penny," belong to an earlier generation, to a pre-Romantic approach in which Hungarian Gypsy elements were assimilated into the wider musical language in a nonconfrontative way, rather than the Romantic approach, which tended to underscore the musically alien and surprising. On the other hand, to lump Schubert in here is indefensible; Schubert's uses of the *style hongrois* are among the most memorable, and are often raw and immediate in their presentation. Liszt even finds himself castigating those who compose in the "Gypsy style" and those who actually do research in this area:

> In point of fact there came a time in Hungary when every musician was obliged to make himself acquainted with [Gypsy music]; for every amateur insisted on hearing it, even if he did not try to fabricate some. Then, natually, the smaller folk among virtuosi began to navigate for certificates of merit and to compete with one another in this school. They were not satisfied with hearing this music in its traditional versions, though sometimes they were contented with mere annotation. Soon, however, the more ambitious embarked upon what they called "correcting" and "embellishing" these works.
>
> The natural end of all this was to "compose" in Gipsy style; for the caprice of the mode and the vogue it had attained was sure to inspire mediocrities of inferior talent with this idea; those who have no real individuality still often having a certain skill in imitating; especially when the general infatuation in favour of a style compels their admiration.
>
> Science [i.e., scholarship] also began to be mixed up with the movement, excited by an interest both lively and unanimous. The idea was to collect traditions and to follow them up to their origin; a particularly unpromising enterprise and one which, as we have indicated, met with very little success. For want of any real source of information, archaeology was brought into play; and unearthing ancient instruments and retracing their history was associated with following up the origin and story of the most popular Gipsy melodies.[61]

The complaints about modern composers using the style, and research being done as to its origins, seem incomprehensible; is the author disavowing his own efforts? Moreover, criticism seems clearly directed at all Hungarian composers then laboring to fashion a national musical language. Liszt also seems to be threatened by real research: one may be excited by this music, but *only* in the way he is. Other compositions are wrong, other research is wrong (although he himself did travel to hear the Gypsies play), any other approach is wrong.

It takes nothing away from Liszt's own *style hongrois* compositions to point out that the book is a profoundly inconsistent document; the authorship problems, the lack of rigor, the plethora of misinformation, and self-contradiction on many points make it something that can be used only with great care. What the book does provide, however, is clear testimony from the mid-nineteenth century as to how the *style hongrois* was heard, and what it meant to listeners, as seen by one of the style's greatest exponents. In evaluating Beethoven and Schubert, Liszt says:

> Both these composers, however, and especially the first were inspired by the inexpressible suffering, as also by the audacious defiance therein expressed.
>
> Beethoven in particular had a sort of vague intuition that certain pains, suffocations of the soul, intolerable oppressions and moral inanitions, having attained a state of delirium beyond either medical aid or remedy by natural means, could only be expressed under Bohemian forms—which are as foreign to our civilization as the sentiments themselves.
>
> This genius, therefore, after having himself tasted the dregs of the chalice of human suffering, seemed, toward the end of his life, to have arrived at the condition of soul from which Bohemian feeling first proceeds; and thus to have more than once remembered Gipsy art in his later works.[62]

That is to say: inasmuch as the Gypsies were felt to have suffered more deeply than the people around them, so their music was held to express deeper grief and suffering than more typical musical languages of the time. The result, as we have seen, is a clear code that may be expressed with the equation: Gypsy music = suffering + defiance + animal-level joys and griefs. In sum, when standard musical discourse was found wanting, when sentiments were too deeply felt for conventional forms of expression, only then would the *style hongrois* find its proper motivation and use.

VII

> During dinner, a small orchestra of dark Zingari performed some national airs after a fashion of its own—that is to say, an extremely *naïve* and wild one—and these, alternating with the speeches and

> toasts, and amply seconded by the burning wines of Hungary, excited the revolutionary fever of the guests to excess.
>
> —HECTOR BERLIOZ (1846)[63]

It is clear, now, that the *style hongrois* did not suffer from the same temporal and expressive limitations as other exotic musical styles. It emerged as an eighteenth-century topic or style, that is, one of a large number of possible subjects for musical discourse, and continued to grow and develop throughout the Romantic era, to the point that by mid century it was fully established as a separate and extraordinarily vivid musical dialect in which entire pieces would be composed. In comparison, by the late nineteenth century its contemporary eighteenth-century styles such as the "Turkish" style (to which it was originally closely related)[64] or the "sensibility" (*Empfindsamer*) style were long dead. Moreover, reinforced as it was by the continual presence of Gypsies, both playing their music and enduring mistreatment, this style took much longer to pale, to lose vividness, and become the familiar cliché of fin-de-siècle operettas.

In fact, the Romani presence itself is one possible cause for the relatively long life span of this style. As the *style hongrois* imitated and idealized the music of people who lived nearby, it was an Exotic Among Us who was being evoked, not a country, people, or culture that most listeners would never dream of encountering.[65] This kind of evocation of the "native exotic" would of course become a more familiar pattern in twentieth-century America, with the flowering of musical exotica based (or supposedly based) on Native American and African American musics, but lay in direct contrast to other nineteenth-century exoticism.

Another remarkable thing about the use of the *style hongrois* by such composers as Schubert, Liszt, and Brahms is the resultant intersection of art and popular musics. Schubert's choice of Gypsy music for finales, an idea he inherited from the Viennese Classicists and that would become almost a cliché later in the century, actually represents a mixture of "high" and "low" styles in one work that would hardly be acceptable in the twentieth century. In Schubert, it does not shock us as much as it might today because our associations of the *style hongrois* with light and popular music are simply too distant. But at least one twentieth-century commentator, J. A. Westrup, writing of the C Major String Quintet, was clearly uncomfortable with the mix:

> The finale is a light-weight, popular in expression and free from tension, above all devoid of any hint of approaching dissolution. The clouds that hovered over Schubert's head in 1824 seem to have lifted. He ends his last chamber work in the

> genial friendly mood that his associates must have known so often when they met together for recreation. . . . We might have wished that the Quintet should end otherwise, that the finale should capture the lofty tone of the first movement. We may not want to be reminded of the open-air café and the Hungarian band. But Schubert saw no reason to segregate music into compartments—and Brahms agreed with him. We must either frankly accept his view or confess a disappointment.
>
> . . . The influence of the café and the theatre is everywhere. Its presence is not necessarily disconcerting. It is only when it is obviously at war with its context that we feel a sense of embarrassment. To dismiss these incongruities is no compliment to Schubert. . . . Better the String Quintet with its uncomfortable finale than no quintet at all.[66]

Westrup's comparison of the first movement's "lofty tone" with the café style gives pause (and, of course, we might now suspect that this use of the *style hongrois* suggests that "the clouds that hovered over Schubert's head in 1824" had *returned,* not lifted). As composers such as Schubert, Liszt, and Brahms are now chronologically remote and charter members of our musical canon, such mixes of high and low style shock far less than they originally may have and, because of the familiarity of repeated listenings, challenge our expectations not at all.

A final observation identifies something that is, in today's ethnically aware environment, anomalous. The Hungarian Gypsy musicians, in keeping with the professional and commercial approach they have always taken to their music, are often perfectly willing to play up to the stereotype in any way desired; acting the part has always been integral to this kind of entertainment. Whether The Gypsy Exults, or The Gypsy Weeps, it is the musician's responsibility to play up whatever musical affectation pleases the paying customer. (In contrast, few African American musicians would probably be willing to participate in a revival of one of the "jungle extravaganzas" of the Black and Tan era.) Here we must beware of well-meaning but facile judgments. This is professional activity, a business in which Romani musicians take great pride. The musicians who practice this style in its totality, and those who imitate them, understand the entertainment equation in a way that critics prefer not to and are not squeamish about playing stereotyped parts to a greater artistic and commercial end.

Indeed, the pervasive Gypsy-as-musician image survives yet, and may be offered to the wider public for political reasons, as something positive about the group in question that the public can safely digest. In early 1996, for example, a Bosnian Gypsy refugee in Berlin made the following statement to a reporter from the *Frankfurter Rundschau:* "If the whole world were like the

Romanies there would be no war. . . . Our kalashnikov is the violin, our grenades the accordion, our bayonets our dances."[67] To a Europe long accustomed to anti-Romani brutality, maintenance of a positive stereotype may be a far better defense than a high-minded denial of stereotypes of any kind; the familiar Gypsy activities of music and dance are almost certainly a better shield than angry assertions of rights as ethnically foreign, stateless refugees in newly reunified Germany would be.

What the *style hongrois* amounts to, in sum, is an attempt by art music composers to catch magic in a bottle. The lands evoked were not that distant, and the people evoked were neighbors, if only until they moved on. The body of associations with this music and its practitioners was so broad and well understood that the style could be relied upon to produce a powerful effect. This could be the deep grief and proud defiance that Schubert and Liszt perceived, the wild celebration that so appealed to Brahms, or even the Hungarian patriotic sentiments experienced by Berlioz and his fellow diners. The *style hongrois,* in other words, was far more than one more exotic musical style intended to evoke the distant and alien; it gave expression to emotions so immediate, so deep and personal, that conventional music was simply unequal to the task.

Cutthroats and Casbah Dancers, Muezzins and Timeless Sands: Musical Images of the Middle East

RALPH P. LOCKE

WESTERN COMPOSERS have evoked the Middle East in astonishingly diverse ways. The lurid pounding of the Bacchanale ballet in Camille Saint-Saëns's opera *Samson et Dalila* (1875), for example, could hardly be more different from the philosophical stateliness of the men's chorus to Allah with which Ferruccio Busoni brings to a hushed close his massive Piano Concerto (1902–3). The present essay traces several threads in this rather vast repertoire of musical representations of the Middle East, focusing on the nineteenth century, with some glances forward to the twentieth.

The "Middle East" (or, as it is called in Europe, the "Near East" or even sometimes just "the East" or "the Orient") can be understood narrowly, as consisting only of Turkey, Egypt, and the Arabian Peninsula (including Palestine/Israel); or broadly, as extending both westward to include the rest of Islamic North Africa (long known to Arabs as the Maghreb and to Westerners in previous centuries as the Barbary Coast) and eastward to Persia (Iran).[1] In the European artistic imagination the region sometimes stretches still further east, to India and Ceylon—though of course stopping short of the Far East—and as far south as Madagascar. Sometimes clear distinctions were made between the ancient (biblical, Greek, etc.) Mediterranean world and that of more recent centuries, but, as we shall see in *Aida* and other works, sometimes not.[2]

The chapter chooses freely among works set in various of these geographical locations and proceeds more or less chronologically, in the hope of revealing certain trends, sudden shifts, and stubborn continuities over time. Among the main themes it develops are the new kinds of musical exoticism that began to set in after the decline of *alla turca,* the relationship between exoticism and representations of gender and sexuality, and the discouraging impact of musical modernism on overt explorations of the musically exotic.

Throughout our discussion five interrelated issues recur, some persistently, others fleetingly: (1) To what extent do the works reflect, or even claim to reflect, the lived reality of the Middle East? (2) Conversely, to what extent do the works construct a fantasy Middle East upon which Westerners can project their own desires and anxieties? (3) How are these various "reflections" and "fantasy constructions" carried out: primarily through extramusical devices (titles, programs, costumes, sets) or specifically musical ones? (4) If "Oriental" musical devices *are* present, how do these devices resemble (and differ from) those of other dialects of Western musical exoticism, such as Hungarian Gypsy, Tyrolean, Native American? (5) Looping back to the first of these questions, but more concretely now: In what ways might these Oriental devices derive from (and perhaps also misrepresent) stylistic features of one or another (actual) Middle Eastern musical tradition?

Art and Truth, Art and Ideology

How one attempts to address such themes depends on one's basic assumptions about how "cultural products" (including works of art) relate to and work within various social contexts. We can encapsulate two of these contexts by the words "truth" and "ideology."

The relationship between Eastern-tinted musical works and questions of factual truth is rarely simple and direct. The works do not claim (or do not *only* claim) to represent objectively—as if they were travel books or newspaper reports—the Middle East as it really is. Rather (or also), they present themselves as fictions, objects intended to provide entertainment or invite aesthetic contemplation. This is particularly true of comic operas; one favorable early review of François-Adrien Boieldieu's *Le calife de Bagdad* (1800) specifically praised it for having all four essential ingredients of a perfect *opéra comique,* including "a plot that is not believable" and "words that there is no point in hearing" (the other two were "amusing situations" and "tunes that it is pleasant to recall").[3]

Even so, certain "Oriental" musical works perpetuate images of the Middle East and its ancient or recent inhabitants that range widely: from the idealized and the true but one-sided to the noxious and defamatory. Indeed, the very fictiveness of art works (e.g., of comic operas, as just noted) serves to disguise or make palatable some demonstrably prejudicial portrayals of other peoples and places. In fairness, though, one should also note that some works that invoke the Middle East do, at certain moments, manage to capture with precision one or another feature of the group or place being depicted or, at the very least, give a sense of how a distant place—that particular distant place? *any* distant place?—feels to a visitor from abroad. And the best of them are "true" in a nonfactual, perhaps mythic sense: they constitute visions of a beckoning, amusing, or scary "nowhere land," a land that Westerners would like to think is very different from their own but is in fact more a projected self-image, however deformed to hide the painful resemblance.[4]

Similarly complex is the relationship between a musical work and what I am calling the "ideology" of its day. Many of the works discussed here, especially those written in France in the nineteenth and early twentieth centuries, seem deeply imbued with imperialist ideology, especially the variant of it—often called "Orientalism"—that deals with the Middle East. Edward Said defines Orientalist art works—including musical works—as "texts that happily co-existed with or lent support to the global enterprises of European and American empire."[5] Marilyn Butler rephrases the issue somewhat more concretely: "Poets, travel-writers, novelists [and musicians] undoubtedly belong in a discourse through which the British [and the French and others] teach themselves about India [and the Middle East and North Africa] and acquire the national will to be there"—be there, that is, in a position of command and control.[6]

One might think that these two extramusical factors, truth (verisimilitude) and imperialist ideology, are related in some simple way, namely, that an ideologically justified system of conquest and exploitation that many today find reprehensible must have been supported by or reflected in cultural images that were counterfactual and therefore fantasy laden, misleading, mystificatory. In practice, though, works of art can also serve the ends of empire through images that are "true" (i.e., more or less accurate reflections of some aspect of Middle Eastern reality), including carefully researched costumes and sets in Orientalist paintings and operas, or relatively faithful transcriptions of dance tunes or sacred chants.

It should also be stressed that the "cultural work" that is done by the arts when they invoke another society (whether or not that society has been colonized by the West) is not necessarily as repressive and regrettable as the short quotations from Said and Butler suggest. It should not, that is, be assumed that the worldview that musical and other cultural texts of this sort support is necessarily pro-imperialist. Quite the contrary, as Said himself elsewhere emphasizes: art has the potential for formulating a resistant or "antinomian" reponse (in part through modernist irony) to "Western control over the non-Western world"[7] or at least—if we accept the possibility of multiple valid readings of a given work—for allowing itself to be *interpreted* as critical of certain generally accepted policies. Indeed, a given work may communicate (or be understood as communicating) both acceptance of imperial policies and unease with those same policies and their ramifications. For example, in Léo Delibes's *Lakmé,* the English attempt to rule India is presented as neither heroic and admirable nor utterly vile but something in between: necessary or at least unavoidable, and also obtuse and misguided. No doubt the French perceived the folly of colonial efforts more readily when the colonizers were their own hereditary rivals from beyond the Channel. But this does not rule out the possibility that the eager reception of *Lakmé* in the France of its day and decades thereafter also reflected some (mostly unspoken) discomfort with the costs and risks of French colonizings, notably in Algeria.[8]

Orientalist Art: Its Creators and Public

With all this, one must not forget that works about the Middle East may touch on issues other than empire: issues of sexual politics in the home culture, for example, or of individual psychology.[9] Indeed, one traditional explanation has it that nineteenth-century exoticism was primarily the response of hypersensitive artists not to the Middle East at all but to the "enervating, corruptive, brutalizing" world of urban Europe (the words are Flaubert's, in fact).[10] Such artists sought, as the literary sociologist César Graña has put it, a world in which "the spontaneous relationship between daily existence and the natural aesthetic dimension of life" was still possible or even normative, where "ideality and reality were one, where a customary act echoed the depths of a human truth, and where even a casual gesture was a moment of beauty."[11] Such a wording may seem to point to Gauguin in Tahiti, but elements of the Middle East, too—such as an Egyptian maiden glimpsed gracefully filling a jug, Rebecca-like, at a well—could call up just such a response from harried Europeans.[12]

Graña's remark, though, is incomplete. First, it emphasizes only one side of the European view: the East as sentimental-pastoral ideal; it ignores the flip side: the East as diabolical and threatening. This exotic aspect, too, can be seen to have some domestic (endotic) motivation. As Chris Bongie puts it, the West's obsession with Turkish brutality—with summary trials, public hangings, vengeful beheadings—evinced not only revulsion but also a certain attraction, grounded in an "individualistic" dismay with "an increasingly bureaucratic and impersonal society" at home. "The scene of torture exemplifies an Other way of life that has yet to be brought under the panoptic gaze of modernity."[13]

Second, Graña's remark about the exotic "moment of beauty" neglects to note that purportedly positive, idealizing images of another culture emphasizing its "naturalness" and "spontaneity" can veil from sight the complexities of that other culture as fully as do frankly negative stereotypes.

Finally, Graña's formulation emphasizes only one side of the artist-public relationship: it glorifies the importance of the exotic to the person who creates an exotic work of art but leaves unmentioned the individuals and groups that consume the work. Paintings of—and books of Oriental tales about—scimitar-wielding warriors or Barbary pirates were widely purchased and admired; ballets about Middle Eastern dancing women (*almahs* or, in French, *almées* or *bayadères*) were rapturously applauded by audiences across Europe and America.[14] Such works clearly tapped yearnings and anxieties that were not at all unique to the artist, writer, or choreographer and composer but rather widespread among city folk everywhere in the West.

Still, it is true that numerous creative artists were extraordinarily attracted to learning about and even visiting distant regions, perhaps because of that feeling of apartness from the mainstream of urban and industrialized society. Some of the most significant Orientalist writers, painters, and composers traveled to Egypt or the Maghreb; others harvested fresh images and useful kernels of information from travelers' accounts and scholarly books—for example, the articles and detailed plates in the twenty-two-volume *Description de l'Egypte* (1809–28), which was the published result of intensive on-site research by Napoleon's team of savants (including one well-informed musician, Guillaume Villoteau). In contrast, most consumers of culture neither traveled abroad nor read anything about the region that was more reliable than the occasional magazine article. Inevitably, they received their most potent and memorable images of the Middle East from products of craftsmanship and artistic imagination, including not only novels and paintings, book illustrations and carved furniture, but also musical works—especially ballets and operas, with their extraordinary capacity for telling stories, evoking places, conveying passions.

Alla Turca *and Alternatives, 1800–1835*

These multifarious images and evocations varied greatly from place to place, art to art, genre to genre. In the eighteenth and early nineteenth centuries, the visual arts and imaginative literature (echoing travel books and scholarly essays) depicted the Orient as peopled by a wide range of stock characters, including the reflective or world-weary sultan-poet; the devout, hardworking boatman of the Nile; the wise and patient Muslim cleric; the ruthless Barbary Coast pirate; the beautiful, melancholy Persian princess; and the indolent, perhaps pipe-smoking Turkish harem woman.[15] In contrast, for the general music-loving public throughout the Western musical world, there was, during the decades around 1800, basically one recognizable sonic image of the Middle East: the *alla turca* style, a complex of generally noisy timbres and figures derived from the military music of the janissary corps (or from Western impressions thereof; see Mary Hunter's essay in this volume). This style quickly found a home in comic operas, where it tended to be invoked in conjunction with portraits of male Islamic power, especially those tending toward the noble, frightening, or ridiculous (or some combination of these three).[16]

Boieldieu's *Le calife de Bagdad* (1800) and Gioachino Rossini's *L'italiana in Algeri* (1813) illustrate how the familiar Turkish jangle continued to be used, sometimes in a rather automatic, highly conventional fashion, especially for ceremonial choruses heralding the arrival of tyrants, jailers, executioners (impalers, to be precise), Barbary pirate gangs, or other figures of oppressive male authority or organized (and Ottoman-tolerated) criminality. Albert Lortzing's first opera, *Ali-Pascha von Janina* (1824), feels even more like a kind of cultural "afterbeat," being modeled closely on a near-canonical instance of *alla turca* characterization: Mozart's *Entführung*. The energy in the work comes less from the overly familiar musical devices than from the striking timeliness of the story: the libretto is based on a rather grisly anecdote (perhaps spurious) about the infamous Ali Pasha, an Albanian chieftain who had played a complex and much-debated role in the Greek war of independence until he was murdered by Ottoman soldiers in 1822, two years before Lortzing's opera.

Reconnoitering the Musical Territory

The evidence of these and other early nineteenth-century works suggests that by around 1830 *alla turca* and its attendant dramatic types (e.g., the boorish tyrant) were becoming somewhat shopworn, tiresome to composers and perhaps increasingly predictable to audiences. Indeed, several Middle Eastern works in these early decades of the century were beginning to explore fresher musical and musico-dramatic images, either instead of or in addition to *alla turca*. Giacomo Meyerbeer's *Il crociato in Egitto* of 1824 twice emphasized the beauty of nature: in a drone-laden garden scene in 6/8 and a seaside barcarolle (both for chorus). Carl Maria von Weber's *Oberon* (1828, though its libretto contains the standard prowling harem guards) and Luigi Cherubini's *Ali-Baba* (1833, though its libretto features the forty thieves and cutthroats of the beloved Arabian Nights tale) made novel and creative use of "authentic" Eastern tunes found in books.[17] Beethoven, too, may have relied on a source—such as reports or transcriptions of Arab or Turkish music—for certain aspects of his Chorus of Dervishes in *Die Ruinen von Athen* (1811).[18]

The idea of Beethoven or the others copying—at whatever remove—an authentic Islamic or other non-European musical source may at first sound unlikely. But it was precisely during their day—that is, in the first decades of the nineteenth century—that the precursors of the modern field of ethnomusicology, inspired by Johann Gottfried von Herder and other folklorists, were beginning to undertake occasional and, in some cases, extensive on-site transcriptions of the music of Egypt and neighboring lands and to publish the results. The respected organist, composer, and music scholar Georg Joseph Vogler (1749–1814, known as Abbé or Abt Vogler) traveled widely throughout Europe and along the coast of North Africa; thanks to transcriptions given him by diplomats, he was able to include in his organ recitals (of which he gave some two thousand during his lifetime) not only such items as *Terrace Song of the* [North] *Africans* and *The Mohammedan Confession of Faith* but also tunes from such places as Greenland and China.[19] Weber and Meyerbeer had both studied devotedly with Vogler: the former in Vienna, 1803–4, the latter in Darmstadt, 1810–11.[20] As for Beethoven, the already-famous composer once stood listening at a party—together with Cherubini, actually—as Vogler improvised upon the keyboard "endless variations on an African theme which he himself had brought back from its country of origin."[21]

And Vogler was of course a mere dabbler compared to the serious students and disseminators of Arab music in decades to come, including G. A. Villoteau (one of Napoleon's savants), Edward William Lane, and Salvador-Daniel. The last-named made available to many musicians the pathbreaking transcriptions that he had notated on field trips to North Africa in the 1850s.[22]

The Growing Interest in the Middle East around 1840

The 1830s and 1840s saw a sudden burst in the production and eager reception of compositions that took up the challenge of portraying the Middle East seriously and imaginatively. Some of this can be attributed to the work of the scholars noted above or, in exceptional cases, to direct contact with the music of the region. But any phenomenon this complex has many overlapping "causes."

Some of these causes are musical, yet have little directly to do with the non-Western world. For instance, it was during these very years around 1840 that the issue of program music was being widely discussed for the first time (thanks in part to the works and essays of Hector Berlioz and Franz Liszt); as a result, a piano piece or programmatic symphony about distant places and peoples might naturally become a lightning rod for debate in the press and at social gatherings. Exotic musics of various kinds invaded musical life during these years, in large part through theatrical dance (a point to which we shall return) but also through the piano: some exotic pieces were technically modest (though they could of course be quite complex in other ways, as the Chopin mazurkas demonstrate); others were flashy and virtuosic (Louis Moreau Gottschalk's Creole and Caribbean pieces; Liszt's Hungarian Rhapsodies—see Jonathan Bellman's first essay in this volume). The long tradition of stage and symphonic works drenched in other topoi, such as pastoral/Alpine ones, now received fresh impetus through the emphasis, especially in Auber's ballets and Meyerbeer's grand operas for Paris, on using music and choreography that reflected locale and historical period (a parallel phenomenon to the exquisitely researched costumes and sets in these same stage works). And 1843–45—the years surrounding the composition and eager reception of Félicien David's *Le désert*—are the very years in which the polka dance craze (originating, apparently, in the Czech lands) swept Paris, London, and the United States.[23]

But it was the Middle East (and, by extension, India) that became particularly resonant in the mid-1840s, taking second place only to southern Spain as a favored location for operas and ballet. For this the reasons are more strictly nonmusical. By 1829 Victor Hugo felt impelled to note, in the preface to his collection of poems *Les orientales,* that all eyes of Europe were turned toward the Ottoman Empire and neighboring regions: "The Orient has become, for both the intellect and the imagination, a sort of widespread preoccupation, to which the author of this book has conformed perhaps unconsciously."[24] The French wrested Algeria from Turkish control the next year (1830) and soon began to colonize it, as they would later colonize Tunisia and Morocco.

Paris specialized in turning news bulletins into goods and leisure-time activities. In the mid-1830s people strolling on the boulevards encountered, in addition to the usual beggars with monkeys and the children peddling buttons, "men dressed up as Turks in blue blouses offering perfumed sweets that could be smelled from afar."[25] At the Jardin Turc (on the Boulevard du Temple), a fashionable clientele sipped coffee—still a somewhat exotic treat—while listening to, in this case, scarcely exotic music: a small orchestra playing waltzes by such composers as the young Jacques Offenbach. And visual artists such as Louis Daguerre (the future founder of photography) transported audiences with painted dioramas, such as "The Crucifixion, with the City of Jerusalem," and a glorious one of "The Inauguration of Solomon's Temple" that, by adroit changes in colored lighting from front and back, seemed gradually to fill with a crowd of pious Hebrews.[26]

Increasingly, Europeans were also touring or even settling in the Middle East: first in the "Holy Land" regions—Egypt, Palestine, greater Syria—then, around 1840, in the Maghreb. Some individuals were pursuing a spiritual or aesthetic quest (e.g., Chateaubriand, Lamartine, Delacroix); others came on military, governmental, or commercial missions (e.g., the young musician Ernest Reyer, who lived in Algeria in 1839–48, working with his uncle in a French government office). Over the ensuing decades, European-style luxury hotels were constructed to meet the demands of these individuals plus an increasing number of simple vacationers fleeing winter's chill.[27]

People who did not travel could consult guide books, travelers' memoirs, and published collections of photographs (e.g., by the writer Maxime du Camp) or detail-laden drawings and etchings (including mammoth-format ones by the British artist David Roberts) that conveyed images of the region's villages, beasts of burden, and crumbling ancient monuments.

Middle Eastern musics were not so easily captured and (however onesidedly) represented. As regards the musics of the biblical world, including ancient Egypt, the few surviving primary sources were (and remain today) frustratingly opaque. Current-day music of the region was mostly known through the few brief and misleading fragments available in books and in the occasional book-plundering musical work (e.g., Weber's aforementioned *Oberon*). Musicians and music lovers would not be able to discover for themselves the richness and complexity of the musics of the Middle East until travel became more widespread later in the century (in both directions: a Tunisian instrumental ensemble held forth at the Paris International Exhibition of 1878).

David's Le désert *(1844): An "Ode-symphonie" and Travelogue*

The single most crucial moment in the musical portrayal of the Middle East, therefore, came in 1833, when a young Western composer, eschewing books, journeyed to Turkey, Egypt, and Palestine, and kept his ears open. Félicien

David made the journey not on his own but as one of several dozen followers of the Saint-Simonian movement, a "utopian socialist" movement that was suppressed by the government in 1832. Several small boatloads of disciples made their way to Turkey and Egypt, where they hoped to locate the Female Messiah, whose imminent appearance the leaders had been predicting. During his two years in "the East," David gathered musical impressions, which he arranged for piano and published, upon his return to France, under the collective title *Mélodies orientales* (1836), but few copies were sold.[28]

David's second major tribute to the Middle East, *Le désert,* achieved instantaneous and, indeed, international success a scarce eight years later (1844). He dubbed the work's genre "*ode-symphonie,*" comprising as it did both spoken narration (in verse) and orchestral and vocal music (the vocal forces being, in this case, solo tenor and male chorus).[29]

Part 1, "L'entrée au désert" (The entrance to the desert), begins with the narrator, supported by long-held notes in the strings, evoking the grandeur of the endless arid realms. Next, a male chorus—which represents, for the moment, the "grains of sand" themselves, singing "unutterable harmonies from everlasting silence"—praises, in pantheistic fashion, the omnipresence of Allah. A caravan arrives from the distance, beginning *pianissimo* and building to *fortissimo,* then adding the chorus ("Come, let us trot, move along our way, sing, go gaily and in freedom!"). A brief sandstorm rises up and then dies down.

Part 2, "La nuit au désert" (Night in the desert), takes place after the caravan has "planted its tent" at some apparently unpopulated spot. A tenor aria proclaims the beauty of the night, comparing it to the pleasures of loving a woman. In two orchestral numbers the audience must imagine dancers and dancing. The first, "Fantasia arabe," is energetic and perhaps evokes the competitive displays of horsemanship that formed one widely accepted meaning of the word *fantasia* in the nineteenth century. (The second, an orchestral evocation of dancing women, is discussed further below.) Male members of the caravan then sing in praise of "freedom in the desert," in contrast to "you pale city dwellers"—is this *vous* the audience?—who stay behind in "your tombs of stone"—apartment houses? concert halls?—instead of sleeping in tents under the stars. Part 2 draws gently to a close with the "Rêverie du soir," in which tenor soloist and unison men's chorus voice their erotic yearnings, then fall asleep.

In the concluding part 3 ("Le départ de la caravane": The caravan sets forth), the sun rises; the muezzin (tenor, again) calls the worshipers to prayer (in Arabic); the caravan resumes its march toward the horizon and vanishes "like a morning mist"; and the sands restate their praise of Allah.

The travelogue-like plot and the spoken dialogue were both novel features, and they combined to give an impression of "you are there" that was unlike anything previously done. The effect was further increased by David's enterprising use of several authentic tunes and motives and by the muezzin's scraps of Arabic.[30] No fewer than four movements were based on tunes collected by David in Egypt or Syria: "Danse des almées," "Fantasia arabe," "Rêverie du soir," and "Chant du muezzin." Still, probably the single most attractive movement is the aforementioned "Marche de la caravane." Apparently not based on any "air arabe," the number combines features of West and East: in character and form it echoes the "Marche des pèlerins" from Berlioz's *Harold in Italy,* but its second statement (example 5.1) is varied by an oboe descant line that, in its soloistic freedom, evokes mental images of a player of the *zurna* improvising atop his lumbering camel.

Ex. 5.1. Félicien David, *Le désert* (1844), "Marche de la caravane," second statement.

The Advent of the Oriental Woman, and of "Kradoudja"

Less often mentioned at the time than the various aspects of (seeming) authenticity was the work's no less distinctive treatment of gender. To begin with, at no point in the work are women involved as performers. One number, though—the orchestral "Danse des almées"—is quite pathbreaking in that it vividly evokes images of curvaceous women dancing with supple arm and torso movements; the beckoning quality is intensified by the curling melody's being given to a solo oboe, perhaps understood as the equivalent of the Arab *mujwiz* (example 5.2). When one contrasts the sterner view of Arab customs in "Le harem" (from *Mélodies orientales* of eight years earlier), one suspects that David was now beginning to yield to popular taste.[31] Indeed, several successful stage works had already presented Eastern dancing women to Paris audiences, though with music of relatively conventional cut, notably Daniel-François-Esprit Auber's *Le dieu et la bayadère* (1830) and Johann Friedrich Burgmüller's *La péri* (1843), a ballet set in Cairo to a scenario by Théophile Gautier (based on his own *faux*-Arabian tale, "The Thousand and Second Night"). Paris had even hosted two months of public performances by a troupe of *bayadères* (plus instrumentalists) from India in 1836, and Gautier had lauded them in his newspaper column.[32] The 1830s and 1840s, in short, mark the moment when the Middle East becomes female, which it will then remain past the end of the century.

Ex. 5.2. David, *Le désert*, "Danse des almées."

These decades likewise mark the arrival of a fascination with Middle Eastern music (however narrowly or broadly one defines the region). By the mid-1840s the lure of Middle Eastern music had become quite explicit and was quickly commodified: two (supposed?) Arab tunes different from those used by David began to be performed and published in adaptions suitable to concert hall and parlor. The first, a *Marche marocaine,* attained brief success in 1845 in a virtuoso piano arrangement by Léopold de Meyer.[33]

In contrast, the second Arab tune was a love song, or at least disseminated as such, to judge by its French title: "Kradoudja, ma maîtresse." It was also to have a longer and more varied career. This tune is purportedly of Algerian origin and seems to have first attained renown as a musical "marker" of Middle Easternness in France: the wildly fashionable pianist-composer Franz Hünten (a permanent Parisian, though German-born) published a *Fantaisie arabe* based upon it; the dance-orchestra conductor Philippe Musard turned the tune into a quadrille, musically prosaic but graced with a glorious cover vignette; and the poet and critic Théodore de Banville alluded to the song several times in the years 1846–50. Narrow in range and obsessive in its melodic patterning, it would have a second vogue in America, being published at least five times around 1895 (thanks to dance performances by a woman called "Little Egypt" at the Columbian Exposition in Chicago, 1892–93). Even today this "Hootchy Kootchy Dance," as it is often known, probably remains the "exotic" tune best known throughout the Western musical world.[34]

Simplicity: A Chosen Marker and Its Treatment

The single most striking feature of such tunes as "Kradoudja/Hootchy Kootchy," de Meyer's Moroccan march, and the scraps of Arab music used by David in *Mélodies orientales* and in *Le désert* is their simplicity. (David's muezzin chant is the exception that proves the rule.) Arab art music has long been marked by elaborate, flexible, highly decorated instrumental and vocal improvisation upon one of dozens of *maqāmat* (roughly: scale patterns, many using intervals finer or broader than those in the Western scales) and accompanied by a vast and subtle variety of accompanimental rhythms. But next to none of that can be sensed in these European-published *airs arabes,* which are mostly square, primarily Aeolian-mode tunes (often consisting of two parallel phrases with, respectively, "open" and "close" endings), narrow in range and accompanied by some version of the accompanimental figure shown in example 5.4. This rhythm is well attested in many transcriptions and can still be heard today in improvisations by Egyptian and other musicians, but the latter of course regularly enrich it with a dazzling variety of cross-rhythms, of which the *morceaux arabes* of the 1840s give no hint.[35]

The use of simple materials was conditioned by many factors: the limitations of Western notation and Western instruments and performance traditions (both of which allowed no room for microtonal scales); the limitations of Western hearing and of the Western conception of the musical "work," when confronted with the very different complexities of non-Western music (e.g., improvisational layering); and, always, the underlying assumption that non-Western culture was inherently less elaborated (more primitive), more easily reduced to a few concrete images (the harem, impoverished Nile boatmen) and musical devices (frank repeated rhythms, a florid oboe solo, melodies stuck in a single modal rut or hovering around a single pitch). This electively simple vocabulary or collection of "signifiers" may seem stultifying; in practice, though, it provided composers from the 1840s onward with a style whose distinctive and obstinately stable features would, in their very stubbornness, contrast with the suppleness, nuance, and variety of harmony and orchestration that were becoming major preoccupations in the world of Western concert music.

Piano Works, Songs, and the Orient as Female

Pieces for amateur performers were the cheapest and quickest way for composers and publishers to respond to the Arab vogue. The Hünten and Musard pieces noted above, a fantasy by Henri Herz (1844) on the Arab dance from Burgmüller's aforementioned *La péri,* David's *Mélodies orientales* (reprinted in France and picked up also by Schott in Germany, within a year of the premiere of *Le désert*), and later, a remarkable "Mauresque" by Emmanuel Chabrier (1881), are all more or less suitable for an "intermediate" piano student.

German *Lieder* and French *mélodies* were similarly scaled to the abilities of amateurs; this, combined with the presence of a sung verbal text, made such "art songs" a particularly important genre for delivering and embroidering current images of the Middle East. Several of Schubert's songs anticipate the trend (e.g., "Geheimes," the "Suleika" songs, and "Mahomets Gesang," all of 1821, and "Der Gott und die Bajadere" of 1815). Over the next five decades, songs full of Oriental colors flourished, including notable examples by Georges Bizet ("Adieux de l'hôtesse arabe"), Edouard Lalo, Charles Gounod, Anton Rubinstein, Edvard Grieg—a "Song of the Odalisque" that gives full vent to her aching, unrequited love for her sultan—and Saint-Saëns, leading finally out of the parlor and into the concert hall with Maurice Ravel's *Shéhérazade* (1903) for mezzo-soprano and orchestra.

Arab hostesses, Sheherazade, odalisques: clearly, these songs continue the trend, noted in *Le désert,* toward greater emphasis on female sensuality as the chief signifier, alluring and mysterious, of the imagined Middle East. This trend is well known in paintings of the period: the famous harem women of Jean-Auguste-Dominique Ingres and Eugène Delacroix, ca. 1825, are but the beginning of a tradition that reaches a climax of decadent voluptuousness and sometimes barely disguised prurience around the 1870s in works of Jean-Louis Gérôme, Lecomte de Nouÿ, and others.[36] Similarly, in Orientalist songs (such as most of those just mentioned) the Middle East itself becomes, in a sense, female, a realm in which issues of power and control can be forgotten by the happily complicit listener. The songs make increasing use of curvaceous melodic lines (directly analogous, at times, to curling smoke or wafting breeze or to the draftsman's decorative line known, precisely, as "arabesque"), floating harmonies of various kinds, and ear-caressing accompanimental textures.

A French Wave of Oratorios and Operas

What is true of song was that much more true of large-scale pieces requiring numerous performers and presuming the presence of a paying audience (oratorio, opera, ballet, and orchestral pieces): the rapid increase in number of works, and the increasing emphasis on feminine sultriness. Musical Orientalism reached its greatest level of elaboration in a number of such works, many of them by French or French-inspired composers. Giuseppe Verdi's *Aida,* for example, was built on a scenario by a French Egyptologist, and its music is in various ways modeled on the French grand operas of Meyerbeer, not least the latter's own "Middle Eastern" contribution, *L'africaine.*

David's oratorio-like *Désert* was followed by several similar works that inch their way toward including women as active characters. Ernest Reyer's secular oratorio *Le sélam* (1850, to a text written for the purpose by Théophile Gautier) eschews spoken narration but otherwise repeats or reworks many of the features of David's *Désert* (e.g., muezzin call and hymn to the night, here combined in a single number). The two most successful moments are a spookily effective women's chorus in which "sorceresses" exorcise the *jinns* (spirits who haunt houses, spreading their "bat wings in the darkness") and a concluding march of pilgrims returning from Mecca.[37] Reyer, having lived in Algeria, was able to assure the public, in his program note, that his "Conjuration des *djinns*" described a scene of "superstition" to which he had been an "eye- and earwitness" in Constantine.[38] Around the same time, the young César Franck and then Hector Berlioz produced biblical oratorios, respectively *Ruth* (1843–46, rev. 1871) and *L'enfance du Christ* (1850–54); the former contains a few cautiously charming numbers (e.g., chorus of Moabites), the latter a brilliantly imagined spinning dance for the soothsayers, presumably inspired by recent verbal descriptions of whirling dervishes. In both, of course, the female roles are appropriately respectable—tender and devoted and not much fun.[39] (Much the same can be said of Robert Schumann's *Das Paradies und die Peri* from around the same time—1843).[40]

It took the operatic and ballet stage to free the exotic woman from the constraining propriety of oratorio and *ode-symphonie,* allowing her to become the focus of detailed, sometimes obsessive attention on the part of the tenor (or male dancer, in the case of ballet) and, of course, the audience. Three mid-century French operas, written under the influence of *Le désert, Le sélam,* and the poems of Hugo and Gautier, populate the stage entirely with natives of the region in question. Such operas tend to function, in James Parakilas's words, as "dream[s] of a different life into which the audience escapes when the curtain rises and from which it awakens when the curtain falls."[41] That they thereby served to distract attention from the realities of Western exploitation of, and geopolitical scramble over, the Middle East should not go unremarked.

David's *Lalla-Roukh* (1862) contains some of his most fragrant and delicate evocations: hearing it, Berlioz rightly felt that David had found his way again after several less distinctive works. Still, it pales in comparison to two operas by Bizet: *Les pêcheurs de perles* (1863) and the one-act *Djamileh* (1871). These Bizet works are, admittedly, somewhat uneven (in part because of problematic librettos), but they turn masterful whenever the scenarios allow the evocation of a mysterious setting, religious ritual, or tale of long ago. What is particularly interesting is how they differ in their manner of evoking the East.

Though *Les pêcheurs de perles* is officially set in Ceylon (the outermost eastward arm of the "Middle East," as we noted at the outset), almost nothing in the music is specifically "Oriental," no doubt because the action was originally located in pre-Columbian Mexico and was only shifted to the South Asian island after Bizet had begun composing. And yet, so magically Other is the music that it seems a perfect complement to what is more an erotic fantasy than any kind of even remotely realistic depiction. Particularly remarkable is "Je crois entendre encore," the tenor Nadir's nostalgic aria about the many bygone times that he, hiding at night in the shadows of the palm trees, observed his beloved priestess from afar as she parted her long veil to the evening breeze. The melody line (taken by the solo oboe, then the lyric tenor) hangs obsessively around the dominant and lowered sixth and seventh degrees to such an extent that it seems to form an independent compositional layer in E Phrygian over the more conventionally tonal A minor accompaniment (example 5.3).

Ex. 5.3. Georges Bizet, *Les pêcheurs de perles* (1863), Act 1: Nadir's aria, "Je crois entendre encore."

Djamileh (based on Alfred de Musset's tale "Namouna") offers an even richer mixture: numbers that are specifically Middle Eastern jostle against more of Bizet's uniquely "Other" writing. The opening of the prelude (a grotesque march that will recur at the entrance of the slave merchant) features a descending serpentine oboe line in chromatic triplets that announces "Cairo!" to us, whereas the first number, an SATB chorus of boatmen (and apparently boat boys, represented by the women), is decorated with weird descending chromatic thirds that whisper "Land of Mystery!" The string chords with which Bizet connects the prelude and chorus are richly suggestive of a place where almost anything may happen. The ballad for Djamileh herself (example 5.4) opens with a winding descent in Aeolian mode, except that the fourth degree, intriguingly, is sometimes raised, sometimes not; quiet chords in the strings enunciate a simple drumbeat-type rhythm in 2/4 with subdivided first beat. And a descending chromatic oboe solo, accompanied by a nicely syncopated rhythmic pattern, forms the basis of the music to which the *danseuse* who is the "true pearl" of the slave dealer's inventory displays her art.

Ex. 5.4. Bizet, *Djamileh* (1869): Djamileh's ballad.

Instrumental Evocations from Many Countries

Well into the twentieth century, France was to remain the center of Middle Eastern evocation (e.g., Saint-Saëns, Ravel), and perhaps of musical exoticism generally (e.g., Olivier Messiaen, Pierre Boulez), no doubt in large part because of the country's unique position as both a major musical center (along with Germany and Italy) and a major colonial power (along with Britain and, eventually, the United States). But the fascination spread far and wide, to countries having little or no colonial presence (e.g., to Norway, in Grieg's incidental music to Ibsen's *Peer Gynt:* "Arabian Dance" and "Anitra's Dance").

One distinctive category of Orientalist music—we might call it the "instrumental evocation"—seems to have been particularly attractive to composers from a number of widely dispersed countries, including Russia (Mily Balakirev's large-scale, virtuosic piano piece *Islamey*, 1869, rev. 1902) and America (Arthur Foote's *Four Character Pieces from the Rubaiyat of Omar Khayyam* for orchestra, op. 48, 1900). The resulting pieces vary widely in "specifity" of evocation. Lalo's orchestral suites from *Namouna* (1881–82) include a particularly effective marketplace scene; they derive from a failed ballet, as does the long-popular suite from the *Ballet égyptien* of the Lyons-based composer-conductor Alexandre Luigini (1875; the ballet was first performed in Algiers). Pierre de Bréville's three-movement *Stamboul* (1875) for orchestra or piano has a muezzin call in its slow movement. Alexander Borodin's *In the Steppes of Central Asia* (1880) features hypnotic rhythms that perhaps evoke (camel) steps more than steppes, and Mikhail Ippolitov-Ivanov's *Caucasian Sketches* (1894) contain a flavorful example of the (by this date) nearly obligatory florid-oboe slow movement. Most of the aforementioned evoke a series of scenes, as does the Saint-Saëns *Suite algérienne* (discussed below). In contrast, César Franck's symphonic poem *Les djinns* (1884) for piano and orchestra, based on a famous poem by Hugo, describes the changing aspects of a single scene, namely (as in the Reyer), an exorcism of evil spirits.

The master of Middle East travelogues remains Saint-Saëns, who produced several such works for orchestra, for virtuoso pianist, or for the two in combination. Some of these, such as *Africa* for piano and orchestra (1891), are rather like Liszt's Hungarian Rhapsodies for piano (or Saint-Saëns's own *Rhapsodie d'Auvergne*), in that they consist of a single, somewhat fluid movement that surveys the music of the given region or ethnic group. The second movement of Saint-Saëns's Fifth Piano Concerto (1896) is just such a Middle Eastern rhapsody and has caused the whole work to be known, misleadingly, as "the Egyptian concerto."[42]

A similar "Rhapsodie mauresque" forms the second movement of his *Suite algérienne* op. 60 (1880) for orchestra and is perhaps the most successful evocation of non-Western music-making before Colin McPhee's gamelan-inspired *Tabuh-tabuhan* (see Mervyn Cooke's essay in this volume). According to Saint-Saëns's own program note (published in the score), this movement is set in one of Algiers's many cafés and represents Moors (Arabs) doing dances that are "by turns lascivious and unrestrained, to the sounds of flutes, folk fiddles [*rebabs*], and hand drums [*tambourins*]." The sequence of moods does indeed resemble what one might encounter in a very short (here three-section) *nawba* or suite by an Algerian or Tunisian ensemble, and these sections (as is also typical) contrast in meter and also mode. (The movement's key signature, two sharps, is differently interpreted in each section.) The first section, in 6/8, starts and ends with tunes in A Mixolydian and E Dorian (example 5.5); the middle of this section, though, is set in a Western-style D major and features Beethovenian modulating fugatos, quite unknown in traditional Arab music though clearly depicting, here, the frenetic increase of tension in the dancing. The second section of the movement, in 2/4, is in a kind of "relative minor" to D, namely B Aeolian (the flatted seventh, A natural, is given a downbeat accent at cadences). The third and last section begins with nothing but a solo flute playing a crisp 3/4 tune against duple drumming (timpani and *tambour de basque*), but then builds and builds in loudness and harmonic richness; the tune is in D Mixolydian (C naturals written in throughout) but always cadences on its fifth degree (making it A Dorian) until Western conventions prevail in a straightforward D major coda.

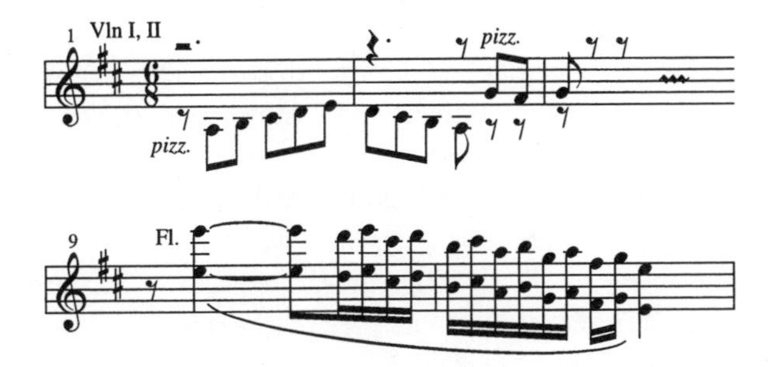

Ex. 5.5. Camille Saint-Saëns, *Suite algérienne,* op. 40 (1880), mvt. 2: "Rhapsodie mauresque," mm. 1–3 and 9–10.

The other movements of the *Suite algérienne* similarly focus on sounds (mostly musical ones) that a tourist might have heard on a trip to Algeria. Indeed, the whole work can be said to parallel the glorious travel posters (some designed by distinguished artists such as Etienne Dinet and Léon Cauvy) that advertised the diverse attractions of Algiers or Tunis, all under the protective umbrella of the French government and its various ministries and agencies (e.g., the Paris-Lyons-Marseilles railroad).

Varieties of Orientalist Opera

Despite these triumphs of purely instrumental evocation, it was of course opera, with its wealth of concrete signifiers—costumes and stage set, sung text and bodily gesture—that proved the most natural vehicle for embodying images (quasi-realistic or utterly fantastic) of another region or culture. Such operas are enormously varied, depending on the meanings that the composer and librettist projected onto the chosen locale. These added meanings, however, can render quite illusory the sense of a specific era (one of the supposed advantages of the genre) by suggesting "now" even in a work describing the Middle East back "then." For example, the old-fashioned "Turkish Captivity" opera (to use Parakilas's categories) gained fresh vigor in Verdi's early *I lombardi alla prima crociata* (1843), for the plot (about Crusaders and Ottomans and their respective cruelties) is overlaid with contemporary concerns about the tyranny of empire (the repressive rule of Austro-Hungary over Italy).

This solution was not widely adopted. Few operas, at least among those that achieved any notable success, dealt with the recent or present history of the region. For instance, aside from Meyerbeer's idiosyncratic *Il crociato,* there was no important opera of the "Soldier and the Exotic" sort about Algeria or Egypt, even though British and French soldiers and businessmen were spending months and years of their lives in these countries, often in intimate involvements with various local inhabitants (whether female or, in some cases, male). Or was it not "even though" but "because": was the Orient of the present day (and the relatively recent past, e.g., the Crusades) now becoming unfashionable in intellectual and artistic circles precisely because travel to the Middle East was becoming so widely available?

Whatever the reasons, serious Middle East operas—at least the ones that established themselves in the repertoire—were mostly now set back in ancient times.[43] Such ancient-world operas, however, are often rich in allusions to the inhabitants of modern-day North Africa and Arabia. (In that sense, they resemble *I lombardi* after all.) Such "allusions" take different forms and tones, as can be seen in *Aida* (1871), in several operas by Jules Massenet, in Karl Goldmark's *Die Königin von Saba* (1875), and in Saint-Saëns's *Samson et Dalila* (1875).

For one thing, the Orientalism may cut several different ways, depending on which group seems to be identified primarily as Other. In *Samson et Dalila* the Hebrews are, in musical terms, the God-fearing proto-Christians, whereas the Philistines are lascivious and violent heathens, given to drunken revelry (in the famous Bacchanale ballet), sacrilegious rituals, and vicious mockery. Effectively, this makes the Philistines the Middle Easterners or Arabs of the opera (or even, paradoxically, the Jews, in their mockery of Samson, who is clearly portrayed toward the opera's end as a prototype of the suffering Christ).[44] In Massenet's *Hérodiade* (1883), by contrast, imperial Rome is the stylistic norm (brassy ceremonial music of a typically French-Grand-Opera variety), against which the Hebrew religion is represented by a delicate "Danse sainte" before the Holy of Holies and by a florid prayer ("Schema Israël") that Massenet learned from a synagogue cantor in Paris, and the cult of John the Baptist by a women's chorus singing a particularly lovely canticle in nearly pandiatonic style. More fully Middle Eastern is the music—some of the strongest in the opera—for characters clearly represented as exotic even to the Jews and Christians: merchants and slaves from "different countries" (Act 1: example 5.6), and female slaves from Nubia, Greece, and Babylon, who recline "in lascivious and picturesque positions" around the reclining Herod in his bedchamber (Act 2: example 5.7).[45] (Example 5.7, as Rodney Milnes has noted, seems likely to have served Chaikovsky as a direct model for the "Danse arabe" in *The Nutcracker.*)[46]

Ex. 5.6. Jules Massenet, *Hérodiade* (1881, revised 1884): foreign merchants and slaves in Act 1 (orchestral part only).

This last feature of *Hérodiade* draws our attention to a crucial feature of exotic operas, generally: the stylistically most "different" moments tend to be located at the beginnings of scenes or acts and tend to involve the orchestra alone, or the chorus, or dancers (but little or no solo singing). The beginning of Act 3 of *Aida,* for example, gives new life to the traditional linking of the exotic and the natural world: the staccato tonic pedal, spread over four octaves in the violins, while the solo flute executes modal "arabesque" phrases, like little tunes heard in the distance, evoke a scene of placid beauty, including perhaps twinkling stars reflecting off the nearly still water of the wide river. The visible and audible setting is more than mere decoration, since it indicates with exquisite clarity how far from the hubbub of the Egyptian court Aida has had to come to be alone—she is about to sing her aforementioned romance—

Ex. 5.7. Massenet, *Hérodiade:* Babylonian, Greek, and Nubian women slaves, Act 2, mm. 11–17 (orchestral part only).

or, for that matter, to converse freely with the two people dearest to her: her father and her beloved Radames.

Reading the Local Color

The tendency to restrict the most overtly exotic music to the chorus and to numbers without singing (preludes, ballets) has sometimes been seen as a defect in these works of the high-water Orientalists (and, for that matter, those of their predecessors, including Boieldieu, Rossini, and David, though nobody objects when Mozart does the same, or Beethoven in *Die Ruinen von Athen*). In *Hérodiade,* complains one recent critic, "exotic allure . . . is not integrated into the drama of the characters."[47] Joseph Kerman seems to have something similar in mind when he blames *L'africaine* and *Aida* (and *Turandot*) for setting the pattern for a "careless application of local color" in opera.[48] (In *Tu-*

randot he finds "bogus orientalism lacquered over every page of the score"; the remark presumably would apply also to the operas of Massenet, though Kerman does not deign to mention them.) The implication in such remarks is that the foreignness, because musically confined to environmental numbers, comprises mere surface decoration, without "organic" function: "local color or exoticism for its own sake," as Kerman warns (in the case of *Turandot*).[49]

Such accusations are not without basis. Some opera ballets, in particular, can seem largely decorative (though intelligent staging and choreography can strengthen what might otherwise seem a weak link). We can willingly admit that the dance sequence in Act 2 of *Thaïs* (1894), for example, largely reinforces a point that the opera has already made more than adequately: the superficiality of the hedonistic world in which the actress and courtisan Thaïs has been living (before meeting the Cenobite monk who succeeds in reforming her but who then, to his own distress, falls in love with her). The ballet, one senses, was inserted largely to satisfy convention; hence there may be good reason to omit it and to use, instead, the "bridge" passage that Massenet later composed for the purpose.

More often than not, though, one can adduce several different ways in which exotic local color adds to the work's richness. First of all, Oriental-style numbers, such as ballets, tended to be enormously appealing to audiences (and performers) back then, as they still are today. Composers surely realized this since they often presented one or more such excerpts on an orchestral concert to drum up interest in a new opera or made four or more into an orchestral suite (which might, in some cases, have a longer life than the stage work itself).

Second, such "entertainments" are often crucial in establishing the social and gender context of an operatic plot: for example, the power of its monarch or its army chiefs to command dancing from women who come from neighboring regions, or the difference in lifestyle from Western norms (as reified in the style of these numbers, e.g., in the clearly lascivious *Samson* Bacchanale).[50]

Third, such environmental applications of exoticism—analogous to the opera's sets, costumes, and foreign names—can frame the *rest* of the opera (the nonexotic numbers) for its listeners, guiding their reactions to what the characters say and do. We accept the unrestrained, predatory sexuality of Saint-Saëns's Delilah not only because we know her reputation from the Bible but also because she makes her first entrance with the scantily clad, frond-waving Philistine maidens and because she dances with them to a mesmerizing Aeolian-mode tune, ravishingly orchestrated.

Fourth, numerous works show a defter interweaving of exotic and "normative" styles than critical nostrums admit. In Act 1, scene 2, of *Thaïs* (set in ancient Alexandria), Massenet uses exotic tunes in straightforward ways, for example, to set the scene and to portray certain characters, such as Thaïs's theater buddies or the two "beautiful fun-loving [*rieuses*] female slaves." More notable, though, is his ability, in the great quartet between these two slaves (Crobyle and Myrtale), their dissolute young owner Nicias, and the aforementioned Cenobite monk Athanaël (whom the slaves are bathing in perfume and dressing in jewelry and fine robes), to allow the women's exquisitely playful and arabesque-laden music (example 5.8) to float to the surface in the orchestra much of the time but then to fade out whenever Nicias urges Athanaël to enjoy the women's rather teasing attentions and when the latter prays for strength against these demons of lust and delight.

Ex. 5.8. Massenet, *Thaïs* (1894), Act 2, quartet.

Fifth and last: even when the main characters are associated (as they often are) with music that is nonexotic in style, the resulting dramatic effect may be quite different from what the critics cited above imply. It may, in particular, invite empathic identification with the Other through what Carl Dahlhaus might term a principled refusal to exoticize.[51] Verdi's Princess Amneris, for example, may be *surrounded* with exoticizing music of various kinds, but the music that she herself sings—music in which she longs, suffers—never comes labeled as Other. Indeed, during the trial of her beloved Radames, she comes to experience an anguish ("Numi, pietà") that is figured as indubitably sincere, Verdi's music here relying on a marker of grief—the repeated descending two-note sob—that draws authenticity from its use in Italian madrigals of the sixteenth century and the passions and sacred cantatas of J. S. Bach. Something similar can be said of Aida herself. Though certain passages in her music—and references to her by other characters—are made to sound exotic through a combination of several features (oboe solos, chromatic melodic lines, high pedals in the violins—the latter forming, as noted earlier, part of a scene of placid natural beauty),[52] some of her most heartfelt statements, including her own plea to the Fates (e.g., end of Act 1), are free of Otherizing accent and thus, presumably, cause us to feel, as if we ourselves were Aida, the agonizing bind in which circumstances of war and politics have placed her.[53]

Seeing (and Seeing through) Gender Stereotypes

The question of whether the sung music "sounds" Oriental has naturally led us to the many fascinating women in these operas and, more generally, to questions of the representation of gender.

The male characters, especially the religious and political leaders, are often marked by dogmatism or fierceness. In *Samson et Dalila,* the two leading male Philistines, Abimelech and the High Priest, are given words and actions no doubt calculated to make the characters hateful to the audience. The satrap Abimelech obsessively ridicules Israel's (the West's) God and then attacks Samson with a dagger; the High Priest, soon after, gives vent to an ugly, genocidal rage against the Israelites ("I will wipe them out without trace!") that, unlike the analogous fuming of Mozart's Osmin against the Christians, is treated with no shimmer of comic distance. Indeed, the roles of Abimelech and the High Priest might be thought irredeemably racist and offensive, the very kind of thing that no right-thinking opera house director would choose to mount today, and that no sensitive operagoer could take pleasure in witnessing, were it not for the music, which sharply differentiates the two characters and brings them alive. Since neither is characterized musically as Oriental, they can both end up being perceived not as Others at all but rather as contrasting models of the dangerously sectarian political/religious leader, not an unknown quantity in France or anywhere, then or now.

The choral throngs in Orientalist operas are sometimes treated as extensions of these male leaders (e.g., choruses of priests). Often, though, they represent, more unambiguously than do the leaders, the inhabitants of the Middle East—in part by the sheer transporting impact of a stage filled with browned-up bodies in loose robes and burnooses and carrying scimitars or whatever, but also because the chorus usually gets to sing at least one scene-setting number of their own in exotic style. The chorus members sometimes seem innocently interested in going about their own lives. Or they may show humane feelings (as in their pleading for the lives of the Ethiopian prisoners, in *Aida*, against the objections of Ramfis and the stern Egyptian priests). Or they may pick pointless fights with members of other tribes (quarreling groups of merchants and slaves "from different countries" at the beginning of *Hérodiade*). Or they may let themselves be led by the nose (e.g., the Philistines in the last act of *Samson*), a commentary, presumably, on the modern-day peoples of the region.[54]

Still, it is the Oriental women characters who seem increasingly to be what many such operas are about, as is indicated in the preponderance of operas bearing a woman's name as title, such as *Aida* and *Thaïs*. (Saint-Saëns's manuscript of his *Samson et Dalila* is headed simply *Dalila*.) Many of the leading ladies in these operas are outright seducers (Delilah) or have some rather purple past (Thaïs); similarly, in Act 2 of *Parsifal* (1882) the garden of a castle "richly Arabian in style" is conjured up by the sorcerer Klingsor, complete with a chorus of Flower Maidens wearing pastel veils and singing the most mellifluous lines in the entire opera, in order to entrap our tenor hero.[55]

A powerful instance from Central Europe is the title character of the once widely performed *Die Königin von Saba* (The Queen of Sheba) by Karl Goldmark, a Hungarian-born Jew. The plot deserves to be summarized, as it shows how the image of a Middle Eastern femme fatale could be elaborated to make a full-length opera that was at once fantasy-rich—not least in its obsessive linking of ripe femaleness and luxuriant plant life—and morally comforting.

The Queen of Sheba is explicitly referred to by other characters as the "Star of Arabia." Saba (as she is simply named in the score) is, like Delilah, the sort of seductive foreign beauty who, colonial soldiers were told, might bring crashing down their military career and hopes of a proper married life. We first learn about her from the young Hebrew warrior and diplomatic envoy Assad (tenor): when he was once in Lebanon on a mission, she came to him naked amid lush greenery by a river—symbolic natural surroundings, again—and wrapped her arms around him. Now, arriving in Judaea with her retinue, she turns and lifts her veil for him to recognize the face that only the wise but apparently somewhat aged King Solomon (baritone) is supposed to view. In Act 2 she lies in wait for him (at night, again outdoors) as her handmaiden Astaroth (a "Mooress"), in a modally fascinating vocalise (example 5.9), lures the anguished tenor to be with the Queen.

Ex. 5.9. Karl Goldmark, *Die Königin von Saba* (1875), Act 2: Astaroth's wordless and unaccompanied song.

At the end of the story, Assad is in exile in the desert (a setting symbolic of his now-wasted emotional state), and the Queen tries one last time to seduce him in order to "pay" him for his sufferings (her repulsive verb: *zahlen*). He angrily sends her away and, watched over by his true beloved Sulamith, sinks to the ground and dies—punished in body for having so long yielded to a sacrilegious desire (at one point he had even declared, in front of Sulamith, King Solomon, and the priests of Jehovah, that he worshiped only this human "goddess") yet also redeemed in soul for having finally rejected temptation and chosen the path of virtue. Saba's punishment, at opera's end, comprises a last and fitly merciless nature image that is the polar opposite of her beloved nighttime gardens and rivers: she is engulfed by a rising sandstorm.

One other complex aspect of voice and gender should be isolated and emphasized here. Saba is a mezzo, as are numerous other exotic women in opera (e.g., Sélika in *L'africaine,* Amneris in *Aida,* Dalila in *Samson et Dalila,* the title roles in Massenet's *Cléopâtre* and Bizet's *Carmen*). The lowish voice implies a kind of worldly wiseness (including a willingness to manipulate or deceive) that, in operatic women, often comes along with open sexual desire and independence of will. The Middle East seems to have been a perfect setting to allow such women characters to proliferate. Egyptian women entertainers, for example, embodied many a visitor's fantasy of what a woman could be like when free from the complementary European constraints of demureness (represented by the proper Victorian woman) and shame (the prostitute, hiding in the shadows).

Into the Twentieth Century: Musical Style Absorbs the Middle Eastern

Goldmark's opera is an emblematic case also in regard to a phenomenon discussed earlier: the stylistic disparity between the exotic numbers and the rest of the opera. Astaroth's love call (example 5.9), the ballets, and the numerous other orchestral numbers (extensive preludes and marches) are more original and attractive than the rest, which is highly conventional, square-cut, and dramatically slow. This disparity, seen to greater or lesser degrees in many "Middle Eastern" works of the period, must at some point have been understood as suggesting a valuable new direction: if the evocation of the Orient (and especially of its sexiness) was so appealing to composers and audiences alike, why encapsulate it, seal it off, in a few dance numbers and orchestral interludes? Why not instead try to let this quality expand out into the entire work? This is exactly what many composers of the next generation (around 1900) seem to have thought.

Their motivation was no doubt reinforced by certain aesthetic tendencies of the day. Formalist and organicist views of art combined to make a highly semantic use of local color seem—by virtue of its inherently *inorganic* relationship to the style prevailing elsewhere in the work (or in the composer's oeuvre, generally)—distracting, woefully superficial, expendable, cheap.[56]

Less familiar to us today than formalism/organicism is a very different turn-of-the-century aesthetic trend: symbolism. Writers and creative artists who inclined toward symbolism tended to view music and the other arts as a realm of magic, of the otherworldly (including mystical ponderings), or else of the this-worldly (sensual gratification, anxiety) carried to excess. The Middle East, seen through a symbolist lens, not only retained its longstanding fascination but also could now serve more than ever as a locus for the mingling of the dangerous, the transcendant, and the unpredictable. The painter Odilon Redon, the ballet impresario Serge Diaghilev, the writers Pierre Loti, J.-L. Huysmans, and Victor Segalen, the composers Claude Debussy, Maurice Ravel, and Karol Szymanowski—all saw the Orient as a primarily imaginative space in which one might take refuge from the sordid ugliness or prosaic utilitarianism of the urban West or, for that matter, of the real Middle East, with all its now-obvious limitations. After all, a serious artist could no longer pretend that the (supposedly more or less timeless, undeveloped) Orient being invoked was either the real one, visitable by tourists, or else its ancient precursor, revealed more or less accurately in history books. As a result, notes Chris Bongie, the Orientalism of the decades around 1900 tended toward a "fatidic pessimism":

any place of purity or refreshing vitality that it conjured up as a "refuge from [the] overbearing modernity" of real life was understood to be a product of active imagining.[57]

Composers were right to feel that a real-life alternative to the West could no longer be found in the Middle East (if, that is, it ever could have been). Cities such as Algiers and Cairo had been so reshaped and built up that whole *quartiers* now resembled, and functioned as, European cities. Furthermore, there were periodic uprisings and other acts of resistance on the part of the native populations (e.g., in Egypt, against the European imperialists and their native representatives, 1881; in Persia, 1906; and in Turkey, 1908–23). This formed a clear reminder that the principle of Western superiority (hence of ethically and religiously mandated control) over the darker races—still a keystone of most Western political thinking around 1900—could prove impossible to carry out in practice and was, in the end, a flattering but unsustainable illusion.

Not surprisingly, therefore, what now began to fascinate the Orientalist artist (and, as always in such formulations, his or her audience as well) was the Orient as idea rather than reality (or even half reality), the Orient as a scent capable of setting off fantasies. The Orient now favored was frankly mythical, ungraspable, unreal, which is to say *more* real than any place in history book or atlas, because it conveyed more of certain oft-unspoken aspects of life—sadness, delirium, yearning, brutality, ecstasy—than art had hitherto dared to encompass.

It is at this point that Middle Eastern traits become profuse in musical works having no connection to Arabs, Turks, or Persians. Modal structures of the most varied kind abound in Debussy and Bartók, including distinctive uses of the octatonic scale. (This scale had carried both Middle Eastern and supernatural associations in the hands of Mikhail Glinka, Nikolai Rimsky-Korsakov, and other Russians.)[58] The neighbor-note triplet figure that meant Persia and Central Asia to Rimsky-Korsakov and Borodin now features prominently in Debussy's *La mer* (1903), even though the work is not generally associated with the Middle East but with Japan (understandably, since the cover of the score bears a woodcut by Hokusai).[59] Ravel, in his ballet *Daphnis et Chloé,* paints the sunrise over mythical ancient Greece—the birthplace of "the West"—with similar "Eastern" figures. More generally, the love of surface decoration that is so typical of art nouveau and that made artists look toward the Middle East for inspiration is everpresent in such pieces.[60]

Richard Strauss's *Salome* (1905) can stand as paradigmatic for works in which Orientalist attitudes and stylistic devices are at once everywhere and nowhere. The Arab style proper appears only in Salome's "Dance of the Seven

Veils," which goes through several distinct moods: these include a slow section that at once beckons erotically and staggers almost drunkenly and, as conclusion, a pounding dance reminiscent of the end of the "Bacchanale" from Saint-Saëns's *Samson.* For the rest, Strauss himself felt that he filled the opera with "truly exotic harmonies which sparkle like taffeta, particularly in the stirring cadences"; "operas hitherto based on Oriental and Jewish subjects," he opined further, "[have] lacked true Oriental color and scorching sun."[61] Such a remark remains truly puzzling, when one considers that audiences and critics, over the intervening century, have received *Salome* in a very different spirit: not as an evocation of the Middle East but as a case study in psychology and obsession.

The Popular Middle East and the Modernists

Still, the more typical nineteenth-century view of the Middle East as exotic, as not-Us, did continue, but primarily in popular rather than "high" culture. The "musical travelogue" approach took ever-new forms in illusionistic exhibits at world's fairs and the like (such as the "Mareorama," or sea voyage, at the Paris 1900 fair, complete with phonographic Arabic and Turkish music),[62] but also in music for silent films and for light concerts. Erno Rapée's *Motion Picture Moods* anthology (1924) contains pieces bearing such titles as "In Sight of the Oasis" and featuring such reductive signals of Arabness as swirling melodies full of augmented seconds.[63] (More recent outcroppings within this tradition are *Lawrence of Arabia*—with music by a well-versed Frenchman, Maurice Jarre—and the Walt Disney film *Aladdin,* itself taking off from the 1940 *Thief of Baghdad.*) In 1920 Albert Ketèlbey produced the immortal *In a Persian Market,* an "intermezzo scene" for band or small orchestra; reprehensibly demeaning or delightfully tacky—opinions will differ—is the pentatonic plea for alms, sung by members of the orchestra and harmonized entirely with open fifths and octaves over a tomtom beat, the result sounding rather like stereotypical American Indian music.[64]

Popular song, too, served as a vehicle of vicarious travel, especially for the French, many of whom would at some point in their lives travel to North Africa or, if not, might receive picture postcards from soldiers or business people stationed there.[65] In the same way that American popular songs of the first half of the twentieth century evoked the tropical splendor of Caribbean islands that were becoming a major vacation getaway, the French entertainment industry captured (and reinforced) the nationwide, yet often blinkered, fascination with the colonies that were increasingly seen as making up "greater France." Popular songs carried titles such as "Baraki Barako" (1906), "Sous le soleil marocain" (1925), "La caravane, ou La fille du bédouin" (1927), "Nuit d'Alger" (recorded by Josephine Baker, 1936), and "Ali ben Baba" (recorded by Maurice Chevalier, 1942).[66] Similarly, the music of these pop songs made recurrent use of certain long-standard markers of Arabness (e.g., accompanimental rhythms such as in example 5.2).[67]

What makes these impoverished musical "works" undyingly fascinating, though, is the way in which they were performed by gifted, even seductive entertainers. These singers jauntily parodized North Africans' pidgin French, their accents ("b" instead of "p," and lots of guttural "kh"), and their funny Koran chanting. Reed players in the backup band played squeaks and wails recalling, for the ignorant, Arabic music for *zurna*—that is, when the number in question wasn't a straightforward Western-style march song celebrating the hundredth anniversary of France's victory over Abd-el-Kader, or a pseudo-sultry ballad filled with escapist blather nearly identical to that in mid-nineteenth-century opera librettos ("Nuits coloniales, nuits d'étrange volupté . . . nuits de rêve, nuits d'amour!").[68]

No wonder that composers of serious music began running the other way. And are still running. When Pierre Boulez defends his own borrowings from non-Western music, he specifically contrasts them to the "clumsy appropriation of a 'colonial' musical vocabulary" that he says marks "the innumerable short-lived *rhapsodies malgaches* and *rhapsodies cambodgiennes* that appeared during the early years of the present century."[69] One wonders if his gut reaction is being fed entirely by such minor or mostly long-forgotten pieces. (*Rhapsodie malgache,* for example, was composed in 1945 by the now obscure Raymond Loucheur.) Or might he not also be be reacting, perhaps without being quite aware of it, to the *chansons coloniales* just mentioned, which form a (less pompous) analogue to the pseudo-Moorish/Byzantine Palais du Trocadéro (built for the Exposition Universelle of 1878 and torn down in 1935) or, on a smaller scale, the many French public spaces (e.g., movie theaters, Masonic halls) that were decorated with Sahara scenes, camels, and—blending modern and ancient, Algeria and Egypt—pyramids.[70] Or might he even be recalling with a shiver the (to his mind kitschy?) Nautch Dances and the like by the barefoot pioneers of modern dance, such as Loïe Fuller, Maud Allan, and Ruth St. Denis?

Critics, too. A lingering formalist and organicist bias guides the remarks of Kerman and others cited above.[71] If, such critics still seem to feel, the exoticism is on the surface, it cannot be organic, nor therefore can it be artistically cogent. Only once it is absorbed into the prevailing musical language of a composer—an achievement of first-generation modernists, such as Strauss and Debussy, that was carried further by Igor Stravinsky, Messiaen, and others—does it become clean enough to praise, precisely because it has shed most of its allusive power, its reference to a world beyond the West, its claim to "represent" another culture.[72]

But that is the magic of *Oberon, The Pearl Fishers, Aida:* the works play, often somewhat messily, with—wallow in or anguish over—distinctions between ethnic observer/desirer and ethnic observed/desired, between "mainstream" and "margin," between hegemonic/metropolitan and disempowered (sometimes resurgent, sometimes supine) subaltern.[73] One day human society may finally be free of such versions (inherently skewed toward the destructive and exploitive?) of the basic (universal? inevitable? ideologically neutral? infinitely malleable?) epistemological distinction between Self and Other. At present, though, they remain widespread, defining, troubling, infectious, sometimes poisonous, and nearly always at once sharp and blurry. So long as such asymmetrical ethnic dichotomies retain their resonance, their central role in shaping both social reality and people's feelings about it, the musical works and other cultural representations that have been predicated upon them will continue to inspire, fascinate (sometimes creepily), and teach us about ourselves and our own continuing obsessions and hopes, fantasies and fears.

How Spain Got a Soul

JAMES PARAKILAS

The corruption of the three-quarter measure does not express Austria, nor the Spanish way of executing a *gruppetto* the soul of Spain.

—ARTUR SCHNABEL[1]

SCHNABEL is evidently speaking here about national style rather than exoticism. Austrian music could hardly have seemed exotic to him, and the form of his sentence makes his Spanish example simply a reinforcement of the Austrian one. But he could not help exoticizing Spain. He could ask his audience—and he was writing here for an American lecture-hall audience—to consider the Viennese waltz and Spanish dance music as parallel in that each had a characteristic rhythmic "feel," but he could not erase the difference in his listeners' ways of thinking about the two musical traditions. The waltz was a dance they danced, and the well-known claim of Viennese musicians to a distinctive way of playing the waltz beat (Schnabel's "corruption of the three-quarter measure") was a claim of Viennese primacy within a tradition that united all Western nations. Spanish dances did not belong to his listeners—to non-Spaniards—in the same sense; they were dances to watch others dance, on stage or on screen, signifying "Spain." It seems that Schnabel could not help using the hackneyed expression *the soul of Spain,* either, though we do not find him talking about the soul of Austria. This essay is concerned with discovering how Spain came to be imagined as a place with a soul, a soul that *could* be expressed in a musical sound . . . a rhythm . . . a "way of executing a *gruppetto.*"

Spain did not get, or need to have, a soul in the days when it was uniting to drive out its Moorish rulers . . . discovering and conquering a New World . . . defending Catholicism against the Reformation . . . dominating Europe and European culture. Only after its Golden Age, when its power—even the power of its name—was gone, did it acquire a soul, as if a national soul were the compensation offered to the powerless. In this case, though the decline in power was gradual, the soul was produced abruptly, through a radical demotion, or marginalization, or exoticization that turned the nation whose rulers had once called themselves "the Catholic monarchs" into a place that was barely part of Europe.

This transformation was produced in Paris; it was the French who needed Spain to be exotic. They had long looked to their Latin neighbors, especially the Italians, for cultural leadership. But in the Napoleonic years the French found themselves engaged in a Europe-wide struggle in which they were the only Latin power left, having to come to terms with the arts and ideas, as well as the military, industrial, and commercial might, of mostly Protestant German and English neighbors. Perhaps unconsciously, the French kept themselves in the running by detaching themselves culturally from their less powerful, less progressive Catholic Latin neighbors. By 1830, for instance, a prize to study in Rome, which had still been a revered pilgrimage site for northern artists in the time of Mozart and Goethe, could seem like cultural exile to Berlioz.

The exoticizing of Spain, in other words, was part of a larger process by which artists in the northwest quadrant of Europe—especially French artists—turned the rest of the continent into an exotic cultural margin, or borderland, between themselves and the utterly alien cultures beyond Europe. This process in turn created the possibility of solidarity among artists of the marginalized cultures. Glinka, in his awareness that Spain and Russia seemed equally exotic to Parisians, could identify with Spain and Spanish music as no nineteenth-century French musician could. In fact, French and Russian composers have long been paired as the greatest, or first, masters of Spanish music (by listeners who did not distinguish Spanish music from music about Spain).[2] The present study treats the two groups less as a pair than as an opposition—between French musicians, for whom the representation of Spain in music has been an exercise in rendering their neighbors exotic, and Russian musicians, for whom it has meant finding a mirror of their own cultural situation in the corner of Europe most distant from themselves.

And what has it meant to Spanish musicians? Especially when they were making music for other Spaniards, they have not always needed to concern themselves with how to represent Spanishness. In the exoticization of Spain, then, have they served simply as unwitting suppliers of themes and rhythms for foreigners to expatiate upon? Or, given Manuel de Falla's generous crediting of Debussy—in a famous remark that will be revisited here—with having shown Spanish musicians the way, should we regard them as Johnnies-come-lately at purveying Spanishness? Hardly. Important Spanish musicians, driven by the provinciality of their country (the very condition that gave Spain its exotic appeal) to make their careers abroad and to address their music to foreign audiences, were actively involved in the creation of the exotic "soul of Spain" all along. And Falla's entire career can be seen as a restless, resourceful struggle with the exoticism of the "Spanish." Within the history being told here, the *auto-exoticism* of Spanish musicians represents a third strand, and by no means the least important. Furthermore, it provides one of the earliest case histories of the condition, common to musicians in many parts of the world today, of being able to produce a marketable art only by exoticizing oneself and one's culture.

The history will be told here in a chronological series of "acts," within which new players will take up recurring themes.

Act 1: The 1810s
War, the Disappearing Grandee, a Bolero, the Alhambra

The Napoleonic Wars gave the French not just a general motive for exoticizing most of Europe, but also an experience of Spain that would model for them a new image of Spain as an exotic locale. This experience, anything but exotic in itself, was Napoleon's invasion and occupation of Spain, lasting from 1808 to 1813. What distinguished that campaign from others the French fought under Napoleon was that it was begun with the abdication of the Spanish royal family and fought against a leaderless people. Within the French public, which had been taught by its Revolution to cherish its own ability to defend itself without a king, there was enormous sympathy for the Spanish *guerrillas* (a word that this war brought into the French language, as into English), even as the horrible struggle was decimating a French army. François René de Chateaubriand, for instance, describes the French public as responding to the Spanish fighters as if they were the leaderless Greeks of Xenophon's *Anabasis:* "The resistance of the Spanish to Bonaparte, of a disarmed people to this conqueror who had vanquished the best soldiers in Europe, excited the enthusiasm of all hearts capable of being touched by great devotion and noble sacrifices."[3]

This admiration had no suitable stereotype of the Spanish to fix on. For centuries, the French literary and theatrical imagination had defined Spain for itself through the figure of the grandee, that male character of noble estate who represented either the highest ideals of chivalry or the impossibility of living up to such ideals: the Cid, as recreated by Corneille and others . . . Don Quixote and his many French derivatives, such as Le Sage's Gil Blas . . . Don Juan, as restaged by Molière . . . Beaumarchais's Count Almaviva. But from the time of the Napoleonic campaign in Spain, as Léon-François Hoffmann has written, the French were "no longer limited to admiring the Conquistador or the high-spirited captain, as in the seventeenth century, since the humblest peasant was shown to be capable of heroism."[4] Political events made it possible for the first time for French culture to model an image of a Spain without grandees.

A story from the beginning of the Napoleonic campaign illustrates one side of this modeling process, the erasure of the grandee.

SCENE: THE HALLS OF MONTEZUMA

Gaspare Spontini's *Fernand Cortez, ou La conquête du Mexique,* produced at the Paris Opera in 1809, was a miscalculation in political imagery—Napoleon's miscalculation. "There is no doubt," David Charlton writes, "that Napoleon contrived to angle the work, even during composition, to make Cortez's bloodless conquest of Mexico 'legitimize' his own policy towards Spain, namely in replacing the Bourbon king and subordinating the Inquisition (represented in the opera by fanatical Aztec priests)."[5] It is certainly striking that this opera, in which Cortez allegorically represents Napoleon, is virtually the only work named after Cortez in the long history of "Montezuma" operas. But the role reversal within the parable (the Spanish conquistador onstage representing Napoleon conquering real-life Spain) seems to have proved tricky. Whether because the opera represented the plight of the Mexicans too affectingly (as Anselm Gerhard has it) or the bravery of the Spanish too gloriously (as Gerald Abraham has it) or for more obscure reasons, the French authorities suspended its successful run, at least temporarily.[6] And for decades after the French debacle in Spain, though the Paris Opera produced work after work celebrating the great age of discovery and conquest, those works noticeably favored Portuguese over Spanish conquistadors: Gaetano Donizetti's *Dom Sébastien, roi de Portugal* (1843), Félicien David's *La perle du Brésil* (1851), Giacomo Meyerbeer's *L'africaine* (1865).

While the grandee . . . the conquistador . . . the Spanish ruling class were being erased, or at least backgrounded, as symbols of Spain, other figures, at once humbler and more exotic, were being promoted into that role in French musical culture. To some extent, this promotion was achieved by a sleight of hand, substituting a new figure for an old one while maintaining the same discourse of "Hispanism." The guitar, for instance, long associated with the Spanish aristocrat serenading his lady from below her balcony, continued to serve as a symbol of Spain even as it was given a new association with dancing Andalusian Gypsies. The same transformative process was carried out in the literature and visual arts of the period, most spectacularly by the painter Edouard Manet. An assiduous copier of classic and modern Spanish master paintings in Paris and in Madrid, Manet seems to have modeled virtually all his "Spanish" paintings and prints—images of singers, guitar players, dancers, bullfighters, and Gypsies—on the composition and look of Velázquez and Goya paintings of Spanish royalty and aristocrats.[7]

This list of Manet's Spanish "types" reads like the list of characters in the opera *Carmen* (1875) by his friend Georges Bizet. But let's not jump ahead of the story: the full list of exotic Spanish types was not yet determined when Napoleon was ruling France. One of these types, however—the smuggler or bandit—was already being introduced to France during Napoleon's Spanish campaign,[8] and it was a Spanish musician, the great tenor Manuel García, who brought it there in a song. In 1809, newly arrived in Paris, García appeared in his own monologue opera *El poeta calculista.* The hit song from this opera, the polo "Yo que soy contrabandista" ("I am a smuggler"), which in Spain was being turned into patriotic songs of resistance to the French, served in France to popularize the image of the Spanish smuggler as a symbol of resistance to political authority.[9] Two decades later Prosper Mérimée would continue the romanticization of that image, writing that in Spain, "to be a highway robber was, in the eyes of many people, to serve as the opposition, was to protest against the tyrannical laws"; and he described himself as "almost ashamed," after months of travel in Andalusia, never to have encountered one of these robbers.[10] Meanwhile, García's song remained popular enough, at least in liberal/Romantic artistic circles in France, to inspire Liszt's *Rondeau fantastique sur un thème espagnol (El contrabandista)* of 1837 (discussed below), which in turn inspired a story by George Sand. And another four decades later, in Bizet's *Carmen,* the Spanish smuggler would still represent to Parisian audiences the life of freedom from authority. García's energetic song (see example 6.1) had given this figure a memorable musical profile from the start, making it adaptable for comic as well as romantic purposes on the stage.

One other character type, this one musical by nature and an even more important part of the new exotic image of the Spanish, was also established in

Ex. 6.1. Manuel García, "Yo que soy contrabandista," mm. 1–27.

the Napoleonic era: the Spanish dancer, above all the female Spanish dancer. For almost two hundred years now, the "soul of Spain" has been lodged above all in the body of the Spanish dancer, evoked by music that plays on the rhythm of one or another of the famous Spanish dance types. For that reason, it seems to me, Christiane Le Bordays misjudges in her otherwise admirable study of French musical Hispanism when she characterizes the "Spanish" style by means of a catalog consisting largely of melodic formulas—Phrygian cadences, triplet turns (Schnabel's *gruppetto*) and other embellishments, chains of descending thirds, and so on. Those formulas, to be sure, all help make music recognizable as "Spanish," but the rhythms of Spanish dances, which she mentions only secondarily, do more than place the style; they embody its exotic eroticism.[11]

In some cases, as a Spanish dance became exoticized, a change occurred in its character, by the familiar sleight of hand: a dance of genteel Spaniards in the eighteenth century would be transformed into a dance of the nineteenth-century French stage, imagined as a dance of the Spanish people. And the character of the music for this dance would change accordingly. The process was already underway even before the Napoleonic invasion of Spain.

SCENE: TOLEDO, THE HOME OF TWO BLIND SINGERS

It is evident, for instance, in Etienne-Nicolas Méhul's comic opera *Les deux aveugles de Tolède* (The two blind men of Toledo), which was premiered in Paris in 1806. Benoît-Joseph Marsollier's libretto is both plebeian in subject and exotic in origin, being adapted from his own earlier libretto *The Two Blind Men of Baghdad,* based on a story from *The Arabian Nights.* Though the Spanish setting does not make itself felt in the music of the opera itself (instead, a waltz—one of the first ever heard on the French stage—breaks out in one of the airs), the overture is dominated by the rhythms of the Spanish bolero, an effect well appreciated by the original audiences, according to Elizabeth Bartlet.[12] In fact, Parisians had known the bolero for about a decade before then; already by 1800, in Boieldieu's *Le calife de Bagdad,* they were expected to recognize "Spain" when a character picked up a guitar and strummed a bolero rhythm in a catalog aria of national styles.[13] Yet it is still hard for us to imagine the precise effect it would have made on them to hear a bolero in an overture, separated as we are from them by centuries of subsequent boleros, capped by Ravel's bolero-to-end-all-boleros. It is possible through analysis, though, to reveal an innovation of monumental importance to Western musical history being carried out in this modest bolero and others of its time.

Méhul's bolero begins, after an introduction, with a vamp (see example 6.2). This vamp is what makes the music a bolero: the dance is identified musically here by an ear-catching rhythm (even eighth notes in a 3/4 meter, with a subdivided second eighth) in the "rhythm section" that need not ever appear in the melody. When the melody is finally heard, from the clarinet, it has its own, more changeable, less identifying rhythms. This is already a revolution: there was no such division of rhythmic function between melody and bass in the social dances of earlier centuries, not even in "Spanish" stage dances such as the fandangos of Gluck's ballet *Don Juan* (1761) and Mozart's *The Marriage of Figaro* (1786); even the waltz—the contemporary of the bolero—had a rhythmically undifferentiated bass; but much of the future of Western popular dance and of popular music in general lay in such defining bass rhythms, many of them Spanish or Hispanic. And there is more. The bolero rhythm in Méhul's vamp is carried not by a bass line but by a repeating chord, evidently inspired by guitar strumming. A movement with no line: this was as revolutionary an idea in the Western musical tradition as Monteverdi's *stile concitato*—a characterization with no line—two centuries earlier.[14] And in its mixture of energy and stasis, this music conveys the Spanish dancer's unmistakable—and, compared to French social or stage dancers, quite exotic—combination of self-possessed bearing with passionate movement.

Ex. 6.2. Etienne-Nicolas Méhul, Overture to *Les deux aveugles de Tolède,* mm. 29–41.

SCENE: THE ALHAMBRA

One last exotic element that entered the French musical image of Spain in this period was not a figure but a locale: Granada, the last stronghold of the Moors in Spain and, with its Alhambra, the place that most strikingly symbolized Spain's Moorish past—symbolized, that is, a Spain not European in origin and not Christian in religion. The centuries-long struggles between the Spanish Moors and Christians had long figured in the literature and other arts of France, but they had generally been viewed from the Christian side. In 1809, though, a new French translation of Pérez de Hita's sixteenth-century *Civil Wars of Granada* reminded French readers of the legends of Moorish Granada—the Moor's Last Sigh, the massacre of the Abencerrajes—and inspired the creation of new artistic works that focused on the Moors themselves. A politically artful strategy was at work: if the French invasion made Spain more fascinating than ever to the French, it also gave French artists reason to represent a Spain far removed from the one so furiously resisting that invasion.

One of these representations was Chateaubriand's story *Les aventures du dernier Abencérage,* written in 1810 though not published until 1826.[15] In this story the Moor Aben-Hamet, last survivor of the legendary family of the Abencerrajes, living in North African exile decades after the fall of Granada to the Christians, makes a pilgrimage to the city of his ancestors and falls hopelessly in love with the Christian Blanca, who turns out to be descended from the Cid. For the history of musical exoticism, the most notable element in this story is Chateaubriand's account of the dance Blanca performs for Aben-Hamet, sealing his destiny "with no return." If it seems odd to us that the Christian should be seducing the Moor with exotic wiles—since, after all, such later works as *Carmen* established a convention of exotic women seducing unexotic men[16]—Chateaubriand describes this dance and its music so as to suggest that Spanish culture as a whole was infiltrated by the arts of the more exotic peoples of the peninsula. Blanca is said to "surpass the most accomplished Gypsy women" in her dancing; the dance she chooses is the Zambra, an "expressive dance that the Spaniards borrowed from the Moors." She removes her veil, puts on her castanets, and sings as she dances to an accompanying guitar:

> She turns her head, seems to call out to someone invisible, tenders a rosy cheek to the kiss of a new husband, flees in shame, returns radiant and consoled, marches with a noble, almost soldierly gait, then flutters anew over the lawn. The harmony of her steps with her singing and with the sounds of the guitar was perfect. Blanca's

> slightly veiled voice had an intensity of the sort that stirs the passions to the quick. Spanish music, composed of sighs, lively movements, sad refrains, and sudden stops in singing, offers a singular mixture of gaiety and melancholy.[17]

In this passage Chateaubriand, perhaps reliving experiences of his trip to Granada in 1807, captures in language an entire "syndrome" of Spanishness, uniting movement and sound, that was not to be transported whole to the French stage for decades to come.

What was transported immediately to the stage of the Paris Opera was the setting of the Alhambra, and with it the idea of Moorish Spain. Luigi Cherubini's *Les Abencérages, ou L'étendard de Grenade,* was created there in 1813.[18] While the story (by Etienne de Jouy) is even more centered on Moorish characters than Chateaubriand's, Cherubini's music has nothing particularly Moorish about it; instead, it offers many musical stereotypes of the Spanish, combined in a wonderful hodgepodge. The dance scenes include both a fashionable bolero (Act 3) and a set of variations (Act 1) on the centuries-old *folies d'Espagne* (of which the third itself has a bolero rhythm). The courtliness of the medieval Moorish court is established with . . . a gavotte (Act 1). The one Christian among the principals, Gonsalve de Cordoue, represents the musical tradition of medieval Christian Spain by singing a romance (Act 1), accompanied by harp and a chorus of troubadours (bolero rhythms infiltrate this number, too). And the dancer François Albert played the guitar while dancing—the first use of the guitar in the Paris ballet in a century.[19]

The Moorishness lies entirely in the sets, in scenes laid in the Lion's Court, the halls, and the gardens of the Alhambra. The opening of the third act, above all, introduces into French opera the new stereotype, the new vision, of "Moorish" Spain. The score describes "a lonely part of the Alhambra gardens; a Moorish funeral vault on the left; the River Darro in the background; moonlight." The Moorish princess Noraïme, alone in the garden, is about to sing her love lament, to be joined by her lover, the banished Moorish commander Almansor, who has smuggled himself into the Alhambra in disguise. This Spain is an Oriental garden paradise, an imaginary sensual refuge, protected by its ancient stone walls, its darkness, and its disguises from harsh realities—realities like that other, hostile Spain from which the French army of occupation was about to be driven, within a few months of the premiere of this opera, defeated by the British army under Wellington at the battle of Vittoria. But Cherubini's music for this scene is surprisingly neoclassical and chaste: apter for a Fidelio, perhaps, than a Noraïme. Were we expecting something more atmospheric? But in the absence of a foretaste of, say, Glinka's *Memories of a Summer Night in Madrid* or Debussy's "Perfumes of the Night," Cherubini and his collaborators can at least claim the credit of having brought the dreams of nights in the gardens of the Alhambra into the musical arena in the first place.

Act 2: The 1830s and 1840s
Critics, Dancers, Tourists

SCENE: THE FRENCH BORDER WITH SPAIN

It is May 1840, and the Parisian critic and poet Théophile Gautier, passionate appreciator of the Spanish dancers who appeared in Paris theaters, has decided to see Spain for himself. At the moment of crossing the border, however, he is seized with self-consciousness—or so he tells us in his newspaper account of the moment, one of a series he later collected to form his *Voyage en Espagne:*

> In a few more turns of the wheels I will perhaps lose one of my illusions and see the Spain of my dreams vanish—the Spain of the *Romancero,* of Victor Hugo's ballads, of Mérimée's novellas, of Alfred de Musset's stories. In crossing the frontier I am reminded of what the good and witty Heinrich Heine said to me at Liszt's concert, with his German accent full of "humour" and malice: "How will you manage to speak about Spain once you have been there?" [20]

It is above all this consciousness of tension between a "Spain of my dreams" and a Spain really "there" that distinguishes Gautier and his entire Romantic generation of Parisian writers, artists, and musicians in their vision of Spain.

Though the French government continued to intervene militarily in Spanish affairs in the decades after the Napoleonic occupation, it was now possible for French intellectuals to think of Spain as a tourist site, as a playground for their fantasies of the Other. In a flood of illustrated guidebooks to Spain, as in the travel accounts and stories of Gautier and the authors he mentions, a very new French pilgrimage route to Spain was mapped: instead of hugging the northern coast, like the medieval French pilgrim, to reach the Christian haven of Santiago de Compostela, the modern tourist-pilgrim headed south, to Andalusia, to seek what was least Christian, least European in Spain.[21] For Gautier, traveling south from Madrid to Granada was "like passing suddenly from Europe to Africa."[22] But the point of the pilgrimage was never to discover the "true" Spain, never to make one's illusions vanish. If anything, it was to make oneself more conscious of those illusions, more conscious of the "Spain of one's dreams" as a put-on.

The nature of the mid-nineteenth-century French obsession with Spain is epitomized in Gautier's inspired sense of put-on in his dance criticism, as well as in the *Voyage en Espagne.* A famously flamboyant dresser himself, he is always intrigued by costume—whether the Spanish costumes of Paris dancers or the French fashions of middle-class Spaniards—as a form of tourism, as a means of playing with an identity not one's own.[23] In his travels, in his writings, he tries on the "Spain of my dreams" as a costume, to see how disconcerting it looks on him, to see what it shows him about France, just as Mérimée's middle-class character Don José, in the novella *Carmen* (1845), tries on the costume—and life—of an exotic "Spanish" type, the bandit, or as Manet's Parisian subjects, two decades later, would pose self-consciously in exotic Spanish costumes. The use of Spanish costume for identity games is apparent above all in the license it provided for cross-dressing—for gender put-on—whether in a male impersonator's parody of the Austrian ballerina Fanny Elssler's celebrated Spanish dancing, mentioned by Gautier in his very first review of Spanish dance,[24] or in the macho costumes of Manet's *Young Woman Reclining, in Spanish Costume* and *Mlle V . . . in the Costume of an Espada.*

In all of these artistic productions the put-on is too transparent, too self-advertising, to serve primarily as a put-down of the Spanish. Gautier can be dismissive of the Spanish, as when his disappointing first experience of Spanish dance in Spain, after years of admiring the version seen on the Paris stage, leads him to this outburst: "Spanish dances exist only in Paris, just as seashells are found only in curiosity shops, never at the seashore. O, Fanny Elssler! . . . even before we came to Spain, we suspected that it was you who invented the *cachucha!*"[25]

But the ultimate object of his mockery here is Paris fashion, and himself as its representative; he knew, after all, where seashells came from. And even before he left Paris, he was capable of using the authentically Spanish dancer Dolores Serral to take the measure of her foreign imitators and, with them, the Paris scene:

> For Dolores the *cachucha* is a faith, a religion. It is obvious that she believes in it, for she performs it with all the emotion, passion, guilelessness, and seriousness that it is possible to summon up. Fanny Elssler and Mlle Noblet dance it a little like unbelievers, more to satisfy a whim or to brighten up the opera glasses of that bored sultan, the public, than out of any real conviction. Also, they are both spirited flirts, amusing but not erotic, which is an unpardonable sin in a *cachucha* or a *bolero.*[26]

As the *cachucha* is hardly known even as a name any more, it is worth looking into this dance and its music. Fanny Elssler's "invention" of the cachucha when she danced it in the ballet-pantomime *Le diable boiteux* in 1836 was historic only in that she was bringing Spanish stage dancing from the commercial Paris theaters onto the stage of the Paris Opera for the first time. The dance itself had already been popular in Spain for some time, part of the tradition of social dances cultivated as stage dances in the "bolero school" *(escuela bolera).*[27] Unlike the even more popular bolero, for which any number of different musical works was composed, the cachucha was danced, apparently, to the single song from which it took its name (see example 6.3). It's hard to hear any exoticism in this song; the influence of Italian opera on the Spanish theatrical tradition is all too evident in its melody in thirds and its mincing double chromaticisms. But in what may sound to us like another thoroughly unexotic, Italian, and specifically Rossinian feature of the music—the endless repetition of alternating four-measure phrases (tonic-to-dominant and dominant-to-tonic)—may lie the potential for exoticism in the dance. If these phrases were performed with the *accelerando* and *crescendo* that such Rossinian writing invites and were danced in the way Gautier described—"hot-blooded and impetuous dancing, with its exaggerated movements and its free gestures"—the cachucha can easily be imagined creating a sensation at the Opéra, the home of French classical ballet.[28]

Ex. 6.3. "La cachucha," arranged and freely adapted into French by Paul Lacome, in Lacome and Puig, *Echos d'Espagne: Chansons et danses populaires* (Paris, 1872), mm. 17–24.

SCENE: THE SALLE PLEYEL

In "Spanish" music written for concerts or the salon or parlor, where there was to be no costume and no dancing, it fell to the notes to convey everything—the sexually charged atmosphere, the liberating experience of the dance, the arch tone of the role playing. As a consequence, composers of "Spanish" songs and instrumental pieces in midcentury Paris inevitably resorted to the one musical type that could reliably convey everything "Spanish": the bolero. The self-conscious exoticism of the Parisian bolero can be heard in Liszt's song "Gastibelza" (1844, on the poem "Guitare" of Victor Hugo); in Berlioz's song "Zaïde" (1845, on a poem by Roger de Beauvoir, written in several versions, one with piano and optional castanets!); in L.-J.-A. Lefébure-Wély's *Boléro de concert* (1860s) for—believe it or not—organ. This tradition is capped by the song "Madrid," published in the 1880s by Pauline Viardot-Garcia, the most Parisian musician of the García family.[29] In this song she turned Alfred de Musset's poem of 1829 into a showpiece of bolero clichés, including the guitar figuration, the vocal turns and descending thirds, the modal moves, and a musical click of the heels to finish.

One of the earliest works in this tradition, Chopin's Boléro for piano (1833), raises intriguing possibilities of a cross-national put-on. This work, composed within a few years of Chopin's arrival in Paris, is often regarded as a polonaise in disguise, on the grounds that the two dances share the same rhythm (the bolero rhythm seen in example 6.2) and Chopin had already shown that he had the polonaise in his blood.[30] But hold on: there are features of this Boléro that belong specifically to the bolero tradition, dating back at least to the Méhul overture, rather than to Chopin's own practice to date with the polonaise—the strumming of one chord in the characteristic rhythm, the use of that strumming on its own—here as a "break" rather than a vamp—as well as melodic features more Spanish than Polish (see example 6.4).[31] But what sets the Boléro unmistakably apart from those earlier Chopin polonaises—which never surrender their polonaise pulse for an instant—is its playfulness about its own identity. It tries on, for instance, two completely different introductions—one glitteringly instrumental *(Molto allegro),* the other self-contained and vocal *(Più lento)*—before the bolero proper begins. Even then, the music slips abruptly out of its bolero act into the utterly different rhythm, character, and even tempo of a nocturne (the episode in A-flat, mm. 156–67), only gradually, oh-so-gradually allowing itself (over the course of the following thirty measures) to be lured back into its bolero steps.

Could it be that Chopin learned more about writing polonaises from his

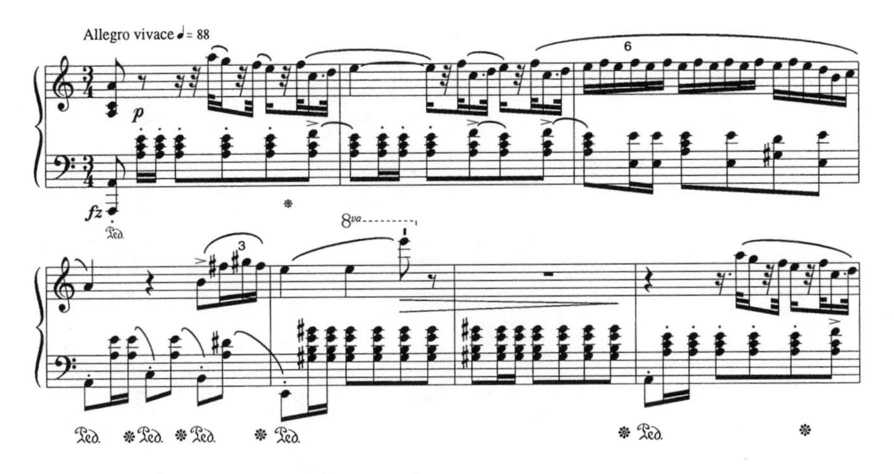

Ex. 6.4. Frédéric Chopin, Boléro, op. 19, mm. 200–206.

experience with the bolero than the other way around? Certainly, if you go through the polonaises he wrote after the Boléro (starting with the two of op. 26), you find an increasingly Boléro-like willingness to don and doff any and all conventions of the polonaise, until in the Polonaise-Fantasy, op. 61, he barely puts them on at all. And in part, what he puts on instead in these works are bolero items. In the F-sharp Minor Polonaise, op. 44, for instance, just before changing—for the first time in any of his polonaises—to a tempo alien to the polonaise *(Doppio movimento: Tempo di Mazurka),* Chopin introduces a remarkably extended break that seems to have been conceived for the guitar, built on a turn figure that could be heard as a Polish equivalent of the Spanish *gruppetto* (example 6.5). In a sense Chopin is taking advantage of coincidences in rhythm and character between a Spanish dance and a Polish one to express, like Glinka, the sympathy of one marginalized European nation for another. But while he is playing on a common bond between those nations, he himself is playing the Parisian: it is the Parisian put-on of the bolero that provides his terms of exchange between the bolero and the polonaise.

SCENE: A SALON IN FLORA BERVOIX'S PARIS MANSION

Similar complexities can be found whenever Italian composers of this period write "Spanish" music in their operas. There is always a question of whether as Italians they belong with the French exoticizers of Spain or with the Spanish

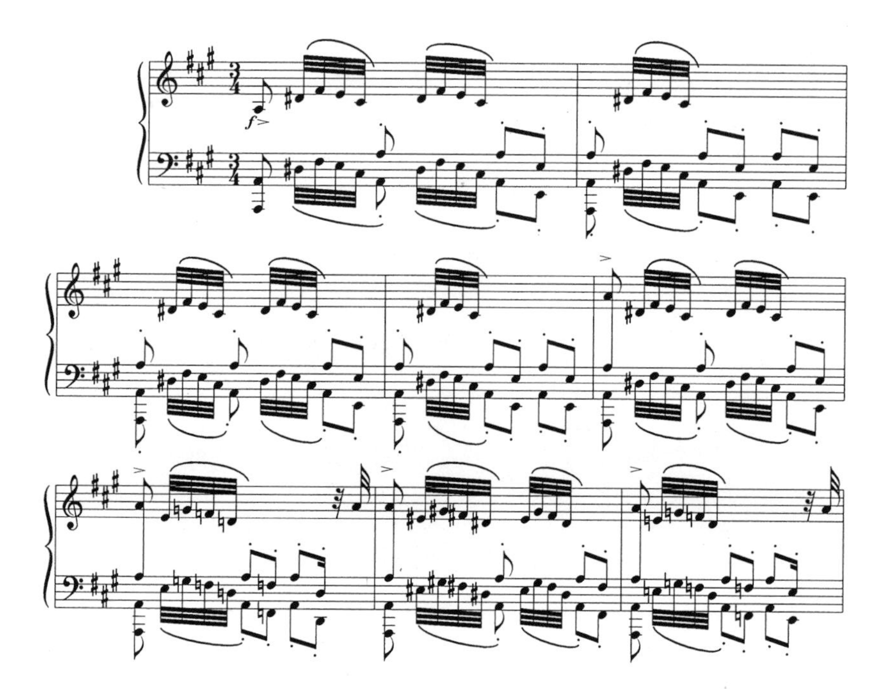

Ex. 6.5. Chopin, Polonaise, op. 44, mm. 83–90.

as victims of French exoticization. Was not Italy, after all, marginalized by the same means as Spain, and for the same reason, within French culture? Were not an Italian exoticism and a Spanish exoticism mixed more or less indiscriminately together in French opera whenever the plot provided a pretext, as in Auber's *La muette de Portici* (1828)? Yet no Italian composer of the time could avoid the influence or the lure of Paris. A book could be written about Verdi's Spains, and much of it would have to do with French mediations: "Spanish" operas that he wrote for the Paris Opera (*Don Carlos*) or that his librettists drew from French sources (*Ernani*); characters of the exotic Spanish types long found in French opera, notably bandits (*Ernani*) and Gypsies (*Il trovatore, La forza del destino*); and everywhere—not just in dance numbers—the rhythms of the bolero.[32] Did it make Verdi at all uncomfortable, as an Italian, to play the Frenchman exoticizing Spain? It might be a sign of his discomfort, or perhaps fascination, with the issue, that Verdi was drawn at least twice (*Ernani* and *Il trovatore*) to subjects that pose traditional Spanish character types against exotic ones (the grandee against the bandit or Gypsy), contending with each other not only for primacy but even for their identity.

By contrast, he can seem unguardedly Frenchified in the few scenes of his operas in which unexotic characters self-consciously put on an act of Spanish exoticism. This happens twice in *Don Carlos:* in Princess Eboli's Veil Song (a Counter-Reformation Spanish princess standing outside a Castilian monastery exotically singing a Moorish legend about seduction in the gardens of the Alhambra!) and in the later "night in the garden" scene—with music described by Julian Budden as exoticism "of the boulevardier variety"—in which Eboli masks herself as the queen. We might expect this concession to French taste—this depiction of characters self-consciously playing the exotic, with all the condescension that implies about the exoticized object—in the one "Spanish" opera Verdi wrote for Paris.[33] But what about that most absurd instance of "Spanish" exoticism in all of Verdi's operas, the chorus of Gypsies followed by the chorus of matadors and picadors who arrive at Flora's party in the second act of *La traviata*? This time it is an Italian opera, and nothing to do with Spain. Are these choruses just "an echo of the musical world of *Il trovatore,*" as Roger Parker would have it?[34] It seems to me that it may be a case of Verdi turning the tables, that the exoticized object here is, for once . . . the Parisians. These are Flora's rich Parisian friends, after all, masquerading as Gypsies and matadors, singing and dancing *à l'espagnole,* as rich Parisians were known to do. Would not Verdi's Italian audiences have enjoyed this divertissement not simply as a put-on of the Spanish, but even more as a send-up of the Parisian put-on of the Spanish?

SCENE: THE SPANISH BORDER AGAIN

Glinka visited Spain for two years, starting in 1845, five years after Gautier's trip there. Like Gautier, he set out for Spain from Paris. His accounts of his travels are mostly letters written to friends and relatives back in Russia, not to a newspaper for publication. Yet they are no less fascinating than Gautier's, partly for the contrast they provide to Gautier's "take" on Spain, partly as companions—not merely as background—to the two Spanish Overtures that are the major musical products of Glinka's visit. The contrast with Gautier is apparent from the moment Glinka crosses the border. As he reports in his *Memoirs,* "I arrived in Spain on 20 May, my own birthday, and was in total ecstasy." Not the words of someone worried about losing his illusions. And more than a year later, his ecstasy had turned into identification with Spain, when he wrote to his mother that "I like it so much in Spain that it seems like I was born here . . . here my spirit is able to rest from all its sad adventures."[35]

Glinka's identification, like that of many tourists who feel themselves surprisingly "at home" in a foreign land, contains both a sense of a common bond with his own country and a sense of difference. The common bond, not surprisingly, he expresses as a common un-Frenchness: the inhabitants of Valladolid, he writes, "are extremely affectionate and unpretentious, which is quite new after Paris, and in many ways it reminds me of our Russia, as do many things in Spain." On the other hand, Spain clearly represented to him a sorely needed change from Russia, and not just because it was far away, but because of specific differences. To a Saint Petersburger, for whom warm evenings were "white nights," the summer evenings in Spain, both warm and dark, opened up a new world; they were literally something to write home about: "Nights are enchanting. There is a splendid park here in Madrid, the so-called Prado. At night it's a fascinating spectacle."[36] And when he memorialized those evenings in the music of his Second Spanish Overture, "Memories of a Summer Night in Madrid," his music had the exoticism of "nights in the garden" not vaguely imagined but intensely remembered, clung to, in all their vivid distinctness.

Glinka's letters from Spain in fact read like the reports of someone bent on *not* exoticizing the Spanish, someone bent on getting past any stereotypes, either of the people or of their music. He studied the language assiduously; learned to sing and play Spanish songs, dance the dances, play the castanets; transcribed songs from the singing of muleteers and Gypsies. He expresses an ethnographer's satisfaction at uncovering an untainted Spain:

> If [Spanish or foreign maestros living in Spain] sometimes perform national melodies, they immediately disfigure them and give them a European character, even when they are purely Arabian melodies. For me to attain my goal I have to run to coachmen (*arrieros*), workmen, and common people and listen very attentively to their singing. The melodic turns, placement of words, and ornamentation are so original that even now I have been unable to capture all the melodies I have heard. I am speaking here of purely Spanish folk music.

But with the satisfaction comes the frustration of discovering that the "purely Spanish" was not national. In describing his attempt to attain "a perfect understanding of Spanish folk music," he confesses that "my study is attended by great difficulties, since everyone sings differently."[37] The more closely he examined Spain, it seems, the harder it got to find its soul.

What did he make of these discoveries and frustrations and ruminations when he composed his "Spanish" music? He had been in Spain only four months when he wrote the first of his Spanish Overtures, the "Capriccio brillante on the Jota aragonesa." Perhaps he had not yet discovered, as he would within another four months, that "jotas come in many different types and subdivisions."[38] In any case, it is striking that the Spanish theme he chose for this work was not of the purest sort, not one of those innumerable variants with details so "original" as to elude "capture." He chose the *jota aragonesa* that had already been thoroughly captured, transcribed, perhaps "disfigured," nationalized, and transported to the stage, the same *jota aragonesa* that Liszt and Gottschalk and other composers were also to make arrangements of and that would appear in many a nineteenth-century anthology of Spanish folk music (see example 6.6).[39] And how did Glinka arrange it? In 1840s "brilliant" style, brilliantly orchestrated and brilliantly developed, so that it sounded like nothing so much as the festive music of Berlioz's recent "Italian" works, *Harold in Italy, Benvenuto Cellini,* and *Romeo and Juliet,* which he had no doubt come to know, along with their composer, in Paris. In short, it may be hard to see how this work would have been any different if Glinka had never been to Spain.

Ex. 6.6. Mikhail Glinka, Spanish Overture No. 1, "Capriccio brillante on the Jota aragonesa," mm. 24–31 (harp part only).

The best answer to that question may come from considering whom Glinka was writing for. Evidently he was thinking of Spanish audiences in the first place (not the audiences that French composers of the nineteenth century thought of), since just before he composed it, he wrote: "Literature and the theater here are better than I would have supposed, and therefore, having looked around, I think I might undertake something for Spain."[40] He was following the hallowed tradition of introducing oneself to foreign audiences with music one had composed on favorite themes of their own. Even this gesture of national flattery places the "Capriccio brillante" beyond the faddish exoticism of Glinka's earlier Bolero for piano, composed in 1840, before he had even been to Paris.[41] And writing something "for Spain" could have had the added sense, for him, of showing Spanish musicians, from his experience working with Russian folk music as well as his knowledge of the latest French orchestral techniques, some ideas on how to make a national concert music, of potentially international as well as national interest, out of their folk music. From another part of the margins of Europe, a lesson in auto-exoticism.[42]

His Second Spanish Overture, "Memories of a Summer Night in Madrid," is an altogether different matter. He did not write even the first version of it until after he left Spain; evidently he intended it primarily for audiences outside of Spain. Its title evokes a Spain viewed from outside—from memory, as a scene and a spectacle—rather than from inside—as a dance. And its material is as varied as that of the "Capriccio brillante" is singular. Some of that material came from Glinka's transcribing, all of which was behind him by then; he reported in his *Memoirs* that "a certain *zagal* (muleteer on the stagecoach) would come to me and sing folk songs, which I then would try to capture and record. I especially like two *Seguidillas manchegas (airs de la Mancha),* and later I used them in the second Spanish overture."[43] The constant shifting from one folk or popular theme to another in this Second Spanish Overture, besides suggesting the carnival atmosphere of the Prado on a summer night, allows Glinka to display the enormous musical diversity he had found in Spanish music. He shifts freely among rhythms and modes and characters; revels in folk textures, monophonic and even heterophonic (see example 6.7); and ends with a festive combination of the elements already aired.

This display of musical diversity provided a solution to the problem of how to get the exoticism of Spanish music—the real, difficult-to-capture musical exoticism he had found in "purely Spanish folk music"—into an orchestral work. The solution was to represent Spanishness not by trying to capture all the originality of one melody's "melodic turns, placement of words, and ornamentation," but by exhibiting the considerable range of the Spanish musical language within a single work. During his time in Spain he had wrestled with the task of translating from the medium of folk music to that of concert music, constantly underestimating the difficulty of the task. A characteristic misjudgment was his attempt to make an opera singer of the folk singer Dolores García, whom he brought from Granada to Madrid for the purpose and later sent home to her family, saying that "she would never be an artist."[44] He was neither the first nineteenth-century composer nor the last to misjudge in that way. But in this overture, written as soon as he left Spain, he seems to have been one of the first to get around the difficulty of "national" concert music by a scheme that was still serving Bartók and others nearly a century later: the

Ex. 6.7. Glinka, Spanish Overture No. 2, "Memories of a Summer Night in Madrid," mm. 9–18 of the "punto moruno."

scheme of letting the diversity of a country's music stand for its uncapturable essence, its soul.

MEANWHILE, ELSEWHERE ON THE SPANISH CONCERT CIRCUIT

Glinka was not the only foreign musician visiting Spain and showing an interest in its music then. When he arrived, in fact, Liszt was already there, creating a much greater stir as a performer than Glinka could as composer and as student of Spanish music. Their paths seem not to have crossed in Spain. But they used Spanish music in somewhat similar ways, and Liszt's interest, as a Hungarian, in the music of other "marginal" European peoples raises the possibility of considering him as more "Russian" than "French" in his musical Hispanism, at least from this point on in his career. Liszt wrote his own work on a combination of Spanish themes during his tour, the *Grosse Konzertfantasie über spanische Weisen,* though it is not clear that he performed it on the tour or therefore that he conceived it, like Glinka's "Capriccio brillante," as an act of flattery to his hosts. The themes he used in this work all come from the international repertory of the "Spanish": the *Figaro* fandango, the *jota aragonesa* that Glinka also used, and the cachucha. Whatever attention he paid to Spanish folk music showed in improvisations he did for his hosts rather than in any written composition comparable to Glinka's Second Spanish Overture.[45]

In some ways Liszt's most fascinating engagement with Spanish music came in his fantasy for piano on García's song "Yo que soy contrabandista" (example 6.1), a work he wrote in 1836, eight years before he toured Spain. This piece, the barely remembered *Rondeau fantastique sur un thème espagnol* is no act of flattery, but a magnificent "analysis" of the song, testing the sources of the power of each of its apparently simple phrases. He subjects the opening measures, for instance—nothing but alternating measures of tonic and dominant harmony over a dominant pedal—to a number of enrichments without sacrificing their repetitive energy, just as Bizet was to do with a very similar passage of another García polo in the final entr'acte of *Carmen.*[46]

Liszt's most thought-provoking (if perhaps thoughtless) choice of a theme to represent Spain, on the other hand, appeared in a work he wrote around 1863, decades after his tour of Spain: his *Rhapsodie espagnole,* also for piano solo. This time he combines the *jota aragonesa* with the *folies d'Espagne.* In a sense the venerable *folies d'Espagne* stands for Spain here exactly as it did in Cherubini's *Les Abencérages* of five decades earlier. But there seems something almost willfully naïve in Liszt's use of the theme after having noted, when just back from Spain, that it "is the title of a song perfectly familiar abroad, but one that I never heard while in Spain."[47] It seems, that is, like the characteristic nineteenth-century naïveté of failing to distinguish between two kinds of "national" music: a nation's folk music and the music chosen, often from abroad, to represent that nation. In this case, though, we can also ask if, by bringing together the courtly *folies d'Espagne* and the folk, or popular, *jota aragonesa*, Liszt was not imagining a kind of synthesis, even a reconciliation, of two opposed strands of Spanish history, two competing images of the Spanish. And perhaps, in drawing music of Spanish court life into an exotic, nationalist rhapsody, Liszt can be seen not so much to be reviving the practice of Cherubini as to be anticipating that of Ravel and even Falla.

Closer to Glinka in his "Spanish" compositions, in fact more "Russian" than Liszt in his whole relationship to Spanish music, was another piano virtuoso who toured Spain: the American Louis Moreau Gottschalk.[48] Gottschalk's Spanish tour of 1851–52, comparable in length to Liszt's, produced a considerably longer list of "Spanish" works, in enormous variety. At one extreme in this list are brilliant concert pieces based on the favorite Spanish themes that everyone else used, such as the *jota aragonesa*. At the other extreme are less brilliant works showing signs that he sought out and transcribed Spanish folk music with the same kind of dedication as Glinka. One of these works is the *Chanson du gitano* written in Cordoba in 1852 and apparently derived from music he heard performed by Gypsies there or elsewhere in Andalusia. As an early instance of imitation of the Andalusian *cante jondo* by an outsider, it is remarkable for its reliance on the hypnotic plainness of the song's repetitions. The *Manchega: Etude de concert*, written in Seville in 1853, is remarkable in another way: its interest lies in its counterrhythm, the interplay of two different meters maintained between the two hands throughout the piece (see example 6.8), an effect that Glinka described hearing in Spain but did not incorporate into his own compositions.[49]

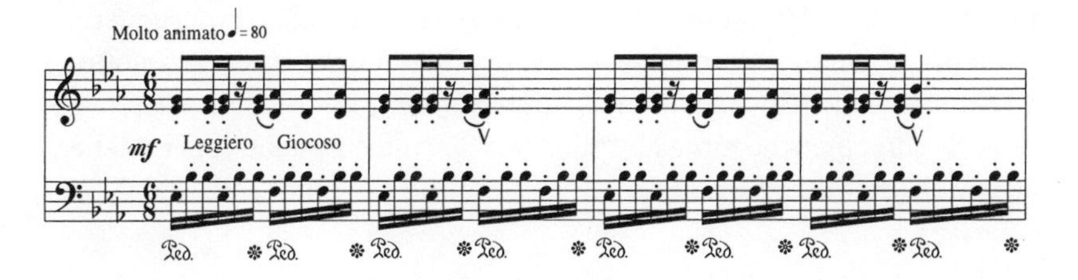

Ex. 6.8. Louis Moreau Gottschalk, *Manchega: Etude de concert*, mm. 1–4.

For Gottschalk, as for Glinka and to a small extent Liszt, the opportunity to discover and treat Spanish folk music fulfilled a need beyond the pleasing of

Spanish audiences, a need created by the composers' own exoticism. This was the need to find in a marginalized culture some musical material with usably exotic traits, so that they could fashion from it concert music that would offer a distinctive and impressive alternative to mainstream (French-German-Italian) concert music. Not surprisingly, all three composers after their Spanish tours turned back to the music of their own marginalized cultures in the same spirit.

This "Russian" method of celebrating the validity of the Spanish in music may seem utterly at odds with the "French" method of celebrating it as a fantasy. But the two methods are bound together by a common concern to represent the Spanish as distinct. If this seems more of a slim thread than a common bond, consider the two together in contrast to a third method, the "German." From arias and variations of Carl Maria von Weber to Hugo Wolf's *Spanisches Liederbuch* (1891), from Conradin Kreutzer's *Nachtlager in Granada* (1834) to Eugène d'Albert's *Tiefland* (1903), the Spanish theme looms as large in German and Austrian music as in music elsewhere in the nineteenth century. But the Spanishness quite consistently takes an unexotic form there; instead of representing the distinctness of the Spanish, this music on the whole represents the Spanish *Volk* as stand-in for the German. The keynote is sounded late in the eighteenth century by the prominence Johann Gottfried von Herder gives to Spanish romances in his momentous collection of international folksong texts. For the next century the musical sons of Herder, when they wrote "Spanish" *Lieder,* would choose imitations of medieval Spanish romances (Loewe's Moorish ballads) or translations of Spanish traditional and folk poetry (Schumann's two Spanish collections and Wolf's) for their texts—not choices that many French composers would be caught making.[50] And how did they make their Spanish subjects sing? In the Schumann and Wolf collections (as even in Wolf's opera *Der Corregidor*), the predominant musical color is of folk style—German folk style—with just an occasional number in bolero rhythm as a needed reminder of the allegory at work.[51] This strategy served a number of purposes, but the marking of cultural distinctness was not one of them. Brahms may have adored Bizet's *Carmen,* but like other German-speaking composers he turned his thoughts down the Danube (or, as Metternich put it, down the Landstrasse) when he wanted to write exotically.

Act 3: The 1870s and 1880s
Gypsies and Fiddlers

Now for the part of the story everyone remembers, the music that still most strongly represents the exoticism of Spain: *Carmen* and orchestral works of

Lalo, Chabrier, and Rimsky-Korsakov (to be followed in a few decades by works of Debussy, Ravel, and the "Spanish school"). What kind of edge do these later works have over the earlier ones, and why did it take so long (seven decades in France) for this edge to develop? Or maybe the question should be this: In the period when European powers were extending their imperial power all around the globe (except for Spain, which was just losing the remains of its exotic empire in the Spanish-American War), why was "Spain" not given up as a theme in European music in favor of more exotic exoticisms? The answers to all these questions have a lot to do with Spain's intermediary status. Spanish performers, that is, could serve as intermediaries, inspiring new kinds of "Spanish" music by non-Spanish composers and stepping onstage everywhere in the West, as few non-Western performers could, to deliver "authentic" performances of them. Moreover, Spain itself represented an intermediary exoticism, a more manageable, imaginable exoticism than that of Japan or Fiji or Timbuktu, an exoticism with both its European and its non-European sides, a meeting ground for Don Josés and Carmens. It was an exoticism worth pursuing in the industrial age because it represented a part of Europe that still had a soul.

SCENE: OUTSIDE A PRACTICE ROOM AT THE PARIS CONSERVATORY, 1857

Behind that door thirteen-year-old Pablo de Sarasate is practicing. He came from Madrid a year ago and has already won the first prize in violin and solfège here. But what is he practicing? When he tires of his scales and études, does he try out his fandangos and malagueñas? Hard to say. He has not come to Paris to learn to play Spanish, to become Sarasate. There's no model for that. He's come for the training and opportunity that Paris offers violinists, from wherever.

In a couple of years he'll begin touring the world. In the meantime he is starting to meet French composers who will write memorable works for him: Camille Saint-Saëns (the "Introduction and Rondo Capriccioso" in 1863) and Edouard Lalo (the Concerto in F of 1873 and the *Symphonie espagnole* of 1874). They will not hesitate to capitalize on his Spanish identity, his skill at Spanish styles on the violin, as well as his Paris-perfected virtuosity, in those works. What's so remarkable about that?

The combination, actually. "Spanish" had not particularly meant "virtuosic" in instrumental music before Sarasate, except perhaps in the music for guitar—that "Spanish" instrument—by Fernando Sor (1778–1839), another Spanish musician who migrated to Paris. Even in the "Spanish" works of virtuoso pianists such as Liszt and Gottschalk, the virtuosity generally takes the form of digital embroidery around a fairly plain Spanish melody or passage. So where does the "Spanish" bravura of the violin writing in Lalo's *Symphonie espagnole* come from, a bravura apparent from the player's first entrance (example 6.9) and inseparable from the melody itself? From imitating *cante jondo* or some other passionate, rhapsodic form of Spanish vocal music? Up to a point, perhaps, but there is clearly a violinistic model behind this too, and the violin was not an instrument associated with Spanish rhapsodic music of any kind. It seems most likely that Lalo was drawing on the rhapsodic violin style of another European exoticism, the celebrated style of the Hungarian Gypsy fiddlers, reconstructing that style around the traits of Spanish dance and vocal music.

Ex. 6.9. Edouard Lalo, *Symphonie espagnole,* op. 21, mm. 5–12 (solo violin part only).

Sarasate's championing of the *Symphonie espagnole* no doubt contributed to the promotion of Lalo's career when it was at a low ebb. But by the same token, Lalo can be said to have invented Sarasate in this work—to have invented for Sarasate the style on which he would build his career. A glance at the list of compositions Sarasate wrote for himself before the *Symphonie espagnole* came along in 1874 shows mostly fantasies on popular operas (*Don Giovanni* is the closest thing to a Spanish theme among them); immediately afterward, though, he began the long series of his own Spanish numbers with the *Gypsy Melodies* and *Spanish Dances.* And it was not just a style that Lalo was inventing for him, but a role: the role of Spanish ambassador to the concert halls of Europe and the Americas, the translator of Spanish melody . . . Spanish rhythm . . . Spanish soul . . . to the non-Spanish medium of concert music for violin.[52]

It cannot have been an easy role to play. To fulfill international expectations of the Spanish "type," his music and his playing had to be passionate; to match the manners of the concert hall, they could not be too passionate. His music settles for elegant lyricism. The more successfully he cultivated the role of the Spanish fiddler, the more he played into condescension abroad when he insisted on breaking out of that role, as when he performed Beethoven in Berlin. No wonder he looks so guardedly out of his portrait by Whistler.[53]

And the difficulty did not end with Sarasate. Classical musicians from Spain still have to weigh the advantages against the costs of presenting themselves as specialists in their own exoticism—the cost, notably, to how seriously they may be taken outside that specialty. Would Pablo Casals have been acclaimed for his Bach if he had been willing to play on his Spanishness as a musician? But what about a Spanish mezzo-soprano such as Teresa Berganza? Can she avoid *Carmen*, even if her heart is in Mozart and Rossini? For the program of the Edinburgh Festival, where she first played Carmen (well into her career), she wrote down her thoughts on the role, and in the tortured arguments of this essay can be felt the painful double bind of the Spanish musician: the bind of needing to prove that she can play Carmen while needing to deny that Carmen—the role that epitomizes the exoticization of Spain—is exotic.

The sense of a crusade both personal and political is evident in this essay from first ("My greatest wish at this moment is to be able to erase for good from the public's mind and imagination the false idea of Carmen") to last ("I shall also do my best to present to the public the image of a real Spain"). And what is her idea of the true Carmen? "Deep contemplation of this character surely recalls to mind the fact that Mérimée describes her as a gipsy woman. This very special detail, instead of clouding the features of Carmen's femininity, on the contrary helps to make them still clearer, from the important fact that it bars her from belonging to any specific nation or culture."[54]

What can this mean? That every Western country has its Gypsies, and therefore Carmen is not specifically Spanish? Berganza is certainly dedicated to lifting the role out of any Spanish context: Mérimée gave Carmen, she says, "her universal validity as a literary figure"; her calm in the face of death allows her to be compared with "the great tragic figures of classical antiquity." And Berganza fights valiantly against the age-old Northern stereotypes of the exotic embedded in the role: "Carmen is not a prostitute: she works in a factory to earn enough to keep herself and save sufficient money to enable her to visit her mother." Berganza's Carmen does not embody the exotic Spanish; she does not really, or merely, belong to Spain at all; yet she is supposed to represent "a real Spain": it is only a misunderstanding of Mérimée and Bizet, she says, that has given rise, in traditional productions of the opera, to "the scenic representation of a novelettish Spain" (*una España folletinesca*—literally, a magazine-romance or pulp-fiction Spain). In the end, in her struggle to make *Carmen* a place where she can feel comfortable with her own Spanishness, Berganza has sought to enlist the authors of the novel and the opera in a battle against fiction itself.

SCENE: A PUBLIC SQUARE IN SEVILLE; A TOBACCO FACTORY ON THE RIGHT . . .

Of course, Bizet was not worrying about how it would feel for a Spanish singer to be caught in the role. He conceived the opera for Parisian performers and already had the Parisian mezzo-soprano Célestine Galli-Marié in mind for the title role by the time he completed it. Furthermore, while the work was in production, it was that singer whose belief in it and in her role sustained Bizet against the fears of those involved who wanted to compromise his conception. Her understanding of the role would have been formed by her life in the theaters of Paris. The daughter of a Paris Opera singer, she was born in 1840, the year of Gautier's letters from Spain, and grew up, like Bizet and the librettists Henri Meilhac and Ludovic Halévy—native Parisians all—in a period when new representations of the exotic Spain appeared on the stages of Paris every year—plays, vaudevilles, operas, ballets, spectacles of every sort.[55] From that source, adding even to the stock of characters in Mérimée's story, the librettists drew every last shopworn stereotype of the exotic Spaniard—the bullfighter, the smuggler, the comically ineffectual soldier who is supposed to police the exotic characters, the *cigarière,* and above all the Gypsy woman, singing, dancing, telling fortunes, changing lovers at will. In fact, on the opening night, when the curtain went up on the third act of the opera, much of the audience apparently tutted that that scene of smugglers in their mountain retreat simply aped an Offenbach *opéra bouffe, Les brigands* (1869)—also to a libretto by Meilhac and Halévy—that had been revived in Paris only a few months earlier.[56] The creators and the audience, in other words, were equally conscious that the work belonged to the Parisian tradition of the Spanish put-on, even if this time, following Mérimée, it led to a far grimmer outcome than usual.

It is not simply a matter of plot and sets, of course; Bizet's music too uses all the usual Spanish stereotypes and gives them all a serious twist. There is, for example, no bolero as such in the opera, but the Toreador Song is a bolerified march (or rather, an alternation between a bolerified march—"Votre toast"—and a plain, unexoticized march—"Toréador, en garde!"), a perfect musical neologism for showing Don José, and the audience, who the "real" *hombre,* the "real" soldier in the show is. The Habanera, which seems today like the biggest cliché in the opera, virtually in all of opera, subject of countless spoofs, progenitrix of countless habaneras and tangos, actually represented the freshest genre of "Spanish" music in the opera at the time. Bizet may have lifted the notes of the number wholesale from a song thirty-five years old, Sebastián de Yradier's *canción habanera,* "El arreglito," but the genre of the habanera, which Yradier apparently introduced to Spain by publishing this song in 1840, was still far from established in the Parisian theatrical and concert repertory of Spanish exoticism before Bizet came along.[57] Nevertheless, he adapted the song in line with the tradition of exotic Spanish dance music stretching back at least to Méhul. Like Méhul's bolero, that is, Bizet's Habanera derives its seductive exoticism from two rhythmic patterns rubbing against each other, an insistently maintained bass rhythm against a melodic rhythm that can take several forms on the first beat, usually conforming to the bass rhythm only on the second beat. Most seductive of all is the effect of the triplet eighths in the melody against the dotted rhythm of the bass.[58] All of these elements can be found in Yradier's song, but he does not maintain the bass rhythm—nor, consequently, the interplay of rhythms—as hypnotically as Bizet (see example 6.10); but then, his number, a teasing dialogue of lovers who only gradually reach an accommodation, has need of its changes of character, whereas Bizet's has need of its rhythmic consistency to overwhelm the spectator with the power of Carmen's movements.

Ex. 6.10. Sebastián de Yradier, "El arreglito," from *Chansons espagnoles del Maëstro Yradier,* mm. 8–15.

We may not have much idea what Galli-Marié's Habanera looked like—no one in Paris would have expected her to perform the Cuban steps to the dance—but it's important to remember what an extraordinary thing it was for a composer to require such dancing from an opera singer as Bizet did here. The performer who plays Carmen is called on to be Elssler (playing castanets, too, let's not forget), Malibran, and Bernhardt rolled into one, and if Galli-Marié could do it all, it's no wonder she threatened to resign rather than let Du Locle (director of the Opéra-Comique) or the librettists or anyone tone down her role.[59] If the genius of Mérimée was to show in Don José a middle-class character putting on the life of a smuggler, the genius of Bizet surely was in giving center stage in *his* version of *Carmen* to a woman who puts on all the attributes of exotic womanhood—the dancing as well as the singing, the seductiveness as well as the refusal to be dominated by a man. The character Carmen, unlike Don José, may not put on an alien identity, but for women singers, as well as for the women in particular within the audience, the role of Carmen is the ultimate put-on, the ultimate fantasy, of exoticism. And if by the end of the opera she has left her dancing, her seducing, her exotic music behind,[60] if by the time of the Card Trio she is expressing herself in music "both intimate and tragically sweet" (the words are Berganza's, and here she is right on the mark), music, that is, stripped of any attributes of exoticism, it is not that she has left all stereotypes of exoticism behind. What is she doing in that scene, after all, but reading her fortune in the cards, along with her sister Gypsies, and believing superstitiously in the fate they decree? No, the miracle of *Carmen* is what gripping musical drama Bizet made within the very magazine-romance stereotypes of Spain that Berganza deplores as not "real." It is that he put real "soul" into the put-on Spain.

SCENE: STAGE LEFT, A CAFÉ IN SEVILLE; STAGE RIGHT, A STUDY IN SAINT PETERSBURG

In a *café cantante* in Seville sits Emmanuel Chabrier, with his wife, listening to the Gypsy musicians sing and play guitar, drinking from bottles of Manzanilla as they are passed from hand to hand, transfixed above all by the dancing of the women. It is October 1882, and he is already contemplating "an extraordinary fantasy, very Spanish, with the memories of this splendid trip,"[61] which he will produce for the Paris public in hardly more than a year as his *España* for orchestra. What is most remarkable about Chabrier the tourist is that he seems to ogle and transcribe at the same time; from Seville he writes to his publishers back in Paris:

> But, my friends, you really haven't seen anything if you haven't witnessed the spectacle of two or three Andalusian women billowing their bottoms, in time both with the cries of *anda! anda! anda!* and also with the eternal clapping—with a marvelous instinct they beat the 3/4 in counter-rhythm—while the guitar unobtrusively follows its rhythm, you hear them do as follows (with their hands):
>
> as others beat the strong beat of each measure—each of them beating more or less at her pleasure: it's an amalgam of the most curious rhythms. Moreover, I'm notating it all.[62]

In his study in Saint Petersburg, Nikolai Rimsky-Korsakov is poring over a recent collection of Spanish folksongs, *Cantos y bailes populares de España,* compiled by José Inzenga. It is 1887, and having just scored a success with his *Fantasia on Two Russian Themes* for violin and orchestra, he has decided to complement it with a violin fantasy on Spanish themes. The moment is more propitious now for exploring Spanish folk themes through published collections than it was a decade and a half earlier when Bizet, embarking on the composition of *Carmen,* went to the conservatory library in Paris and asked to see whatever was there by way of Spanish song; several major Spanish folksong collections, more scientific than any that came before, have been published in the intervening years.[63] In the course of writing the work, Rimsky will turn it from a virtuoso showpiece for violin into a virtuoso showpiece for the whole orchestra, though the solo violin will still assert itself prominently at various points. He will conduct this work, the *Capriccio on Spanish Themes* (generally known in English as the *Capriccio espagnol*), with great success, first in Saint Petersburg and then in Paris, at the Universal Exposition of 1889.

A curious exchange has occurred here: the French composer has taken on the role of the "Russian," and the Russian has taken over as "Frenchman." It was Chabrier for whom, as for Glinka, a trip to Spain was the experience of his musical lifetime, and Rimsky-Korsakov who, like Bizet or a host of earlier French composers, was content to build the "Spain of his dreams" out of a few Spanish tunes that found their way to him. It is the Frenchman who sought out the originality and "truth" of Spanish folk music, the Russian who worked with the exotic stereotypes. The Frenchman even followed Glinka in the structure of his work—*España* follows Glinka's "Capriccio brillante" as a single movement straying not at all from the rhythmic character, and not very much from the key, of its principal theme, which in both cases is a *jota*—while Rimsky's Capriccio is a divertissement, a suite of contrasting Spanish musical types.

What made this exchange possible? More than the personalities of the two composers. In France exoticism had taken a turn for the realistic. Through its colonial experiences, through frequent world fairs in Paris, and in the case of Spain through tourism on a large scale, the French public developed an appetite for the exotic as an endless process of discovery, no longer as a game to be played and replayed with stereotypes. It is not simply that Chabrier decided to go looking for undiscovered folk treasures in Spain; the Paris critics expected it of him and praised him for it. Louis Bourgault-Ducoudray, for instance, wrote in his review of the premiere of *España:* "Chabrier . . . belongs to that school of musician-explorers who paint after nature and occupy themselves above all with creating the *true.*" At the same time, Spain was making itself new as a tourist site. What Chabrier was after most of all, and what he found in that café in Seville and others like it in Cádiz and Granada, was *cante flamenco,* and the experience he had of it had simply not been available to tourists of the time of Gautier and Glinka and Gottschalk. They did hear Gypsy music in those cities, but if the evolutions of flamenco music and dance in the intervening decades are difficult to establish now (indeed, are subjects of heated debate), the changes in the presentation of them to tourists are incontrovertible. With the establishment of the *cafés cantantes* in the Andalusian cities by midcentury, flamenco performers developed a way of making a living performing for tourists. They developed, in other words, self-consciousness about exoticizing themselves and their art. The self-consciousness of these Spanish musicians and the appetite of the French composer and French musical public for the undiscovered and "true" in Spanish music could not have existed without each other.[64]

An equally great change had overtaken Russian attitudes toward the exotic in the decades since Glinka. Cultural power was now measured to a great extent in terms of empires, and the Russians had one of the largest of any nation in the world. With a curious ambiguity of perspective, Russians could still consider themselves cousins of the Spanish as a people defined by their rich tradition of folk music, yet they could also consider Saint Petersburg one of the centers of world cultural power, no longer a place on the margins. While his Spanish contemporaries, whether they worked mostly inside Spain (Chapí, Bretón, Pedrell, Granados) or mostly outside it (Albéniz), could almost never escape dealing with the theme of Spain, Rimsky was empowered by his country's geopolitical eminence to sit at home and conjure up out of a book any exotic musical world he chose—Russian, Spanish, or Arabian. He could move from one to another without changing his techniques of conjuring, which include the violin solo (Sarasate may in some oblique sense be behind the solos in the Capriccio, but who could be behind the ones in *Sheherazade,* written a year later?) and the framing theme. In the expansiveness and exuberance of the *Capriccio on Spanish Themes,* the Russian composer can be heard inheriting the self-confidence of a French composer, a Bizet, as a creator of exoticism.

Chabrier's exoticism on the other hand depends on his own research. Bourgault-Ducoudray may have thought of *España* as "painting from nature," but Chabrier had a tradition behind him as well: like Cézanne, who claimed to be "doing Poussin over again, from nature," he was doing Glinka over again, from (folk) culture. Much more than even Glinka's Second Spanish Overture, *España* is filled with tunes, rhythms, and ideas that the composer transcribed in Spain. Though they may have come from all over Spain, Chabrier did not make a tour of Spain out of them. Nor, though the piece is extraordinarily cohesive, does it represent any one genre of Spanish music, any one vignette, any one place or region. It is defined, in fact, not so much by Chabrier's collecting as by his analysis: it is in effect a study of the rhythmic phenomenon of twos within threes, in all the richness that he found in Spanish music. The whole work is in a quick triple meter (3/8): in the letter from Seville quoted above, he observed that all the music he was hearing, except for the tango, was in triple time. But at the very beginning of the work the triple time is disguised by six measures of pizzicato chords on every other eighth-note beat, and in this tug of the heard against the unheard Chabrier announces the rhythmic "theme" that he will pursue throughout the work. The introduction gives way to the principal melody (a *jota* melody that he transcribed somewhere on his Spanish travels), the first of several themes built of two-beat motives within the triple time. The later trombone theme (example 6.11) uses a different two within the three: two duplets per measure (two beats stretched to take the time of three)—a rhythm he heard in a *café cantante* in Granada, beaten by a man holding a cane between his legs, sitting next to the guitarist playing in triple time.[65] The response to this phrase is the *jota* theme (woodwinds in example 6.11, second system), with a variety of accompaniments, each making a different two-beat pattern, just like the duple patterns (such as the one transcribed above) that each of the women in Seville clapped "at her pleasure," all together creating "an amalgam of the most curious rhythms." We owe *España* to Chabrier's trip through Spain not only because such an "amalgam of curious rhythms" was not to be found in any book, in any published transcription of folk music, of that day, but because it was from his experience in Spain, analyzing as he ogled in that café in Seville, that Chabrier derived the relationship between the intricate workings and the exotic impression, between the constantly changing rhythmic combinations and the unvaried vitality, of *España.*

Ex. 6.11. Emmanuel Chabrier, *España*, orchestral score, p. 32, m. 5, to p. 34, m. 2.

Rimsky-Korsakov too had a model, beyond his book of transcriptions. His model is perhaps most evident at the beginning of the fourth movement of the *Capriccio on Spanish Themes:* the "Scene and Gypsy Song," apparently based on an Andalusian Gypsy song. What kind of a scene are we to imagine here? The opening, with its snare drum roll and its choir of trumpets and horns (example 6.12), hardly suggests the music making in a *café cantante.* The start of a bullfight, perhaps? But then, what to make of the subsequent cadenzas for violin, for flute, for clarinet, and for harp? What is especially striking about this whole long opening is its state of suspense; the snare drum roll in particular, extending surprisingly through the violin cadenza, arrests any possibility of movement. And it is this long suspension of movement, oddly enough, that suggests the model at work here: the ballet. The long period without a danceable rhythm could provide time for a stage to fill with dancers not dancing but waiting to dance, time for the building of an excitement to be fulfilled by the buoyant bolerolike rhythm that eventually carries the opening brass theme through the rest of the movement.

Ex. 6.12. Nikolai Rimsky-Korsakov, *Capriccio on Spanish Themes*, op. 34, mvt. 4, "Scena e canto gitano," mm. 1–6.

What we are being asked to imagine here (and the idea can be extended fruitfully to the whole Capriccio) is not Spain directly, but a ballet about Spain. It is an approach to the subject that makes perfect sense in a work written for Saint Petersburg, since ballet was the main vehicle for Spanish exoticism there. Marius Petipa, the French dancer and choreographer who became the main arbiter of Russian ballet for the entire second half of the nineteenth century, learned Spanish stage dance (of the bolero school) in Madrid in the early 1840s, would have stayed in Spain and founded a national school of ballet if he could have, and instead migrated to Saint Petersburg, where he made Spanish dance one of the favorite forms of ballet exoticism.[66] So while Chabrier was bringing a taste of flamenco to Paris as the latest Spanish sensation, Rimsky was evoking Spain through the Spanish dance that had caused a sensation in Paris half a century before, in Gautier's day, and had been kept alive in Saint Petersburg ever since. However faded the memory of that dance was in Paris by then, Rimsky's evocation of it was vivid enough to cause a stir when he brought his Capriccio there for the Universal Exposition in 1889.

Act 4: The Turn of the Century
Memories, Histories, Transformations

To French musicians like the twenty-five-year-old Debussy and the fourteen-year-old Ravel (just entering the Paris Conservatory), the Universal Exposition opened up many new musical worlds, not just the worlds of East Asian music—a celebrated encounter—but also those of Spain. They heard both the exoticized Spain of Rimsky-Korsakov and the direct import: Gypsy musicians from Granada performing flamenco music and dance.[67] In a sense the exposition represents the privileged vantage point of French musicians at that moment in history, heirs of a century-long and continuing tradition—largely though not exclusively French—of exoticizing Spain in music, and at the same time students of the newest musical discoveries from Spain itself. From this position Debussy and Ravel created a musical Spain unprecedented in the layers of memories it brought together; even Falla would have to travel to Paris to learn from them how to fashion a musical Spain so deep with memories—so rich in history—before he could return to Spain to figure out how to de-exoticize it.

Not that Debussy's Spain is the same as Ravel's. Debussy's is amazingly focused, an obsession with a single image, a single Spanish locale that he never visited, while Ravel's is encyclopedic, embracing the whole range of that century-long tradition of exoticism and adding an important new theme to it. Debussy's Spain, fixed in locale, is adrift in time, a "place" where pasts and present float in and out of each other, while in Ravel's Spains the sense of a bygone time is not only definite, but is the entire point of the music.

For all the differences between the two, an investigation of Debussy's Spanish music properly begins with a piece by Ravel. This piece, a Habanera originally written for two pianos (as part of the *Sites auriculaires*) and first performed in 1898, was withdrawn by the composer, eventually finding a place in his *Rapsodie espagnole* for orchestra (1908). By then Ravel was feeling defensive about the piece because Debussy, who had heard the two-piano version and borrowed the score, meanwhile reworked most of the ideas of the piece in his "Soirée dans Grenade" (from *Estampes*, 1903). Actually this Habanera touched off more works of Debussy than Ravel knew. As a teenager Debussy had written a few songs on "Spanish" poems of Musset and Gautier, but these belong, by their music as well as their texts, to a much earlier "act" of this story. In his twenties, he had been required or asked to set a cantata and later an opera on Spanish epic themes, but he had first resisted, then abandoned those projects.[68] Before he heard Ravel's Habanera, in other words, he was not evidently drawn to the Spanish exotic. Once he heard it, he reworked the same few ideas from it—and a single extramusical "image"—in four different "Habanera" movements, written over the course of a decade and a half. What's more, he began this process, as we shall see, in a work written, like the Ravel, for two pianos. In fact, while Ravel went on to write Spanish works in every medium, Debussy stayed with the piano—which meant staying with the Spanish pianist Ricardo Viñes, who premiered most of the piano music of Debussy and Ravel—except in his largest work on the Spanish theme, *Ibéria* (from his orchestral *Images*).

What evidently caught Debussy's ear in Ravel's Habanera is that Ravel takes the stock elements of the genre and, by inverting them, liberates them in function. That is, he turns the stock triplet- to duplet-eighth rhythm of habanera melodies—Yradier's, Bizet's, Chabrier's, everyone's—into a bass rhythm, and the stock bass rhythm—continuous in the Bizet, less so in the Yradier—into a melodic rhythm (example 6.13).[69] Then he switches back and forth between the stock arrangement and the inverted one, and in so doing he makes each rhythm an independent element, not tied to any one function, either conventional or unconventional. And Ravel gives these elements, these rhythms, not only independence of function, but independence from each other in harmony and in timing (the melodic elements entering unpredictably against the ostinato pattern). All of this deconstruction follows logically from that simple differentiation of bass and melodic rhythms in the Méhul bolero.

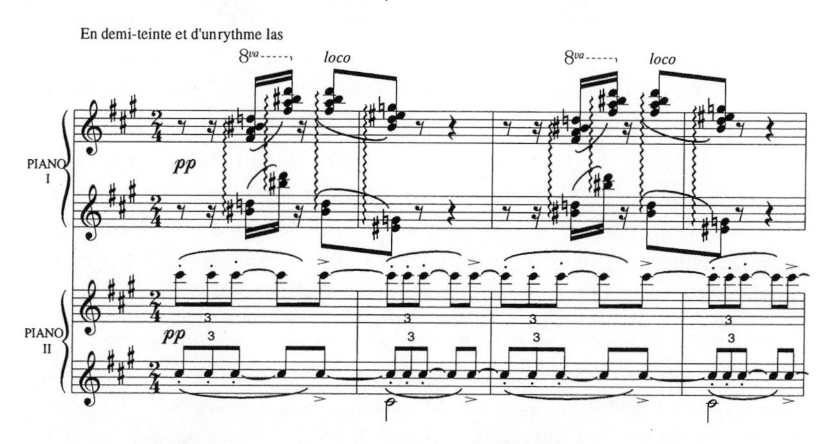

Ex. 6.13. Maurice Ravel, *Sites auriculaires*, Habanera, mm. 1–4.

SCENE: THE ALHAMBRA; ORANGE TREES TIPPED WITH SILVER; FOUNTAINS SPARKLING IN THE MOONBEAMS

Debussy made this transformation of the habanera a means of evoking a specific Spanish image—a place and an atmosphere long established in the canon of the Spanish exotic: night in the gardens of the Alhambra. His habanera, like Ravel's, is no longer a specific dance but a source of musical elements that float freely through the imagination. Debussy uses it to situate a dreamy persona in a tranquil imagined spot—the Alhambra garden—from where many different Spanish sounds can be "heard": Gypsy music from the streets of Granada far below, Moorish music from the distant past. This scenario in all its particulars was not suggested by Ravel's Habanera. To some extent it was available to Debussy from the tradition of Spanish exoticism stretching back to Chateaubriand and Cherubini. But the title of Debussy's first work on this theme suggests a more specific source.

This work is *Lindaraja,* a piece for two pianos that would have hurt Ravel's feelings as much as "La Soirée dans Grenade" if he'd known about it, but Debussy never had it performed or published. Its title puzzled Debussy scholars until François Lesure revealed that Lindaraja is the name of a terrace of the Alhambra, which he supposed Debussy saw pictured in a French illustrated magazine.[70] It would have been like Debussy to respond to pictures of this garden terrace or of the arabesque-covered Balcony of Lindaraja (*Mirador de la Daraxa*) that looks out onto it. But suppose instead, or in addition, that Debussy was reading the book that every European since Pushkin and Gautier, even Spaniards, had read to learn about the history, the legends, and above all the atmosphere of the fabled citadel: Washington Irving's *The Alhambra* (1832). There he would have learned that the name Lindaraja belonged to a beautiful Moorish maiden who lived in the Alhambra, and in the chapter "The Mysterious Chambers" he would have found a Poe-like tale that could well have suggested the whole structure of associations on which he plays, first in *Lindaraja* and even more clearly in his later works on the same subject. In this tale Irving describes his own nights spent alone, wandering the ancient, ruined halls of the Alhambra:

> The moon . . . gradually gained each evening upon the darkness of the night, and at length rolled in full splendor above the towers, pouring a flood of tempered light into every court and hall. The garden beneath my window, before wrapped in gloom, was gently lighted up, the orange and citron trees were tipped with silver;

the fountain sparkled in the moonbeams, and even the blush of the rose was faintly visible. . . .

Lindaraxa once more walked in her garden; the gay chivalry of Moslem Granada once more glittered about the Court of Lions! Who can do justice to a moonlight night in such a climate and such a place? The temperature of a summer night in Andalusia is perfectly ethereal. . . .

Sometimes the faint click of castañets rise from the Alameda, where some gay Andalusians are dancing away the summer night. Sometimes the dubious tones of a guitar and the notes of an amorous voice, tell perchance the whereabouts of some moon-struck lover serenading his lady's window.

Such is a faint picture of the moonlight nights I have passed loitering about the courts and halls and balconies of this most suggestive pile; "feeding my fancy with sugared suppositions," and enjoying the mixture of reveries and sensation which steal away existence in a southern climate; so that it has been almost morning before I have retired to bed, and been lulled to sleep by the falling waters of the fountain of Lindaraxa.[71]

Debussy, in *Lindaraja* (1901), his first experiment in capturing this scene, uses the four hands of his pianists to bring together a "mixture of reveries and sensation." Curiously, though he borrows Ravel's idea of working with the individual rhythmic elements of the habanera, he never uses the dotted "bass" rhythm (too strongly suggestive of dancing?), but instead keeps the dreamier "melodic" triplet rhythm sounding almost incessantly through the 185 measures of the piece. In example 6.14 it is "mixed" with a motive in a mirroring rhythm (suggesting the lulling fountain?), as well as with a wailing melody (*expressif*), flamenco-like in its close intervals (the "notes of an amorous voice" from the city below?).

Lindaraja is a more fascinating work than most commentators have allowed. But it is only with "La soirée dans Grenade" (Evening in Granada), written two years later, that Debussy found the means to shape such sounds into a compelling portrayal of the figure in the garden who hears or imagines them—a portrayal matching that of Irving's narrating self. Here he draws on the same sorts of "reveries and sensation" as in *Lindaraja,* but in a richer, more fluid "mixture," paradoxically—or miraculously, for Falla calls the work "a miracle"—requiring only two hands. This time it is the dotted "bass" rhythm of the habanera that sounds almost without break through the piece. Another distant wailing melody is heard, again framing the piece: it is the first theme to be heard over the habanera ostinato and the last to return. Toward the end "the dubious tones of a guitar" are heard (*léger et lointain*), another distant "sensation," twice interrupted by one of the "reveries."

Ex. 6.14. Claude Debussy, *Lindaraja,* mm. 9–18.

But Debussy's materials here are not all identifiable musical "sensations," nor is interruption his only technique of "mixture." Just before the guitar "tones," for instance, we hear thematic elements of all sorts mixed together in an astonishingly compact passage of transformations and infiltrations (example 6.15). The process begins when the *tempo giusto* theme drifts, as it has never done before, upward from its key. Before that leaves off, the theme previously marked *très rhythmé* slips quietly back in (middle staff). The pedal point in the bass shifts (from C-sharp to E) to accommodate the new theme, but its shift is not quite synchronized with the moment when one theme supersedes the other. Meanwhile the *tempo giusto* theme (in the upper staff) gives way to an ostinato figure, in the habanera dotted rhythm. But that rhythm, which from the start of the piece has served as a bass ostinato, often on a single tone, now blossoms into a descant in chords.

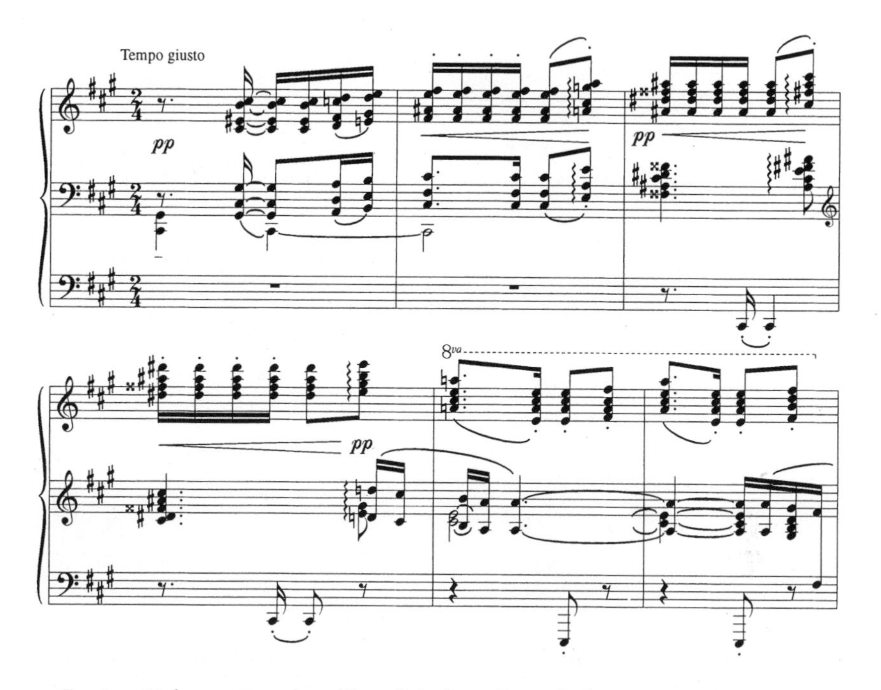

Ex. 6.15. Debussy, *Estampes,* "La soirée dans Grenade," mm. 94–99.

Overlappings . . . asynchronies . . . functional fluidities—all contribute to the impression of a mind indulging its reveries. In the opening and closing sections, with their "notes of an amorous voice" and "dubious tones of a guitar," we feel that our nocturnal visitor to the Alhambra has a mind open to the external world. But what is that mind open to during the greater part of the piece that extends between those opening and closing passages? In the passage of infiltrations just examined, for instance, we are rehearing two themes we heard before; both are presenting themselves now as memories, recollected less stably, less fully, more quietly than the first time. But what did they represent then? The *très rhythmé* theme at its first sounding was the longest uninterrupted thematic span, and its beginning the loudest, most forceful moment, of the entire piece. But after only two measures at full force it began to fade, and it went on fading for its remaining sixteen measures. The fading tells us that even in its first, more forceful appearance, this theme—the most passionate of the piece—does not represent anything as it is being experienced. It is remote, like all the passions of this piece. Whether those are the imagined passions of the Alhambra's ancient Moorish inhabitants or the overheard passions of the modern-day Spaniards in the city below or even the observer's own remembered passions—and we can imagine all these types at various times in the music—they all amount to someone else's passions.

It is a curious kind of exoticism that Debussy invents in "La soirée dans Grenade." The figure in whose mind all the "reveries and sensation" of the music play is receptive to Spains past and present, to the setting of the Alhambra, to sensations from outside himself, to the passions of the Other. But the Others themselves are excluded from the scene: this is a Spain with a soul, but with no Spaniards, at least none visible. In Debussy's scenario, as in Irving's, the Alhambra is vacant but for its one foreign visitor, so that we, prevented from projecting the passions of the music on anyone else present, are compelled to hear them as belonging to that visitor's mental process. Far from putting on anything Spanish, Debussy's figure—his persona as tourist—holds himself aloof from it, the better to receive whatever impressions of Spain he has positioned himself to receive.

This pose of receptivity pushes the concept of exoticism virtually to the breaking point. If it seems an extremely disengaged method for constructing Spanishness in music, all the stranger that Falla, of all people, should have written of "La soirée dans Grenade" that "the whole piece, down to its smallest details, brings Spain to us." The praise might have sounded strange to Debussy himself, who once wrote to Dukas of his wish to make people feel "that for a moment they had been dreaming of an imaginary country, that's to say one that cannot be found on the map."[72] When Falla says as well that "we are far away from those *Sérénades, Madrileños,* and *Boleros* which the manufacturers of Spanish music used to give us," it's hard not to notice that he has had to leave *Habaneras* off the list. Yet Debussy, while depending over and over on habanera rhythms in his "Spanish" output, never "manufactured" a habanera as such, and perhaps such respectful reticence—his avoidance of the kind of musical detail that would put a false image of Spaniards on display—was crucial in winning Falla's respect. Still, for Falla there is also a positive side to that reticence: "In *Soirée dans Grenade* everything is directed towards one aim: the creating of atmosphere."[73] What remains to explain about Falla is why he went beyond allowing a Frenchman that formula for evoking Spain, to adopting it himself and advocating Debussy's Spain as a model for other Spanish composers.

But first let's consider why, once he had produced this miracle of atmosphere, Debussy, with his notorious dread of repeating himself, would have gone on composing "Spanish" works: the three-movement *Ibéria,* the middle movement of which is his third nocturnal habanera, and two of the Preludes, of which one—"La Puerta del Vino"—is a fourth habanera, named for a gate of the Alhambra. Our answer, while it should describe all the ways in which these later works represented new ideas, should not fail to concede that he *was* also repeating himself: the scenario of night in the Alhambra garden clearly became an obsession with Debussy.

In *Ibéria* his obsession clearly led him to expand on what he had achieved in "La soirée dans Grenade": to surround his persistent image of the Alhambra with other images of Spain and to expand the techniques he had worked out in "La soirée dans Grenade" for representing a mind receiving competing impressions. If when he started composing it he described *Ibéria* in letters as a work for two pianos (like *Lindaraja* and Ravel's Habanera), nevertheless whenever he decided to orchestrate it, he was expanding his instrumental resources of evocation over both his previous "Spanish" works.[74] And the orchestration makes it particularly clear that *Ibéria* represents Debussy's summation of contemporary music on the theme of Spain, each of the three parts absorbing and saluting, but also expanding on, the achievements of a recent "Spanish" work.

The first part, for instance, "Par les rues et par les chemins," is Debussy's take-off on Chabrier's *España.* It is composed in the same fast triple meter (though Debussy does not stick to it, as Chabrier does), has the same compelling dance energy (so different from the spirit of Debussy's "nights in the garden" music), and offers a composite impression of Spanish dance music, rather than a musical image of one locale (Debussy wrote that he was "hearing the sounds of the roads [*chemins*] of Catalonia at the same time as the music of the streets [*rues*] of Granada)."[75] It expands on *España* in that it explores the same rhythms that Chabrier explored there—the same possibilities of duple patterns within or against the triple meter. But whereas Chabrier's explorations were guided by the principles of interaction among players, singers, clappers, and cane beaters in a flamenco performance, Debussy both follows those principles and goes beyond them. In addition to giving separate instruments different duple rhythms to play against the 3/8 meter, for instance, he sometimes moves from one duple rhythm to another within a single instrumental part (from quarter notes to dotted eighths in example 6.16). And whereas in the Chabrier it is the coordination of phrases that allows individually simple rhythms, played off against each other, to create the giddying impression of rhythmic freedom, in the Debussy, especially in certain quiet, relatively dreamy moments, what creates that impression is precisely the opposite: the discoordination—of motives that overlap each other and even of harmony, with different motives occupying different parts of a rich chord (as in example 6.17).

Debussy's vantage point, in other words, includes Chabrier's—that of the tourist in the *café cantante* putting together all the different rhythms that are sounding at once—but extends to that of the tourist in a reverie assembling sounds from many times and places of a recollected or imagined tour of Spain.

Ex. 6.16. Debussy, *Images* for orchestra, no. 2: *Ibéria,* mvt. 1, "Par les rues et par les chemins," rehearsal no. 7, mm. 1–4 (2d violin part only).

In the second part of the work, "Les parfums de la nuit," the contemporary music he salutes—and outdoes—is his own earlier music of nights in the gardens of the Alhambra (and in a sense Ravel's Habanera as well). The outdoing consists partly of furthering the process that Ravel began—abstracting the habanera. Here, though the habanera is undoubtedly the genre behind the whole movement, no single habanera rhythm sounds continuously. Instead, fragments of habanera rhythms are heard in a hundred guises—four measures of the dotted rhythm from the tambourine here, a melody with the habanera triplet (but slowed to half the normal speed) from the French horn there. It is heard more often as a melodic than a bass rhythm, as at the opening, when the oboe plays a fragmented melody in the dotted rhythm (mm. 1–4). A whole-tone habanera melody, marked "expressive, a bit drawn out," for oboe!—it seems that Debussy is combining the habanera here with the "notes of an amorous voice" overheard from the silent Alhambra, combining, that is, the first two elements sounded in "La soirée dans Grenade" into something more abstract, less specifiable than either. In fact Debussy does not so directly invoke the act of overhearing this time, despite having an orchestra at his disposal, with its power to specify musical sources. He lets us hear echoes of music not from the streets, but from "the Streets"—the previous movement. Early on, the oboe replays (in the seventh measure after rehearsal number 39) the most "expressive," most "amorous" of the melodies in "Par les rues" (the one it plays in example 6.17); toward the end of the movement (rehearsal number 48) flutes, trumpets, and strings play the main theme of "Par les rues." Here is no "mixture of reveries and sensation," but a mixture of abstracted and recollected sensations, all equally converted into reveries; here the Alhambra be-

Ex. 6.17. Debussy, *Ibéria,* "Par les rues et par les chemins," rehearsal no. 14, m. 3 to rehearsal no. 15, m. 3.

comes not the single locale of Debussy's Spanish imaginary, but the single locale from which his imaginary tourist can dream of still other Spains.

Everything about the third and final movement, "Le matin d'un jour de fête," seems a response to Rimsky's *Capriccio on Spanish Themes:* the orchestral effects, ranging from the multiple-stop-filled violin solo to the pizzicato strings making like a big guitar; the wholesale reworking of earlier themes in the finale; the transition without pause from a nocturnal movement into a sunlit finale. Actually, the beginning of Debussy's finale, in which the dreams of "Les parfums de la nuit" are successively infiltrated by the waking sensations of "Le matin d'un jour de fête," deserves to be distinguished not only from smooth transitions by Rimsky-Korsakov and other composers, but also from infiltrations in *Ibéria* and earlier works of Debussy: here the delicious state of reverie at the moment of awakening is attributed not just to the narrating figure, but also to the Spanish subjects of the narration. As Debussy, after a pleasing rehearsal of the work, reported about this transition: "*It sounds as though it's improvised. . . .* The way it comes to life, with people and things waking up."[76]

In the movement as a whole it seems as if every perfumed motive from "Les parfums de la nuit" is transformed (along with several from "Par les rues et les chemins") by exposure to the light of day. To cite just one example, a motive appearing late in "Les parfums," where it is marked "expressive and stressed in its sweetness" (beginning at the *sans lenteur* after rehearsal number 50), turns—who can say why—into the violin solo in "Le matin" (rehearsal number 61), the "fantastic" display of a street fiddler, mocked by the crowd (the answering wind instruments). This idea of mocking a phrase previously treated so tenderly may be more indebted to the *Symphonie fantastique* than to the *Capriccio on Spanish Themes,* but Debussy is using the technique to exorcise a specifically Spanish image, in fact using it with a vengeance on a whole web of themes, the whole "syndrome of Granada" (in François Lesure's phrase) that had obsessed him.

The exorcism took, pretty much. After *Ibéria* there were several more Debussy Spains, but none of perfumed moonlight. "La sérénade interrompue," in the first book of Preludes for piano (1910), borrows as obviously from Isaac Albéniz ("El Albaicín" from book 3 of his *Iberia,* 1907) as Debussy's earlier "Spanish" piano pieces do from Ravel. The most striking sign of the borrowing is the full-blown imitation of the sounds of the serenader's instrument, the guitar—no longer the merely schematic representation found in "La soirée dans Grenade" and "Le matin d'un jour de fête." It is possible that the humor of the piece too owes something to Albéniz, whom Debussy praised for "the special sense of humor peculiar to his country of origin (he was a Catalan)."[77]

Not that Debussy is imitating any particular humorous passage of Albéniz. But Albéniz in his *Iberia* poked some fun at folk music making (the flat-footed habanera of a street organ, complete with misfirings of the valves, in "Lavapiés"),[78] and the example of his Spanish friend may have served as a kind of permission to Debussy, who makes a joke of exoticism itself in "La sérénade interrompue." He interrupts the "true" Spanish music of the serenader, at his most impassioned cadenza, with the distant sounds of a "Spanish" march by none other than Debussy himself (from "Le matin d'un jour de fête"). But—and this is a departure for Debussy—he also mocks the Spanish serenader, who flies into a rage from which he barely recovers, only to slink off into the night. Though all Debussy's exotic musical explorations depended directly on the European imperialism that reigned unchallenged in his lifetime, he was also one of the first European artists to express consciousness of the ill effects of imperialism—by expressing, here, a discomfort with both the arrogance and the piety of musical exoticism.

"La Puerta del Vino," in the second book of his Preludes (1913), marks a return to the Alhambra, but by daylight. It is another habanera, with all the same musical elements, the same musical "sensations," as "La soirée dans Grenade"; but now, instead of infiltrating each other, they are posed against each other, according to Debussy's indication, "with brusque oppositions of extreme violence and passionate softness." These contrasts were inspired, according to Falla, by the contrast of midday sunlight and shade in a postcard Falla had sent Debussy of the Puerta del Vino, one of the gates of the Alhambra.[79] The music has, in any case, a glare to it—Debussy marks it "ironic" at one point—that allows no effects of perfume. Until the end, that is, when with a slight let-up in tempo (*un peu retardé*) one of the phrases of "passionate softness" makes midday shadows seem like moonlit radiance—an effect of musical fauvism, turning the color schemes of reality inside out—and for just two measures the music echoes—distills—the ecstasy that Debussy had once projected on the moonlit Alhambra.

Later still came *En blanc et noir* (1915). At first he was going to call those movements for two pianos *Caprices,* and he wrote to his publisher Durand while working on them that he'd "made a slight change in the colour of the second of the *Caprices* . . . it was too profoundly black and almost as tragic as a 'Caprice' by Goya!" That movement, a portrait of the battlefield, written during the bleakness of World War I, was associated in his mind—as the original title suggests—with the *Caprichos* of Goya, that is, with Goya's bleak vision of human nature, colored by his experience of the Napoleonic occupation of Spain. And if Debussy eventually made the music less graphic and the title less specific (though still "graphic"), it stayed associated in his mind with Spanish art: "These pieces draw their colour, their emotion, simply from the piano," he wrote once they were published, "like the greys' of Velázquez."[80] But there is no trace of an exotic Spain here, and to the extent that Debussy was comparing the situation of France, invaded by Germany as he was composing the work, to that of Goya's Spain, invaded by France a century earlier, he had found in an unwilled identification with the weak the bitterest possible reason to forswear exoticism altogether.

SCENE: THE SPANISH COURT, THE SIXTEENTH CENTURY

Ravel was as deeply affected by World War I as Debussy but was not inclined to draw the same conclusions about exoticism, at least about the exoticizing of Spain, not because he was less sensitive than Debussy, but because his musical Spain had different, more personal roots. As Falla puts it, "Ravel's was a Spain he had felt in an idealized way through his mother," who was Basque but had lived in Madrid and spoke fluent Spanish. Or, as Ravel himself put it: "My mother used to lull me to sleep singing guajiras. Perhaps it's because of this link that I feel so attracted to Spain and its music."[81] In other words, Spain was his familial exotic—that foreign place to which he was so connected by his own history that it felt neither alien nor naturalized, both exotic and innate, to him. Ravel was not the first composer with Spanish roots to write music of exotic Spain; Lalo had distant Spanish ancestors. But Ravel's sense of connection to Spain through his mother led him to produce not only the richest output of "Spanish" music by any non-Spanish composer but even, within that output, some works exploring a kind of exoticism not dreamed of by musicians for whom Spain was simply exotic.

The list of Ravel's "Spanish" works extends from the two-piano Habanera, written in 1895, during his student years, to the last music he wrote, the songs *Don Quichotte à Dulcinée* of 1932–33. It includes piano music, orchestral music, a folksong arrangement, original songs, a ballet, and an opera. The Habanera starts a line of works that, whatever they have to do with his personal-familial Spain, also invoke and enrich the long, largely Franco-Russian tradition of Spanish exoticism. In the "Alborada del gracioso," part of the solo piano suite *Miroirs* (1905), he made his contribution to the genre of guitar-inspired piano music, just as Albéniz was about to embark on the composition of his *Iberia.* His *Rapsodie espagnole* (1907) is, overall, his tribute to the *Capriccio on Spanish Themes,* if anything outdoing Rimsky-Korsakov's already stunning orchestration. But there is a more complex relationship in the work, that to Debussy. The third movement of the *Rapsodie* is an orchestration of his earlier two-piano Habanera, a gorgeous piece of orchestration, but retaining the notes of the piano piece exactly, while the date "1895," prominently placed under the title *Habanera* in the score, stakes his claim to priority over Debussy's "Soirée dans Grenade" in this genre of musical evocation. But then, what is the first movement, the "Prélude à la nuit," but a borrowing in turn of the specific night-in-the-garden scenario of "La soirée dans Grenade"? Except that Ravel also adapts a variety of two-within-three rhythms (suggested by Chabrier's *España*?) to this scenario, this atmosphere. And perhaps Debussy was inspired by a violin theme in this movement to imitate it in his next night-in-the-garden piece, "Les parfums de la nuit." The questions of priority hardly matter any more, but it is clear that Ravel in this work was deeply enmeshed in a common enterprise of Spanish exoticism.

He had already struck out into territory of his own, though, in the second "Spanish" work of his student years, the "Pavane pour une Infante défunte" (Pavane for a deceased Infanta) of 1898. The work in fact breaks the tradition—the "rules"—of Spanish exoticism by evoking the Spanish court of the Golden Age, the Spain of Velázquez and the young princesses who endlessly sat—or rather, stood—for him to paint. Did Ravel not know that that Spain was off-limits for exoticizing? That the whole nature of the "Spanish" enterprise for French artists was to efface Spain's Golden Age and with it any memory of a Spain whose power the French had feared and whose culture they had emulated? There is surely nothing exotic or in any conventional way "Spanish" about the sound of this piano piece. In the prevailing staccato notes of the inner voices Laurence Davies hears Ravel "presumably endeavouring to imitate the faint pluckings of a lute or vihuela,"[82] but the same conceit appears whenever Ravel and his contemporaries evoke courtly music (in the Passepied from Debussy's *Suite bergamasque* of 1890, for example), and the plucking could belong to the harpsichord as easily as to the vihuela. The real exoticism here is of time rather than place; the border Ravel is crossing is 1789, not the Pyrenees. The title he dreamed up for the piece speaks of vanished worlds: if the Spanish setting belonged to a part of his family history irrecoverable except through his mother's lullabies, the specific music that he chose to evoke here belonged to the court life that had vanished from Spain, as from Europe generally. And the Pavane is exotic in sound only insofar as, through its stiff courtly rhythms, it palpably trembles with nostalgia.

The kinds of Spanish music more conventionally associated with exoticism—popular song and dance, folk music, *cante flamenco*—were not such appropriate vehicles for nostalgia. They had not, after all, disappeared. According to the beliefs of the day, they barely even changed over time.[83] Ravel's setting of a Spanish folk song in his multinational collection of *Chants populaires* (1910) has therefore no sense of a bygone era or culture about it; it belongs to a more ethnomusicological enterprise, a comparative exoticism. But his last "Spanish" music, the songs *Don Quichotte à Dulcinée* (1933), apparently simple works, effect a remarkable fusion of styles from every category of Spanish traditional music to recreate—or so it seems—the Spanish Golden Age as a living musical world. The theme of Don Quixote, like that of the Cid, had never lost its appeal in France; Massenet, for instance, had exoticized both themes in operas (1910 and 1885 respectively). Ravel's three songs for Don Quixote use the techniques of exoticism, too, but so as to specify a time as well as a place. Each of the songs takes the rhythm of a different Spanish folksong genre: the "Chanson romanesque" has the alternating 6/8 and 3/4 of the guajira (Ravel remembering those lullabies again?), the "Chanson épique" the 5/4 of the Basque zortzico, and the "Chanson à boire" the cross-rhythms of the *jota*.[84] But nothing is quite as it seems: the slow rhythm of the "Chanson épique"—a prayer—does not feel at all like that of a folk dance; instead, it works with the song's chantlike melodic lines and organumlike parallel harmonies to evoke the Catholic church music of the past—actually, of an age even older than Don Quixote's (example 6.18). But Ravel specifies "Spain" in another way: the accompaniment gives urgency to Don Quixote's prayer the way flamenco music gives expression to pain, with chords of crushing dissonance—"Spanish guitar" chords like those of the "Alborada del gracioso" (example 6.19). In this music there is no nostalgia, only Ravel's conviction that all the traditions of Spain's musical heritage can be melded into a single musical language to sing of Spain's past.

In the decades between the Pavane and the *Don Quichotte* songs, Ravel composed two "Spanish" stage works, the opera *L'heure espagnole* (staged in 1911) and the ballet *Boléro* (staged in 1928). Each displays a distinctive attitude toward the past, though in these cases the reference is more to past "Spanish" exoticisms than to past Spains. In the score of *L'heure espagnole* the period of the setting is not even specified; the setting is simply "a Spanish watchmaker's shop." It takes the first line of text to tell us that the watchmaker lives in Toledo, and Ravel, in an interview just before the first production opened, praised the costumes as "copies of models by Goya." Goya certainly provides a fitting period costume for the work. Ravel may have claimed to have done his "utmost to make my work express Spain,"[85] but though there are "Spanish" rhythms and vocal embellishments galore in this work, they are rather indiscriminately applied, and in many instances they form a barely audible substratum to the

Ex. 6.18. Ravel, *Don Quichotte à Dulcinée,* "Chanson épique," mm. 1–5.

Ex. 6.19. Ravel, *Don Quichotte à Dulcinée,* "Chanson épique," mm. 12–14, piano part only.

singing. It is as if Ravel were writing a tribute to *The Barber of Seville* (1816), thinking longingly of Rossini's age as the last time when Spain could be represented in music without making an issue of its Spanishness, and then simply colored his tribute with enough Spanish exoticism to acknowledge what had gone on in music since then.[86]

Boléro turns that formula inside out: it makes an issue of Spanish exoticism without being about Spain at all. In taking us back to the bolero, that earliest genre of the Spanish mania in France, he revives the "Spanish" put-on of Elssler's and Gautier's day, rounding out, in the process, his lifelong survey of the exotic-Spanish tradition.[87] He was writing, in fact, for a ballet to be danced by a latter-day Elssler, the Russian dancer Ida Rubinstein, backed by a *corps de ballet* of twenty men—not the couple's dance of the old *escuela bolera* or even a formula from flamenco tradition, but an anticipation, perhaps, of the "flamenco" extravaganzas created by Spanish national dance companies later, during the Franco era.[88] Ravel's music is a piece of musical clockwork, though utterly different in rhythm from the clockwork introduction to *L'heure espagnole,* and from the sound of the music we cannot be surprised to learn that Ravel wanted the ballet set in a factory.[89] But then, what becomes of the sensuality that was supposed to be at the heart of the bolero and the whole long line of Spanish exoticism? He was not thinking of a cigarette factory in Seville, presumably. There is actually room for sensual movement in the early minutes of the work: its bolero rhythm, however clocklike, suggests the floor-bound movements of the bolero dancer, as Gautier contrasted them with the ballerina's leaping and lifting: "luxuriating in the rhythm and casting amorous glances, as they do in Andalusia . . . and without sending the hem of the skirt flying into the air."[90] By the end, though, sensuality, and with it any trace of exoticism, is overwhelmed by repetition, by volume, by the machinelike coordination of so many instruments and dancers. Like Debussy, Ravel eventually sacrificed the tradition of Spanish exoticism to his consciousness of the conditions of modernity; unlike Debussy, he salvaged for himself—for subsequent exploration in the Don Quixote songs—what had always been for him an alternative Spain, a Spain of the distant past, which he presented as almost pre-exotic.

SCENES: ALHAMBRA GARDENS BY MOONLIGHT; THE COURTYARD OF AN INN, WITH A PUPPET THEATER; DEEP IN THE ATLANTIC OCEAN

Manuel de Falla followed a similar path, but from the perspective of the one exoticized. He was intensely conscious that it was through exoticism—French Spains in particular—that Spanish musical traditions had been transformed into modern Spanish music. In his article "Claude Debussy and Spain," for instance, already cited above, he credits Debussy with teaching Spanish composers to use guitar harmonies that they had "neglected, even despised as barbaric" and then sums up the whole matter, the circular exchange between the exoticizer and the exoticized: "if Claude Debussy has found in Spain a source of one of the most beautiful facets in his work, he has paid us back so generously that it is Spain who is today his debtor."[91] Writing an obituary tribute, and for a French publication, Falla could afford to be generous to Debussy, while staking a balancing claim for Spain as a "source." But there is more than diplomacy at work here. Falla spent most of his thirties (1907–14) in Paris, where he cultivated the friendship of Debussy and Ravel among others, studied their "Spanish" works, and developed his own Spanish art under their influence. In the remaining thirty years of his life, even while undergoing extraordinary stylistic evolutions, he never altogether escaped the Spanish exoticism he had learned in Paris. Nor did he ever lose his consciousness of foreign, especially French, musicians and listeners as potential hearers and judges of his work.

Because of his persistent engagement with a foreign view of his own culture, his astoundingly methodical lifelong study of exotic musical Spains, and his equally methodical transformations of the exoticizing ideas he studied, Falla makes an exemplary case of auto-exoticism—as a political plight, as a psychological condition, as an artistic dilemma. We can ask, for instance, why, if it was French culture that expressed the strongest need to exoticize Spain—the strongest need to define Spain by its difference—why Falla should have felt so drawn to France. Did not he feel condescension from the French in their exoticization of Spain, resentment that his country was made the object of their musical ogling? In his published writings, at least, there is no trace of that. The simplest explanation may be that he accepted the premise of French difference from Spain, though on his own terms. It may have suited his own needs to believe in one Catholic, Latin country that, unlike his own, could be as modern as, and artistically and intellectually more advanced than, any of its Protestant, Germanic competitors.[92] Holding that belief about France would have left him room to celebrate the difference of Spain—the beauty and value of its unmodern cultural traditions—in his own music, even as he produced that music by following the most advanced French concepts of exoticism.

The most powerful evidence for such a motivation in Falla is the persistence of his adherence to the model of exoticism. In many accounts of Falla's career, it is true, the exoticism of Debussy and Ravel is described as casting its spell over Falla for only a short while after he left Paris—for not very long after his "impressionist" *Noches en las jardines de España* (Nights in the Gardens of Spain), completed in 1915. Burnett James, for instance, writes that around 1920 Falla "turned, artistically, from Andalucía to Castile, from, that is, the periphery of colourful, atmospheric, exotic Spain to the true centre of classical Spanish thought and feeling."[93] But the foregoing history of exotic Spain in music permits the argument that Falla had so many models of Spanish exoticism before him that in his whole artistic development he could turn from one model to another without ever leaving exoticism behind.

Falla's cultivation of historical styles in works like the Harpsichord Concerto (1926), for instance, can be seen not as a turn away from exoticism altogether to neoclassicism (albeit with Spanish sources), but as a turn toward history as a kind of exoticism (and with more Spanish color than Ravel used in the Pavane). In fact, already in 1919 Falla was finding a place for eighteenth-century style within a generally exotic context, that of *The Three-Cornered Hat:* the Corregidor's Dance (in part 2) is a minuet, or rather a mockery of a minuet, and the mockery is achieved in part by giving it an exotic "Spanish" twist, changing the meter from 3/4 to 6/8 at cadences. On the other hand, a work described as "possibly his most openly neoclassical composition,"[94] the song "Psyché" (1924), which Falla says he imagined as music performed for the Spanish queen looking out from her window in the Alhambra in 1730, nevertheless has passages of short "flamenco" trills (example 6.20) strongly reminiscent of those in the Alhambra movement of *Nights in the Gardens of Spain* ("En el Generalife"). If anything, Falla was obsessed with the theme of nights in the gardens of the Alhambra longer than Debussy, and in his last work, the "scenic cantata" *Atlántida* (unfinished at his death in 1946), there is a final reminder of that arch-exotic image, couched within another historical vision, in the narration of the dream that Queen Isabella dreamed one night in the Alhambra.

Merely in switching and mixing models of Spanish exoticism, Falla does not of course distinguish himself from Ravel. We have to consider his oeuvre in other ways to discover what marks its auto-exoticism, its insider's perspective. One sign of that is his study of other models, other composers who represented the music of their own people as exotic. These models take us away from French and back to Russian, or more generally to Slavic, composers. One of the earliest signs of this study is Falla's Mazurka for piano (around 1900), recently discovered and published for the first time, in perfect imitation of Chopin's style. Here Falla is studying how Chopin represented the most "different" music of Polish folk culture to a cosmopolitan European audience.[95] Falla's puppet opera *El retablo de maese Pedro* (Master Peter's Puppet Show, 1922) has been compared to Stravinsky's small-scale theatrical works of the same period, starting with *The Soldier's Tale,* and we can be sure that, having earlier heard in Stravinsky's music "a very conspicuous national character," he was keeping his eye on Stravinsky for new models of music theater suited to a

Ex. 6.20. Manuel de Falla, "Psyché," mm. 1–8 (strings omitted in mm. 1–7).

composer whose national material was internationally recognized as exotic.[96]

A deeper sign of Falla's Spanish perspective is his concern with authenticity, which he judged unnecessary for foreigners writing "Spanish" music—he excused Debussy from that standard[97]—but addressed in many ways in his own music. One of the simplest examples is that he wrote his obituary homage "Le tombeau de Claude Debussy" (1920) for guitar, the instrument that Debussy had always imitated in his "Spanish" works without actually employing. Deeper evidence lies in Falla's manifold and knowing use of Spanish melodies, Spanish styles, Spanish texts throughout his work. When he turns an episode of *Don Quixote* into a puppet opera (*El retablo*), for example, he is dealing with the classic text of his national literature, as Massenet and Ravel in their musical *Don Quixotes* were not.[98]

Authenticity, of course, provides no defense against the highly charged response that a work of auto-exoticism would naturally meet in its own country, and the reception of Falla's work was certainly more politically charged in Spain than in France and elsewhere.[99] But in representing Spain to both Spain and the rest of the world, Falla faced still other problems. In works like the ballet *El amor brujo* (1915) and the *Fantasia bética* for piano (1919), Falla was evidently seeking to replace "those *Sérénades, Madrileños,* and *Boleros* which the manufacturers of Spanish music used to give us" with a more authentic, more intense musical representation of Spain. To do that he drew on Andalusian flamenco as his representative Spanish music. But how could he keep Spanish audiences, on the one hand, from quarreling about the propriety of that choice and foreigners, on the other hand, from inferring from it that Spanish music was all "primitive"?

Likewise, Falla's music has proved influential on later composers, Spanish and foreign, depending on what position they have been in to respond to his struggle with exoticism. Joaquín Rodrigo, for instance, in his *Concierto de Aranjuez* (1939) or his *Fantasía para un gentilhombre* (1954), can be heard dealing in the exoticism of the Spanish courtly past—following the examples of Falla's Harpsichord Concerto and "Psyché"—in preference to the more folkish or primitivist exoticisms of Falla's earlier music, exoticisms that had become politically suspect in Franco-era Spain. By contrast, it has been precisely the primitivist side—the *Amor brujo* side—of Falla's exoticism that has appealed to composers in the Americas from Alberto Ginastera to Miles Davis and George Crumb; they have assumed a "Russian" role toward that exotic Spain, finding in it a reflection of their own musical identity, European and non-European at the same time. After all, it was at least partly through the exoticism of *El amor brujo* that Miles Davis and Gil Evans found in flamenco music a European musical tradition sufficiently powerful on their terms that they could naturalize, or assimilate, it into the Jazz idiom in *Sketches of Spain.*[100]

In the last analysis Falla could exoticize his own country because he was a nationalist and because exoticism coincides in many respects with nationalism, as the sentence of Schnabel's revealed at the opening of this chapter. He never doubted, for instance, that Spain had a soul, even if the nationalist—the insider's—perspective on the soul of Spain was in a sense the opposite of the exoticizer's—the outsider's. For exoticism, that is, the problem was to find what makes Spain different from other cultures, especially from one's own, while for nationalism the problem was to find what makes all Spanish cultures alike. But while Falla faced the nationalist problem, the solutions he resorted to had all been developed in the workshop of exoticism. From his "Andalusian" style—

that is, flamenco style exoticized into a "national" Spanish style—he moved, especially after 1920, to experiments in historical exoticism. This move can be seen as an attempt to find beneath the social, political, and regional divisions of Spain—which had been intense throughout his life and were becoming catastrophic—a stratum of history that all Spaniards shared. His quest took him deeper and deeper into history, from the eighteenth century and the Golden Age to the ancient mythology of Atlantis. But if Falla was addressing national divisions in *Atlántida,* he was also—as in any auto-exoticist project—placing his country in relation to the outside world. The work locates Iberia in the prestigious classical Mediterranean world—an answer to the exoticist tradition of marginalizing Iberia—but also in the middle of the Atlantic, looking toward the discovery of the Americas, but at the same time cut off from Europe. In that sense it is both Falla's ultimate exoticization of Spain from Europe and his one act of withdrawal from the European, especially French, representation . . . marginalization . . . embrace . . . of Spain.

That act of withdrawal—de-exoticization, perhaps—still resonates in Iberia, not necessarily in its musical culture, but quite evidently in the Portuguese novel *Jangada de pedra* (The Stone Raft), José Saramago's 1986 fantasy of Iberia breaking off from Europe at the Pyrenees and floating out alone into the Atlantic.[101] It seems to be a danger of exoticism that those who are its objects, when they conclude they cannot overcome their exotic relationship to the centers of power, begin to consider that they might be better off with no relationship at all.

"Entoiling the Falconet": Russian Musical Orientalism in Context

RICHARD TARUSKIN

IN RUSSIAN the word "Orientalism" may be rendered either as *orientalizm,* or more commonly *orientalistika,* which are perfectly good Russian words (well, Russian words anyway), or as *tema vostoka*—the "Eastern theme." The "Eastern theme" is neutral: from a study with that phrase in the title one expects inventories, taxonomies, identification of sources, stylistic analysis. "Orientalism" is charged: from a study with that word in the title one expects semiotics, ideological critique, polemic, perhaps indictment.

In fact, it is Orientalism in Russian art music, and especially in opera, that I shall be addressing, not the "Eastern theme." One could not possibly do the latter justice in anything less than a book, what with the hundreds of Russian operas, ballets, tone poems, instrumental pieces, and songs with Oriental subject matter that appeared over a rough century between Catterino Cavos's *Firebird* and Stravinsky's.[1] Any adequate taxonomy of this richly variegated material would first have to separate it into what we might call intra-imperial and extra-imperial categories (which already raises the specter of Orientalism), dividing the intra-imperial (following the movements of the Russian army) into Siberian, Caucasian, and Central Asian phases, cutting the extra-imperial first into vastly unequal Near and Far Eastern shares, and then apportioning the Near Eastern into Arabian, Persian, Turkish, and Levantine strains. So prevalent for a while was the "Eastern theme" that when Vladimir Stasov, the great mythologizer of Russian music, looked back in 1882 at "Twenty-Five Years of Russian Art" (the title of one of his most famous essays), he could name "the Oriental element" as one of the four distinguishing—and, of course, progressive—features of what he called the "New Russian School," the others being skepticism of European tradition, "striving for national character," and "extreme inclination toward program music."[2]

Leaving taxonomy aside, we are left with Orientalism: the East as sign or metaphor, as imaginary geography, as historical fiction, as the reduced and totalized Other against which we construct our (no less reduced and totalized) sense of ourselves. As Stasov implied, as we knew to begin with, and as we have been forcibly reminded by postcolonialist writers, it is not possible to separate this constructed East from "the real one." The East is the East only to the West: the very act of naming it is already constitutive and heavily invested, consciously or not, with theory. There can be no investigation of it that is not both itself an ideological critique and subject to ideological critique in its turn.

The only question is how overt shall we make our critique, and how bluntly accusatory. If I had wanted to put my enlightened scholarly and human perspective on display by attacking Alexander Borodin's *Prince Igor,* the focus of the Dallas symposium that instigated my writing on the subject, it would have been all too easy. I could have pointed out that throughout *Prince Igor*'s notorious eighteen-year gestation (1869–87), its plot was being uncannily reenacted in real life: Russia was just then competing avidly with Britain in what Kipling (and others) called the Great Game, a protracted imperialist war in Central Asia against a Muslim Holy League led by the Khan of Bokhara. I could have shown that, along with most of educated Russia, Borodin and Stasov enthusiastically endorsed this war, which came to an end only with the Soviet debacle in Afghanistan. As evidence I could have cited virtually all the differences between the libretto—or, better yet, Stasov's original scenario—and its literary source, the twelfth-century epic (unless it turns out to be an eighteenth-century forgery after all) known as *The Lay of Igor's Campaign* (*Slovo o polku Igoreve*).

Regarding the relations between the Russians and their antagonists in this epic, the Pólovtsï, there were two main inventions: on the one hand there was the egregious Ovlur—an unidentified name in the *Lay* but in the opera a turncoat Good Indian straight out of Fenimore Cooper—who arranges Igor's escape; on the other, there was the interpolated love intrigue between Igor's son Vladimir, who does exist in the *Lay of Igor's Campaign,* and Khan Konchak's daughter, Konchakóvna, who does not. Later, it will be evident that Konchakóvna was an absolutely essential character for the sake of her music. The pretext for her invention, however, was slim: just a few lines in the *Lay* between Khans Gzak and Konchak in which they briefly consider "entoiling the falconet by means of a fair maiden," as Nabokov translated it.[3]

Stasov's scenario ended with an epilogue Borodin never composed, in which the wedding of Vladimir and Konchakóvna was celebrated after a second, successful campaign. It was a transparent derivation from the last scene of Glinka's *Ruslan i Lyudmila,* the opera on which *Prince Igor* was modeled in countless ways, great and small. Except for the final chorus, which would have incorporated the last few lines of the *Lay* (including the famous concluding Amen), the epilogue had no precedent in Russian literature or history, yet it epitomized the scenario's ideology: while in captivity Igor would not assent to a marriage that would make his son a Polovtsian, even postponing his escape to prevent it; and yet he rejoices at home in the same marriage when it "annexes" the Khan's daughter as a Russian and a Christian.

Thus *Prince Igor,* which chiefly differs from the more innocently "magical" *Ruslan* precisely by virtue of its aggressive nationalism, finally made overt the pervasive subtext to nineteenth-century Russian essays in orientalism: the racially justified endorsement of Russia's militaristic expansion to the east. "We go with trust in God for our faith, our Russia, our people," the operatic Igor anachronistically proclaims, very much in the spirit of Tsar Alexander II. In fact, Borodin's exquisite "musical picture" *V sredney Azii* (*In the Steppes of Central Asia*), was explicitly composed—along with Modest Musorgsky's orchestral march "The Taking of Kars" and Pyotr Chaikovsky's lost "The Montenegrins Receiving the News of Russia's Declaration of War on Turkey"—to glorify Alexander's expansionist policy. It was intended as an accompaniment to one of a series of *tableaux vivants* planned in celebration of the tsar's silver jubilee in 1880.

These, then, are some of the points I might adduce were I interested in "unmasking" *Prince Igor,* or in making Stasov and Borodin out as a pair of feckless "Orientalists." But that would be a bore, and so I will not mention them. Yet (to drop the Ciceronian mask and don another), just as the prosecutor knows that the jury cannot really disregard the inadmissible evidence just because the judge had so instructed them, I do intend these "unmentioned" points to equip us with a context and a subtext. If one is going to talk about Oriental style as a sign, one must specify its referents.

Foundation thus laid, I shall try from here on to let the music speak for itself by way of examples chosen and arranged so as to let a certain semiotic point emerge. Again, I have scamped the inventory and the taxonomy. Some kinds of musical Orientalism passed the Russians by. There is no Russian equivalent to Félicien David's Symphonic Ode, *Le désert* (about which, see Ralph Locke's essay in this volume), famed for its transcription of the muezzin's call to prayer; Islam as such seems to have left the Russians cold. There are many kinds of specifically Russian musical Orientalism that I will not mention either. Some, like biblical Orientalism, while very prominent and telling, are not particularly relevant to *Prince Igor.* Others, like the representation of Oriental military hordes, or of barbarian magnanimity, are very pertinent indeed. But instead of covering the whole field with a thin film, I prefer to concentrate on one aspect and get somewhat beneath the surface.

As already suggested, Russian Orientalism can be divided into periods roughly corresponding to the phases of Russian imperial expansion. The heyday of Russian romanticism, as every lover of Pushkin and Lermontov knows, coincided with the Caucasian campaigns. One of the best-loved souvenirs of that period (at least by musicians) was an untitled lyric by Pushkin dating from 1828:

Ne poy, krasavitsa, pri mne
Tï pesen Gruzii pechal'noy:
Napominayut mne onye
Druguyu zhizn' i bereg dal'nïy.

Uvï! napominayut mne
Tvoyi zhestokiye napevï
I step', i noch'—i pri lunye
Chertï dalyokoy, bednoy devï.

Ya prizrak mïlïy, rokovoy,
Tebya uvidev, zabïvayu;
No tï poyosh;—i predo mnoy
Yevo ya vnov' voobrazhayu.

[First stanza repeated.]

[Sing not in my presence, O beauty,
thy songs of sad Georgia;
they remind me
of another life, a distant shore.

Alas! they remind me,
thy cruel melodies,
of steppes, of night—and 'neath the moon
the features of a poor far-off maid.

This lovely, fateful vision
I can forget on seeing thee;
but you sing—and before me
I envision it anew.]

Between 1829 (the year of the poem's publication) and 1909, at least twenty-six settings of it were published by Russian composers (and a couple of non-

Russians, too, such as Pauline Viardot, who set it as a concert vehicle for her Russian tours).[4] We shall consider three, beginning with the one by Mikhail Glinka, the patriarch himself, which he published in 1831 at the age of twenty-seven, five years before his first opera, *A Life for the Tsar,* was performed and he became a "Nationalist." Subtitled "Georgian Song," it incorporates the first two stanzas of the poem (the opening is given in example 7.1).

Ex. 7.1. Mikhail Glinka, *Ne poy, krasavitsa,* opening.

According to the composer's memoirs, the melody of this song, which he learned from the poet and playwright Alexander Griboyedov, was an authentic Georgian tune, the very one to which Pushkin reputedly composed the poem.[5] From the music alone there is no way of guessing that. Nothing about the song sounds the least bit exotic. The diatonic melody seems perfectly ordinary to Western ears, Glinka's harmonization humdrum, the prosody straightforward. Already we have a warning that musical Orientalism is a matter not of authenticity but of conventions—conventions that had not yet been established by 1831.

Now, compare Mily Balakirev's setting, published under the actual title "Georgian Song" a generation later in 1865 (see example 7.2). It has Eastern export written all over it. The melody is full of close little ornaments and melismas with telltale augmented seconds (even though the singer—that is, the speaker of the lines—is not supposed to be an Oriental), and the beautiful woman has evidently brought her band with her. It is easy to find authentic recorded prototypes for this setting, much as we can imagine Balakirev, who spent a good deal of time in the Caucasus, encountering them *in situ.* Folkways FE 4535 (*Folk Music of the USSR,* compiled by Henry Cowell) has two conveniently consecutive cuts, the first of which exemplifies the melodic style, the second the oriental orchestra with its characteristic drum pattern.[6]

Ex. 7.2. Mily Balakirev, *Ne poy, krasavitsa,* opening.

The interesting thing is that these "prototypes" are Armenian, with strong Turkish and Persian influences, not Georgian. Georgian folk music does not sound anything like them, or like Balakirev's "Georgian Song," and obviously Balakirev knew that perfectly well. But he wanted us to get the point, and that meant sacrificing verisimilitude to "artistic truth," what the Russians call *khu-*

Ex. 7.3a. Sergei Rachmaninoff, *Ne poy, krasavitsa,* op. 4, no. 4, opening.

dózhestvennaya pravda. The critic Hermann Laroche, pondering the matter of what I have called biblical Orientalism, put it this way: "In what does [Alexander] Serov's masterly characterization of the extinct Assyrians [in his opera *Judith*] consist, or [Anton] Rubinstein's of the ancient Semites [in his "sacred opera" *The Tower of Babel*]? Obviously in one thing only: the composers have successfully reproduced *our* subjective idea of the Assyrians and the Sem-

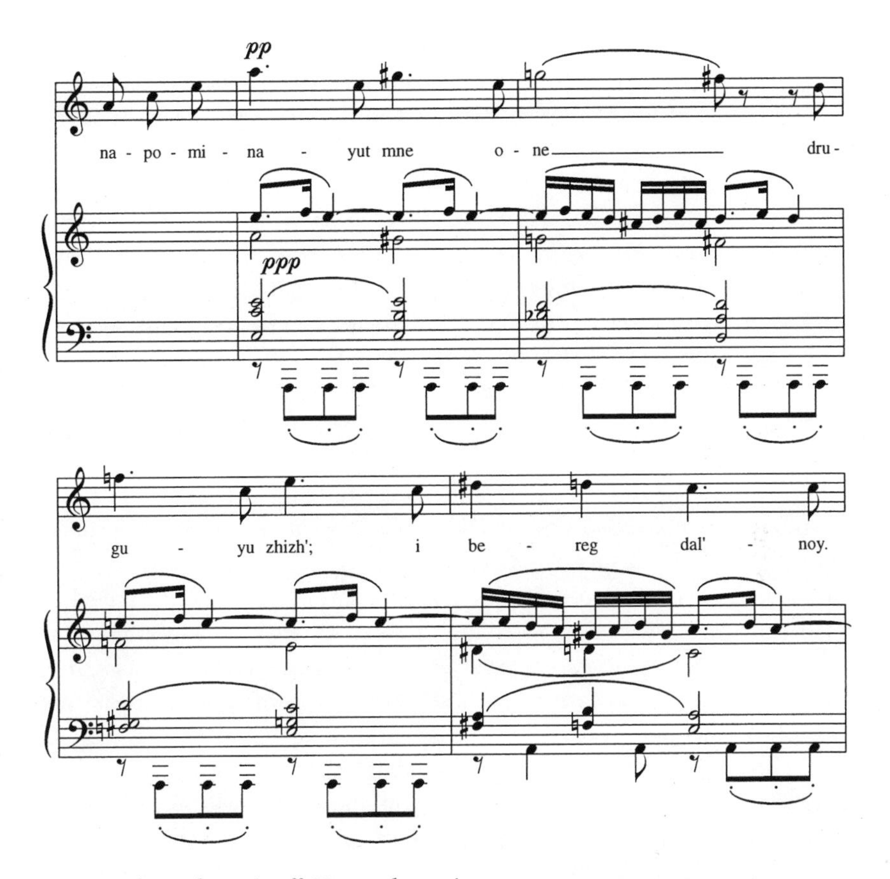

Ex. 7.3b. Rachmaninoff, *Ne poy, krasavitsa,* op. 4, no. 4, mm. 39–42.

ites"—as Balakirev reproduced his contemporaries' idea of the contemporary Orient, indeed as Romantic composers, increasingly a rare breed in Russia, usually did.[7] So far we have had an example that was authentic but not exotic, and one that was exotic but not authentic. It is the latter that we take for verisimilar, hence "truly" Oriental. But Balakirev's setting has little going for it except its seeming verisimilitude, an infusion of stereotyped local color that connotes little and does nothing to redeem what might seem a negligent reading of the poem.[8] If that seems an injustice, compare a third setting of Pushkin's poem, the most famous one, written by Sergei Rachmaninoff another generation later, in 1892 (the same year as the Prelude in C-sharp Minor), when the composer, a prodigy of nineteen, had just been hatched from the Moscow Conservatory (see example 7.3).

Rachmaninoff's setting is far less verisimilar than Balakirev's, and makes no pretense at authenticity. Yet, with hardly an augmented second, it speaks the sign language of Russian Orientalism in a highly developed form, adding a great deal to our experience of the poem. We can trace that language back to Glinka (though not to his "Georgian Song"), passing optionally through Balakirev, but necessarily through Borodin and *Prince Igor,* which was first performed only two years before Rachmaninoff composed his song. The young composer was evidently emulating the opera, although the opera was not the source of the tradition in which he was participating. Rachmaninoff was also probably responding to Balakirev's setting, to judge from the way the voice, on its first entrance, dramatically interrupts the melody with a recitative, interpreting the first line of the poem, with its request not to sing, as an actual command to leave off singing.

His setting also has conspicuous melismas: not little decorative authentic-sounding ones like Balakirev's, which sound strange in the mouth of the poet-speaker, but great sweeping ones that have a motivic consistency deriving from the opening neighbor-note. The neighbor-note motif is usually sounded in pairs or in threes, with ties that connect resolution tones to the next preparation tone. The result is a syncopated undulation that is sounded in conjunction with two other distinctive musical gestures to complete a characteristic semiotic cluster: a drone (or drum) bass such as even Glinka had suggested, and—most important of all—a chromatic accompanying line that in this case steadily descends along with the sequences of undulating melismas.

To anyone privy to the tradition on which it depends, the song's opening ritornello quite specifically conjures up the beautiful Oriental maiden the song is about—not the one singing, but the one remembered. The ritornello also tells us that she was the poet-singer's erotic partner, for the cluster of signs (undulating melisma, chromatic accompanying line, drone) evokes not just the East but the seductive East that emasculates, enslaves, renders passive. In a word, it signifies the promise or the experience of *nega,* a prime attribute of the Orient as imagined by Russians. The word, originally spelled with a *yat* (a vowel confiscated by the Bolsheviks after the revolution) and drawled voluptuously by those who know that fact, is usually translated as "sweet bliss," but it really connotes gratified desire, a tender lassitude (or "mollitude," to rely once more on Nabokov's vocabulary).[9] In opera and song, *nega* often simply denotes S-E-X *à la russe,* desired or achieved.

The syncopated undulation itself is iconically erotic, evoking languid limbs, writhing torsos, arching necks. The drum bass and the melismas are an echo of the stereotyped musical idiom Balakirev had primitively evoked, *nega*'s necessary ticket of admission (for Russian necks do not arch and writhe). It is the descending chromatic line—neither iconically nor stylistically verisimilar, but a badge worn by exotic sexpots all over Europe (cf. a certain Habanera)—that completes the picture of the seductive East. The climax of the song—undeniably a climax despite the soft dynamic—occurs at the setting of the last two lines, when the chromatic line is suddenly transferred from the middle of the texture to the voice part, at the top (shown in example 7.3b). It is by no means a unique or original touch; in fact it is rather typical. Indeed, everything about Rachmaninoff's setting is both typical and extreme. No masterpiece of the genre, it lays on the *nega* with a trowel, what with the threefold sequential repetition of the undulating melisma, and particularly with a chromatic line that descends through almost an entire chromatic scale. When it comes to suggesting *nega,* less can definitely be more.

Having arrived at Rachmaninoff's locus classicus by way of antecedent settings of Pushkin's Georgian song, let us turn around a press back again in time to discover the origins of the particular Orientalist trope it embodies. Borodin has been already named as immediate predecessor. Before getting to *Prince Igor,* it will be useful to have a look at a little-known spinoff from the opera, a posthumously published song entitled "Arabian Melody" ("Arabskaya melodiya"), composed in 1881 at the request of the contralto Darya Leonova. It is a harmonization of a "khasid" (*qasida*), a North African improvisatory vocal solo to the text of a classical Arabic poem, which the composer found in a book his librarian friend Stasov procured for him, Alexandre Christianowitsch's *Esquisse historique de la musique arabe aux temps anciens* (Cologne, 1863). In the source the melody is labeled "Insiraf Ghrib," meaning a fast section from a *qasida* performed in the evening. Notwithstanding, Borodin's setting is a slow one, marked *andante amoroso* (alternating, it is true, with piano ritornelli marked *allegro passionato*). The text, about the lover's sweet death in love, is Borodin's paraphrase of Christianowitsch's French translation of the Arabic original. Translated into suitably archaic Italian, it could pass for a madrigal text. The melody is another Oriental tune, like that of Glinka's "Georgian Song," that happens to coincide with a normal Western diatonic mode, and so does not immediately give away its origin to the Western ear. What marks Borodin's song as "Oriental" is the snaking chromatic accompanying line, so obviously related to the one in Rachmaninoff's "Georgian Song." While the song is often performed by male singers (notably Boris Christoff in a well-known recording), it is important to keep in mind that it was written for a contralto; the voice range, too, was a marker, as we shall see. Borodin would never have composed such a song for a bass (see example 7.4).

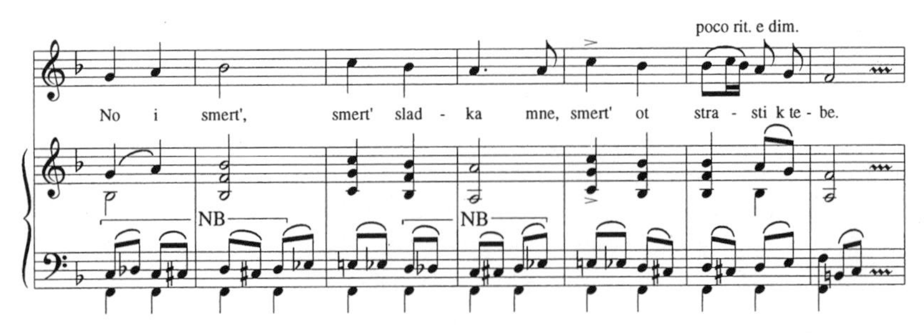

Ex. 7.4. Alexander Borodin, "Arabskaya melodiya," second strophe.

Where Rachmaninoff's chromatic line made a straightforward descent, Borodin's is serpentine, adding a new dimension of erotic undulation. The point at which the change of direction takes place is significant. The line descends to the fifth degree, then passes chromatically up to the sixth, then down again through the same interpolated half step, joined now by a middle voice that proceeds to repeat the same double pass twice, not counting a couple of extra undulations between the fifth degree and its chromatic upper neighbor. When the climax is reached ("But even death is sweet to me, the death born of passion for thee"), the rhythm of the undulation is excited into diminution, and begins to spread out to neighboring scale degrees, ontogeny thus foreshadowing phylogeny, as we know from Rachmaninoff.

The reversible chromatic pass between the fifth and sixth degrees is in fact the essential *nega* undulation, as a little snatch from the Chorus of Polovetsian Maidens at the beginning of *Prince Igor*'s second act will prove (see example 7.5). Brief as it is, this little passage summarizes with great economy everything we have learned thus far: the text is about creature comfort and gratified desire (in this case the image of nocturnal dew following a sultry day is acting as *nega* surrogate); the sopranos contribute the melodic undulation, here a sort of pedal; the altos contribute the harmonic undulation, from the fifth degree to the sixth and back through a chromatic passing tone each way; and the orchestral bass instruments supply the drum/drone. Even the ritornello at the end is a marker, for it is played on the English horn. We will encounter that timbre again.

Ex. 7.5. Borodin, *Prince Igor,* no. 7, 10 mm. before rehearsal no. 2.

Now we are equipped to get the full message from the most famous music in all of *Prince Igor* (see example 7.6). The famous Polovetsian Dance displays the whole cluster—melodic undulations tied over the beat, a chromatic pass between degrees 6 and 5, pedal drum/drone, English horn timbre—just as they are displayed in the "Oriental" theme that confronts a Russian one directly in the "musical picture" *In Central Asia.* The theme makes its first appearance, predictably enough, as a long English horn solo. Illustrated here is the final statement, in which the chromatic inner voice grows to encompass a whole scale, as in Rachmaninoff's modeling of it, and is climactically repeated in an outer voice, in this case the bass (see example 7.7). It was a telling touch—and, again, a typical one—to extend the length of each phrase to five bars through one extra languorous undulation ("please, just once more . . ."). What it tells us is why those hedonistic Central Asians were simply no match for the purposefully advancing Russians.

Ex. 7.6. Borodin, *Prince Igor,* no. 17, 4 mm. after rehearsal no. 2 (orchestra only).

What I have been calling the "markers" have long been recognized as essential features of Borodin's personal style (compare Ravel's *A la manière de Borodine* for piano [1913], where they all pass in review). They did achieve what we might call maximum strength in Borodin—who, by the way, though the illegitimate son of a Georgian nobleman, was born in Saint Petersburg and never visited the Orient—but they were none of them his invention. Compare the beginning of the Maidens' Dance from Act 2 of Anton Rubinstein's *The Demon,* composed in 1871 after Mikhail Lermontov's famous romantic poem set in Georgia (see example 7.8). It, too, could be titled "A la manière de Borodine." Or conversely, Ravel's piano piece could have been entitled "A la manière de Rubinstein."

Ex. 7.7. Borodin, *In Central Asia,* mm. 175–90.

Ex. 7.8. Anton Rubinstein, *The Demon,* Act 2, Maiden's Dance.

But both would have been misnomers; the origin of the style, as of so much in Russian music, lay in Glinka—in particular, in the third act of *Ruslan i Lyudmila,* the opera Glinka based on the mock epic Pushkin had written between 1817 and 1820, during the first flush of Russian Orientalism. The setting of Glinka's third act is the magical garden of the sorceress Naína, who keeps a chorus of sirens handy to enchant errant heroes. It goes without saying that these seductresses sing Oriental tunes of promiscuous origin. Their first is called the Persian Chorus, and it set the tone for all the exercises in *nega* evocation that we have been examining (see example 7.9). Here is the fount and origin, the passage that established the voluptuous undulation and the chromatic pass as emblems to be displayed by Oriental singing or dancing girls in future operas and songs. Glinka claimed the melody was truly a Persian one that he heard sung by a Persian-born secretary of the Saint Petersburg Ministry of Foreign Affairs. The claim must be true, because Glinka was not the only one who used the tune; it also figures in the middle section of Johann Strauss's *Persischer Marsch,* first played in Vienna's Volksgarten in December 1864 to welcome the visiting shah. To compare Strauss's boisterous march with Glinka's dreamy chorus is revealing: what made the chorus a marker of *nega* and a model for generations to come were the elements Glinka brought to it, not any "Oriental" essence. As an impassioned authority has observed, "Orientalism overrode the Orient."[10]

Ex. 7.9. Glinka, *Ruslan i Lyudmila,* no. 12, mm. 93–104 (Naína's part omitted).

Nowhere is this dictum better corroborated than in the archetypal embodiment of the Oriental luxuriance in Russian opera: Ratmir, the first of Naína's victims in the magic garden. He is an easy mark. One of three suitors in quest of the abducted Lyudmila, Ratmir is a young khan of the Khazars, a nomadic Turkic tribe famous for its eighth-century conversion to Judaism and indigenous to areas recently acquired as of 1817 by the Russian empire. Pushkin introduces him as being "full of passionate daydreams," and that is why he fails on his quest: he simply cannot keep his mind on it. The fact that he is cast as a trouser role for a contralto has been ascribed to the composer's insistence on writing a major part for Anna Vorob'yova, the singer who had made a sensation in the trouser role of Vanya the orphan boy in Glinka's first opera, *A Life for the Tsar.* But the contralto timbre also symbolized the torpid and feminized East.

Ratmir's big aria in Act 2 of *Ruslan* shows him literally torpid, wandering into Naína's garden in a state of exhaustion, complaining that the "sultry heat has replaced the shade of night," and longing for the sweet bliss of sleep. At this point he is musically characterized by a pedal bass, by the melismas he sings, and by an ornate English horn obbligato—in other words, by the trappings of local color. The melody is supposedly a Tatar (i.e., Mongol) tune Glinka had learned from the great seascape painter Ivan Aivazovsky; a near relative of it figures in David's *Le désert* (see example 7.10).

Ex. 7.10. Glinka, *Ruslan i Lyudmila,* no. 14 (cavatina), opening.

This is obviously no characterization of a hero. It is the portrait of a loser, and so will the same set of markers characterize the ill-fated Georgian prince

Sinodal thirty years later in Rubinstein's *The Demon.* Through a traditional tenor, Sinodal becomes an honorary contralto, emasculated by his Ratmirish melismas and the pedal bass. Note, too, the extraordinary economy of the English horn obbligato, which dooms the singer as lover even before he opens his mouth (see example 7.11). When the bass moves, it does so to reestablish the tonic through the chromatic pass we have learned by now to associate with *nega.* This, too, is something Sinodal shares with Ratmir—though not in the example we have so far examined.

Ex. 7.11. Rubinstein, *The Demon,* Act 1, scene 3, Sinodal's arioso.

For all his impotence Ratmir is a noble character, and to Glinka that meant that Ratmir's big musical number had to get the full cantabile-cabaletta treatment. We have seen the opening of the cantabile; in the cabaletta, Ratmir has one of those "passionate daydreams" of his, mopishly recalling his harem. It has raised many eyebrows, this cabaletta, for it is cast as no Oriental dance, but in what Glinka frankly marks "Tempo di valse." David Brown, Glinka's most recent biographer, wrings his hands over the "stylistic non-sequitur" here, by which "the languishing oriental, approaching the height of passion, is converted into a waltzing westerner." "Glinka," he concludes, "betrayed Ratmir badly in *Ruslan and Lyudmila,*" and this proves that he was "simply unable to express real physical passion in music."[11]

Is "real physical passion" what Ratmir is all about? Of course not. Ratmir is an avatar of *nega,* the passive, feminine embodiment or enjoyment of "*molles délices,*" as Nabokov has it.[12] Let us recall what constitutes *nega* in music at a minimum: tied or syncopated melodic undulations, and the reversible chromatic pass between fifth and sixth degrees of the scale. Now, look at the offending waltz, in which the text, not by Pushkin but by a poetaster named Valerian Shirkov, makes a rare, explicit reference to *nega.* Leaving that term untranslated so that it may incorporate all of its associations, the words are these: "A wondrous dream of quickening love rouses the fire in my blood; tears scald my eyes, my lips burn with *nega.*" And now the cabaletta (example 7.12).

Ex. 7.12. Glinka, *Ruslan i Lyudmila,* No. 14 (cabaletta).

The voice part is nothing but syncopated neighbors and appoggiaturas that could easily be extended into Rachmaninoff's quintessential Oriental melisma, and the English horn does nothing but signal the chromatic pass, immediately reversed in the bass so that it becomes a harmonic undulation—a veritable mug. Far from playing the character false, the waltz is another locus classicus of Oriental languor seen through European (or perhaps Eurasian) eyes. Again, Orientalism overrides the Orient. Putting the two halves of Ratmir's aria together, we have a complete catalogue of the devices that would be mined by Russian composers bent on depicting that languor all the way to Rachmaninoff and beyond.

Now, the climax. Ratmir never achieves it; it had to wait until *Prince Igor,* in which the ultimate Ratmir surrogate finally made his/her appearance. Konchakóvna is unique in the annals of opera: an ingénue role played by the throatiest contralto imaginable. Ratmir's voice range, as we see, has by now become an indispensable signifier. In the Act 2 love duet with Vladimir, Igor's son (the ostensible heroic tenor), her voice coils all around and beneath his to startling effect. The falconet is indeed "entoiled by means of a fair maiden"—and emasculated. Nor has there ever been such an emphasis on raised fifths, flattened sixths, and chromatic passes in general. Rather than compile a tedious list, and because it is impossible to present the entire score here, let us just note a few salient points.

In the introduction to the duet, which is cast over the harmony of the dominant ninth, Konchakóvna's part obsessively applies the flattened sixth to the fifth while Vladimir, having gone through a variety of other passes, finally takes up hers at the closing fermata. As the duet proper begins, she turns around and, ascending this time, makes another pass at him, from raised fifth to sixth, while he yelps in response, his repliques narrowed down to the sign of chromatic passing in its minimal, most concentrated form—four separate two-note chromatic descents—what we might call the very morpheme of *nega.* The orchestral bass meanwhile gives out one of those complete chromatic descents that signal *nega* at full sensual strength. Again she entoils him, and he replicates her pass; they reach their first climax on a question ("Will you/I soon call me/you your/my wife?"), supported in the orchestra by a prolonged harmony rooted on the flat sixth, which finally makes affirmative—indeed, climactic—progress through the dominant to the tonic. The change from question to affirmative reply itself takes the form, for Vladimir, of a chromatic inflection (an earlier sustained high A-flat now trumped by a sustained high A-natural). While they hold their final notes the orchestra harps repeatedly on the hypnotic undulation of fifth degree and flattened sixth. Vladimir is now thoroughly lost: Ratmirized, his manhood *nega*ted, rendered impotent with respect to his (and his father's) mission, he must be left behind. No less than Ratmir, he has been the victim of a sinister Oriental charm.

While something that could certainly be indulged for its own sake as soft-core pornography, the Orientalist trope associated with *nega*—a flexible amalgam of ethnic verisimilitude, sensual iconicity, characteristic vocal or instrumental timbres, and Glinkaesque harmony—nevertheless functioned within the Victorian conventions of its time. In most of the examples discussed (and in any number of others) *nega*, associated with the Orient, is held up as a degenerate counterpart to more manly virtues associated with Russians. It marked the Other—marked it, in fact, for justified conquest.

It is moreover ironic that, owing in large part to Stasov's influential privileging of "the Oriental element" in modern Russian music, the perceived absence of that Other-signifying factor in a composer's work could result in his being regarded as somehow less Russian (ergo, less valuable) than a Musorgsky or a Rimsky-Korsakov or a Glinka. I refer, of course, to Chaikovsky, the one major Russian composer of the period so far unmentioned, whose only overtly Orientalizing numbers consist of two late and relatively insignificant items: the Arabian Dance in *The Nutcracker,* and the Moorish physician Ibn-Hakia's aria in the one-act opera *Iolanta,* which shared a double bill with *The Nutcracker* on their joint premiere during the last year of the composer's life (18/30 December 1892). And yet Chaikovsky made obvious and telling, if unadvertised, use of the Orientalist trope quite early in his career, in the love themes from *Romeo and Juliet* (1869; revised 1870, 1880), composed just as the composer was getting over his infatuation with the soprano Desirée Artôt, the one woman known to have aroused his sexual interest. (She had disappointed him by marrying the Spanish baritone Mariano Padilla y Ramos.)

The frank sensual iconicity of this music is often remarked upon. Usually it is the throbbing, panting horn counterpoint that is so recognized, but the themes themselves evoke *nega* just as surely by means of the familiar chromatic pass between fifth and sixth scale degrees. Moreover, the first love theme (the one generally associated with Romeo) features, on its first appearance, the equally familiar English horn timbre (see example 7.13). Juliet responds to Romeo's advance by mirroring his descending chromatic pass with an ascending one that is then maintained as an oscillation (osculation?), while Romeo's ecstatic reentry is prepared by reversing the pass and linking up with the striking augmented-sixth progression that had launched Chaikovsky's "balcony scene" to begin with (see example 7.14). At the climax, delayed until the recapitulation, Chaikovsky enhances carnality by adding one more chromatic pass at the very zenith of intensity to introduce the last full statement from which the love music will then gradually subside (see example 7.15). Russian music would not get steamier than this until Scriabin discovered *Tristan,* a good three decades later.

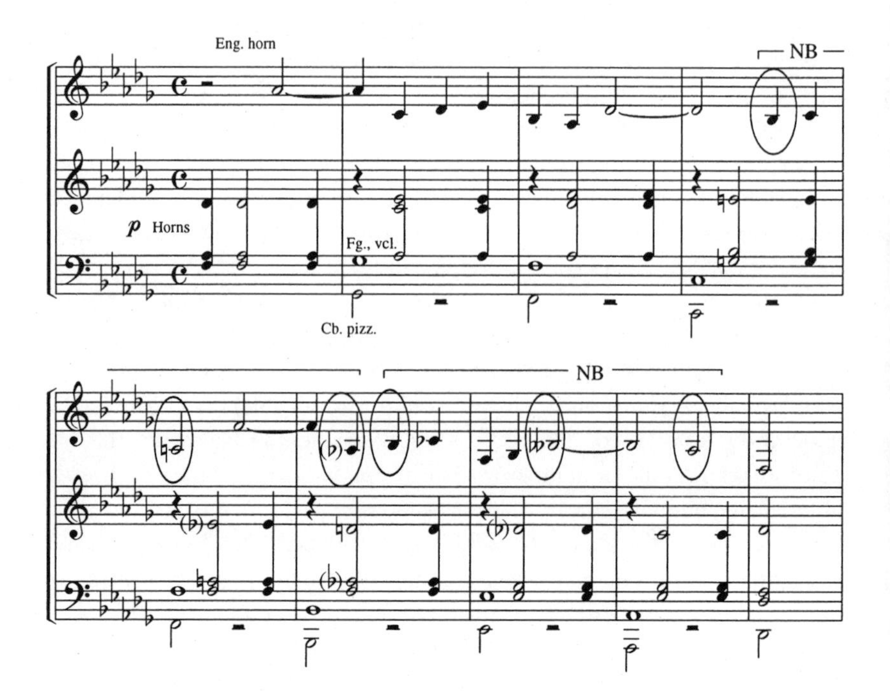

Ex. 7.13. Pyotr Il'yich Chaikovsky, *Romeo and Juliet* (1869 version), mm. 156–64.

A contemporary who recognized both the Eastern *topos* and its erotic subtext was Balakirev, a connoisseur nonpareil of musical Orientalism and the inspirer and dedicatee of Chaikovsky's "Overture-fantasia." In a marvelously cruel letter to Chaikovsky of 1–13 December 1869, he reacted to the four main themes of the work, which Chaikovsky had sent him for inspection while composition was still in progress. Here is what he had to say about the big love theme:

> . . . simply enchanting. I often play it and have a great wish to kiss you for it. It has everything, *nega,* and love's sweetness, and all the rest. . . . it appears to me that you are lying all naked in the bath and that Artôt-Padilla herself is rubbing your tummy with hot scented suds. I have just one thing to say against this theme: there is little in it of inner spiritual love, only the physical, passionate torment (colored just a wee bit Italian). Really now, Romeo and Juliet are not Persian lovers, but European. . . . I'll try to clarify by example. I'll cite the first theme that comes to mind in which, in my opinion, love is expressed more inwardly: the second, A-flat major, theme in Schumann's overture *The Bride of Messina.*[13]

Ex. 7.14. Chaikovsky, *Romeo and Juliet* (1869 version), mm. 164–76.

Indeed, Schumann's long wet noodle of a love theme, which reaches no climax, does seem as if by design to moderate the orientalism of Chaikovsky's, diluting the chromatic passes and replacing the lascivious English horn with a chaste clarinet.

Balakirev's letter confirms the surmise that Chaikovsky used the Orientalist trope metonymically, to conjure up not the East as such, but rather its exotic sex appeal. The little tease about Artôt is provocative indeed, precisely because it is so plausible. If, as Balakirev seems to suggest, Chaikovsky had cast himself as Romeo to Artôt's Juliet, then the theme becomes a self-portrait. And if so,

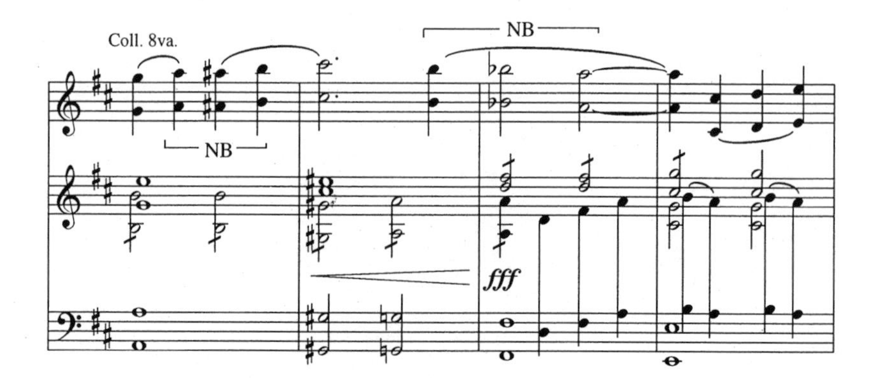

Ex. 7.15. Chaikovsky, *Romeo and Juliet* (1869 version), mm. 366–69.

then it is another instance where, in a manner oddly peculiar to the Russian Orientalist strain, the eastward gaze is simultaneously a look in the mirror.

The further irony is the relationship between the original "imperial" opposition of exotic Oriental versus Russian conquistador and what, viewed from further west, was an exotic, Orientalized Russia. Some sense of this skew can be gained from a list of the Russian compositions through which Sergey Diaghilev and his ballet company conquered Paris in their first two *saisons russes* (1909–10). Besides the Polovetsian Act from *Prince Igor,* they included the "Apparition of Cleopatra" from Rimsky-Korsakov's opera-ballet *Mlada;* the Dances of the Persian Slave Girls from Musorgsky's opera *Khovanshchina* (presented, like the *Mlada* music, in an omnium gatherum choreographed by Mikhail Fokine under the title "Cléopâtre"); the Arabian Dance from *Ruslan i Lyudmila,* presented as part of another Fokine *salade russe* entitled "Le festin"; Rimsky-Korsakov's *Sheherazade,* choreographed by Fokine to a murder-in-the-harem scenario by Alexander Benois; and Stravinsky's *Firebird,* the first original ballet Diaghilev ever commissioned. Clearly, *nega* was having a field day in Paris, and Stravinsky's first ballet was created in part to supply a new infusion of semi-Asiatic exotica-cum-erotica, the sex lure that underpinned Diaghilev's incredible success.

Of course, *nega* had a meaning for the French vastly different from what it meant to the Russians. For the French it meant Russia, for to them Russia itself was East and Other. The heavy emphasis on Oriental luxus in his early repertory was something Diaghilev had calculated coldly, one could even say cynically. It accounts for the disproportionate popularity of Russian musical Orientalia in the West to this day, and for the mistaken notion (abetted by Stasov's influential propaganda) that it was one of the main modes of Russian musical expression, if not (next to folklore-quoting) the dominant one. The ploy eventually held Diaghilev captive, preventing him from presenting to the West the musical artifacts of the European Russia with which he personally identified.

That Russia, the one with which Chaikovsky is usually identified, is still considered in the West to be less authentic than the more familiar exotic, Oriental, and phantasmagorical Russia. But Musorgsky can put matters in perspective for us. When asked by the younger composer Nikolai Kompaneysky why he never finished his opera on Flaubert's *Salammbô,* the future composer of *Khovanshchina* replied: "We had enough of the Orient in [Serov's] *Judith.* Art isn't a pastime; time is precious." [14]

"I'm an Indian Too": Creating Native American Identities in Nineteenth- and Early Twentieth-Century Music

MICHAEL V. PISANI

FEW EXAMPLES in the American musical literature better illustrate the native North American as an exotic "Other" than does Irving Berlin's "I'm an Indian Too." When Berlin wrote this song in 1946 he engaged musical idioms that for decades had been associated with the American Indian. Such contrived but potent signifiers, as we will see, were the descendants of more generic European exoticisms and were often merely adapted to suit the North American locale.

In Berlin's Broadway musical *Annie Get Your Gun,* the sharpshooter Annie Oakley eagerly longs to become an Indian, although it is quickly evident that the proud image of the Indian she portrays exists largely in the popular imagination. Annie's Indian inhabits a minor-key world and is accompanied by two ever-present musical "friends" (example 8.1a): a tom-tom imitation in open fifths in the bass, and a descending chromatic line in the middle of the harmonic texture. The opening melody suggests a five-note or pentatonic scale, but the subsequent emphasis on the lowered seventh scale degree ("A Sioux, ooh-ooh! A Sioux, ooh-ooh!") belies the true modal derivation—Aeolian or natural minor. The flute countermelody (mm. 9–11) provides a hint of true pentatonicism, a common feature in American Indian musics. The B section of the song (example 8.1b) slips easily into the relative major. But Berlin artfully colors the key of E-flat with the added sixth (C) in several ways: in the melody itself (mm. 27–28) and in the accompaniment's C-minor chords and its regular alternation of the fifth and sixth scale degrees (B♭–C) in the "tenor" voice.[1] Annie's melody begins in a pentatonic vein but then, for "I may hide away," dissolves into that most generic of early twentieth-century exoticisms, the whole-tone scale.

Ex. 8.1a. Irving Berlin, "I'm an Indian, Too," from *Annie Get Your Gun* (1946), mm. 2–13. Words and Music by Irving Berlin / © Copyright 1946 by Irving Berlin / Copyright Renewed / International Copyright Secured All Rights Reserved.

The roots of these musical "Indianisms" (which continued to serve similar semiotic ends as late as the 1950s in the film scores of Hollywood Westerns) go back at least to the eighteenth century. But it was largely in the nineteenth century, wherever cultural issues of nationalism and exoticism were played out, that music and message began to coalesce in the form of "musical portraiture." The exotic veneer of such portraiture can best be examined and explained not through traditional musicological procedures but in the context of what the Americanist Mick Gidley calls "cultural archaeology"—in other words, viewing music as cultural artifact.[2] In raising some of these issues, I realize the danger of treading upon ideologically slippery ground, given the long history of misrepresentation and misunderstanding in Indian-White relations. Yet this complex relationship as manifested in narrative poems, spoken drama, the

Ex. 8.1b. Berlin, "I'm an Indian, Too," mm. 26–34. Words and Music by Irving Berlin / © Copyright 1946 by Irving Berlin / Copyright Renewed / International Copyright Secured All Rights Reserved.

novel, and in traditionally European forms of musical expression—character pieces, cantata, opera, and so on—seems to have developed from one of deep antipathy and mistrust to one of cooperation and, in some cases, identification. The biased viewpoint of the nineteenth century's Indian wars, reinforced through popular images in dime novels and early Western films, could not easily be dispelled. The leveling of hostilities since the 1890s between nonindigenous and Native peoples was a slow and unsteady process and, while at present it remains far from complete, it has come a long way since the days when the Indian was a source of crude amusement in stage and song.

Savages, Noble or Otherwise

Between 1830 and 1850 no less than thirty-five "Indian plays" graced the American stage (many unpublished and mostly well received).[3] The popularity of

John Augustus Stone's *Metamora, or The Last of the Wampanoags* (first performed 1829) and its charismatic leading actor, Edwin Forrest, were largely responsible for initiating this wave. Stone's melodramatic play placed Metamora (Prince Philip) in the untenable position of a morally virtuous leader while at the same time providing clear evidence of his heathen nature. Such incongruities apparently went unnoticed. The historical Indian plays of the 1830s and 1840s held a certain allure for urban Americans living primarily in the Eastern regions of the continent, who were mostly too young to remember any of the incidents depicted and who probably had had little if any contact with Indians.

The Indian dramas reflected two contrasting views concerning the Indians that were prevalent in European and American literature during the first half of the nineteenth century. One of these was the Indian as "noble savage," an image popularized by Montaigne, Dryden (who coined the epithet in his long poem *The Conquest of Granada*, 1670), and Rousseau. According to the literary critic Michael Castro, the concept of the noble savage presumed that "humans in the 'natural' state . . . were basically good, and that what corrupted such goodness was the influence of civilization itself." In his original setting, "the noble savage was naturally dignified, poetic, serene, generous, essentially egalitarian, economically stable, and living in harmony with nature. In contrast, the civilized person appeared insecure, materialistic, selfish, warlike, oppressed and depressed by brutalizing class differences, and essentially out of touch with or opposed to nature."[4] American authors from Philip Freneau to Washington Irving adopted this essentially European view in their writings. Irving's grand and heroic portrayal of King Philip of Pokanoket (1814) accentuates the chief's amiable and lofty character and his proud love of natural liberty, thereby firmly placing the historical figure in the tradition of European-style philosopher-princes.

Published musical settings in the late eighteenth and early nineteenth centuries tended to sympathize with this lyrical view. The most internationally famous musical representation of the noble savage was the anonymous "Death Song of the Cherokee Indians," to words first published by Anne Hunter in 1784 (see Miriam K. Whaples's essay in this volume, especially example 1.9). Defiant in the face of torture and possible death, the Indian sings his noble song to the end, unflinching against the pain of injustice.

The rhythmic Scottish snap (or "iambs")—here on "(tor)mentors" and "threats"—was identified in the eighteenth century as a topos of folk song of the British Isles. Later, as traditions of folk song spread through publications, it became evident that this same rhythmic feature could be found in Eastern

Europe as well as in North America among indigenous peoples. This supposedly anonymous Death Song, brought to Scotland from America by "one conversant with the Indian tribes," became popular on both sides of the Atlantic and was used thereafter in eighteenth-century ballad operas and even in nineteenth-century hymn collections. The song experienced a revival in America in the 1830s following the Cherokees' removal from their home land in the southeast to Indian Territory (present-day Oklahoma). During this time, other songs about Indians—heavily influenced by the contemporary American rage for Italian *bel canto*—were also sung during family music making in the parlor.[5] The emigrant Bohemian composer Anthony Philip Heinrich lent his wild fantasy to the Cherokee and other Native American causes with large-scale piano and symphonic compositions. These stream-of-consciousness works depict the noble savage in bold but impulsive Beethovenian strokes combined with an extravagant Italianate lyricism.[6]

The Indian plays of the 1830s and 1840s, like most plays at the time, used descriptive (and very likely some original) music. Owing to the vulnerability of nineteenth-century American theater music manuscripts, however, little of the music from the decades of the Indian plays seems to have survived. Yet by the 1850s at least two Indian parodies with surviving music (or at least reconstructable musical scores) created sensations of a different sort. Travesties such as John Brougham's *Po-co-hon-tas* (1855) and Charles Walcot's *Hiawatha, or Ardent Spirits and Laughing Water* (1856), according to one theater historian, were responsible for laughing the earlier Indian dramas off the New York stage.[7] The burlesques, which contrafacted traditional opera arias and popular songs to effect their humor, reduced the Indian to a laughingstock, a subject unfit for serious drama. Several musical extravaganzas and comic operas on Indian subjects followed, though the Indians in these cases were thinly disguised white Americans who happened to be dressed as Indians, like those in the British-American ballad operas of the eighteenth century (James Hewitt's *Tammany, or The Indian Chief* and John Bray's *The Indian Princess, or La Belle Sauvage*). Edward Everett Rice's *Hiawatha* (1880) and others like it no more suggested believable Indians than Gilbert and Sullivan's roughly contemporary British types clad in kimonos suggested believable Japanese. With few exceptions, the first serious plays to challenge these Indian caricatures did not appear on an American stage until the twentieth century (contemporary with a burst of activity in Indian subjects on the opera stage).

Older than the literary view of the noble savage was the "brutish savage," an image engendered by reports from the early European explorers who encountered cannibalism and human sacrifice among the natives. As images of the noble savage tended to overpraise the virtues of all Indians in the New World, the brutish savage idea tended to vilify them unjustly. The brutish-savage stereotype that persisted throughout the eighteenth and nineteenth centuries, according to Castro, "represented a chauvinistic affirmation of the 'progress' of Western civilization—and a *moral* rejection of what was *different* in Indian cultures, i.e., Native-American attitudes toward religion, nature, sexuality, and property."[8] The preoccupation with savagery—scalp hunting, for example—which imparts the thrill of danger to novels of James Fenimore Cooper, Mark Twain, and others, played upon fears of these earlier (real or purported) practices of various Indian tribes. The war dance, often presented as the prelude to scalp hunting, is one such representation in music of the brutal inhabitants of North America.

One finds composers writing music for Indian war dances as early as the eighteenth century. In the case of Rameau, his "Les sauvages" for harpsichord resulted from attending a performance by two visiting members of the Natchez tribe to Paris in 1725.[9] In general, any American topic in opera, ballet, or other dramatic work before 1850 would result in a piece that portrayed the savages of that world. One such piece was Félicien David's highly popular ode-symphony *Christopher Columbus, or The Discovery of the New World* (Paris Conservatory, 1847).

David's quick duple dance (example 8.2a) is in a minor key and generally has strong accents on beats one and three. Few observers today would detect anything remotely American Indian about this music. But two conspicuous features attract attention: the accompanimental rhythm, quarter-eighth-eighth, and David's constant use in the melody and occasionally in a countermelody of three descending notes in quick sixteenths (the first always accented, as seen in example 8.2b).

Ex. 8.2a. Félicien David, "Danse de[s] sauvages," from *Christophe Colomb* (1847), opening.

Ex. 8.2b. David, "Danse de[s] sauvages," mm. 18–23.

An Indian war dance from about thirteen years later likewise exhibits few features identifiably North American. The savage in Hans Lumbye's "Indian War Dance" for orchestra (1860) is a heathen, pure and simple. The Danish Lumbye, known as "the Strauss of the North," wrote music for parades, dances, celebrations, and other civic events as music director for the Tivoli Gardens. The "Indian War Dance" was originally part of a ballet—*Fjernt fra Danmark* (*Far from Denmark*)—about the New World.[10] This "Polka Marsch" (example 8.3a) opens with spry, Mephistophelian octave leaps downward in the melody (often accentuated by grace notes), and later harps on "terrifying" (or at least ominous-sounding) diminished seventh chords (example 8.3b, mm. 13–14). Offbeat punctuations by the bulk of the orchestra create a heavy, "primitive" feel. Not evident in the piano score is Lumbye's liberal use of the tambourine (a typical European mid-nineteenth-century instrument to evoke the "exotic" Middle East).

One might expect that war dances composed in America (closer to the indigenous source, as it were) would exhibit less generic exoticisms. Before 1850, however, this was rarely the case. A typical "Indian March" (example 8.4) such as that from Alexander Reinagle's *Columbus* (1797) reflects a standard patriotic style (with "Turkishisms") typical of the British-American theater music of the era. About 1850, however, music making in America underwent profound

Ex. 8.3a. Hans Christian Lumbye, "Indiansk Krigsdands" ("Indian War Dance"), *Folkeudgave af H. C. Lumbye's Kompositioner II,* opening.

Ex. 8.3b. Lumbye, "Indiansk Krigsdands," mm. 8–16.

changes. The European revolutions of 1848 resulted in massive immigration from many European countries, and the influx of musicians to the United States led to a dramatic rise in the amount of musical creativity. With them, Europeans brought musical tastes that embodied more complex notions of nationalism and exoticism, ideas that had shaped European art and culture since the eighteenth-century revolutions and that would now begin to take root in America. Before these notions, American descriptive music remained provincial and modest in conceptual grasp and technical resources; it would have been virtually impossible to consider music as a discourse through which one culture could attempt to define the culture of another.

Ex. 8.4. Alexander Reinagle, "Indian March," from the play *Columbus* (1797).

Two highly individual war dances stand out in post-1848 American music history. The first of these is embedded in Robert Stoepel's *Hiawatha* (1859, with text based on Longfellow's 1855 epic poem *The Song of Hiawatha*). This dramatic symphony (along the lines of those of Berlioz and David) premiered in Boston, a Longfellow stronghold. Longfellow himself took an interest in the symphony and attended rehearsals.[11] In excerpts from Longfellow's journal selected and published by his brother, the author noted that "the music is beautiful and striking; particularly the wilder parts,—the War Song and the Dance of Pau-puk-keewis."[12] In addition, a few surviving letters confirm an ongoing intimacy between the two men that resulted from Stoepel's project.

The two movements that Longfellow identified—and that also captured the attention of John Sullivan Dwight and other major critics—exhibit Stoepel's most imaginative writing. They border on an exoticism that, with the exception of that seen in Louis Moreau Gottschalk's works, was rare in American music at the time. Though we do not have any surviving evidence of music for the 1830s and 1840s Indian dramas, Stoepel's music for Indians no doubt reflects his experience of composing melodramas for some of the best theaters in England and America.[13]

"Pau-Puk-Keewis's Beggar Dance" is the earliest known example to capture the mood, spirit, and musical contour that would, nearly half a century later, become permanently associated with the Indian in the Western mind. Besides the relentless four-beat drum imitation in the bass and the minor-mode harmonic accompaniment, the opening of this passage—which one reviewer called "more Scotch than Indian"[14]—includes several distinguishing features: (1) the "snapping" iambic rhythm (here strongly emphasized with a thirty-second note); (2) the defining melodic parameter of one full octave, which, after two or three phrases, ascends to a third (and sometimes a fifth) above the uppermost parameter; (3) the tendency of the melodic shape to cascade downward; and (4) several repetitions of the final or "tail," often embellished by a few descending emphatic inflections. The music appears to be following the poem's imagery (example 8.5):

First he danced a solemn measure,
Very slow in step and gesture . . .
Treading softly like a panther.

Ex. 8.5. Robert Stoepel, "Pau-Puk-Keewis's Beggar Dance," from *Hiawatha: Indian Symphony* (1859), mm. 3–10.

With the snapping rhythm, Stoepel alludes to a folk-song idiom (impossible, of course, to pinpoint out of context as definitively "Indian," Scottish, or any other culture). Stoepel's use of the reiterating pedal point on open fifths reminds one of other Europeans who used the same device for rustic types; Mendelssohn in his overture to *A Midsummer Night's Dream* is perhaps the most vivid example. Two remarkable melodic features of this passage are the pentatonicism implied in the phrase (A–D′–A–G–F–E–[F]–D) and the falling third (F–D) at the cadences. Stoepel even suggests something of the social nature of Indian music in the ensuing pattern: two bars of solo melody and drumbeat accompaniment, two bars of a communally harmonized response. Nowhere in the entire cultivated musical literature of the early and mid-nineteenth century does there exist such a clear borrowed example of what the ethnomusicologist Robert Stevenson might call "unalloyed aboriginal song."[15] It is impossible, however, to know whether Stoepel had been able to witness any of the traveling Indian troupes. (Native Americans did perform throughout the East. Longfellow wrote in 1837, for example, of observing Black Hawk's powwow on the Boston Common.)[16] Stoepel may, while traveling from his conducting engagements in New Orleans (1856), have joined his actress wife in Saint Louis before returning to New York, and could potentially have had occasion along this route to hear Native Americans sing. Unlike other Indian music written by Europeans and Eastern Americans in the mid-nineteenth century, Stoepel's music suggests a firsthand acquaintance with American Indian rituals. It also grants us a refreshingly innocent view of the depiction of Indian life through musical gestures before such gestures became stereotypical in the later nineteenth century.

Another American war dance can be found in *The Arcadian* by George Frederick Bristow (1825–98), an American composer, organist, pianist, violinist, and one of the first concertmasters of the New York Philharmonic. Like Berlioz in his *Episodes in the Life of an Artist,* Bristow originally intended the *Arcadian* as a "Grand Cantata" for vocal solos, chorus, and orchestra to follow *The Pioneer: Symphonie for Grand Orchestra* (1872). Although the cantata is not known to have been performed, Bristow led the orchestral portion in 1873 under the title *The Arcadian Symphony* (and this is the version still available today). The symphonic portion consists of two parts, each with two movements: 1.a. Allegro appassionato, b. Adagio; and 2.a. Indian War Dance, b. Allegro con spirito.[17]

Consistent with others who had written Indian war dances, Bristow (example 8.6) chose a minor key. Right from the start, he emphasized the descending melodic 3–2–1 (the same figure in David and in the "tail" of Stoepel's melody). The distinctive clarinet tremolo in measure 2 was possibly intended to suggest tongue-wagging or "whooping" sounds, and the piccolo grace notes to the top E creates an effect of a shriek. Bristow relies on the chromatic ♯4–5–♭6–5 in the bass to create a generic exotic atmosphere (mm. 5–6, 8–9, etc.). From measure 13, Bristow invokes the image of warriors dancing around a tom-tom with the heavy ponderous rhythm—four equal eighths in the strings, reinforced by the timpani. (In the climactic statement of this theme, Bristow scores two timpani in fifths and adds the triangle, the latter associated with Turkish music and not at all North American.) The descending octaves with grace notes in the melody, like those in Lumbye, evoke wild leaping in the dancing.

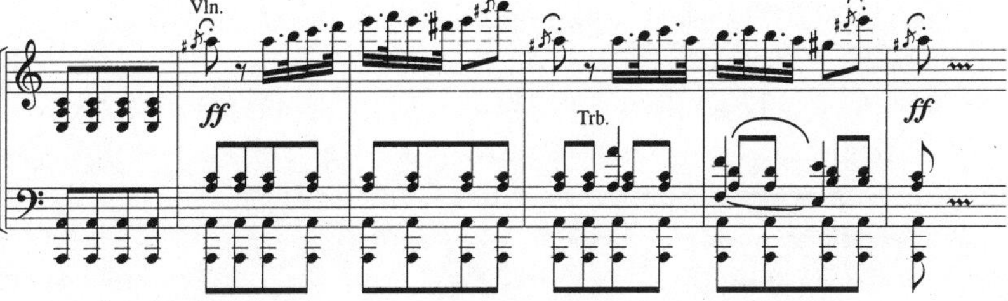

Ex. 8.6. George Frederick Bristow, *The Arcadian Symphony,* fourth movement, "Indian War Dance" (1872), opening.

It might be helpful, having examined a few nineteenth-century war dances, to categorize some of their most distinctively "exotic" style characteristics and to note their use (and possible origin) in other, non-"Indian," pieces or repertoires.[18]

1. "Rural" or "elemental" sustained fifths affecting a bagpipelike drone or resonance in nature: used, for example, by Beethoven in the opening of the Sixth and the Ninth Symphonies and by Wagner in *The Flying Dutchman*
2. "Pastoral" or "rude peasant" rhythm (long-short-short): this may originally be related to the dance forms of the sixteenth-century *canzona* and the seventeenth-century "Canarie";[19] in the late nineteenth century it is commonly found as an accompaniment to the English morris dance, a spring ritual

3. "Gypsy-Turkish" devices (labels from Jonathan Bellman's "lexicon"):[20] a "thumping 2/4," "harmonic stasis," "ornaments and exaggerated dynamics effects to imitate percussion," repeating fourths and drone fifths as harmony, melodic figures such as 1–♯4–5 or 1–2–3–♯4–5 to depict the total savage abandon of the passions and intoxication of the senses
4. Folk idiom (not in the context of the National, or Self, but of the Exotic, or Other): gapped scales, pentatonic suggestion accompanied by minor-key or modal harmonies to create sense of "far away" in a traditional Western European context; this includes Scottish or "Celtic" melodies, many of which were understood by continental Europeans to reflect an exotic land and culture[21]
5. The "lurid": slithering chromatic motion in the bass or inner voice; excessive use of grace notes; use of the tambourine and other "noisy" percussion (also "Turkish"); woodwind tremolos; abrupt, repetitious music gestures (the ♯4 resolving upward or downward was also used in this context)
6. "Oriental" devices: doubling of melodies at the fourth, fifth, or octave, and usually with pedal points; the Oriental idiom also exaggerates the intervals of the gapped scales, often 2–4 and 6–8
7. The three-note descending 3–2–1, usually given out in the rhythm two sixteenths and an eighth or two eighths and a quarter (short-short-long): this rhythm becomes an exotic feature in itself; even when the three pitches vary, it serves as a typical across-the-board device specifically used for Indians

These characteristics seemed to serve as a ready-made toolbox of exotica whenever nineteenth-century European or European-trained American composers undertook Indian topics. American musicians, especially those working between 1890 and the 1920s, could hardly remain oblivious to Indian culture, which, along with other "exotic" cultures, began to emerge into the American mainstream during those years. These exotic devices took root and for decades constituted the standard language for the musical depiction of Indians. We can see such characteristics as the pastoral long-short-short rhythm and the heavier reiteration of open fifths, for example, in a later stage work, *Wanita, or The Indian Maiden's Mission,* a light opera or "musical burlesque" by Ralph Lyman Baldwin (Boston, 1892). It would be difficult to find a more paradigmatic expression for war-mongering Indians than the rustic topos combined with the contrived, descending, minor-key pentatonic melody.[22] Although Baldwin's "fake Indian" style today appears a gross oversimplification and misrepresentation, this was probably how most Easterners viewed Native American music in the early 1890s. "Old Three-Tones-in-His-Voice" jested the Boston critic

Philip Hale of Indian performers.[23] It is less surprising to find these features in later British theater music (John Crook's "Indian Dance" in the score to J. M. Barrie's *Peter Pan,* 1905) or concert music (Frederick Cowen's orchestral "Indian Rhapsody," 1903). But to find downward octave leaps with grace notes, cello "grunts," and slithering chromaticism in a 1910 work by John Philip Sousa ("The Red Man" from *Dwellers in the Western World*)[24] only goes to show how firmly ingrained these exoticisms were in the European American's description of the Indian. The tradition carried over into the "Indian intermezzo," Tin Pan Alley's contribution to Indianism, and also into music composed for silent films. One classic example by John Zamecnik, a Dvořák pupil at the National Conservatory, was used to accompany "Indian attacks" and was published in *Sam Fox's Moving Picture Music of 1914* (example 8.7).

Ex. 8.7. John Zamecnik, "Indian Attack," in *Sam Fox's Moving Picture Music* (1914).

This chronological overview illuminates a previously unacknowledged aspect of Indianism in the nineteenth century: because a relatively minor composer—Baldwin—used these now formulaic "Indian" devices in a stage work in 1892 and Stoepel, a stage music composer forgotten by the 1890s, had already used them in 1859, we can conclude that such idiomatic devices originated on the stage and largely remained there (most of the music is now lost, of course) until first Bristow and then later others, most notably the New Englander Edward MacDowell, brought them into the concert hall.

The third and fifth movements of MacDowell's Second Orchestral Suite ("Indian"), completed in 1895, were firmly grounded in the war dance tradition. MacDowell was considered the first major composer to use Indian themes in a composition. But this credit must be firmly qualified: he used "published" Indian themes—those from Theodore Baker's 1882 thesis.[25] For the substance of the work, however, he drew heavily from many of the idioms in the categories outlined above.

Two themes from the third movement, (incipits in example 8.8a), are from Baker's study (much of which Baker collected from Iroquois sources at the newly established Carlisle Indian School in Pennsylvania), but the origins of these two themes differ tremendously: the first four bars of the principal theme (mm. 1–16) are taken from an old modal English or Celtic tune (from a Narragansett Indian Christian hymn book of the 1840s), whereas the contrasting pentatonic tune (mm. 17ff) is a Seneca-Iroquois melody in the oral tradition from western New York State.

Ex. 8.8a. Edward MacDowell, Second Orchestral Suite ("Indian"), 1895, two contrasting "Indian" themes from the opening of mvt. 3, "In War Time."

Ex. 8.8b. MacDowell, "Indian" Suite, mvt. 1, "Legend," mm. 38–53.

Ex. 8.8c. MacDowell, "Indian" Suite, mvt. 5, "Village Festival," excerpt.

Features such as, in example 8.8b, the 3–2–1 (G–F♯–E) and 5–♯4–3 (B–B♭–G) with violin trills as an ominous pedal point, and in example 8.8c, pentatonic exaggeration in the melody, the flute and piccolo grace notes, and the accompaniment of oscillating fourths in the bass—just to name a few—illustrate MacDowell's reversion to generic exotic techniques just at the time when American audiences were on the verge of a more sympathetic appreciation of the Native American character and a more accurate familiarity with North American musical traditions.

Hiawatha *and the Later Nineteenth Century*

By the time Longfellow published his epic poem *The Song of Hiawatha* (1855), the concept of the noble savage in literature, however widespread in the general populace, had virtually ceased to hold intellectual interest. In the concert hall, however, *Hiawatha* was the beginning of a long conservative tradition that lingered some sixty years. After Robert Stoepel in 1859 (and he was not the first), there followed dozens of settings of excerpted texts from the poem, as well as programmatic orchestral works based on it. Longfellow's poem remained influential for over fifty years, roughly until World War I. Most cantatas, such as Arthur Foote's *The Farewell of Hiawatha* (1886) or Frederick Burton's *Hiawatha* (performed 1898), and symphonic poems, such as Louis Coerne's *Hiawatha* (1893), do not employ actual or ersatz Indian music. A few later vocal settings do, however, though neither Carl Busch in *The Four Winds* (1907) or Frederick Converse in *The Peace Pipe* (1915) heralded the themes in their scores by citing their derivation (as did Arthur Farwell for the Indian-based pieces published in his Wa-Wan Press, 1901–11). Hiawatha compositions in the later nineteenth century often explored Romantic nature imagery or mythological archetypes and may be aligned aesthetically to their European counterparts: for example, that of Grieg's music for *Peer Gynt* or Sibelius's settings of *Lemminkäinen* or other *Kalevala* legends.

Some Europeans attempted to capture a North American Indian atmosphere in their Hiawathas. One of these was Samuel Coleridge-Taylor, the Anglo-African composer. A vague "Indian" tone pervades much of *Hiawatha's Wedding Feast* (1898, the first of three Hiawatha-based cantatas). The opening of the work (example 8.9) presents the principal thematic germ of the cantata in the soprano and alto voices: a theme based on open fourths, fifths, and octaves. (Richard Strauss, Coleridge-Taylor's contemporary, also used motives based on these intervals in *Salome* and other works to represent archetypal figures from myth or antiquity.) Coleridge-Taylor uses the pastoral "rude peasant" rhythmic accompaniment beginning in measure 7. The accompaniment evokes a familiar topos of the war dance, but also that of the rustic image of the Indians as forest dwellers. The Scottish snap allusion to the noble savage also energizes the melody in measures 10–13. A new harmonic feature, associated not with war dances but with the nationalist flavor of Edvard Grieg and Ralph Vaughan Williams—is the strong coloristic effect of the move from the tonic to the minor submediant and back again (mm. 5–7).

Such exoticisms remain relatively subdued throughout the cantata trilogy. Like the large-scale choral works of his contemporaries Sir Arthur Sullivan, Charles Hubert Parry, Edward Elgar, and Frederick Clay, Coleridge-Taylor's cantatas are conspicuous for their uniformity of color and extreme soft-pedaling of exotic influences. In one single important instance, however, Coleridge-Taylor went beyond an apparently nineteenth-century English obsession with homogeneity to construct one of the most powerful and haunting climaxes in the entire work. In that moment he conceived an Indian world that, to my knowledge, had never before existed and, through imitation by others, would resonate well into the next century. Fearful of losing his dying Minnehaha, Hiawatha rushes into the forest to pray to Manitou, but his prayers prove

Ex. 8.9. Samuel Coleridge-Taylor, *Hiawatha's Wedding Feast* (1898), choral opening.

futile. The previously ponderous 3/4 undergoes a dramatic transformation in the orchestral interlude (example 8.10). The melody is accented and less languid, the bass line becomes more active, and an *accelerando* leads to an *allegro* in 4/4. The unique events occur following the double bar: (1) the underlying harmonic motion of i^6_4 to V with open fifths (the latter reinforced and power-

Ex. 8.10. Samuel Coleridge-Taylor, *The Death of Minehaha* (1899), Hiawatha's prayer to Manitou.

fully sustained in the brass); and (2) short three-note and two-note musical cells in the melody (especially the falling thirds B♭–G—in the recognizable Scottish-snap rhythm—and A–F–D). This singular orchestral moment (which leads to an equally mighty choral outburst in an "empty" and "madden'd" pentatonicism) suggests the evocation of a primitive world of strange gods and the overwhelming, unsympathetic force of nature through the elemental quality of the open fifths.

Though the Hiawatha cantata trilogy was performed in whole or in part many times in the United States during the first decade of the twentieth century, its American life was short. But it attained ritual status in England. During the composer's remaining years (from 1900 to 1912) it was considered "the most popular English oratorio"; Novello publishers profited enormously from it.[26] It was after 1924, however, that Coleridge-Taylor's cantata trilogy benefited from the Indianist craze then being fueled by the popular music and film industry. After several attempts by organizations in England to give Hiawatha in operatic form, a British producer, Thomas Fairbairn, devised an extravaganza using Coleridge-Taylor's music. For these events, beginning on 19 May 1924, he claimed the whole vast arena of Royal Albert Hall, as well as the stage platform, to be draped in scenic decoration. Masking the organ, he suspended a backdrop of snow-clad mountains, pine forests, and wigwams. He costumed some five hundred choristers—braves and squaws—in full Indian regalia and war paint and directed them to make a dramatic first entrance with whoops and hollers, and to participate physically throughout the evening by arm waving and other gestures. He also engaged skilled lighting technicians, who, among other things, created the illusion of falling snow at the opening of the second part. In addition, actors were hired to pantomime the various characters, since the score called for only three vocal soloists. Eugene Goossens conducted. A corps de ballet of one hundred also participated, and the composer's son, Hiawatha Coleridge-Taylor, conducted an interpolated ballet at the Wedding Feast to music drawn from Coleridge-Taylor's *Three Dream Dances.*[27] The performances were such a success with the public that they became an annual event. The spectacle reportedly continued even through World War II, after which it was discontinued. The conductor Malcolm Sargent later took over from Goossens, and at least one Native American, the Mohawk baritone Oskenonton, took the role of Hiawatha from 1930 to 1945.[28]

Clearly, Coleridge-Taylor's *Hiawatha* was many things to many people. Performances produced a range of different responses from that of the Duchess of Sutherland, who reportedly was deeply moved by the 1899 Hanley Festival performance, to the enthusiasm of several African American choruses who performed it in the United States, to those elicited by the hyperexoticized London productions. It is possible, as I have shown, to identify a few elements of musical exoticism in the score. But the music's strong appeal could not have been limited solely to these rare and isolated incidents.

A significant, if controversial model for Coleridge-Taylor and other later composers of "Indianist" pieces was Antonín Dvořák's Symphony "From the New World," written and performed in New York, 1893. Compared to the other works in this study, this symphony's relationship to *The Song of Hiawatha* has a veritable deluge of compiled information.[29] Briefly summarized, the sketches for an unwritten Hiawatha opera went into the symphony. The opening music of the scherzo was originally intended to accompany the Dance of Pau-Puk-Keewis at the Wedding Feast. In Longfellow's words, Pau-Puk-Keewis dances

> Till the leaves went whirling with him,
> Till the dust and wind together
> swept in eddies round about him. (11:107–9)

Longfellow portrayed the trickster in this canto as handsome and beloved of women, but as we find out later in the poem, he has a destructive personality. Several features of both the war dance and the noble savage tradition have been sublimated into the musical texture of Dvořák's scherzo, especially the two sixteenths and an eighth rhythm, repeated over and over in both the melody and the accompaniment (example 8.11). The famous opening normally reads as an echo of Beethoven (the scherzo of the Ninth Symphony) but in this context also recalls the primitive octave leaps of some earlier war dances. In these four measures Dvořák captures "the sound of drums and voices"; in measure 13 and following, he captures "the sound of flutes and singing." Dvořák uses repeating strings to create a subtle tom-tom effect. Later, the spinning violin countermelody seems to suggest the "whirling" leaves in Longfellow's poetry.[30]

Unlike the more unadulterated war dance, most late nineteenth-century composers who were drawn to *Hiawatha* tended to use exotic musical features more subtly and often sublimated them to the Romantic's love for expressing nature.

Realism and Idealism

By late in the nineteenth century, earlier poetic images of the Indian were on the retreat, only to be supplanted by more complex and, at the same time, equally reductive views. The Indian presence had come to be perceived as a terrible threat to Western expansion, and defensive tribal groups were increasingly being vilified in American popular culture. Horace Greeley wrote (1869) of diverse European Americans and the hardships suffered during the settlement of the vast and fertile Mississippi Valley and while driving back "the dominion of the brute and savage."[31] The sturdy American pioneers whose characters shaped the frontier and who created the cities that sprung up as if

Ex. 8.11. Antonín Dvořák, Symphony no. 9 in E minor, "From the New World," mvt. 3, opening.

miraculously across the Western half of the nation were little interested in romantic notions of drawing room Indians.

Some Americans, however, did sympathize with the plight of the Indians, and their numbers grew during the socially sensitive years of the Progressive Era, from 1890 to 1920. Many of those voicing sympathies with the Native Americans were women. Among the earliest and most eloquent was Helen Hunt Jackson, whose passionate and somewhat propagandized *A Century of Dishonor* (1881) led to changes in government policy. Another emphatic voice was that of Alice Cunningham Fletcher, who spent years living among the Omaha and Nez Perce peoples and, through her connections with the Peabody Museum of Harvard University, continued to be an active voice for Indian culture throughout the late nineteenth century. Fletcher (1838–1923) was a pioneer not only for Indian studies but for also American music, a cause she is known to have taken up as early as 1873.[32] She constantly nudged composers to acknowledge Indian culture in their music. Some did, especially after demonstrations of music based on Indian themes during the Congress of Musicians at the Omaha Exposition in 1898 illustrated that the fusion of Indian and Western European culture was at least plausible, if not wholly successful. Earlier expressions, such as the Larghetto from Dvořák's Sonatina for violin and piano (1893), were couched in imprecise terms of sympathy for the Indian. One apparent subtext of the Larghetto was later made explicit in a version lightly adapted by Fritz Kreisler, who popularized this "Indian Lament" on his concerts. Dvořák used two pentatonic themes, one in minor (the harmonic setting itself suggests pentatonicism and avoids the leading tone) and a contrasting one in major (example 8.12). For the second, Dvořák provided an ostinato accompaniment of 6–5–6–5. This simple accompaniment is an original "Indianist" musical device that became virtually synonymous with musical expressions of the "frontier." Through extramusical association, it has come to represent the binary activity involved in movement: the clip-clop of horses' hooves, or the action of pistons which drive a train engine. It has also been used in countless instances to suggest the westward movement of wagon trains across the prairie. (Recall that Irving Berlin later used this same ostinato, only reversed, in the contrasting middle section of "I'm an Indian Too.")[33]

Between the Civil War and World War I the noble savage/heathen savage dichotomy central to the European view of the American frontier began to dissolve. America's growing confidence in itself as a nation and the need to project an identity for that nation was one decisive factor in determining the image and degree of presence of the Native American. The Indian image in the country was shaped principally by three relatively separate developments:

1. The establishment of the reservation system across the United States
2. The growing presence of the Indian in popular culture about the American West: "types" in popular fiction (faithful friend and servant, the idler or drunkard, the stoic, the beautiful Indian maiden, remnants of a vanishing race, etc.) and Wild West shows
3. An increasingly methodical documentation of Indian life through photography and recording devices (public organizations, such as the Smithsonian Institution and the American Folklore Society, and privately funded expeditions)

Published studies of Indian music begin to circulate among scholars in the 1880s, beginning with Theodore Baker's 1882 dissertation and continuing with the transcriptions of noted Indianists such as Franz Boas, Benjamin Gilman, Alice Fletcher, and others. At first this documentation reached only specialists in the field. But the invention of the recording cylinder proved a great boon

Ex. 8.12a. Fritz Kreisler, "Indian Lament" (1914), adapted from Dvořák, Sonatina for violin and piano (1893), Larghetto, mm. 1–5.

Ex. 8.12b. Kreisler, "Indian Lament," mm. 44–51.

for the dissemination of notated Indian music—indeed, for all kinds of folk music—as the repetitive capabilities of the device assisted transcribers in the notation process. In the 1890s articles on Indian culture, including music, began to circulate widely in literary magazines and elsewhere. The idea of transcribing and printing Indian music grew outward from projects sponsored by the Smithsonian. John Philip Sousa, for example, credits several regional contributors for the tribal Indian melodies he harmonized in his collection *National Patriotic and Topical Airs of All Lands* (1890). By 1900 most of the music written in America on Indian subjects had gone far beyond Coleridge-Taylor and Dvořák in intensity in the engaging of real or supposed elements of Native American musics.

Alice Fletcher's benchmark 1893 publication (aided by Francis La Flesche, who, as a Native American co-author, not only took musical dictation but persuaded Omahas visiting Washington, D.C., to contribute) proved to be one of the most influential studies of American Indian music ever published. *A Study of Omaha Indian Music* was particularly significant for musical composition, partly because it included transcriptions and harmonizations by the music historian and theorist John C. Fillmore, who elsewhere defined how monophonic Indian music could be harmonized and made more palatable to cultured tastes. In the annals of early ethnomusicology, Fillmore figures barely at all. But in a study of the Indian as exotic, he suddenly leaps into prominence, not only because of his curious adaptations of Indian music but of the wide application of his theories and his influence on American composers. Of the ninety-three melodies Fletcher chose for her 1893 collection, Fillmore found seventy-six of them adapted best to a major-key accompaniment, a thesis which contradicted the minor-key settings of previous "savage music." He solved the ambiguity of modulating pentatonic collections within single pieces by adopting a modulating harmonization. Fillmore's solutions for rhythmic subtleties were less creative. His settings reflect the obvious limitations of European instrumental notation, which, when applied to non-Western music in an oral tradition, resulted in an artificial rigidification of the Indian melodies. Nevertheless, Fillmore's rhythmically rigid melodies with their hymnlike accompaniments influenced a generation of American composers who began to turn to Indian music for its spiritual content. Fletcher and Fillmore gave copies of the study to major composers across the country, including Dvořák, urging them to use the transcribed melodies as a source of American folk song for their compositions. It was only after receiving his copy in August 1893 that Dvořák subsequently added Indian music to his list of folk music possibilities (e.g., Negro, Anglo) for an "American" music.[34]

Composers who adapted Indian music after 1890 did so for various reasons. Some idealists constructed their music out of Indian themes in an effort to introduce Indian culture to new Americans through the filter of standard Western musical practices. Some Americanists, seeking to reach a wider public for concert music, drew upon the growing popular interest in Indian subjects. Other composers, looking perhaps for sensationalism, found that older colonial ideas of the American savage suited their taste for local color and found the occasional Indian topic the perfect vehicle for a barbarous, primitive tone in their music. Still others saw in Indian music a parallel with the exotic subjects used by certain prominent European or Russian composers. Few of the composers sympathetic to Indian music before the twentieth century had much actual contact with the peoples and cultures from which they drew. Contact would come slowly through the publication of articles relating to Indian culture and music in notable specialists' and popular magazines in the 1890s and after, and through the displays of world culture on the midways of national and world's fairs: Chicago in 1893, Omaha in 1898, and Saint Louis in 1904.

We can observe the process of appropriation and reconstitution of Native American expressions to the concert hall in two instances of musicians' visits to the world's fairs. The composer and author Frederick Burton (1861–1909), known largely for his posthumously published study of Ojibway music, was also among the earliest in the 1890s to have written and performed a work based on an Indian melody. The Kwakiutl melody was published for the first time in 1893 by the music critic of the *New York Tribune* Henry Krehbiel, who heard it not during fieldwork (as might have been supposed from Burton's suggestion in the score) but in a staged performance on the Midway Plaisance at the World's Columbian Exposition in Chicago on 1 July 1893.[35] Krehbiel notated the song (music only, no text) more or less as he probably heard it, including a quicker drum accompaniment in 6/4 against a more "sluggish" vocal line in 4/4, each filling a measure of equal duration. It was doubtless from the 1893 article, or from subsequent contact with Krehbiel, that Burton obtained the theme that he used for the "Dance of Pau-Puk-Keewis."[36]

The melody's descending pentatonic phrase (example 8.13) focuses on the downward thrust toward its final, and the arrival by a falling minor third is repeatedly emphasized and answered. Burton supplied the whole melody with a predominantly minor setting and even attempted to depict a heterophonic texture by echoing the melody in different voices. Even more original was Burton's continual drumbeat in three against the duple melody. This effect of a primitive ancient culture differs considerably from the jumble of exotica projected by MacDowell in his "Indian" Suite. Burton's primitive setting remained, though, an early experiment that he did not repeat. Most of his later Indian music (the remaining movements of the *Hiawatha* cantata and the "art songs" included in *American Primitive Music*, 1909) stayed well within the perfumed parlor song tradition to which Thurlow Lieurance and others were to contribute.

Ex. 8.13. Frederick Russell Burton, "The Dance of Pau-Puk-Keewis," from *Hiawatha* (c. 1893–98), mm. 1–14.

For "Indian Music Day" some six years later at the Congress of Musicians, which coincided with the 1898 Trans-Mississippi Exposition in Omaha, Nebraska, scholars of Indian music read papers, of course, but for the first time, owing to the efforts of Alice Fletcher, Ernest Kroeger, and a few others, a group of Omaha Indians sang their native melodies to an audience composed largely of trained musicians. Fletcher observed: "This unique presentation not only demonstrated the scientific value of these aboriginal songs in the study of the development of music, but suggested their availability as themes, novel and characteristic, for the American composer."[37]

To correct the problem of limited availability of Indian music, Fletcher published an accessible version of thirty Omaha songs in a small volume that she titled *Indian Story and Song from North America* (Boston, 1900). Instead of supplying specialists in the field of ethnology with detailed and informative field notes, she offered the songs and their accompanying simplified mythologies "in a more popular form," so that "the general public may share with the student the light shed by these untutored melodies upon the history of music." Despite years of living among the Omahas, Fletcher could still write in 1900 of such a collection that "these songs are like the wild flowers that have not yet come under the transforming hand of the gardener."[38]

Younger ethnologists early in their careers had similar expectations for the flowering of Indian music in Western culture (such as, for example, Frances Densmore's use of Arthur Farwell's "Dawn" in 1903 to illustrate the application of Indian tunes to modern composition).[39] Most discarded such notions by the 1920s. The idea did not disappear altogether, however, even among the most critical of later ethnomusicologists. In 1943 Willard Rhodes advocated essentially identical ideas to those proposed in *Indian Story and Song,* though he distanced himself from all earlier responses to Fletcher.

> The romantic approach to Indian music of Edward MacDowell, Arthur Farwell [et al.] in the early years of this century has been reason enough for modern composers to shy at anything connected with Indians, to regard the material as suspect. But the musical revolution and experimentation of the twenties is behind us. For many of our leading composers the effort to translate the soul of America into sound has become secondary to their desire to write good music. This more realistic attitude and less fevered approach prompts one to suggest that the time has arrived when the composers can safely reconsider American Indian music as a source of material.[40]

The avid interest in Native American culture and ethnographic studies led to more diverse approaches to Indian music with greater emphasis placed on distinctive cultures of various tribes, such as, for example, Arthur Farwell's "Pawnee Horses" (1905) or Horace Alden Miller's "Paiute Gambling Song" (1910). Taking this sensibility into consideration, we can divide Indian-based compositions from the 1890s on (both solo instrumental or orchestral) into two types. The first and simplest of these, harmonized transcriptions of Indian monodic music as notated by the Indianists, were generally limited to one specific theme per work. These "tribal portraits" might be texted works for voice and accompaniment, such as Natalie Curtis's *Songs of Ancient America* (1905), Charles Wakefield Cadman's *Four American Indian Songs* (1909), and Thurlow Lieurance's *Nine Indian Songs* (1913), or they might be essentially "songs without words" for piano solo or a small group of instruments, such as Edward MacDowell's "From an Indian Lodge" from *Woodland Sketches* (1896). Many Indian character pieces were also grouped in cycles, such as Arthur Farwell's *American Indian Melodies* (1901), Harvey Loomis's *Lyrics of the Red Man* (1903), Amy Beach's *Eskimos* (1906), Horace Miller's *Melodic Views of Indian Life* (1910), and Henry Gilbert's *Indian Scenes* (1911).

The second type of work, fanciful compositions in which transcribed Indian music provided the foundation for a fantasia, often engaged several themes or even original themes assuming the shape and character of the borrowed ones. Fanciful works consisted of solo pieces such as Preston Ware Orem's *American Indian Rhapsody* for piano (1918); chamber works such as Carl Busch's popular "Indian Legend" for violin and piano (1907) and string quartets on Indian themes by Charles Sanford Skilton (1915), Charles Tomlinson Griffes (1918), Farwell (1922), Frederick Jacobi (1924), and Amy Beach (1921/29); or compositions for large orchestra such as Fillmore's "Indian Fantasia" (1890), Ferruccio Busoni's *Indian Fantasy* for piano and orchestra (1913), Carl Busch's *A Chant from the Great Plains* (1921), and Mario Castelnuovo-Tedesco's *Indian Songs and Dances* (1942).

The promotion and sales of pieces in the first category—instrumental and vocal settings of Indian melodies—fell off dramatically after 1918. Large-scale symphonic compositions of the second type, however, continued to be written and performed until the 1930s and after. Despite the continued appearance of Indian-based works on concert programs, it became clear to many that using Indian themes to create larger pieces of music could not compare with Rimsky-Korsakov's use of Russian folk melodies or Vaughan Williams's use of English folksong. Critics consistently observed that most American culture as they understood it had nothing to do with Indian music. Unlike Russian and English folk music for those cultures, many critics complained, Indian music was not part of the American heritage. (Such objections echoed the simple fact that, throughout the nineteenth and early twentieth centuries, Indians were not citizens and could not vote, hence were not "Americans.") In addition, it seemed unlikely that a tradition could be established based on music that out of context had little more than vague associative power. Only in those cases when Indian idioms were distilled and shaped into idiomatic (if stereotypical) musical topoi did Indian-based music seem to find acceptance among composers, critics, and audiences. Music based on Indian themes, therefore, remained more an exotic phenomenon than, to apply Boris Asafiev's concept, the "intonation" of a national character.[41]

MacDowell, Burton, Henry Hadley, and many lesser-known composers had previously used Indian themes, but Arthur Farwell was among the earliest to identify spiritually with his Indian subjects. Fascinated by this dimension of Indian music, Farwell strove to incorporate greater spiritual and emotional complexity. Despite the title, his "Navajo War Dance" (example 8.14) turns away from traditional Romantic techniques. Farwell composed it originally for piano solo (1905), then adapted it in 1937 for the Westminster Choir in Princeton, New Jersey. Somewhat dark and musically disjointed, its dissonance, rhythmic vigor, and melodic inflections—including Indian vocables later added for the chorus—seem drawn from Farwell's travels in the West and his contact with Charles F. Lummis, and thus actual, rather than imagined, American Indian music.[42]

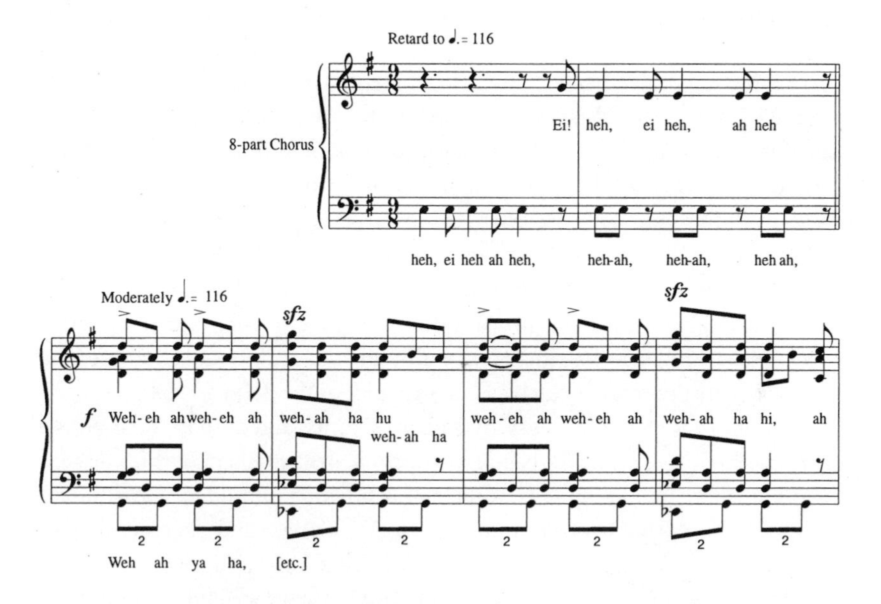

Ex. 8.14. Arthur Farwell, "Navajo War Dance" (1937), adapted from the piano suite *From Mesa and Plain: Indian, Cowboy, and Negro Sketches* (1905), excerpt.

With Farwell, two other American composers, Charles Wakefield Cadman and Charles Sanford Skilton, also portrayed "Indian music" in a distinctively sympathetic way. Not only were these three composers musically prolific, but each was an eloquent speaker on behalf of American Indian culture and its relationship to musical idealism. They believed the music possessed a deep spirituality that much American music, concert or otherwise, lacked. In Skilton's insightful address to the Music Teachers National Association in 1917—later published in the proceedings—he distinguished three methods by which Indian material had been adopted by American composers. Only the third of these, he contended, the "realistic method," preserved the spiritual integrity of Indian music because it maintained its characteristic features, that is, melodic shape and rhythmic accompaniment. (This technique remained somewhat at odds with that of Cadman, whose enthusiasm for American Indian music led him to paraphrase some of what he heard in so-called idealizations.) It was largely owing to the efforts of Farwell, Cadman, and Skilton himself, three leading composers who wholeheartedly embraced and adapted the research of the Indian ethnographers, that a kind of spiritual integrity came to be expected in Indian music rendered in a Western musical context.

Though Cadman sympathized with the agonizing plight of the Indian, one of his most effective songs on a Fletcher/La Flesche melody, "The Moon Drops Low" from *Four American Indian Songs* (1909), presumes the "Indian race" to be disappearing altogether, a concept that persisted in the American mind from the age of Jacksonian "Manifest Destiny" to the 1920s, when Zane Grey published his *Vanishing American.* This idea, still a popular theme in the first two decades of the twentieth century, stemmed from the belief that Indians and their "primitive lifestyle" were slowly dying out. It confused progressive notions of Indian assimilation into "civilized" culture with Wild West portrayals of whites "conquering" Indians and driving them off desirable land into harsh and unsurvivable conditions. In reality, however, the actual number of Native Americans during this time increased within the safety of the reservations. The poem by Nelle Eberhart, written as if in the voice of the defeated Native American, emphasizes the tragic loss of Indian identity and disenfranchisement (example 8.15). This is no Death Song with proud Scottish-snap rhythms (except for the single pointed emphasis in the piano, a telling reminder of lost Indian nobility). The normally crisp iambs "glory," "sinking," and "perish'd" seem pale and inert in Cadman's setting. A sense of lost authority and anguish prevails.

Attempts such as those by Farwell and Cadman at a more sympathetic "Indian realism," however, did not take hold in the public imagination. Even "artistic" character pieces inspired by Indian life such as Harvey Loomis's "Around the Wigwam" and "Chattering Squaw" from *Lyrics of the Red Man* (1904) tended to see the American Indian in an Orientalist light.[43] Loomis used exoticisms normally employed by Occidental composers to depict Oriental situations: pentatonic melodies harmonized in parallel fourths or fifths.

The efforts of the Indian "musical realists" during these years, however, were overwhelmed by a renewed interest in the exotic Indian in more popular venues: the popular Indian song craze, Indian subjects in early silent film, and songs from operetta (such as Rudolf Friml's oft-parodied, almost self-parodying "Indian Love Call"). The rise of vaudeville in the United States demonstrated that Americans loved their clichés and stereotypes. From about 1904, when President Theodore Roosevelt and the commissioner of Indian affairs began efforts to emancipate Indians from the failing reservation system, until the onset of World War I, Indian illustrations, pageant posters, letterheads, logos, postcards, and songs were richly and ornately interwoven with American life. Suddenly it was OK, even desirable, to be Indian, or so the popular songs implied. Even Teddy Roosevelt himself is said to have regretted that he did not

Ex. 8.15. Charles Wakefield Cadman, "The Moon Drops Low," from *Four American Indian Songs* (1909), mm. 20–24.

have "a strain of Indian blood" in his veins.[44] The culmination of this activity, which ironically served to raise public consciousness about the state of America's indigenous peoples, resulted in full Native American citizenship in 1924.

The apex of musical realism in Indian topics seems to have been reached about 1911. By then, Arthur Farwell's Wa-Wan Press was in its tenth year of publication and tens of thousands of musicians had found in its pages ample evidence that a serious American music could and must include the music of Native America.[45] In 1911 alone, Mary Austin's play *The Arrow-Maker* (with music by Elliott Schenck) opened to a successful run on Broadway; the Smithsonian photographer Edward Curtis took his "Indian picture-opera" *The Vanishing Race* to a sold-out Carnegie Hall, following that up with a national tour; and the much-adored operetta composer Victor Herbert turned to grand opera with *Natoma,* a work that premiered in Philadelphia and New York in 1911 and toured to over thirty cities in the following years.

Moreover, some "meanings" continued to accrue to musical devices as composers used them in related contexts. Both Henry F. Gilbert and Victor Herbert, for example, used an exotic topos that stemmed from the "tom-tom" chord from Dvořák's scherzo cited earlier, a sonority of two interlocking fifths (E–B and G–D). Others after Dvořák used this chord as a minor dominant seventh (v^7) or tonic seventh (i^7), either in a programmatic work or positioned with a text that suggested a sense of tragedy and lost grandeur. Puccini may have been among the earliest to do so in a specifically exotic context at the climax of the concluding aria "Tu, tu, piccolo iddio" from *Madama Butterfly* (1904). But by 1911 the chord served to suggest these same qualities, for example, in Gilbert's accompanying score to *A Vanishing Race,* and in the "Indian music" in Victor Herbert's *Natoma.*

Natoma, based on a fanciful story of a Native American woman of the 1820s in the Spanish territories that are now part of California, is perhaps more important for historical reasons than as a successful opera. At the time, the attention awarded Herbert's work set off a wave of experimental attempts at Indian operas.[46] The successful "Dagger Dance" at the climax of Act 2 seems to have been popular for the same reasons that war dances in the nineteenth century were popular. The minor-key setting of the pentatonic theme (example 8.16), the accompanying parallel chords, the short-short-long rhythmic tail, and the pervasive four-beat tom-tom all attest to the exaggerated war dance style. In addition, the musical devices Herbert used to depict the "Indian race" throughout the opera, especially pentatonic and modal melodies and open-fifth accompaniments, seem to proliferate in operatic and instrumental works after that date.[47] Herbert's "Dagger Dance" of 1911 vividly illustrates that in the popular reception of Native Americans, very little had changed sinced the 1890s.

Stylistic Assimilation and American Indian Emergence

Despite persistent popular views of the Native American, the work of the Indian realist composers did carry over into later compositional practices. One example may serve as an illustration. By the time the Bostonian Frederick Shepherd Converse (1871–1940) turned to *Hiawatha* as a source for a concert work, several plays and films on the subject had already brought the romantic aspects of the story into the larger domain.[48] Louis Elson described *The Peace Pipe,* a thirty-minute cantata performed at the Chautauqua Festival in August 1915 and later in Boston as "one of the most effective of Mr. Converse's works . . . a work that is direct, dignified, dramatic and yet simple."[49] Elson's comments read like the fulfillment of Converse's dreams, for the composer had

Ex. 8.16. Victor Herbert, "Dagger Dance," from *Natoma* (1911), mm. 1–18.

earlier expressed his belief in a "new freshness and vitality" in the future American music. "Music will grow simpler—we will go back to less complex forms, to more originality."[50]

Unlike some of his Boston colleagues—Hadley and Parker, for example—Converse did not explore exotic subjects as escapist fantasies. Works set in "exotic" places usually transcended these locales and aspired to deeper, more universal meanings. For example, the tone poem "Ormazd" (1912) portrays the Zoroastrian struggle for good over evil. The dramatic narrative "Hagar in the Desert" (1908) similarly deals with angelic intervention in an ancient setting. The opera *The Sacrifice* (1911) contains a principal Native American character—an old Indian woman—whose stirring tragic prophecy in the opera's first act finds fulfillment in the gradual American takeover of Spanish territory.

When Converse turned to Longfellow's *The Song of Hiawatha* in 1914, he did so not because of an interest in the noble hero, nor in the birth/love/death cycle that was a central feature of earlier settings by Stoepel, Burton, Coleridge-Taylor, and others. He turned his attention to the poem's first scene, the pre-Columbian, prehistoric events of the gathering of the world's tribes and the Great Spirit's prophecy of a deliverer from their savage world.[51] The canto describes the various Indian nations coming together on the great stone quarry at the behest of Gitche Manito (the "Master of Life"). Once the tribes have assembled, the Spirit expresses his disappointment in their warring and petty dissensions. He promises to send them a "guide" (the as-yet-unborn Hiawatha) so they might live in peace and warns them of destruction if they do not heed his counsel. He asks them to wash the war paint from their faces and to make peace pipes from the red stone of the quarry to smoke in remembrance of their brotherhood.

For Indian melodies on which to base his setting, Converse turned not to Fletcher but to Natalie Curtis's more recent *The Indians' Book* (1907), a volume of musical transcriptions widely praised for its accuracy and insightful commentary. He employed a Cheyenne "Morning Song" as a unifying theme for the work. It forms the basis of the orchestral introduction to the first movement and returns throughout the work as if to remind the listener of the presence of a narrator and to place the action firmly in the past tense.[52] The appropriately chosen "Morning Song" was generally sung, as Curtis wrote, "by old men, often from the summit of the hills at dawn."[53] Converse included another theme, a Pima "Blue-bird Song," later in the Great Spirit's sermon.[54] Perhaps Converse knew that the composer Ferruccio Busoni had used the identical theme in his *Indian Fantasy* for piano and orchestra (1913), a work that Busoni performed for the first time in America earlier that year under Leopold Stokowski and the Philadelphia Orchestra on 19 February 1915. Converse probably would have been aware of Curtis's connection to Busoni and the latter's use of Indian themes in an effort to capture, in Curtis's somewhat effusive description, "the boundless horizon, the endless stretch of plains and deserts, the might of the Mississippi, the towering grandeur of the Rocky Mountains . . . the spirit of the real America."[55] The grand gestures in Converse's score suggest that he sought to capture just such a panoramic experience with his music.

Converse's opulent score swells and surges (example 8.17b). In the first four measures, Converse quotes recognizably from the clearly pentatonic Cheyenne song (transposed a third down from Curtis's original, example 8.17a). The orchestral introduction establishes the key of D major, even though Converse harmonizes the melody with a modally ambiguous minor iv in the second measure (G minor with a ♯7). Once the chorus enters, Converse switches this to a major IV. The Cheyenne song continues to shape the choral melody although it is camouflaged (marked with asterisks in the example). The music here suggests the character of the "American West," especially in the 3–2–3–2–1 with dotted rhythm in the fifth measure, and the ascending A to B at the conclusion of the first two choral phrases.[56] At the climax four measures before rehearsal number 12, Converse again introduces the Cheyenne melody in its recognizable form. He remains faithful to the pitches and rhythms, and even retains the vocables, which he assigns to unison chorus. Converse faced a challenge, however, when it came to harmonizing the entire "Morning Song," since it does not fit easily into any one key (Fillmore's problem). From measures 17 to 23, Converse modulates from a secure G major through a fleeting suggestion of D major (evidenced by the C-sharp in the counterpoint) to the unstable E natural minor (or Aeolian mode). The secure tonal stability of measures 17 to 21 comes from the fact that the first phrase of the Cheyenne melody harmonizes easily with a clear tonal center. The melody of the second phrase, however, drops a fourth, and in order to be fitted to conventional harmony would need to migrate to a different tonic center. Converse's solution is to abandon the stability of the major key and move to a modal sphere. In the measures following the arrival of E minor at measure 23, not only does the ♭7 hint at modality, but also the use of the lowered supertonic (with an added seventh) suggests a Phrygian color. The use of modality becomes another Indian topos, an evocation of pre-modernity and even nobility, hence spirituality.

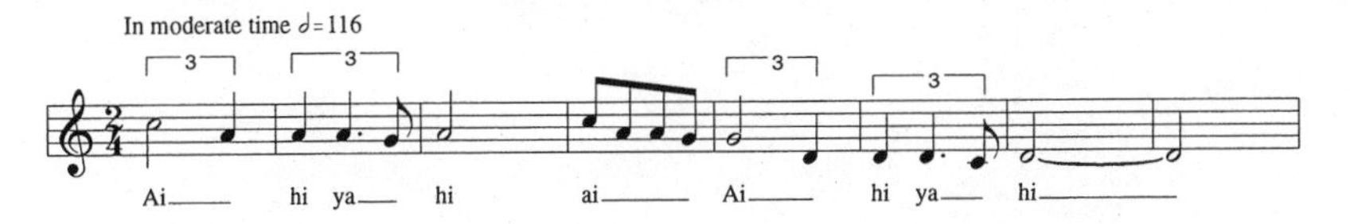

Ex. 8.17a. "Hohiotsitsi Ho-otz," from Natalie Curtis's *The Indians' Book* (1907), p. 172.

One senses throughout this piece that Converse is using musical allegory in a search for meaning beyond the obvious content of the Hiawatha myth. Though the subject matter concerns North America's indigenous peoples and invokes a god and a form of religion clearly not worshiped or practiced in turn-of-the-century Boston, Converse, using musical techniques, tried to bring aspects of Longfellow's myth into his own time. One of these techniques involved an application of well-established "Indian" devices to musical composition in the broader sense. Though some of the techniques I have isolated above had become commonplace in Indianist settings by the time this work was written—not to mention the subject matter itself—Converse transcends common stereotypes through a sense that in his music he had thoroughly absorbed these elements. He engages them not to exoticize his subject but to personalize it. The time is not the remote past but 1915; the Indians are not at war with one another, but it is the white men of the world who are at war.

The phenomenon of reinvigorating aspects of earlier civilizations, real or imagined, for enrichment in the modern world was hardly unique to America. A search for a cultural past in the music of legendary "folk" roots existed

Ex. 8.17b. Frederick Shepherd Converse, *The Peace Pipe* (1915), excerpt.

Ex. 8.17b. (*continued*)

among European composers as diverse as Gustav Mahler, Ottorino Respighi, Béla Bartók, and Leos Janáček, and all four, like their contemporaries Farwell and Converse in America, turned at some point to pentatonicism and open-fifth-related sonorities in an almost universal effort to identify and express tribal views of community. In the 1930s Heitor Villa-Lobos in Brazil and Carlos Chávez in Mexico found inspiration in primitivism, a movement that had swept European art decades before. The Mexican "Aztec Renaissance" of the 1930s had no obvious parallel in the United States, but musical primitivism as unleashed by Stravinsky and others in Diaghilev's artistic circle found abstract echoes later in America, although not with Indian subjects.

About this same time a new generation of American composers, largely educated abroad in French neoclassicism, entered the scene. Aaron Copland, Virgil Thomson, Roy Harris (a student of Arthur Farwell), and others turned away from both the "realism" of Indian themes as an American source and the Germanic training that had formed a foundation for the work of most of the previous generation. The 1890s cachet of Indianism had now become tainted with genteelism and, quite simply, bad taste. "No Indians!" Copland is supposed to have told Martha Graham, who proposed a Pocahontas scenario for the first draft of what would become *Appalachian Spring.*[57] Yet the suggestion of "wide-open" spaces in the widely voiced, sparse harmonic settings—typified by the opening of Charles Griffes's *Two Sketches for String Quartet Based on Indian Themes* (1918)—and the earthy simplicity and directness in some concert music of the 1930s and 1940s came to be irrevocably associated with Americanism: a pastoral simplicity based on the pentatonicism of folk tunes and the spaciousness of parallel chords and open fifths.[58] The influence of the Indianist school lingered, though the source of that influence was suppressed.

Americanism in the 1930s was also associated in part with the pioneer and the vast prairies of the west: in short, it celebrated the whole concept of the West—now where the European American had at last claimed his land—and the official closing, once and for all, of the frontier. "One cannot live in the Great West," wrote Cadman, "without sensing it and thinking how it should sound . . . in terms of rhythm and melody. The composer feels the very pulse of it in his contact with the awesome canyons, the majestic snow-capped peaks and the voiceless yet beautiful solitudes of the desert. . . . It is interesting to know a few have tried to catch these things either with the use of Indian themes or without them."[59]

When Copland composed *Rodeo* in 1942 (without the use of Indian themes), he and choreographer Agnes de Mille imagined cowboys dancing on the prairie. Rugged cowboys—as nineteenth-century photographs of them clearly display—could hardly have been capable of the stylized exuberance that ballet suggests. Yet dancing cowboys seem strikingly appropriate in the context Copland created for them. The unbounded joy of their uniform movements represents no less than a celebratory victory dance; they have won the land. Oscar Hammerstein II's 1942 phrase in *Oklahoma!* —"we know we belong to the land"—could just as well have read "we know the land belongs to us." The only vestige of the cowboy's enemy and of the land's ancestors is a haunting pentatonicism of the melodies, a sense of mystery in Copland's open sonorities and spacious parallelisms, and the vitality of the percussive rhythm.

We can see, now, how European and American composers first borrowed the "idea of the Indian" as a generic pastoral exotic, and in the late nineteenth and early twentieth centuries—during the time when failed assimilation policies began to lead toward a gradual reemergence of the American Indian spirit—adopted a more sober, complex view of Indian spirituality in an effort to enrich their own music. Yet the combination of Indian "realism" as established by Farwell and Loomis, and exoticisms borrowed from Herbert, Zamecnik, and others in conjunction with musical description of the American West, persisted well into the twentieth century, most prominently perhaps in the sound tracks to Hollywood films. Among these were scores by George Antheil (*The Plainsman,* 1936) and Alfred Newman (*Ramona,* also 1936), Hugo Friedhofer (*Broken Arrow,* 1950), Frank Skinner (*Chief Crazy Horse,* 1954), and Franz Waxman (*The Indian Fighter,* 1955).

Some of the patterns we have examined here—exoticized forms of representations alternating with assimilation of Native American elements—would seem to have run their course in mainstream American culture by the 1960s and 1970s. During these years, American Indian dancing and singing achieved greater prominence and visibility, for example, through the pantribal powwow movement. But just as the phonographic cylinder affected the growth and styles of American music in the 1890s, so did the synthesizer and multitrack dubbing shape it once again in the 1970s. The rise of New Age styles in the 1970s and 1980s (and the vast influx of non-Western influences) offered a fresh new medium for representations of North America's Indian heritage. Some layered studio pieces, Laurie Anderson's "Hiawatha," for example, engaged the spirit, if not the letter, of American Indian styles as a form of cultural criticism.[60] Whether consciously applied or passively absorbed, music, as we have seen, played a critical role in the process of acculturation and, even today, persistently draws upon notions of the exotic to lend allure and a sense of timelessness to narratives of the Indian world.

"The East in the West": Evocations of the Gamelan in Western Music

MERVYN COOKE

"IT SEEMS to me certain that future progress in creative music for composers of the Western world must inevitably go towards the exploration and integration of elements drawn from more than one of the world's cultures."[1] When Henry Cowell made this far-sighted prediction in 1948, in response to the strong impact made on him by Colin McPhee's pioneering work in absorbing elements borrowed from Balinese gamelan music into a Western compositional idiom, his prognosis was not merely speculative: even before World War II there had been considerable evidence to testify to a fairly widespread interest in the gamelan music of Java and Bali on the part of Western composers.

The *fons et origo* of all Western derivations from Indonesian music was, of course, the highly original synthesis of Occidental and Oriental procedures attained by Claude Debussy, who had grown up in the midst of the pseudo-orientalism affecting the French operatic stage in the later nineteenth century. Debussy had curtly dismissed Delibes's *Lakmé* (1883) as "sham, imitative Oriental *bric-à-brac*,"[2] but he too was soon to fall under the exotic charm of the East. The famous Exposition Universelle held in Paris in 1889 featured a variety of ethnic musics and included performances on the Champ de Mars by a gamelan from Cirebon, in northwest Java, which played in accompaniment to authentic Javanese dancing.[3] The gamelan in question had been presented to the Paris Conservatoire in 1887 by J. M. van Vleuten, the interior minister of the Dutch East Indies; in 1933 it was installed at the Musée de l'Homme.[4] According to Richard Mueller, in addition to Javanese dance music Debussy also heard the *gamelan angklung* (tuned bamboo rattles) and is likely to have known transcriptions prepared from both genres by Julien Tiersot and Louis Bénédictus (the latter's revived in performance at the 1900 Exposition).[5]

Debussy's first recorded reaction to this experience is to be found in a letter to Pierre Louÿs written on 22 January 1895 in which he asks: "Do you not remember the Javanese music, able to express every shade of meaning, even unmentionable shades, and which makes our tonic and dominant seem like ghosts?"[6] In an article written in 1913 Debussy briefly alluded to one of the most characteristic features of the texture of gamelan music: "Javanese music is based on a type of counterpoint by comparison with which that of Palestrina is child's play. And if we listen without European prejudice to the charm of their percussion, we must confess that our percussion is like primitive noises at a country fair."[7] In the same essay Debussy alludes to Chinese theatrical performances he saw during the 1889 festival; it was this event that also prompted greater awareness of the Japanese art that later became especially favored by the composer. Debussy's final flirtation with an authentic gamelan occurred in 1914, when he considered composing a ballet set in Taiwan that was to have used a Malaysian ensemble with "strange bells, horizontal harps and deep-toned drums."[8]

No convincing argument has yet been advanced to support the view that Debussy borrowed specific musical material from the Javanese performances he heard in 1889, *pace* Mueller's attempts to show that the *Fantaisie* for piano and orchestra composed in the same year derives its melodic shapes from a Javanese piece entitled "Wani-Wani."[9] The most important observation that can be made about the impact of the gamelan on Debussy's style is that the experience intensified techniques that were already latent in his music and that stood well apart from the conventional and soon-to-be-outmoded procedures that had dominated central European tonal music for the previous two hundred years. Debussy's techniques that carry strong resemblances to features of gamelan music may be divided into four categories, to some extent interrelated: scale types, ostinati, polyphonic textures, and sonorities.

Part of Debussy's rebellion against the hegemony of nineteenth-century Austro-German music resided in his cultivation of so-called nonfunctional harmony, which rejected conventional concepts of dissonance, consonance, and resolution. He frequently adopted scales that lay outside the orthodox tonal system, including the ancient church modes and synthetic formulations such as the octatonic and acoustic scales (the latter a major scale with raised fourth and lowered seventh scale degrees, e.g., C-D-E-F♯-G-A-B♭). As Saint-

Saëns's remarked, "the ancient modes are making a comeback, to be hotly pursued by the scales of the East in all their tremendous variety."[10] Both the whole-tone and pentatonic scales favored by Debussy have at various times been likened to gamelan tuning systems. The *slendro* tuning, in which the Javanese ensemble heard at the 1889 Exposition was constructed, theoretically employs equidistant steps within the octave; but there are five such steps, not six (as in the whole-tone scale), and in practice the five tones of *slendro* tend to gravitate towards the distinctive pattern familiar to everyone as the black notes of the Western keyboard (see example 9.1a). This anhemitonic pentatonic scale was well known to Debussy long before his contact with the gamelan, and its early use in his works may have derived from sources as diverse as Russian music (Borodin and Musorgsky), Liszt (whose *Sposalizio* contains pentatonic figurations imitated by Debussy at the same pitches and in the same triplet rhythm in his First Arabesque of 1888), or from numerous European folksong traditions.

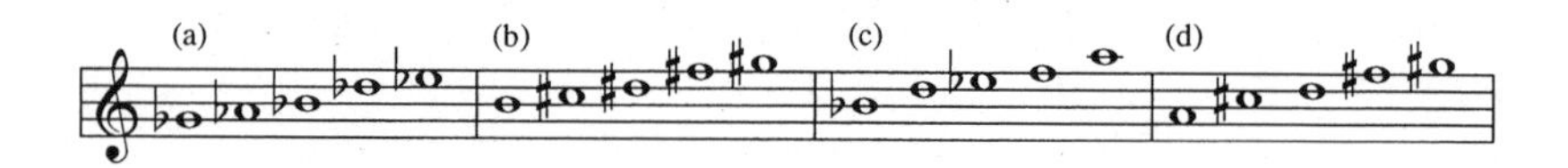

Ex. 9.1. Four pentatonic scales.

In only one work of Debussy's does the pentatonic scale occur prominently in a specifically Oriental context (unless one subscribes to the common speculation that the pentatonic opening of *La mer* was intended to symbolize the sun's rising in the East!). This is the piano piece "Pagodes," published in 1903 as the first of the three *Estampes* and probably inspired by Debussy's second experience of Javanese gamelan at the Exposition Universelle in 1900. Even here the title does not conjure up a specific image of Indonesia (where pagodas are not to be found), but the confluence of pentatonicism and stratified polyphony is sufficiently striking to render a direct gamelan stimulus plausible. At the outset, Debussy forms an anhemitonic pentatonic scale from the pitches B, C♯, D♯, F♯, and G♯ (see examples 9.1b and 9.2), and this formulation provides the tonal material for much of the piece. What is most significant (and usually overlooked) about this celebrated opening, however, is how Debussy anchors his pentatonic scale firmly to the B major triad contained within its five pitches, and even goes so far as to include a B major key signature with its unnecessary A-sharp.[11] This passage, a notably early fusion of Eastern and Western tonal procedures, reflects Debussy's inevitably Westernized perception of the gamelan's pentatonic tuning. Later in the piece, however, he is content to abandon triadic support and allow the pentatonicism to revolve freely without a Western tonal focus (e.g., mm. 11–14), although this approach rapidly yields to another more synthetic treatment in which a pentatonic melodic fragment is harmonized chromatically (mm. 15–18).

Ex. 9.2. Claude Debussy, *Estampes* for piano, no. 1, "Pagodes," opening.

Of wider-reaching significance in "Pagodes" is the tendency toward a stratified contrapuntal texture built up from superimposed ostinato patterns. Although seen here only in embryonic form, in later orchestral works Debussy developed such "layered" textures to a high degree of sophistication. In both piano and orchestral writing, these textures share with the gamelan the direct relationship between tessitura and rapidity of figuration. The slowest-moving element in a gamelan piece is the scheme of punctuation provided by the deepest gongs of the ensemble, usually described as "colotomic" after the fashion in which it systematically dissects the structure. Such colotomic punctuation is loosely represented in example 9.2 by the repetitions of the lowest B/F♯ dyad. Above this rocklike support are superimposed various melodic and accompanimental ostinato patterns, which in gamelan music tend to move more quickly the higher the range of the instrument. Example 9.2 demonstrates three such rhythmic layers, but later examples (such as at rehearsal number 17 in *Ibéria,* the second of the orchestral *Images* of 1906–12) superimpose numerous strata of ostinati in far more ambitious schemes based on the same principle.[12] As with his tonal language, Debussy's preference for these stratified textures represents a further revolt against the traditional contrapuntal and melody-plus-accompaniment textures of most nineteenth-century music.

Although Debussy never resorted to using ensembles of tuned percussion to suggest gamelan sonorities, his music is infused with echoes of the gamelan sound. This is most noticeable in his piano writing, especially where the texture involves bass notes prolonged by the sustaining pedal for considerable periods of time beneath more active figurations. As E. J. Dent observed in 1916, drawing attention to a fundamental discovery associated with the pedal's acoustical function that underlies much twentieth-century piano music, "It is in fact the right-hand pedal which gives the pianoforte an advantage possessed by no other instrument to any appreciable extent. . . . For the principal value of the pedal is not merely to sustain sounds when the finger is for some reason obliged to release the key, but to reinforce sounds by allowing other strings to vibrate in sympathy with them."[13] It seems likely that Debussy's extraordinary exploitation of this phenomenon of sympathetic vibration in his piano music was partly inspired by the gamelan's uniquely resonant tone. As early as 1937 E. Robert Schmitz proposed that "Debussy regarded the piano as the Balinese musicians regard their gamelan orchestras. He was interested not so much in the single tone that was obviously heard when a note was struck, as in the patterns of resonance which that tone sets up around itself. Many of his pieces are built entirely on this acoustical sense of the piano."[14]

Connected with the desire to create a resonant "wash" of sound that reinforced the essentially static nature of much of Debussy's nonfunctional harmony was his self-confessed need (as recorded by Marguerite Long) to make the piano appear as if it were an instrument "sans marteaux" (without hammers). In the finest examples of gamelan music the players miraculously manage to create mellifluous effects, even in virtuoso passagework, in spite of the need to strike every single note with a hand-held mallet.

Later French composers subscribed to Debussy's interest in the piano's sympathetic resonance. Ravel recommended that his 1902 piano piece *Jeux d'eau* be played with copious use of the sustaining pedal in the upper register to emphasize "the hazy impression of vibrations in the air," while Messiaen's early *Préludes* for piano (1929) experimented with what the composer termed "added resonance." Not content to achieve acoustical effects by the use of the sustaining pedal alone, Messiaen went so far as to include deliberately "wrong" notes (played more softly than the prevailing musical material), which function as an illusory extension of the natural sympathetic vibrations set up by the release of the pedal. Significantly, both Ravel and Messiaen shared Debussy's interest in the gamelan. In Ravel's "La vallée des cloches" from *Miroirs*, written in 1905 (close on the heels of Debussy's "Pagodes"), the subtle exploitation of the piano's sympathetic resonances and gently undulating pentatonic ostinato patterns marked *très doux et sans accentuation* directly recall Debussy's example. (Although no explicitly Oriental interpretation is suggested by the title of the piece, Ravel dedicated it to Maurice Delage, who later became well known for his musical Orientalisms.) Particularly prophetic of later composers' gamelan-derived techniques is Ravel's use of low, sustained dissonant notes, which disrupt the prevailing pentatonicism and equally suggest the bells of the title or the colotomic punctuation of the gamelan's largest gongs.

The piano was again used by Ravel to suggest gamelan sonorities in the original duet version of the suite *Ma Mère l'Oye* (1908–10). The third movement is entitled "Laideronette, Impératrice des Pagodes" after the fairy tale "Serpentin vert" by Madame D'Aulnoy (d. 1705), the same source on which Britten's ballet *The Prince of the Pagodas* was later to be based. Orchestrating *Ma Mère l'Oye* in 1911 (also as a ballet), Ravel went one stage further than Debussy by employing a carefully selected percussion group to capture the sonorities of a Far Eastern percussion ensemble more vividly. The combination of xylophone, glockenspiel, and celeste, variously supported by cymbal, harp, and pizzicato string figurations, so uncannily suggests a gamelan orchestra that it may be supposed that Ravel was also acquainted with the sound of the Conservatoire's gamelan. Equally "authentic" is the use of colotomic tam-tam punctuation in the central section, where the celeste is required to play in its unorthodox low register in what again seems to be an attempt to capture a characteristic gamelan sonority. Even if these parallels with Indonesian models were unintentional, Ravel embraces compositional techniques already familiar from Debussy's example, notably anhemitonic pentatonicism and ostinato patterns organized in layers according to principles of rhythmic stratification. Ravel's pentatonic pitches are those found conveniently on the black notes of the piano, and in both pitch content and scoring the movement provided a model for Stravinsky's parodistic "Marche Chinoise" in Act 2 of *Le rossignol* (1913). Ravel briefly returned to chinoiserie in *L'enfant et les sortilèges* (1925), where pentatonicism characterizes the Chinese cup and forms an incongruous element in the "Five o'clock" foxtrot she dances in company with a matching black Wedgwood teapot.

Like Ravel, Bartók owed a considerable stylistic debt to Debussy in his early years, adopting anhemitonic pentatonicism around 1907. In his work, too, pentatonicism stems as much from European folk music as from the Orient. An offshoot of Bartók's interest in pentatonicism was the cultivation of opposing tone clusters on black and white notes to create maximum harmonic tension. The cluster device is reputed to have been a conscious borrowing from Henry Cowell, whom Bartók met in London in 1923.[15] Significantly, Cowell was one of the earliest American composers to have shown an interest in the gamelan, and tone clusters were to figure prominently in the work of most later composers involved with Indonesian music. The only specific reference to Indonesia in one of Bartók's titles, however, is the movement "Island of Bali" from volume 4 of the *Mikrokosmos* (no. 109): here we find an allusion to a specific Balinese scale also used by Poulenc and Britten (see example 9.1c, and below), but no attempt to capture stratified textures of genuine gamelan music. Two years after the publication of *Mikrokosmos* in 1940, Bartók and his wife were to perform Colin McPhee's highly influential transcriptions of gamelan pieces entitled *Balinese Ceremonial Music* (see below) at Amherst College, Massachusetts.[16]

The most explicit borrowing from gamelan music in France after Debussy occurs in the Concerto for Two Pianos by Francis Poulenc, composed in 1932 in the wake of an appearance by a Balinese gamelan at the Exposition Coloniale in Paris during the previous year. The gamelan in question was the *gong kebyar* "Gunung Sari" from the village of Peliatan, later made famous by its Western tours under John Coast and as the source for Britten's *kebyar* borrowings. Commissioned by Princess Edmond de Polignac, the concerto was given its first performance at the Venice festival of the ISCM on 5 September 1932; the soloists were the composer and Jacques Février, with the orchestra of La Scala, Milan, directed by Désiré Defauw. Poulenc commented to Paul Collaer one month after the premiere that "it did in fact stun everyone at the Festival. . . . You will see for yourself what an enormous step forward it is from my previous work and that I am really entering my great period."[17] The concerto was well known to Britten, who performed it with Poulenc at a "Saturday Book" concert at the Royal Albert Hall on 6 January 1945. By this time Britten had already become acquainted with Balinese music through McPhee's two-piano transcriptions, and he can hardly have failed to be aware of Poulenc's gamelan borrowings. In 1955 Poulenc and Britten again performed the work, this time at the Royal Festival Hall, and the timing of this occasion—coming as it does in the midst of Britten's work on *The Prince of the Pagodas*—is undoubtedly significant.

Poulenc described his Concerto for Two Pianos as "blithely bravura,"[18] and the Balinese material it contains is of no greater significance than the composer's habitually haphazard allusions elsewhere in the score to the idioms of composers as diverse as Mozart, Chaikovsky, Prokofiev, and Stravinsky. As is often the case in Poulenc's music, no attempt is made to synthesize this veritable potpourri of stylistic mannerisms, and the explicit reference to Balinese procedures may therefore be considered less satisfying artistically than Debussy's subtle and no doubt largely subconscious manipulation of Javanese textures and scales. Nevertheless, Poulenc's modest handling of Balinese pentatonicism demonstrates a reinterpretation of gamelan scales from a Western viewpoint analagous to that already seen in Debussy's "Pagodes." His contribution to the field of cross-cultural borrowing is also significant in constituting the first use by a Western composer of the other principal pentatonic scale to which gamelans are tuned,[19] which was ignored by Debussy in his exclusive reliance on the anhemitonic variety. The concerto contains five sections based on this scale, the pitches of which presumably correspond to those heard by Poulenc at the Exposition Coloniale: these are identical to the pitches selected by Britten for the majority of his gamelan-inspired effects in *The Prince of the Pagodas*. Britten in fact borrowed these pitches from recordings made by a gamelan from Peliatan (see below), and the coincidence is unlikely to have escaped him.

Poulenc's "gamelan" passages are brief and principally serve to usher in or round off each of the concerto's three movements. The work commences with a flurry of sixteenth-notes based on the pitches of example 9.1c, which are then abandoned apart from a fleeting reappearance in the right-hand dyads of the first piano part at rehearsal number 14. Tonally, the opening gesture is significant: the scale is presented in the context of the tonic key D minor (asserted by the two initial chords), and example 9.1c is therefore inevitably interpreted as part of a Phrygian mode based on D. The most extended passage to use Balinese material forms the coda to the first movement. Poulenc here sets up oscillating sixteenth-note ostinati derived from example 9.1c in an atmospheric texture to be played *mystérieux et clair tout à la fois,* and then presents a simple melody above it (example 9.3). The "gamelan" texture at this point is authentic enough, but the rhythm of the melody is decidedly Western and the theme itself contains one pitch (C) alien to the pentatonicism prevailing in its accompaniment. The melody thus makes explicit the B-flat major tonality that Poulenc perceived to be implied by the Balinese scale, a procedure recalling Debussy's extraction of a B major triad from his pentatonic scale in example 9.2. Poulenc soon adds another additional pitch (G) in the cellos, thereby effecting a further reinterpretation of the scale as part of the Aeolian mode on G. Also notable at this point is the reiteration of the melody from example 9.3 on solo cello harmonics, an ethereal sonority later used independently by both McPhee and Britten to capture the evanescent sound of the Balinese flute (*suling*). Brief reminiscences of the Balinese scale and its associated ostinato-based textures occur at the end of the slow movement (final six measures) and at the conclusion of the work as a whole.

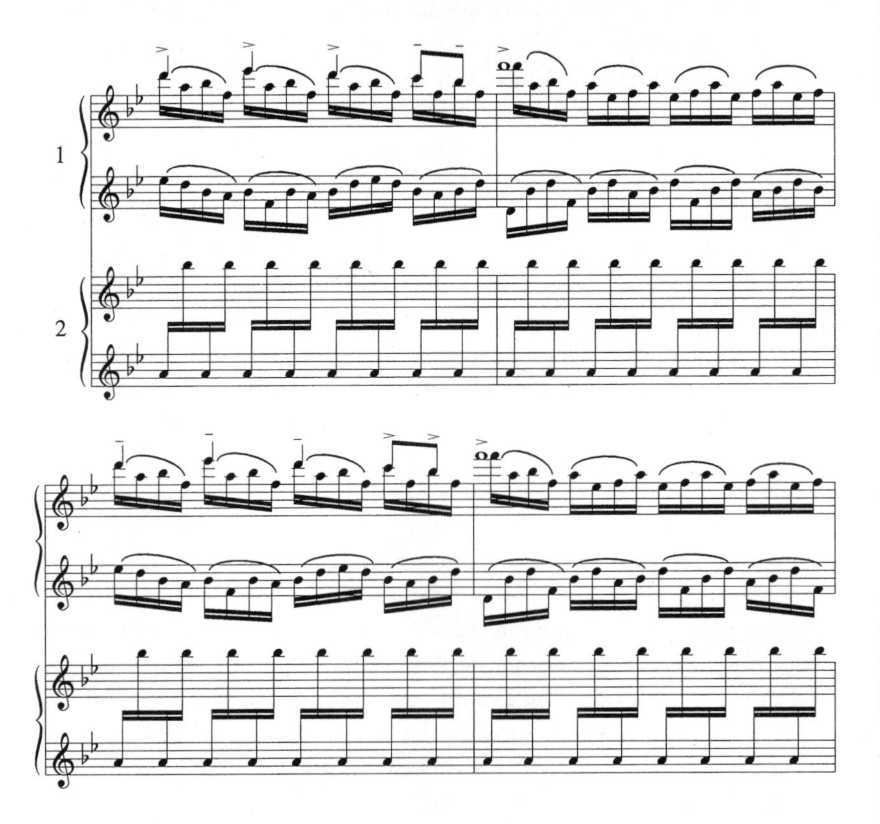

Ex. 9.3. Francis Poulenc, Concerto for Two Pianos, mvt. 1, mm. 173–76.

Poulenc went on to make a further allusion to the gamelan in his opera *Les mamelles de Tirésias* (1944), a work also well known to Britten, who mounted its English premiere at the Aldeburgh Festival on 13 June 1958. Poulenc had originally been engaged to perform a two-piano reduction of the orchestral score with Britten, but in the event the French composer's pathological fear of sea travel forced him to cancel and Britten performed the orchestral parts with Viola Tunnard. Pears took the role of the Husband, and the production (which Poulenc later hailed as "absolute perfection")[20] was directed by John Cranko, who had choreographed the premiere staging of Britten's *The Prince of the Pagodas* in the previous year. The fleeting allusion to Bali occurs at the end of the Prologue, where Poulenc again reworks the sixteenth-note figurations found in the two-piano concerto using pitches identical to those in example 9.1c.

In 1932–33 Percy Grainger transcribed (with the assistance of Norman Voelcker) a recording of "Sekar gadung" for an ensemble of Western tuned percussion and voices, with piccolos representing the *suling.*[21] Grainger went on in July 1935 to draw up with James Scott-Power a full score of a Balinese piece entitled "Berong pengètjèt" from the *gamelan angklung* repertory. Both transcriptions were based on 78 r.p.m. discs recorded in 1928, that of the Balinese piece (Odéon 0-1936a, reissued as Parlophone MO 105) forming the twelfth record in the company's pioneering set "Music of the Orient." Coincidentally, Britten owned a copy of the same disc, although there is no evidence to suggest that he was aware of Grainger's transcription and he did not meet the Australian composer until 1958, well after the completion of *The Prince of the Pagodas.* Grainger's interest in ethnomusicology originated many years before the date of these transcriptions, however: when studying the piano in Frankfurt during the late 1890s he asked his teacher, "If I should win [the Mendelssohn Prize], would they let me study Chinese music with the money?" The reply duly came: "No, they don't give prizes to idiots."[22] His involvement with Western composers' borrowings from the gamelan dates from 1905, when he gave the first British performance of Debussy's "Pagodes" at the Bechstein Hall, London. In 1912 Grainger broke daring new compositional ground in his *Random Round* which explored the phenomenon of stratified polyphony in the context of an aleatory musical structure many years ahead of its time. Each subsection of the work is initiated by a stroke on a Javanese gong and then built up from between ten and twenty melodic variants; choice of variant and tempo are left to the performers' discretion. The motivation underlying Grainger's experiment was the desire to unite performers in spontaneous communal music making, and he commented after a performance of *Random Round* in

London in 1914 that "several of [the 15 musicians] taking part quickly developed the power of merging themselves into the artistic whole. . . . I look forward to some day presenting to English and American audiences a performance of this blend of modern harmonic tendencies with experiences drawn from the improvised polyphony of primitive music."[23]

In 1934, in the midst of working on his gamelan transcriptions, Grainger published a series of twelve lectures under the collective title *A Commonsense View of All Music* that set out his philosophy "to approach all the world's available music with an open mind." The eleventh lecture was called "Tuneful Percussion" (Grainger's idiosyncratic adaptation of the more conventional expression "tuned percussion"), which he deemed to include "Bali bell-orchestras" and "Javanese gong-orchestras." Once more he returned to the cross-cultural significance of Debussy's "Pagodes":

> Of late years the bell-makers of Europe and America have adapted many Asiatic and other exotic tuneful percussion instruments to our European pitch and scale requirements, with the result that we are able to decipher Oriental music from gramophone records and perform them on these Europeanized Oriental instruments whenever we want to. I have tried the experiment of orchestrating Debussy's "Pagodas" (the piano piece he wrote after studying the Javanese gong-orchestras at a Paris exhibition around 1888 [*sic*]) for a complete tuneful percussion group—thus, as it were, turning back to its Oriental beginnings the Asiatic music he transcribed for a Western instrument (the piano). In so doing I am merely giving it back to the sound-type from which it originally emerged.[24]

The lecture was illustrated by a performance of the Debussy piece in its original solo piano guise, followed by Grainger's adaptation for harmonium, celeste, dulcitone, three pianos (twelve hands), xylophone, "metal marimba" and "wooden marimba" (each played by three percussionists), bells, and glockenspiel; the manuscript of the arrangement is dated 1918.[25] Interestingly, Grainger also played on this occasion Ravel's "La vallée des cloches," which he went on to arrange for "tuneful percussion" ten years later. The lecture culminated in a performance of Grainger's own *Eastern Intermezzo* for twenty percussionists.

It was the Canadian-born composer and ethnomusicologist Colin McPhee, however, who deserved the credit for taking cross-cultural borrowings still further than Debussy had dared to attempt. In 1931 McPhee visited Bali for the first time, staying for six months in the region around Kedaton. His involvement with the island's culture became so intense that (after spending three months in Paris) he returned to Indonesia in the following year, building his own house at Sayan and moving in permanently in 1933. McPhee rapidly became established as the leading Western authority on Balinese music, and in 1934 and 1935 he worked with the local composer I Lotring on the modern *kebyar* style of gamelan composition in a special hut constructed on the beach at Kuta. He left Bali in December 1935, but after two years in the Americas, he returned for a final visit in 1936 and stayed until Christmas 1938.[26] After the war McPhee was appointed composer-in-residence at the Huntington Hartford Foundation in Los Angeles, and in 1960 he took up the post of lecturer in composition and Indonesian music at the University of California at Los Angeles. His unsurpassed knowledge of Balinese music was distilled into the encyclopedic volume *Music in Bali: A Study in Form and Instrumental Organization in Balinese Orchestral Music,* published posthumously in 1966. This has remained the standard work on the subject, and it is even used as a textbook at the Balinese Conservatory of the Performing Arts (Konservatorium Kerawitan) in Denpasar—an eloquent rebuff to those of today's ethnomusicologists who scorn McPhee's pioneering work in their discipline as "amateurish."

Certain of McPhee's own compositions were heavily influenced by Balinese procedures, the finest undoubtedly being the toccata for two pianos and orchestra entitled *Tabuh-tabuhan* (1936). Some of McPhee's orchestration is remarkably close to the procedures later adopted by Britten—so close, in fact, that it comes as something of a surprise to discover that Britten probably never heard the work. As Britten and McPhee spent a good deal of time working on two pianos together (see below), it is, however, not inconceivable that McPhee would have shown Britten the score of his work for two pianos and orchestra. McPhee described his approach to the work's instrumentation in a preface to the full score:

> To transfer the intricate chime-like polyphonic figurations of the gamelan keyed instruments and gong-chimes, I have used a "nuclear gamelan" composed of two pianos, celesta, xylophone, marimba, and glockenspiel. These form the core of the orchestra. The various sounds produced by hand-beaten drums are produced by pizzicato cellos and basses, low harp and staccato piano tones. I have included two Balinese gongs of special pitch, and Balinese cymbals, to which are added further gong tones simulated by pianos, horns, etc.[27]

The vigorous outer movements skillfully combine elements borrowed not only from the gamelan but also from Jazz and Latin American popular music, which formed two of McPhee's other great interests. The central "Nocturne" is a setting of a tranquil melody for the Balinese flute (*suling*).

McPhee's most important project as far as his later connection with Britten is concerned was the transcription of certain gamelan pieces for two pianos, three of which were published by Schirmer in 1940 under the title *Balinese Ceremonial Music.* He described the genesis of these transcriptions as follows:

> For the past months I had been engaged in writing arrangements for two pianos of some of the music I had got from Lunyuh, Lebah and even the children. I had already given a little concert and performed a number of these with Walter [Spies], who played the piano very well, on board one of the ships from Java. There had been a "Bali Conference," a visit of Dutch archaeologists, officials and Javanese princes to the island, and two pianos had been sent especially for the event. I was now asked to repeat it in the little harmony club at Den Pasar, and this time I invited the Regents and a few musicians to come and hear what their music sounded like when arranged in this way. They were quite delighted. They had not believed it possible. The percussive sound of the pianos was at times surprisingly close to the sound of the gamelan, and they wondered how only two musicians were able to play all the different parts, the melody, the flowers, the basic tones, the gongs. Only the drums were missing! When it was over the Regent of Tabanan made a quite charming little speech of compliments in which he lamented only that the tuning of the piano did not always match.[28]

The three transcriptions, which originated in 1934, provide a comprehensive introduction to the principal styles of Balinese music, presenting a clear illustration of the two tuning systems on which Balinese gamelans are based: *saih gender wayang* (the Balinese version of Javanese *slendro,* approximating to the intervalic patterns of examples 9.1a and 9.1b) and the more exotically "dissonant" *saih pitu* (commonly found in the pentatonic variant *selisir gong* shown in example 9.1c and related to Javanese *pelog*).

Britten's acquaintance with McPhee and his work dates from the period between 21 August 1939 and 16 March 1942, when Britten and Peter Pears were in residence at the home of Dr. and Mrs. William Mayer on Long Island, New York. The visitors' book from Stanton Cottage, Amityville, reveals that McPhee visited the house as early as 7 September 1939 and was presumably a frequent guest thereafter, since Dr. Mayer took an active and helpful interest in the severe personal problems that plagued the Canadian. During the course of this three-year period Britten and McPhee performed the *Balinese Ceremonial Music* and recorded the pieces in New York in 1941 for Schirmer on a set of 78 r.p.m. discs (513/4).[29] Britten was still involved with McPhee's work in 1944 when he and Clifford Curzon gave the first English performance of the *Balinese Ceremonial Music* at the Wigmore Hall on March 29. The program notes for this concert were provided by Britten himself and were taken directly from the introductory notes written by McPhee for inclusion in the scores published by Schirmer in 1940.

Britten's copy of McPhee's transcriptions is inscribed from McPhee with the words: "To Ben—hoping he will find something in this music, after all. Colin April 1940." This intriguing remark, with its implication that Britten had not yet been convinced that Balinese music was worthy of his attention, is all the more surprising in view of the undeniable influence McPhee's transcriptions appear to have had on Britten's subsequent output. The *Balinese Ceremonial Music* not only introduced Britten to the basic principles of Balinese music but also furnished him with specific material he was later to rework in his own compositions.[30] The second transcription, "Gambangan" (comprising music for cremation rites), contains a distinctive syncopated theme which Britten later incorporated directly into his ballet *The Prince of the Pagodas* (see below, in example 9.5a). "Taboeh Teloe," the final transcription, was ultimately to have a far-reaching influence on Britten's own style. It provides a particularly clear example of the *selisir* tuning at the pitches later adopted by Britten (example 9.1c). The most important feature of McPhee's arrangement is the representation of the three colotomic gong strokes by the dissonant chords in the second piano part, highlighted by pencil strokes in Britten's copy. In the "Sunday Morning" interlude from *Peter Grimes* (1945), Britten transposes both the *selisir* scale and McPhee's punctuating gong triads down a semitone, thus preserving the dissonant effect (example 9.4). It is probably not coincidental that this derivation should occur in a work written while Britten was studying the *Balinese Ceremonial Music* with Clifford Curzon, and McPhee's transcriptions were to continue to leave their mark on Britten's music up to the time of Britten's own visit to Bali in 1956. The *selisir* scale becomes part of Britten's musical vocabulary, alongside the more familiar anhemitonic pentatonic scale. His use of heterophony markedly increases, beginning with the celebrated Prologue to *Paul Bunyan* (rehearsal numbers 11–12), which was written in the United States in 1940, when the composer was in close contact with McPhee. Apart from such obvious textural derivations from the gamelan, Britten's fondness for the sonority of broad gong strokes as a form of punctuation may be found in almost every one of his orchestral scores from the American years onward. Britten's general interest in tuned and metallic percussion reached a climax in *The Turn of the Screw* (1954), which is in several places curiously reminiscent of gamelan sonorities; this suggests that Britten might have heard some of McPhee's tape recordings of live gamelan music, or that some of the composer's gramophone recordings of gamelan music may have been in his possession by this date. It is important to note, however, that whether or not this "gamelan" sound was coincidental or deliberately conceived, the symbolic significance of the celeste and gong sonorities (here representing throughout the opera the fatal allure the two ghosts hold over the children) prefigures all Britten's later conscious reworkings of specific gamelan material.

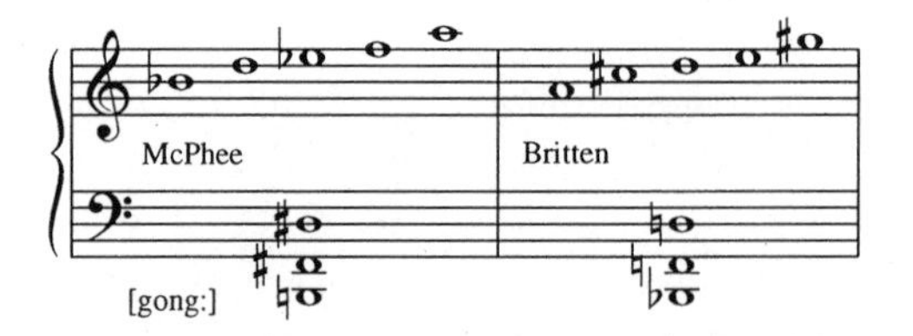

Ex. 9.4. Benjamin Britten's transposition of Colin McPhee's *selisir* scale and gong, used in the "Sunday Morning" interlude of *Peter Grimes.*

There can be no doubt that, by the time of his own visit to the Far East in 1956, Britten's style was in a number of significant respects well suited for the importation of more explicit Balinese material that was to take place in *The Prince of the Pagodas.* Britten's and Pears's world tour commenced in November 1955 with a series of European concerts, and on 6 January 1956 they reached Singapore, where they joined forces with Prince Ludwig and Princess Margaret of Hesse and the Rhine. The Hesses were to accompany the two men for the Far Eastern leg of the tour, and Prince Ludwig wrote an invaluable travel diary that recounts their activities in some detail.[31] The party arrived in Java three days later and attended a dancing lesson in Bandung, which constituted Britten's first experience of a gamelan in live performance. According to Prince Ludwig, the local musicians were delighted when Britten sang out to them the scale on which their music was based, and it comes as no surprise to find that when Britten was exploring the island of Bali between 12 and 25 January he began to compile a detailed set of musical sketches from various gamelan performances. His musical and cultural guide for the Indonesian sojourn was Bernard IJzerdraat, who had at one time performed with the gamelan at Peliatan (a rare privilege for a Westerner) and who assisted Britten with his questions relating to Balinese musical techniques. Most of the gamelan performances witnessed by Britten took place in the small inland town of Ubud, close to the village of Peliatan, and from here Britten wrote to Imogen Holst back in the United Kingdom to declare that the local music was

> *fantastically* rich—melodically, rhythmically, texture (such *orchestration!!*) and above all *formally.* It's a remarkable culture. We are lucky in being taken around

everywhere by an intelligent Dutch musicologist [IJzerdraat], married to a Balinese, who knows all musicians—so we go to rehearsals, find out about and visit cremations, trance dances, shadow plays—a bewildering richness. At last I'm beginning to catch on to the technique, but it's about as complicated as Schönberg.[32]

The most significant event of their stay in Bali was a recording session organized at Britten's request on 23 January, for which "the best gamelan from Ubud" was transported to the studios of Radio Indonesia in the provincial capital, Denpasar. Prince Ludwig recorded his impressions:

In the little studio hall it is like a Turkish bath. After about two hours, the instruments are disposed in the room to everyone's satisfaction. Two pieces are played. . . . Our skulls boom at the fortissimo sections, but there is a great impression of fantastic discipline and of an astonishing empathy in tone and rhythm. We are soaked in sweat and the performers, who are at work from nine to one, are in the same state.[33]

The tape recording resulting from this session was sent to Britten after his return to the United Kingdom by diplomatic mailbag and is now preserved in the Britten-Pears Library at Aldeburgh, Suffolk.

Musical material from Britten's tape recordings and on-the-spot gamelan sketches was to find its way directly into the score of his three-act ballet *The Prince of the Pagodas,* which he had left unfinished on his departure for the world tour. (At least three deadlines for completion of the ballet had been scrapped, but on the very same day that Britten had the recordings made for him in Denpasar, he sent a telegram to the Royal Opera House, London, expressing confidence that the score would be completed by September 1956.) The passages exhibiting the deepest debt to the gamelan occur in Act 2, where Princess Belle Rose finds herself in Pagodaland and the exotic location is represented by an accomplished pastiche of the Balinese *kebyar* style. Britten's "gamelan" is entirely made up of conventional Western percussion instruments, and its music was reconstructed from elements borrowed not only from the Balinese sketches and tape recordings but also from material taken down from various commercial gramophone recordings of gamelan music in the composer's possession.

The two "authentic" Balinese melodies that Britten incorporated are shown in example 9.5. The first (example 9.5a) is identical to the main theme of McPhee's "Gambangan" transcription, although we know from Britten's sketches that he heard it again in live performance during his time on Bali. The second (example 9.5b), used in the ballet to represent the Prince in his magical guise as a salamander, was borrowed from the Balinese tape recordings. Britten's textures throughout this section of the ballet imitate the characteristic stratified counterpoint of the gamelan with unerring accuracy (example 9.6). For the colotomic gong strokes, Britten employs a conventional orchestral gong doubled by sustained double-bass notes of definite pitch; the time-keeping gong known as a *kempli* is imitated by repeated quaver C-sharps on a timpano piccolo and harp *près de la table*; the small metallophones (*gangsa*) and *suling* are represented by rapid figurations on xylophone and two piccolos; vibraphone and celeste provide the slower melody of the deeper instruments (*jegogan* and *jublag*), while three tom-toms serve as substitutes for the two Balinese drums (*kendang*) that lead the gamelan with a wide variety of rhythmic patterns. In other passages the vibraphone acts as a *trompong*, a set of ten horizontal gong-chimes strung in a rack, which often serves as the principal melodic vehicle in *kebyar* music. Britten's percussion section has expanded to include four gongs of different pitches, allowing him to set up sophisticated schemes of colotomic punctuation.

Ex. 9.5a. Balinese melody used by Britten in *The Prince of the Pagodas*.

Ex. 9.5b. Balinese melody used by Britten in *The Prince of the Pagodas*.

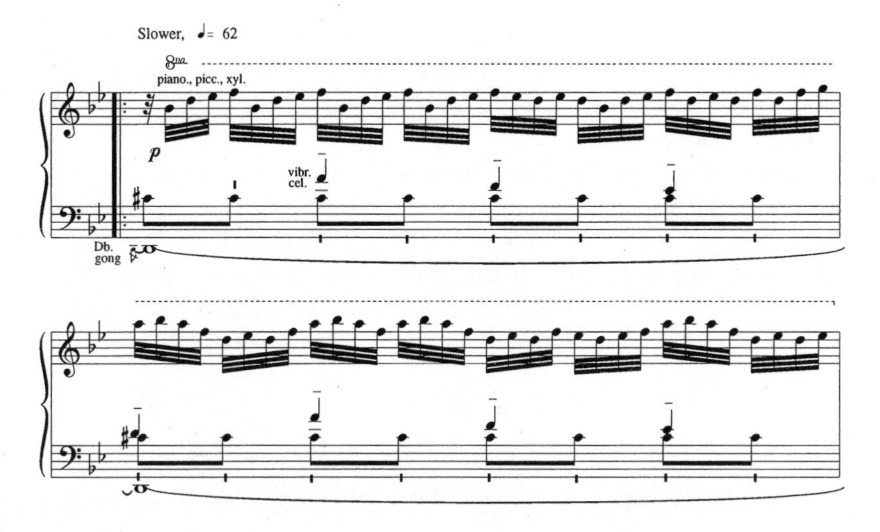

Ex. 9.6. Britten, *The Prince of the Pagodas,* from Act 2, scene 2.

If Britten's "gamelan" music in *The Prince of the Pagodas* makes little attempt to progress beyond highly skilled pastiche, the composer's innate flair for dramatic symbolism was soon to appreciate the potential this distinctive sound world offered for subtle metamorphosis. Nowhere is the compositional synthesis between Eastern and Western elements he later achieved more impressive than in his final opera, *Death in Venice* (1972–73), where he elected to return to the gamelan for a major part of his musical inspiration. In order to capture the allure held over the ageing writer Gustav von Aschenbach by the beautiful young Polish boy Tadzio, Britten cast the latter as a silent dancer accompanied by music predominantly for tuned percussion and colored by gamelan scales, textures, and sonorities. Tadzio's scale (example 9.1d) is identical with a version of Balinese *selisir* notated by Britten on his 1956 manuscript sketches, and it makes its first appearance in the opera in a twelve-tone passage where the pentatonic vibraphone melody to become associated with the boy emerges from a string cluster chord made up from the seven notes not to be found in his scale. As in *Pagodas,* the vibraphone writing directly recalls the idiom of the Balinese *trompong*: indeed, Britten had the earlier ballet sufficiently in mind during work on the opera that he drew up a memorandum of its "gamelan" instrumentation to help him construct similar passages. Example 9.7, from one of Tadzio's silent beach games, shows the same stratification as example 9.6, but here Britten significantly departs from strict Balinese modality. This new tonal flexibility is one of the most notable features of the gamelan dimension in *Death in Venice,* ensuring that gamelan elements function more as allusions than as straight pastiche, and permitting the composer to subject his Balinese-inspired material to considerable tonal and motivic transformations in the interests of dramatic symbolism.[34] A further departure from the earlier ballet is to be seen in the new emphasis placed on wooden tuned percussion instruments in contrast to the metallophones of the *kebyar* gamelans, suggesting that Britten may have been influenced by the xylophones of the *gamelan gambang* or *gamelan pejogedan,* both of which he had heard in Bali in 1956.

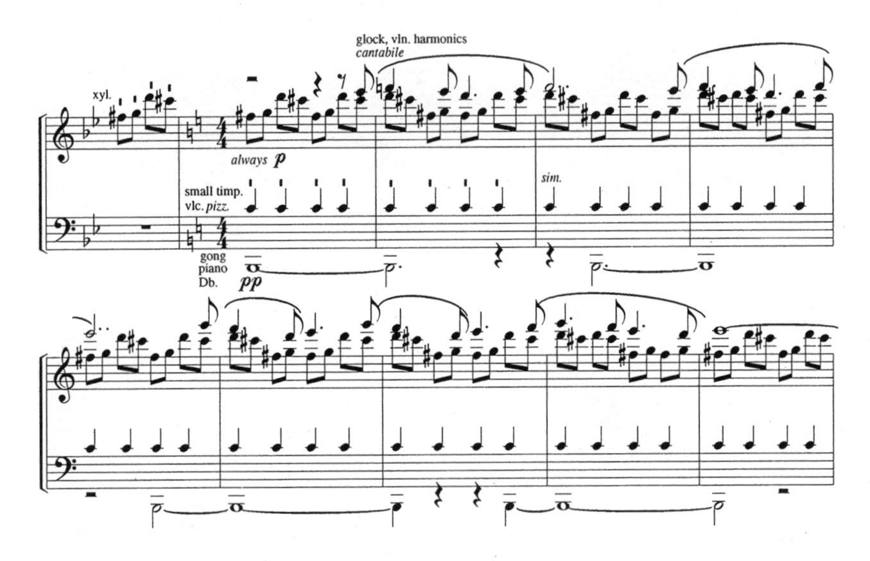

Ex. 9.7. Britten, *Death in Venice,* from Act 1, scene 5.

Death in Venice might not have been the last of Britten's experiments with Balinese music if he had been able to accept an invitation to provide a score for Richard Attenborough's projected film version of Shakespeare's *The Tempest,* to have been shot on location in Bali with John Gielgud as Prospero. Unfortunately Britten's terminal heart condition intervened, and we can only speculate on the exotic musical colors he might have provided if the film had gone ahead. Britten's final opera was destined to be both the culmination and conclusion of his borrowings from the gamelan, embodying a remarkably original synthesis of Western and Oriental procedures and standing as an eloquent monument to its composer's intense involvement with the music of the Far East.

We have seen how Britten encountered Indonesian music for the first time in the United States during the early 1940s, and it is surely significant that his fruitful meeting with Colin McPhee should have neatly coincided with a general rise in the level of awareness of Far Eastern music on the part of American composers. Henry Eichheim had composed a *Javanese Sketch* as early as 1918, and when he subsequently visited Java with Stokowski in 1928 he immediately afterward embarked on an orchestral work entitled *Java* (1929), which shares with Debussy's example its attempt to prolong ostinato patterns in layered textures.[35] Four years later a companion piece, *Bali,* was to follow. Writing to his mentor Henry Cowell in early 1935, McPhee dismissed Eichheim's tone poems as "dished-up impressionism."[36] Cowell (who was at one time Grainger's secretary) had been intrigued by ethnic musics since childhood and began an ethnomusicology lecture course ("Music of the World's Peoples") at the New School for Social Research in New York in the 1920s. Also at this time he discovered the celebrated 1928 gramophone records of Balinese music and listened to them with McPhee. Cowell is best remembered for his systematic exploitation of unconventional timbral effects in writing for the piano, some of which were related to his fascination with the gamelan. Tone clusters (for which he devised a special notation) are first encountered in his piano music at around the same time that Charles Ives was trying them out in his "Concord" Sonata (1911), and a ferocious *ffff* opposition of white- and black-note clusters appears in *Antimony* (1917).

To meet the increasing desire for more eccentric sonorities, the phenomenon of the "prepared piano" emerged in the late 1930s. This blanket term describes the use of various gadgets to modify the normal piano timbre, some of Cowell's innovations having required the strings to be stopped manually or to be struck by using hand-held mallets or plectra. John Cage was influenced by Cowell both in the sphere of ethnomusicology (Cage heard some of Cowell's "Music of the World's Peoples" lectures in New York) and in these radical piano techniques. Cage began by using a gong beater and metal rod to strike the strings in his First Construction in Metal (1939) and went on to introduce the prepared piano in the *Bacchanale* (1940). The latter may have been directly influenced by the sonorities and ostinato patterns of Balinese gamelan music, to which Cowell's lectures had introduced him. His timbral experimentation was not necessarily allied to avant-garde musical material, however, and a work for the etiolated gonglike sonorities of the prepared piano such as *Amores* (1943) is heavily dependent on simple modality and ostinato figurations reflecting Cage's post-Debussian interest in the gamelan. A series of works for percussion ensemble demonstrated this awareness of the gamelan more overtly, especially in the stratified ostinato patterns and *kebyar*-like syncopations of the First Construction in Metal (1939) and *Double Music* (1941). The Second Construction (1940) includes a glockenspiel melody alluding to Balinese scales and punctuated by gong strokes. In 1946 Cage wrote an article entitled "The East in the West" for *Modern Music,*[37] but his Oriental interests were soon to be diverted into the less musically specific realms of Zen and *I Ching* philosophy.

At around the same time that Cage was introducing his prepared piano, his fellow American Lou Harrison (who had studied with Cowell in San Francisco in 1934–35) created a metallic piano sonority by the simple ploy of sticking thumbtacks into the felt covering of the hammers. Harrison collaborated with Cage in some of his percussion ensemble projects of the 1940s, notably *Double Music,* which had used four percussionists and numbered three Japanese temple gongs and six Chinese gongs among its instruments. In 1949 Harrison read McPhee's article "The Five-Tone Gamelan Music of Bali" in *Musical Quarterly* and was sufficiently impressed by it to go to the trouble of writing out all of McPhee's musical examples.[38] In April 1961 Harrison joined McPhee in attending a conference entitled "East-West Music Encounter" in Tokyo; other members of the American delegation were Cowell, Elliott Carter, Virgil Thomson, and the noted scholar of Javanese music, Mantle Hood. In 1963 Harrison's cross-cultural interests assumed an educational dimension when he composed his "Pacifica" Rondo for a youth orchestra comprised of both Western and Oriental instruments. More recent works have included a Double Concerto for violin, cello, and Javanese gamelan (1981), and together with William Colvig he has explored the construction of Western "gamelans" tuned in just intonation and manufactured from thinwall electrical conduit and metal furniture. None of these ventures would have been possible without the extraordinary flowering of ethnomusicology in American universities and the attendant proliferation of genuine gamelans in music departments up and down the country, all ultimately stemming from McPhee's work at UCLA in the 1960s.

If Debussy's emulation of Oriental musical exotica had been symptomatic of a rebellion against the tenets of nineteenth-century Austro-German music, then the so-called minimalist movement that emerged in the 1970s was equally a rebellion against the complexity and pretentiousness of much music produced by the 1960s avant-garde. Minimalist composers saw in the gamelan and other ethnic musics a rhythmic and textural clarity allied to an almost hypnotic repetitiveness, and they absorbed these features into a new idiom that injected a breath of fresh air into contemporary music. Steve Reich studied the drumming of Ghana during the 1970s and became involved with the Balinese gamelan, writing in 1973 that "non-Western music is presently the single most important source of new ideas for Western composers and musicians."[39] These words echoed the prediction of Cowell's made some twenty-five years before (and quoted at the head of this chapter). By the 1980s borrowings from—and more generalized emulations of—Oriental music had become something of a commonplace. An entire disc devoted to gamelan-inspired pieces by young Canadian composers has recently been released, one blending twelve-tone writing with stratified counterpoint, another subscribing to a post-Cageian interest in "ancient Chinese philosophical thought through a Canadian perspective," and another uniting elements as varied as Elvis Presley and Stravinsky in a work designed to be performed on a genuine gamelan from Sunda (West Java).[40] That this extraordinary collection should have originated in Canada is a timely reminder of the seminal importance of that earlier Canadian figure, Colin McPhee.

In an article written in 1933, Cowell declared that the growing tendency on the part of Western composers to borrow material from ethnic musics arose from a "drive for vitality and simplicity. It is not an attempt to imitate primitive music, but rather to draw on those materials common to the music of all the peoples of the world, to build a new music particularly relating to our own century."[41] This remark, strikingly prophetic of the motivation that was to stimulate the absorption of gamelan techniques into the minimalist music of the 1970s, undoubtedly highlights one reason for an interest in Far Eastern music on the part of Western composers. Yet the gradual development of synthetic cross-cultural styles over the course of the past century has proved to be a complex affair, and it remains impossible to isolate a single factor responsible for it. For Debussy, the "vitality and simplicity" of the Javanese gamelan clearly provided a potent alternative to outworn Austro-German modes of musical expression; a similar cultural tension is promoted in Britten's *Death in Venice,* where the composer wished the bright Balinese sounds to contrast sharply with the Germanic self-absorption of Aschenbach's character.[42] But for Britten, and others, the gamelan appears to have had a personal significance extending beyond a surface interest in Indonesian musical techniques. Strong suggestions of supernatural phenomena or of a yearning for an unattainable ideal accompany Britten's appropriations of gamelan effects in his stage works, from the disturbing allure of the ghosts in *The Turn of the Screw,* through the exotic attraction of Pagodaland, to the invocations of peace in *Owen Wingrave* and adolescent beauty in *Death in Venice.* The private significance of these applications of gamelan sonorities has recently been explored by Philip Brett, who has pointed out that Britten, Poulenc, and McPhee were all homosexuals, and that gamelan is a "gay marker" in American music.[43]

On a purely musical level, however, the most satisfying experiments with gamelan material have been achieved by composers who perceived in Indonesian music elements already inherent in their compositional thinking. Both Debussy and Britten had shown themselves to be exploring novel compositional techniques prior to their contact with Indonesian music, and the gamelan acted as a catalyst by throwing up fortuitous musical parallels that focused their attention on the more radical aspects of their own style. As Neil Sorrell has persuasively concluded: "The key word is *influence,* with its suggestion of bringing about a change of course. With Debussy a much more fruitful word would be *confirmation.* It seems far more plausible that what he heard in 1889 confirmed what he had, at least subconsciously, always felt about music, and this experience went far deeper than a desire to imitate something new and exotic."[44]

Similarly, Donald Mitchell has said of Britten's gamelan encounter that "the experience of Bali was not so much the moment of ignition . . . but rather the living confirmation of what Britten had in mind."[45] The only difference in Britten's case arose from his conscious use of specific Balinese material as part of this process of compositional "reinforcement." That the resulting stylistic syntheses have proved to be so enduring adds further corroboration to Cowell's assertion that cross-cultural appropriations "draw on those materials common to the music of all the peoples of the world."

Jazz and Musical Exoticism

GUNTHER SCHULLER

THE TITLE—the thought—immediately prompts a whole cluster of questions. Can Jazz be called an exotic musical language? Was it ever? If so, by whom was it considered such? And when? And why? What is (was) "exotic" about it?

If we concede that Jazz is a musical language—style, idiom, dialect, choose your own word—that developed out of two musical traditions, broadly defined as African (non-Western) and European (Western), and if we further concede that those elements that made Jazz so different, indeed unique (at least in its first sixty or seventy years of existence), were primarily of African descent—a certain type of syncopation, swing, improvisation, call-and-response forms, the close identity of musical and verbal language—then one might readily assert that Jazz was regarded at certain periods and in certain places as an "exotic" music.

To be sure, this was not always a universally held view. Not everyone saw and heard the fascinations of "Negro Jazz." Many, both in Europe and America, considered it irrelevant, beneath recognition, that is, less than exotic, at best a kind of cultural barbarism and hedonism, while many others regarded it as a threat to Western musical culture and, beyond that, a threat to morality and our ethical senses.

But for those with open and curious minds, Jazz—and its predecessors Ragtime and minstrel music, both also Negro musics—did have its fascinations and attractions. Whether people around 1920 (Jazz) or 1900 (Ragtime) used the term "exotic" in reference to these musics I very much doubt. But I am quite certain, regardless of terminology and semantics, that they viewed these "foreign" languages with much the same feelings with which the Viennese viewed "Turkish" music in the late 1700s, or as Parisians saw African art, sculptures, and handicrafts in the late 1800s: a mixture of captivation, allure, fear, mystery, incomprehension—and sheer fascination, especially with their perceived erotic overtones. (It is interesting that the words "exotic" and "erotic," though etymologically unrelated, are often perceived as interrelating and overlapping, as closely associated.)

Most African Americans, of course, would not have conceived of Jazz, Ragtime, and Minstrelsy as exotic, for it was after all their own music. Some other African Americans, on the other hand, considered Jazz, the Blues, and Ragtime as sinful, vulgar music forms, to be assiduously avoided or, at least, to be made aware of their "evil influence." Still other African Americans, especially those who as slaves and ex-slaves were musicians trained in the European tradition, mostly coming to the American south via the West Indies and the Caribbean, may have viewed these indigenous black musics as exotic and strange. There is abundant evidence that many musicians of African descent, trying after Emancipation in the late nineteenth century to assimilate into white musical society, suddenly found themselves forced by economic and racially defined circumstances in the early twentieth century to turn to Ragtime and Jazz, musical languages that previously they had sought to disregard and probably had thought of as unworthy or strange, that is, exotic.[1]

Thus we can see that the question "For whom were Jazz and Ragtime exotic?" has many different answers, viewed from many different social, economic, and aesthetic perspectives. But for most white Americans and Europeans in the early twentieth century, Ragtime and Jazz were, at worst, disreputable and unworthy, therefore practically nonexistent, or at best, remote and exotic.

It was Dvořák, invited to America in 1892 to head a newly founded music conservatory in New York, who began to exhort Americans to appreciate and use Negro and Native American musical traditions, not even—to his credit—as an exotic cultural infusion, but simply as a useful and proud cultural folk heritage. As a Czech (Bohemian) composer who, along with his Eastern European colleagues, feasted on his indigenous folk musics, he could not understand how and why Americans did not put to good use our homegrown, native folk and vernacular traditions. His preachings brought about immediate results in the first waves of "Indianist" movements and a new awareness of Negro musics—spirituals, embryonic forms of Blues and gospel music, secular (work, street, children's) songs, and soon thereafter, Ragtime.

Thus the ground was prepared for an infusion of black musical exotica. It is to Charles Ives's credit (though rarely acknowledged, even today) that he was the first major composer to incorporate black musical elements in his symphonic and chamber works and songs. But there are two things wrong with that assertion, which is correct only when stated in retrospect: namely, that Ives was at the time (1901–2) hardly considered "a major composer" by anybody and, secondly, that he, I am certain, did not regard Ragtime as a form of exoticism. For Ives, who had already brought old church hymns, popular marches, fraternity songs, and Irish-Scottish dance music into his "serious" works, the use of American Ragtime dance rhythms could hardly have been considered a leap into some strange kind of musical exotica. Indeed, for him Ragtime was just another natural addition to an already rich and ongoing, constantly expanding popular musical canon. Ives had never been in sympathy with the efforts of his teachers at Yale and other figures of musical authority of the time to keep "serious" music and more popular musical forms segregated. In Ives's proto-Cageian view of music, all manner of musical forms and expressions could coexist fruitfully and peacefully.

For Claude Debussy, it probably was a quite different matter. In fact, for most Frenchmen, the discovery of Ragtime, as brought to Europe by John Philip Sousa in three successive tours starting in 1900, was a culture shock, seen either as a devastating barbaric degradation of music created by untutored "black savages" or, at the other extreme, as a wonderfully new, rhythmically exciting and energetic export from that unpredictable "New World." And it was not long before Debussy, fascinated with the tantalizing syncopated rhythms of the cakewalk and Ragtime, composed his first tribute to the new idiom, "Golliwog's Cakewalk" (1907), a *Siegfried Idyll*–like gift to his daughter, Chou-Chou. His fascination with Ragtime syncopations did not, however, prevent Debussy from briefly quoting and caricaturing the famous opening motive of Wagner's *Tristan* Prelude. In the midst of "Golliwog's" jaunty dance rhythms Debussy—with outrageous sentimentalizing—parodies Wagner's erotic theme, followed by nose-thumbing Tin Pan Alley chuckles—a tiny snapshot of Debussy's long-time love-hate relationship with Wagner's music and, once again, the juxtaposition of the exotic and the erotic. Not many years later, Debussy contributed two more Ragtime-influenced delicacies to the genre: "Le petit nègre" (1909) and "Minstrels" (1910), both again for piano.

What was it that fascinated "serious" composers with Ragtime? Was it merely the novelty of rhythmic syncopation? If so, why? Had syncopation not been around a very long time? The answer is at least twofold. One, syncopation in classical music, apart from being relatively rare—many famous great composers never used any syncopation at all—was of a different sort from that found in Negro Ragtime; and two, the ragging of rhythms in the melodies and tunes of Ragtime in *irregular* syncopation was juxtaposed with the inexorably *regular* underlying oom-pah accompaniments. It was this contrast between the regular and the irregular—many saw it as more than a contrast, indeed a contradiction, a kind of musical oxymoron—displayed not successively but simultaneously, that captivated people. Undoubtedly many people were drawn to Ragtime's low-life/slumming/sinful aura; most knew, because it was well publicized, that the music was born in the bordellos and honky-tonks of the midwest and south, created by those African-descended exotics: again the connection of the exotic to the erotic.

Syncopation is defined generally as a sudden, temporary "displacement or shifting of the regular metrical accent" (Webster) from strong beats to weak beats. This can be done melodically (horizontally), that is, limited to the melodic or thematic aspects of a piece set against an implied or explicit regular underlying pulse, or it can also be applied vertically to the entire content of a passage, as for example in a series of syncopated chords. Indeed, syncopation cannot occur unless the syncopated rhythms are perceived in relation to a regular beat or pulse. Piano Ragtime, as in Scott Joplin's pieces, for instance, was of the explicit kind, in that the syncopated melodies and rhythms of the right hand were insistently set off against the relentlessly unsyncopated 2/4 eighth-note rhythms of the left hand.

As for the *type* of syncopation that Ragtime offered, it was different from previous sorts of syncopation in two major respects. One, it was set in small rhythmic units, eighth and sixteenth notes (later, in Jazz, in quarter notes and eighths), and thus was bound to occur *within* a single beat, not spread across a series of beats. Second, syncopation in European classical music was phrased "short-long," that is, as notated in example 10.1a. The principle here—however it came about—was that short values would be played short (staccato), long values long (sustained). Ragtime and Jazz reversed that approach, producing an entirely different feeling of syncopation, as shown in examples 10.1b and (for the 2/4 Ragtime version) 10.1c.

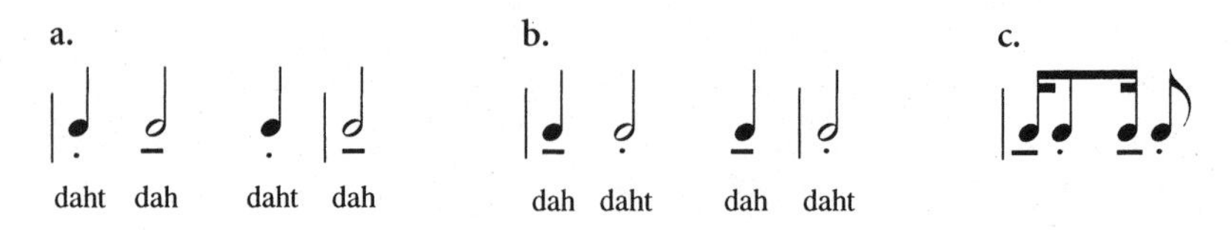

Ex. 10.1a. Syncopation: compared.

Not that everyone in early Ragtime used the "long-short" phrasing, for the Ragtime style, like anything that is new, had to be learned; for many musicians it was an acquired taste. Many formerly classical musicians, switching over to the popular Ragtime craze, brought with them the older traditional way of phrasing syncopations (i.e., short-long). But Ragtime was essentially a dance music, and the black Ragtime innovators (Scott Joplin, James Scott, Tom Turpin, Russel Robinson, et al.) brought a certain degree of swing to the music: not yet a Louis Armstrong kind of swing, which came later, but an earlier sedate form, more like a comfortable, bouncy lilt, which in essence was based on and characterized by the long-short type of syncopation.[2] Eventually most of the best Ragtimers swung their music in that manner, and thus those early twentieth-century syncopated rhythms represented an entirely new aural and physical sensation, not only because of the intrinsic novelty of this particular kind of syncopation, but because of the novel feelings it generated. Our overfamiliarity with such rhythms nowadays, nearly a century later, makes it difficult to appreciate how strange and new such music sounded at the time. But it was perceived as a radical, fascinating breakthrough.

I am not aware of any application of the word *exotic* to ragtime in the critical literature of the time (much of which was vehemently negative—"barbaric," "degenerate," and "dangerous" were frequently used terms), but that surely must have been the sense of the universal reaction to Ragtime, especially among cultured intellectuals and composers in Europe. While some put off Ragtime as the product of the musically illiterate but innately musically gifted Negro "Noble Savage," others recognized the African antecedents of this music. For in truth, the type of syncopation Ragtime featured was an ingenious compression and simplification of the highly complex polyrhythmic, polymetric ensemble musics—drum, ivory horn, and mallet ensembles—of West Africa. Ragtime retained the vestiges, the mildly jagged remains, of those West African traditions, blended with and cleansed, so to speak, by European American harmonic functions and dance or rhythmic forms, especially, of course, the American march as developed and perfected by John Philip Sousa.[3]

By the time Igor Stravinsky discovered Ragtime in 1915, the music was well on its way to being transformed into a newer style that not too long afterward (1917) came to be called Jazz. In the process, Ragtime's notation changed from the universally accepted 2/4 meter (shown in example 10.2a) to 4/4 (example 10.2b). Even Joplin, in his last rag, "Magnetic Rag" (1914), converted to a 4/4 notation, as Stravinsky did in his 1918 Ragtime for Eleven Instruments. Two years earlier, in his *Histoire du soldat,* he had incorporated not only Ragtime (still in 2/4) but another exotic music of the period, the tango, along with the more familiar waltz (which by then had lost most of its exotic/erotic reputation), in three brief dance episodes.

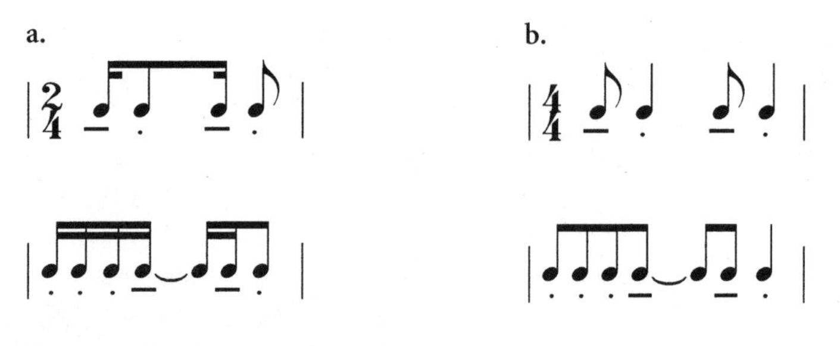

Ex. 10.2a. Ragtime notation.

Erik Satie, always looking for the uncommon, outrageous, and provocative, included bits of Parisian music hall Ragtime as well as pistol shots, sirens, typewriters, and the Cancan in his crowdedly episodic and entertainingly lightweight ballet music *Parade* (1916–17).

American composers of "serious" music, on the other hand (other than Ives), were rather slow in discovering Ragtime as a usable idiomatic element or style, this despite (or perhaps because) of Ragtime's enormous popularity. They probably thought such music was too low-brow, too associated with the underworld and a ragingly commercial Tin Pan Alley. Indeed, it was not until the music had evolved into Jazz that a few composers, such as John Alden Carpenter (*Skyscrapers*) and Louis Gruenberg, began to incorporate Jazz elements into their music. They were soon joined by Aaron Copland, George Antheil, Burlingame Hill, Wallingford Riegger, and, in a sense, George Gershwin. Gershwin, however, approached things from the other direction, that is, from Ragtime to classical music, in his famous 1924 *Rhapsody in Blue,* having come from Ragtime as a pianist and tunesmith and then induced by Ferde Grofé and Paul Whiteman (the latter himself a classically trained violist who had recently moved into the popular field) to try his talented hand at something more than Tin Pan Alley tunes.

Half out of fascination for this new exotic musical breed, half out of patriotic duty—Jazz was, after all, being hailed as America's own homegrown music and musical ambassador to the world—many American composers had a brief flirtation with Jazz that waned quickly by the end of the 1920s. Aaron Copland, for example, made substantial use of Jazz in such works as his concertos for piano and clarinet, but also, in a well-known passage from *The New Music* (1941), dismissed retroactively the relevance of Jazz: "From a composer's viewpoint, jazz had only two expressions: the well-known 'blues' mood, and the wild, abandoned, almost hysterical and grotesque mood so dear to the youth of all ages. These two moods encompassed the whole gamut of jazz emotion. Any serious composer who attempted to work within those two moods sooner or later became aware of their severe limitations."[4] Copland's statement clearly shows the depth of his misunderstanding of Jazz, early on or later. As he communicated to me many times, at best he had been most taken with Jazz's new sounds, inflections, and sonorities, and I am not sure that he ever understood (or wanted to understand) that the Jazz essence really lay in improvisation. Of course, he was not alone in his superficial conception; Maurice Ravel stated repeatedly that Jazz would prove to be the foundation of a national music of the United States,[5] and he proclaimed it an influence in several of his works. But the Jazz he actually knew was the polite, nonimprovised Jazz of the French dance bands of the early-to-mid-1920s; in any case, he later became more negative about Jazz in general, dissociating himself from it and ultimately suggesting that its influence was declining.[6]

Even as these composers and their contemporaries kept a certain (safe?) distance from real Jazz, they were fascinated by its surface characteristics: jaunty, syncopated, Charlestonesque rhythms and the peculiar, seductive, often raucous sounds of saxophones and exotic brass mutes (cup, megaphone, harmon, even the lowly bathroom plunger). They seemed to be totally unaware that Jazz (unlike Ragtime) was essentially an improvised music, much of it spontaneously created, mostly by musicians who could not, or could only barely, read music and could write music in only the simplest, most elementary Jazz-notational terms.

The one European composer who did recognize Jazz's intrinsic improvisatory element—indeed, as many thought, the heart and soul of Jazz—was Darius Milhaud. This bit of wisdom on his part was due not so much to his being a wise Frenchman or a composer of superior intelligence, though he was both, but rather to the happy accident that, when invited by Leopold Stokowski to conduct the Philadelphia Orchestra in 1922 in some of his own works, Milhaud expressed great curiosity about *le Jazz américain* and was consequently taken to hear the real McCoy in Harlem and various other Jazz venues. He was thus the only European composer at that time who actually heard real black Jazz, and he was quickly disabused of the prevalent notion that the polite dance orchestras (such as Billy Arnold's) reigning supreme in Paris and London were "Jazz" orchestras.[7]

In addition, Milhaud brought a small stack of Jazz records with him back to France, studied and listened to them exhaustively, and played them for all his friends. He thus was able to gain a better sense of the spontaneity and looseness, as well as the particular rhythmic and syncopated characteristics of the music, than any of the other important French composers (Georges Auric, Arthur Honegger, Maurice Ravel, Jean Wiéner) who now began to see Jazz as a fascinating exotic novelty.

Milhaud's fine understanding of Jazz—that is, of course, the Jazz of the very early 1920s—is abundantly reflected in his ballet masterpiece *La création du monde* (1923). Several episodes of the work are literally based on or influenced and inspired by the music Milhaud had heard in Harlem and on his recordings, among which were the famous "Livery Stable Blues" by the Original Dixieland Jazz Band and the equally popular "Aunt Hagar's Blues" by W. C. Handy's Orchestra. The similarities between these Jazz sources and Milhaud's transformations of them are striking, especially in the fugue that constitutes the second movement of *La création.* Here Milhaud's thematic material is first stated in the double bass over a percussion ostinato, which approximates what some late-Ragtime, early-Jazz drum virtuosos were playing in those early days (the fantastic Buddy Gilmore, for example, who played with James Europe's famous Society Dance Orchestra). Moreover, this theme bears a close resemblance to many of the more musical "licks" on "Livery Stable Blues." Milhaud's fugue subject features the same typical anacrusis gestures (marked *a* in example 10.3), the alternation of major and minor thirds (Jazz's blue notes, marked *b* in example 10.3), and, of course, the same syncopations and rhythmic displacements (e.g., marked *c* in example 10.3). These stylistic similarities become even more obvious when played on the trombone and trumpet in the second and fourth entries of Milhaud's fugue. Even closer to "Livery Stable Blues," particularly in its fourth and fifth choruses, are the forcefully accented phrases in oboe and cello, bouncing off strong downbeats (in the second phase of the fugue, example 10.4), accompanied by saxophone, horn, and piano in typical Jazz syncopation. The trombone smears Milhaud introduces a bit later were until that time (1923) unheard of in classical music, although by then a commonplace in Jazz, ever since the Original Dixieland Jazz Band's wildly successful first recordings in 1917.

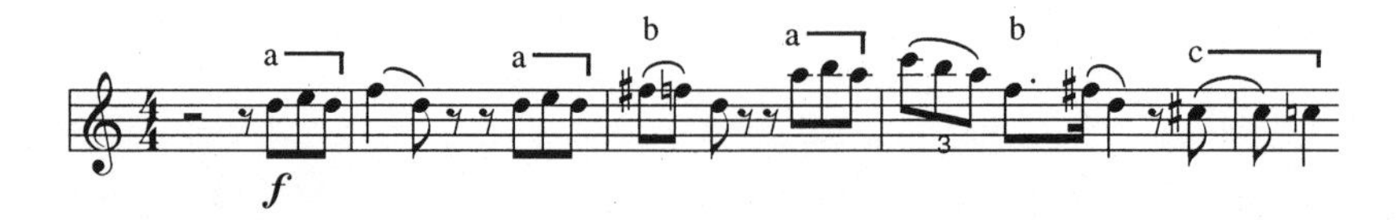

Ex. 10.3. Darius Milhaud, *La création du monde,* fugue subject.

Ex. 10.4. Milhaud, *La création du monde,* fugue, second phase.

The solo "break," featured by many early Jazz players and bands (for example, King Oliver's Creole Jazz Band or Jelly Roll Morton's Red Hot Peppers), makes its appearance in the fourth movement of Milhaud's *Création,* first set forth in a clarinet "chorus" and later recapped in the alto saxophone. This kind of solo playing was as yet new and rare in Jazz, at a time when the New Orleans collective ensemble style was still the vogue. But Sidney Bechet (and a bit later Louis Armstrong) began to espouse that idea as early as 1921, and both of them brought the "solo" concept in Jazz to the fore in the middle and late 1920s. Milhaud probably heard Bechet in New York and may even have heard him leading the clarinets in Will Marion Cook's famous Southern Syncopated Orchestra when they visited France in 1919, and about which Ernest Ansermet, at the time a young thirty-five-year-old conductor, wrote in what must be the first serious critical writing on Jazz:

> There is in the Southern Syncopated Orchestra an extraordinary clarinet virtuoso who is, so it seems, the first of his race to have composed perfectly formed Blues on the clarinet. I've heard two of them, which he elaborated at great length. They are admirable equally for their richness of invention, their force of accent, and their daring novelty and unexpected turns. These solos already show the germ of a new style. . . . I wish to set down the name of this artist of genius; as for myself, I shall never forget it—it is Sidney Bechet.[8]

Interestingly, in Milhaud's work, these solo choruses are accompanied by, in effect, stop-time accompaniments in the ensemble, a technique having acquired considerable popularity among Jazz musicians by the early 1920s, coming out of African American dance patterns and heard as early as Joplin's *Ragtime Dance* of 1906.

By the late 1920s, many more composers, both European and American, had jumped on the Jazz bandwagon. Especially in Europe, the composers and other artists and intellectuals must have still regarded Jazz as an exotic add-on to their music, even though Jazz had by now gained an almost worldwide popularity. It was imitated and played everywhere in one form or another, not only in the capitals and cultural centers of western Europe, but in such far-off places as Czechoslovakia, Hungary, India, Egypt, China, and the Soviet Union (where a lively Jazz tradition of considerable sophistication flourished in the 1920s, until Stalin clamped down on this "bourgeois degradation" around 1928).

In America, however, as Jazz became ever more the quintessential popular music of the United States, one can imagine that for many Americans Jazz simply became assimilated into the cultural fabric, along with Anglo-Irish-Scottish dances, German choral singing, Italian band and parade music, and Argentinean tango music.

In Europe composers began to dabble seriously, if that oxymoron be permitted, in Jazz: one may cite some of Hindemith's early works (*Kammermusik* No. 1); Ernst Krenek's opera *Jonny spielt auf* (which despite its actually limited incorporation of Jazz—limited both quantitatively and qualitatively/stylistically—had a sensational flash success and was within a few years translated into eighteen languages and performed in one hundred cities); Erwin Schulhoff and Boris Blacher, both of whom dedicated their opus ones to Jazz; Kurt Weill's famous and highly successful forays into Jazz (not only, by the way, in the *Threepenny Opera* and *The Rise and Fall of the City of Mahagonny*); Dmitri Shostakovich in Russia; Honegger and Ravel in France; and even in Mussolini's Italy, Alfredo Casella and Mario Castelnuovo-Tedesco.

In a reverse direction, Jazz arrangers and composers in America began to discover "serious" classical music. To them—I can imagine—the music played in Carnegie Hall by the New York Philharmonic must have seemed exotic, naïvely fascinating, and unapproachably distant. In the work of Bill Challis, Ferde Grofé, William Grant Still—all working for the Paul Whiteman Orchestra, which featured among other non-Jazz instruments a violin section—one begins to hear not just Chaikovsky, Rubinstein, and Massenet but quotations and tiny inserts of Stravinsky (*Petrushka*), Wagner (*Tristan*), even Brahms, and of lighter classical fare by Kreisler, Lincke, Romberg, and Herbert.

But suddenly, in the early 1930s, the interest in Jazz on the part of classical composers came to an abrupt halt. It was suddenly no longer exotic: not quite establishment yet, Jazz had been more or less assimilated into the sociocultural landscape and indeed began in some circles to be regarded as an important new mainstream music, with its own distinct history and specific performance practices and traditions.

In all of the music so far mentioned, the Jazz elements and infusions, such as they were, were (1) conceived in very narrow terms, and (2) in any case, never fully realized in performance. Rejecting or unable to understand the improvisatory aspects of Jazz, the composers could not incorporate that all-important ingredient. At best there was a rather superficial understanding of Jazz, a fascination more with its surface than its real content, which is, it appears, in most cases how one culture often views another and hence sees it as exotic, that is, foreign.

Moreover, all of those hundreds of Jazz-captivated works were written for and performed by "classical," that is, notation-reading and nonimprovising musicians, whether it was the Parisian ballet orchestra that premiered Milhaud's *Création* or the Cincinnati Orchestra musicians who first struggled with Gruenberg's 1925 *Jazz Suite*. They could neither improvise nor swing, and in only the rarest instances could they even come close to reproducing the highly idiomatic and varied phrasing and articulative inflections of Jazz. Thus the performances exhibited a certain stiffness, awkwardness, lack of idiomatic feel, that in comparison with real Jazz doomed the whole movement not perhaps to total failure but certainly to a questioning of its validity and contribution to the course of "serious" music.

The whole idea of somehow combining, fusing, incorporating Jazz and classical elements then lay dormant for roughly a decade and a half. It was only in the mid-1940s that a few composers—Leonard Bernstein, Morton Gould, Henry Brant, André Hodeir, myself—began to compose Jazz-related pieces, but, as previously, once again for classical musicians—and this of necessity, because Jazz musicians of that time (with such rare exceptions as Benny Goodman) could not read anything more complex than a Jazz chart and play in the then conventional tonal-chromatic language, essentially the language of the French impressionists of the 1910s and 1920s.

It took another decade or so for the idea finally to germinate that Jazz improvisation, which by the 1950s had developed into an extraordinarily virtuosic and disciplined high art, needed to be considered in any further development along the lines of bringing classical music and Jazz together. But by that time, Jazz had also lost its exotic aura; it was now a great mainstream tradition that, although still meeting resistance to acceptance in some circles, both for social-racial and musical reasons, was now no longer foreign and was de facto more or less culturally assimilated.

The movement eventually acquired the name "Third Stream," exemplifying the offspring from the marriage of the two mainstreams, classical and Jazz. Nowadays it is called by various other more or less commercial labels: World Music, Fusion, Crossover, even New Age. But in its purest, noncommercial incarnation, Third Stream has proliferated greatly in the last three or four decades, embracing not just Jazz but all kinds of ethnic, folk, popular, and vernacular musics, many of which—come to think of it—are being considered by many practitioners and observers as exotic.

Indian Resonances in the British Invasion, 1965–1968

JONATHAN BELLMAN

IN THE mid-1960s' flowering of experimentation in Rock and Pop realms, exotic influences were only beginning to be heard among the new song formats and studio effects. To be sure, isolated exotic experiments had already occasionally appeared. For example, there was a small genre of American Indianist Rock, a kind of vulgar afterbeat to the American Indianist movement in art music (see Michael Pisani's essay in this volume), represented as early as 1960 by the songs "Running Bear (Loves Little White Dove)," written by J. P. Richardson (the "Big Bopper") and recorded by Johnny Preston, and the instrumental "Apache" by the Shadows.[1] The Tokens' famous falsetto-driven novelty single "The Lion Sleeps Tonight" (1961) was based on an African folk song and featured ostensibly African percussion effects.[2] Particularly among English groups (members of the British Invasion, so called because of their influence on the American musical scene), such outward ventures became an article of faith: in 1964 the Kinks (most famous at that time for the hit singles "You Really Got Me" and "All Day and All of the Night") told the British pop music newspaper *Melody Maker* that "we're always looking, searching for new sounds,"[3] and by early 1965 the Yardbirds were listening to medieval liturgical chant and Indian music, also seeking to expand their outlook.[4] But the most recurrent topos in Rock exoticism of the middle 1960s is that of India. Because the heritage of the Raj and London's thriving Indian community made Indian influences more familiar in England than in the United States, this style was predominantly an English phenomenon (though the name "Raga Rock" was coined by a publicist describing a song by an American group).[5] In fact, our perspective of Raga Rock has been shaped by the Beatles, although the story is more complex.

The Beatles

George Harrison's Indian-tinged songs are undoubtedly the best remembered, and as his love for Indian music was profound and ongoing, this is not completely inappropriate.[6] But to remember his work and no other in this context is to ignore the rest of the contemporary London Rock scene.[7] It is also to ignore the testimony of at least one proximately placed individual, which suggests that Harrison's exposure to Indian music did not happen quite the way he said it did.

Harrison's own account, reflecting the mystical inevitability of his adopted Indian perspective, was given in perhaps its most complete form in a *Billboard* interview with Timothy White from December 1992. Harrison speaks here of the filming of the Beatles movie *Help!,* in particular the Rajahama Restaurant scene, which was shot at Twickenham Film Studios on 5 and 6 April 1965. "We were waiting to shoot the scene in the restaurant . . . and there were a few Indian musicians playing in the background. I remember picking up the sitar and trying to hold it, and thinking, 'This is a *funny* sound.' It was an incidental thing, but somewhere down the line I began to hear Ravi Shankar's name. The third time I heard it, I thought, 'This is an odd coincidence.'"[8]

Harrison had found the music faintly familiar and wondered if he had heard similar sounds as a child, when his mother would listen to the shortwave radio, getting broadcasts "from Algeria or somewhere." Then he began to sense that he would soon meet Shankar face to face, which was precisely what happened: "Sure enough, a few months elapsed and then I met this guy from the Asian Music Circle organization who said, 'Oh, Ravi Shankar's gonna come to my house for dinner. Do you want to come too?'"[9]

Harrison and Shankar developed an immediate affinity for one another, and Harrison later went to India to study with him. While the other Beatles were also interested, for Harrison "it unlocked this enormous big door in the back of my consciousness."[10] On 12 October 1965 the Beatles recorded "Norwegian Wood (This Bird Has Flown)," which became the first pop record with an actual sitar on it. The 1966 Beatle album *Revolver* features Harrison's first song composed entirely on the sitar, "Love You To,"[11] and the 1967 album *Sgt. Pepper's Lonely Heart's Club Band* opens side 2 with "Within You Without You," the most developed of Harrison's Indian pieces, an extended song that features

Harrison (and no other Beatles) accompanied by both Indian session musicians and English string players, working from a George Martin arrangement, trying to approximate Indian performance techniques. ("The Inner Light" was a later effort, the B-side of the 1968 "Lady Madonna" single, and also featured Harrison and Indian musicians but no other Beatles.)

There is little that is noticably Indian, other than Harrison's sitar itself (played in a Western fashion), going on at all in "Norwegian Wood."[12] There is no drone, the song is in a waltz meter, and it seems anchored more in the current Western Folk Rock sound than anything more exotic.

By contrast, "Within You Without You" and "Love You To" are full-blown exotic excursions with clear "Indian" markers: persistent drones in the bass, a corresponding harmonic stasis (in these two cases, one harmony sounds throughout each song without changing),[13] and small ornamental slides, particularly in the bass, that suggest Indian bowed instruments. Central to the Indian ethos is the raga-based melodic language Harrison employs. (*Raga* is defined in one standard Indian classical music text as the "modal system of Indian classical music; a melodic mode distinguished from others by a potential variety of elements: selection of pitches [scale type], melodic shape, melodic motive, pitch hierarchy, pitch register, ornamentation, mood.")[14] It is undoubtedly from the ragas that such Indian clichés as the lowered seventh scale degree in major mode, used prominently both ascending and descending, are derived. In addition to this virtually all-encompassing melodic material, "Love You To" and "Within You Without You" use sitar and tablas, and "Within You Without You" uses other Indian stringed instruments as well (svarmandal, tambura, and dilruba).

Predecessors and Contemporaries

The dates are important here, for a simple reason. In late January 1965, three months before Harrison first encountered a sitar on the Twickenham movie set, Ray Davies, the lead singer and primary songwriter of the Kinks, wrote an Indian-influenced song, "See My Friends," which his musical contemporaries found extremely influential. He remembered the episode this way: "We stopped off in India on the way to Australia. I remember getting up, going to the beach and seeing all these fishermen coming along. I heard chanting to start with, and gradually the chanting came a bit closer and I could see it was fishermen carrying their nets out. When I got to Australia I wrote lots of songs, and that one particularly."[15]

It is only fair to mention that one of the Kinks' producers of that time, Shel Talmy, felt that Davies wrote in the Indian idiom only after hearing a song by the guitarist Jon Mark (later a sideman with John Mayall) that Talmy had played for him and suggested as a model.[16] Regardless (it is perhaps only human nature to claim a piece of such a good idea), Davies was able to achieve an Indian sound by substituting a controlled feedback for the sitar drone. He recorded his twelve-string Framus guitar with it placed near the amplifier, then he substantially compressed the frequencies, which resulted in the thin, surging, sitarlike effect.[17]

Historically, the song may have even been more influential than is generally assumed. Barry Fantoni, an illustrator and saxophonist who had been associated with the Kinks from their earliest years, recounts an episode involving some of the Kinks' contemporaries and their immediate response to "See My Friends": "I remember it vividly and still think it's a remarkable pop song. I was with the Beatles the evening that they actually sat around listening to it on a gramophone, saying 'You know, this guitar thing sounds like a sitar. We must get one of those.' They were vandals. Everything Ray did they copied."[18]

Partisan and problematic as this anecdote is, it is not necessarily untrue.[19] "See My Friends" was released in late July 1965; after entering the British charts on 5 August it became a hit, being overall no. 18 for the month of September.[20] This means that it saturated the London airwaves the very month before Harrison and the Beatles recorded "Norwegian Wood" in October, and a substantial period of time before Harrison's later, more recognizably Indian efforts were written and recorded.

Of course, Fantoni's version of events is unverifiable and (not surprisingly) has been utterly ignored in the Beatles literature. However, Fantoni (and the Beatles, if his memory is clear) would not have been alone in finding the song remarkable: the Who's Pete Townshend, another mid-1960s Rock visionary, realized exactly what Ray Davies had done. Here is his assessment: "'See My Friends' was the next time I pricked up my ears and thought 'God, he's done it again. He's invented something new.' That was the first reasonable use of the drone—far, far better than anything the Beatles did and far, far earlier. It was a European sound rather than an Eastern sound but with a strong, legitimate Eastern influence which had its roots in European folk music."[21]

Townshend's point is a crucial one: for a Western pop listener, an Indian Rock blend had to retain a sufficient amount of traditional Western elements to be successful. What Ray Davies did (and Harrison did not do) was to allow more than one chord to enter the picture. Because traditional Indian music is based on drones and not on harmonic progressions, Harrison wrote songs in which the prevailing harmony did not change. In Davies's "See My Friends," almost the entire verse is based on a drone, but the harmony changes at the very end, and a contrasting chord progression appears in the middle section. The overall sound remains jangling, drone-based, and unquestionably quasi-Indian, all that is necessary in a pop-exotic context, and while the flattened seventh scale degree is melodically prominent, it is used with no functional pull to the subdominant whatsoever. The variety expected by Western ears is still provided by the extremely judicious use of contrasting chords.

"See My Friends" is in my opinion at least equaled by the Kinks' only other contribution to the genre, "Fancy," from their 1966 album *Face to Face*, recorded when, of the Beatles' sitar pieces, only "Norwegian Wood" was known. Not only is Ray's Framus-generated drone easier to hear, but there are more *faux*-Indian slides in the bass, and the rhythmic feel suggests a more familiar kind of exoticism: the song's slow-to-moderate 4/4 meter with a subdivided second beat radiates the kind of undulating snake-charmer motion that has signified the Seductive East for a century and a half.[22] The lyrics are somewhat more suggestive of an exotic topos ("My love is like a ruby / that no one can see / only my fancy"), and while the song has a second chord, we hear it only after two full verses over the drone and a vocal flourish. As this chord is a second-inversion subdominant sounded over the same bass, there is no sense of harmonic impetus requiring movement; the drone sounds throughout. It is perfectly set up, and a chord that might have gone unnoticed becomes a major event, highly effective and expressive.

Face to Face was released in October 1966. Davies has dated the composition of "Fancy" after the song "Sunny Afternoon" came out, in June of that year.[23] Positing a July–early August composition date (given recording–release turnaround time, it could not have been much later), this means that he still would not have heard any strongly Indian-influenced songs from Harrison and the Beatles, because "Love You To" was released only in August (John Mendelssohn's claim that "Fancy" preceded "Love You To" by several months is therefore mistaken).[24] But by the same token, since "Love You To" was recorded on 11 April of that year,[25] Harrison could not have been influenced by "Fancy," although (as Fantoni claimed, and as the chronology makes clear) he could well have been by the earlier "See My Friends."

Other sitar-based experiments were taking place contemporaneously. In late June 1965, five months after "See My Friends" was written, one month before its release, and just two to three months after Harrison picked up a sitar for the first time, the Yardbirds released "Heart Full of Soul," a biting, minor-key single with no exotic lyrical content that was an immediate hit on both sides of the Atlantic; in Britain, it was no. 2 for the month of July.[26] Jeff Beck's famous wailing guitar riff had been intended for sitar, which would have put it well before "Norwegian Wood," had the plan been followed through. Here is how Yardbird Jim McCarty remembers the recording session:

> The riff on the demo suggested a sitar, and Giorgio [Gomelsky, the Yardbirds' manager] actually hired an Indian sitar player and tabla player, God knows where from—probably the Indian restaurant where he'd just had lunch. We walked into the studio and saw these two sitting on the floor, in the full gear, with Roger, the engineer, trying to mike up their instruments. We spent a couple of hours trying to get a decent sound, but it didn't work; it sounded terribly thin. Then someone had the bright idea that Jeff could produce a sitar-like effect on the guitar, which he did.[27]

Fine as Beck's lead is, it is regrettable that the sitar recording was unsatisfactory. An outtake from the earlier portion of the session survives, with the sitar part intact (and, indeed, too soft), and the Eastern-exotic flavor is much increased.[28] But overall, "Heart Full of Soul" has markedly less specifically exotic content than "See My Friends," relying as it does on a more familiar Rock beat and more frequent chord changes.

Since it was released a month before "See My Friends," "Heart Full of Soul" would have been recorded before the Yardbirds could have known anything about Ray Davies's Indian experiment, much less Harrison's. In early March 1966 the Rolling Stones recorded "Paint It Black," which featured Brian Jones on sitar and is somewhat related in mood (and lack of Indian lyrical content, despite the use of an Indian instrument) to "Heart Full of Soul."[29] As far as actual recordings, the Stones could only have known about "See My Friends," "Heart Full of Soul," and "Norwegian Wood" at this time; none of the Beatles' developed Indian pieces had yet been released.

All of this serves to illustrate a central point about the genesis of Raga Rock: easily lost in the blizzard of Beatles literature and retellings of Harrison's introduction to Shankar is the fact that experiments with Indian instruments and musical content really happened simultaneously, in several quarters, some months before Harrison's first efforts. Many of the musicians in the London Rock scene knew each other, and while there is no firm data showing that they traded sitar experiments and other Indian exotica around, it is hard to imagine that such influences would not have been "in the air."[30] And while much has been made of the Beatles' "Norwegian Wood" because it was the first pop record to use a sitar, it was recorded well after the Kinks' clearly Indian "See My Friends" was released and was first only because the Yardbirds' recording technology failed.

Music, Drugs, and Meditation

For the public at large, an awareness of Indian culture occurred neither before nor in tandem with these widely disseminated musical experiments; it lagged behind. Yet a clear connection developed between cultural and musical worlds. The main publicists for Indian culture (however imperfectly understood) were the Beatles, and the catalyst would be their infatuation with the Maharishi Mahesh Yogi, a Hindu monk and apostle of Transcendental Meditation (TM), who catered especially to celebrities. And it was through the specious connections between sitar music, the Maharishi, drugs, and the Beatles that Raga Rock acquired its sense of the slightly forbidden.

A Western awareness of India had been growing, particularly as growing numbers of young people found themselves in Asia for other (often drug-related) reasons. It is true that opium poppies were grown in and exported from India, but that country was no more than a medium-size producer of that particular crop. To Indians, of course, there was no connection between meditation and drugs, and the fact that "hippie-type visitors" perceived similarities between the two was insulting and annoying.[31]

Certain Westerners were perceiving a connection they wanted to exist, in other words. To the practitioners of this kind of meditation, which was based on ancient Indian traditions, it was thoroughly traditional, nonsubversive, and nonchemical. The entrance of the Beatles, heroes of the youth culture, onto this particular scene only made the connections easier to make.

The Beatles' well-publicized meeting with the Maharishi would not occur until August 1967, when the other members of the group would come to share Harrison's interest in him. However, as this was more than a year after "Love You To" had been recorded and some five months after the recording of "Within You Without You," Harrison had already been involved with Indian music for some time. For all the appearance of a connection, then, the Maharishi could have had absolutely no role in the Beatles' initial interest in Indian music.

They were with the Maharishi when their manager Brian Epstein died of a drug overdose, and the Maharishi was able to offer them comfort, explaining that death meant little, that Epstein had only gone on to the next stage, that he would be reincarnated. Later, the group even made a pilgrimage to the Maharishi's camp in India to study with him, but they would become disenchanted with him and leave. In fact, Lennon's extraordinarily bitter "Sexy Sadie," from the Beatles' 1968 "White Album" (the official release title was simply *The Beatles*) was originally called "Maharishi"; Lennon agreed to "Sexy Sadie" to avoid legal complications, at the urging of the other Beatles.[32] The lyrics, which otherwise remained unchanged, spoke clearly of disaffection: "She made a fool of everyone. . . . However big you think you are . . . you'll get yours yet . . . we gave you everything we owned just to sit at your table."

That Harrison had been interested in Ravi Shankar long before his interest in the Maharishi and TM, and that TM was based on ancient Indian traditions and had nothing whatever to do with drugs—these were subtleties lost on the transgression-addled 1960s public. Even distinguished cultural critics tended to make facile connections between India and Indian-influenced music, TM, and the much-celebrated and feared culture of drugs and psychedelia.

Richard Poirier, in his 1967 *Partisan Review* essay "Learning from the Beatles," offers this glib commentary on "Baby, You're a Rich Man":

> The sitar, an instrument Harrison studied in India for six weeks with the renowned Ravi Shankar . . . here suggests not the India of "Within You, Without You" evoked on the Sgt. Pepper album, the India of the Bhagavad Gita. It is rather another India, of fabulous riches, the India of the British and their Maharajahs, a place for exotic travel, but also for josh [*sic*] sticks and the otherworldliness of a "trip." . . . [The Beatles were] once close to home both in fact and in their music but [are] now implicated not only in the Mersey beat but in the Ganges sound, in travel to India and "trips" of a kind for which India set the precedent for centuries.[33]

Poirier's clumsy emphasis on the parallel meanings of "trip" and the involvement of various Beatles with LSD was not a rogue action: locating TM on the same line as drugs, if perhaps a bit further along, had been done (intentionally or not) by the Beatles themselves. Harrison put it this way in an interview with the *Los Angeles Free Press:* "Acid is not the answer, definitely not the answer. It's enabled people to see a little bit more, but when you really get hip, you don't need it." Of LSD, Paul McCartney said to Hunter Davies of the *London Sunday Times,* "It was an experience we went through, and now it's over we don't need it any more. We think we're finding other ways of getting there." After offering these two quotations, Poirier opines that "in this effort they're apparently being helped by Maharishi Mahesh Yogi, the Indian founder of the International Meditation Society."[34] As these comments postdated the Beatles' introduction to TM, the implication was clear: TM was the Next Big High after drug use.

Advocates of and publicists for TM were even clearer about the connection between the two, the natural progression from chemical to meditational highs. An odd little volume from 1968, edited by Martin Ebon, entitled *Maharishi, The Guru* and published by Signet books, gives ample evidence of this viewpoint.[35] The book is a collection of rave essays by favorably disposed journalists and followers of the Maharishi, including such pieces as "Beyond Pot and

LSD" and "He Turned Us On!" The Beatles are paraded about in the volume, in two pieces particularly. The first, "The Beatles Without Mask," outlines how TM became the mature choice of these four enlightened young people, who were too experienced to bother with drugs any more. A David Frost TV interview with John Lennon and George Harrison is also included, and the two Beatles talk of their past drug use and of how different meditation was. (By the time the book came out, of course, the Beatles had already broken with the Maharishi.)

So, despite the Maharishi's repeated statements that TM had nothing to do with drugs and his oft-repeated demands that students stay clean for fifteen days before they started learning TM, and despite Harrison's prior Indian experience, drugs and TM were frequently assumed to belong to the same cultural matrix. Here, for example, is the page one advertising blurb from *Maharishi, The Guru:*

> **BEYOND**
> **POT**
>
> **AND**
> **LSD**
>
> is the title of a chapter in this fascinating book. In it, the California hippies tell how they gave up drugs in favor of Maharishi's non-drug turn-on, a trend that can be seen in more and more of the psychedelic generation—and among men and women from all walks of life—as Maharishi tours the U.S. with his message of spiritual regeneration.

A quick browse through the book leaves no doubt as to its tenor and message. Krishna Singh uses the Maharishi's own words in describing the nature of the Transcendental State of Being—a consciousness "absolute" and "pure," beyond all conscious sensory, mental, or perceptual experience. It lies beyond all thinking and feeling, all sense of sight, hearing, touch, smell, or taste.[36]

Moreover, Rock musicians such as the Beatles, by virtue of their mere presence and visibility, lent celebrity status to the TM movement itself. Chester Butterworth enthuses:

> And because they are farther out than most, . . . it was the Beatles who had the first real Western crack at Maharishi's transcendental meditation. George . . . moved from playing the guitar to the sitar. . . . Then he got the other three to share his enthusiasm for everything from incense to Hindu mythology. They don't do things by halves. George had his minicar painted with Indian symbols.[37]

Don McNeill describes the Maharishi's meeting with other musicians on his fall 1967 tour: "The next day, he [the Maharishi] spoke privately with Donovan,

Mick Jagger, and several members of the Grateful Dead and the Jefferson Airplane, an audience which yielded other disciples. 'It was really boss,' [the Grateful Dead's Bob] Weir recalled, 'He turned us on.'"[38] Finally, TM was most clearly situated within the (apparently codified) hippie cosmology by James Crenshaw:

> Since the hippie's avowed aim is to "have an ecstatic, beautiful, productive, wide-awake, self-realized life," experiments with various drugs, especially the mind-expanding variety, appealed to him.
>
> The fact that impressed us most, though, was that "meditation" à la Maharishi is replacing even these drugs for many of the hippie practitioners. It has become more than a substitute for the drug experience. . . . Those who have fallen under the Maharishi's spell would not consider going back to drugs.[39]

The Moody Blues: Raga Rock Becomes a Cliché

By 1968 these pervasive cultural connections had, finally, come to be reflected in the musical world. Moreover, what had been musically experimental had become a kind of convention, as was demonstrated by a prominent album released that year by the Moody Blues, *In Search of the Lost Chord.* The Moody Blues were an English Art Rock band who built a reputation on superb musicianship coupled with a fairly windy mysticism, and this was the first album on which the band members themselves played *all* of the instruments, some twenty of which are listed on the record jacket. These include sitar and tablas, which like other instruments are played by two or more "Members of the Expedition," as the jacket has it. The jacket not only provides an explanation of the mantra concept, and of the word *Om,* but also features a large, geometric figure called a yantra, which "is used much the same way as a *mantra,* though visually."

In glaring contrast to the Raga Rock music of 1965–67, *In Search of the Lost Chord,* taking its cue from the zeitgeist, was completely dependent on the connections between drugs, meditation, and India, and it is about journeys, physical and chemical as well as spiritual. The journeys are, if one takes them literally, somewhat random; a song about the explorer David Livingstone coexists with a song that claims that "Thinking is the Best Way to Travel," while other songs entitled "Visions of Paradise" and "Voices in the Sky" evoke the celestial. More specific songs address both drugs and Indian culture: a frank paean to the LSD high priest Timothy Leary ("Legend of a Mind") amounts to an endorsement of psychedelics, while the sitar-and-tabla-laden "Om" exalts meditation. Of course, if everything is taken metaphorically rather than literally, the album can be seen to deal with The Great Journey (even the lighthearted "Dr. Livingstone, I Presume," which sounds in parts like an English music hall number, features a line, "We're all looking for someone").[40] Still and all, the mystic and philosophic content of the album is superficial, which is why it is so effective in connecting TM, India, drugs, exotic musical instruments and styles, and everything else into the same blandly mystical constellation of mind expansion; any deeper thought on the issue would have exposed the flaws of the approach.

"Om," the final song, has the clearest use of Indian musical elements. The lyrics, predictably, are about meditation, the infinite, and so on. Between the second and third verses, where a guitar solo might be expected, the beat is suspended and a long passage for sitar and tabla uses, rather than a fixed Western beat, the gradual *accelerando* characteristic of Hindustani (North Indian) musical performances.[41] In marked contrast to the earlier "Raga Rock" songs, the lyrical content is complementary to the instrumentation and style involved.

Coming out as relatively late as it did, "Om" lacks the earlier Raga Rock songs' sense of riskiness and immediacy, since the Indian topos and use of sitar were already well established on the airwaves and in musical culture. On the other hand, the Moody Blues' level of musicianship and recording expertise far outshone what had appeared previously. In the brief period since 1965, however, India had acquired much cultural baggage. Far from experimenting, in evoking those associations the Moodies were betting on a sure thing.

In a sense, *In Search of the Lost Chord* conventionalized the subject matter of its lyrics in the same way it did the use of Indian instruments and styles. What had previously evoked the forbidden and experimental was now somehow made accessible, even prosaic. When meditation, LSD, mind travel, India, Voices from the Sky, and even Dr. Livingstone are placed carefully and neatly—almost systematically—next to each other on a record album, the composite effect is less vivid and alluring than safe, in a kind of shrink-wrapped way. One imagines the adolescent record owner: Here is my record album about Journeys: physical, chemical, and spiritual. I keep it on my shelf, right *here*.

The Exotic and the Personal

The various Raga Rock artists had distinct reasons for making use of Indian instruments or styles. Of the earliest wave of Rock exoticists, George Harrison at least had developed a passion about Indian philosophies and ideals when he took interest in Indian music, and he sought to write Indian-influenced songs so as to evoke something for which the normal Rock language was unequipped. But Harrison was, as we saw, not the first to work in this area. The Yardbirds' and Rolling Stones' efforts seem to be purely musical experiments, in contrast, seemingly less attached to any exotic topos or lyrical content than to an attractive new sound. The Moody Blues were so long after the fact that all the symbolism had been spelled out for them already, and they may even (bluntly) be said to have been cashing in. But with the Kinks' Raga Rock songs, Ray Davies had a very different motivation.

Davies had also used the Indian ethos to access the inaccessible, but he was originally singing about an area far more remote and taboo to Rock listeners of the time than mere India. As he put it in an interview with Maureen Cleave, "See My Friends" was about homosexuality:

> It wasn't fiction. I can understand feeling like that. . . . It's about being a youth who is not sure of his sexuality. I remember I said to Rasa [his wife] one night, "If it wasn't for you, I'd be queer." I think that's a horrible thing to say to someone of seventeen, but I felt that. I was unsure of myself.

For the mainstream public, it seems, the real message of "See My Friends" hardly got out at all. Davies even went so far as to discuss the song with Keith Altham of the English music paper, the *New Musical Express,* who was unsympathetic to the song and Ray's explanations about duality, bisexuality, and so on. The resistance to the song may even have been a good thing, Davies felt, lending it a kind of notoriety.[42]

Davies's other Indian-influenced Kinks record, "Fancy," deals not with sexuality but with other matters profoundly personal and revealing: relation to and protection from others, desire, misconceptions. The biographer Jon Savage felt that "'Fancy' stands as one complete statement of Ray Davies's philosophy." Davies himself provided further commentary on the song and its lyrics, crediting his old Framus guitar with the ability to sustain one note, after the fashion of Indian music, and characterizing the line "my love is like a ruby that no one can see" as possessive, and the line "no one can penetrate me" as virginal and self-protective. Even more interestingly, he pointed out that a female friend objected to the words "fancy all the girls you see" on the grounds that they were too specific, but that he disagreed because they made people feel at ease. Sometimes, he felt, a songwriter just had to "put something normal in."[43]

That Davies's friend objected to the explicitly heteroerotic line, the line that masked the issue addressed in "See My Friends," and that he justified it on the basis of not wanting to shock audiences all the time, is revealing. While not explicitly dealing with sexual matters, this song uses an exotic musical language, to that point only heard in the Rock world in "See My Friends" and, to a more limited extent, the aforementioned songs by the Yardbirds and Rolling Stones, to show us the inner man, carefully and successfully self-protected. Perhaps Davies's friend was troubled by the disguising of a key piece of the puzzle: homosexuality, the very issue around which "See My Friends" had centered. The relationship between the two songs was not lost on Savage, who singled out the drone device, hallmark of probably the most obvious and available "Other" music known to Davies, as the vehicle he used to get to his "innermost feelings" in both songs.[44]

Homoeroticism was too dangerous for the world of mid-1960s popular music, where gender roles were clearly spelled out. The thread was not picked up by other Rock musicians (or even, it seems, much noticed by the public). But the Kinks' use of Eastern musical influences to allude to personal and sexual matters is directly in keeping with historical uses of exoticism as signifier for forbidden sexuality, starting with the "Turkish" style, although there is no indication that Davies was aware of any of these "exotic" repertories.

The artistic (as opposed to commercial) success of the Kinks' two Indian-tinged songs relative to Harrison's early efforts in that area illustrates another key point about exoticism in general, touched upon by Pete Townshend. For Western music, whether art music or Rock, to achieve a successful "exotic" effect, it cannot have, ironically, too much ethnomusicological verisimilitude. Our ears are anchored in the familiar. If too much of the home product gives way to exotic elements, the end result sounds like an unconvincing copy of a foreign music: not very evocative, paradoxically, of that exotic frame of reference. There is a profound difference, Edward Said has reminded us, between Orientalism and the actual East. "Fancy" in particular suggests "the Exotic East" to us with every gesture that we Westerns subliminally understand to be Indian: drones, harmonic stasis, flattened seventh scale degrees, keening vocals, hypnotic beat, ragalike melody, and lyrics that suggest that the singer's inner reality is at least as real as the outer, physical one. But the framework remains Western: the beat remains regular, the structure is strophic, and there is a chord change. "Fancy," like "See My Friends," evokes this mood without ever suggesting that we are listening to anything other than Western musicians. The exotic card is thus not overplayed.

In retrospect, it is clear that Raga Rock's most common associations, TM and drugs, were not intended by the Kinks, Yardbirds, or Beatles, but were more the result of other forces active in popular culture, only later to be made explicit by the Moody Blues.[45] The historical pattern is familiar: original intent is superseded by something more resonant to the popular mind. What is striking is how quickly it all happened. Perhaps, in the second half of the twentieth century, this is no surprise after all; an idea is no sooner born than it is available to the world through mass media, and the birth-to-death evolutionary curve of at least the first phase of such a musical-cultural development is bound to be much shorter than it would have been in previous eras. Memories are shorter, and awareness more fleeting. The end result was, in this case, that a stylistic strain in Rock music that sought to evoke the profound, the enlightened, and the timeless appeared and disappeared in the proverbial wink of an eye.

That is, the original form *all but* disappeared; given the speed with which Raga Rock became a cliché, there may have been no other alternative. But Indian influences in Rock and popular musics did not completely cease with the Moody Blues; in fact, they continue to appear up to the present time. On the one hand, after the late 1960s, the approach became broader: more musicians have sought an actual East-West blend, as opposed to merely a piquant taste of the East.[46] But on the other hand, there is a nostalgia factor, too: a 1994 song by Sam (formerly Leslie) Phillips, "Baby I Can't Please You," alternates a flawlessly Beatlesesque Raga Rock chorus with a completely different musical style in the verses, a Mersey Beat sound more reminiscent of the Beatles' "From Me to You." Raga Rock thus becomes less an exotic style than "one of the things the Beatles did," less evocative of the Exotic East than of other homegrown Indian-influenced exotica. There is a delightful irony in this: a stylistic strain in Rock and Roll that referenced the time-worn trope of the Eternal Orient ends up by reminding us more of *us thinking about* the Eternal Orient than the Orient itself. Raga Rock is thus like other musical exotica in that it pairs, perhaps in equal measure, an exploration outward with a penetrating look in the mirror.

Appendix: Selected Discography

The purpose of this brief discography is to give information on availability, as of this writing, of the songs discussed.

BEATLES

Inner Light. *Past Masters,* vol 2. CD. Capitol/EMI 90044.
Love You To. *Revolver.* CD. Parlophone 46441.

Norwegian Wood. *Rubber Soul.* CD. Parlophone 46440.
Tomorrow Never Knows. *Revolver.* CD. Parlophone 46441.
Within You Without You. *Sgt. Pepper's Lonely Hearts Club Band.* CD. Parlophone 46442.

KINKS

Fancy. *The Kink Kronikles.* CD. Reprise 6454.
See My Friends. *Kinks-Size Kinkdom.* CD. Rhino Records 75769.

MOODY BLUES

In Search of the Lost Chord. CD. Polydor 820 168.

SAM PHILLIPS

Baby, I Can't Please You. *Martinis and Bikinis.* CD. Virgin 39438.

ROLLING STONES

Paint It Black. *Hot Rocks, 1964–1971.* CD. ABKO Records 6667.

YARDBIRDS

Heart Full of Soul (commercial release). *Greatest Hits,* vol. 1, *Smokestack Lightning.* CD. Legacy Records 75895.
Heart Full of Soul (sitar version). *Greatest Hits,* vol. 2, *Blues, Backtracks, and Shapes of Things to Come.* CD. Legacy Records 48658.

NOTES

INTRODUCTION

1. Representative examples in this area are cited in the essays by, among others, Miriam K. Whaples, Linda Austern, and Ralph Locke.

2. Similarly, in discussing the interest in Asian religions held by the American Transcendentalists, Arthur Versluis distinguishes between "negative" (that is, disparaging) Orientalism and "positive" Orientalism, which saw in the East eternal truths. Both views, be it said, can be simplistic, and neither does justice to the complexity of the East-West cultural encounter. See his *American Transcendentalists and Asian Religions* (New York: Oxford University Press), 5, 184–234.

3. Joseph Kerman, *Opera as Drama* (1956; rev. ed., Berkeley and Los Angeles: University of California Press, 1988), 207, 210–11, 206.

4. Susan McClary, review of *The Romantic Generation* by Charles Rosen, *Notes* 96, no. 52 (June 1996): 1142.

5. Lawrence Kramer, *Classical Music and Postmodern Knowledge* (Berkeley and Los Angeles: University of California Press, 1995), 204–5.

EARLY EXOTICISM REVISITED

1. The most important recent books include Marcia J. Citron, *Gender and the Musical Canon* (Cambridge: Cambridge University Press, 1993); Susan McClary, *Feminine Endings: Music, Gender, and Sexuality* (Minneapolis: University of Minnesota Press, 1991); Ruth A. Solie, ed., *Musicology and Difference: Gender and Sexuality in Music Scholarship* (Berkeley and Los Angeles: University of California Press, 1993); and Philip Brett, Elizabeth Wood, and Gary C. Thomas, eds., *Queering the Pitch: The New Gay and Lesbian Musicology* (New York: Routledge, 1994).

2. Julia V. Douthwaite, *Exotic Women: Literary Heroines and Cultural Strategies in Ancien Régime France* (Philadelphia: University of Pennsylvania Press, 1992), 5.

3. Walter Preibisch, "Quellenstudien zu Mozarts 'Entführung aus dem Serail': Ein Beitrag zur Geschichte der Türkenoper," *Sammelbände der Internationalen Musik-Gesellschaft* 10 (1908–9): 430–76.

4. Margaret Griffel, "'Turkish' Opera from Mozart to Cornelius," Ph.D. diss., Columbia University, 1975; Thomas Betzwieser, *Exotismus und "Türkenoper" in der französischen Musik des ancien Régime* (Laaber: Laaber-Verlag, 1993).

5. Anke Schmitt, *Der Exotismus in der deutschen Oper zwischen Mozart und Spohr,* Hamburger Beiträge zur Musikwissenschaft 36 (Hamburg: Wagner, 1988), 23; unless otherwise identified, all English translations here are mine.

6. Betzwieser, *Exotismus,* 17–18, n. 11.

7. Miriam Karpilow Whaples, "Exoticism in Dramatic Music, 1600–1800," Ph.D. diss., Indiana University, 1958; Betzwieser, *Exotismus,* 15–16.

8. Peter Gradenwitz, *Musik zwischen Orient und Okzident* (Wilhelmshaven & Hamburg: Heinrichshofen's Verlag, 1977), 9.

9. See Marcel Paquot, *Les étrangers dans les divertissements de la cour* ([Brussels]: La Renaissance du Livre, [1933]), 25–28.

10. Jean Froissart, *Oeuvres,* ed. Baron Kervyn de Lettenhove, *Chroniques,* vol. 15, (Brussels: Devaux, 1871), 88.

11. *Chronique du religieux de Saint-Denys, contenant le règne de Charles VI, de 1380 à 1422, publiée en latin pour la première fois et traduite par M. L. Bellaguet* (Paris: Crapelet, 1840), 64, 66. The nineteenth-century French translator renders *choreas sarracenicas* as "la sarrasine," thus introducing an otherwise unknown medieval dance (ibid., 67). Without comment Marcel Paquot (22n.) identifies *choreas sarracenicas* with the mauresque, which he describes as "a dance without figures; the dancers turned about at their own caprice, beating the ground with the [ball of the] foot and the heel."

12. Froissart, *Chroniques,* 85. The third chronicler has "gens sauvaiges": *Chronique des quatre premiers Valois (1327–1393),* ed. Siméon Luce (Paris: Renouard, 1862), 328.

13. See Margaret T. Hodgen, *Early Anthropology in the Sixteenth and Seventeenth Centuries* (Philadelphia: University of Pennsylvania, 1964), chapters 1 and especially 2.

14. *Chronique du religieux,* 64.

15. The single example before Lully is a *Ballet des Janissaires,* music for which is preserved in the manuscript collection of Philidor l'ainé at the Bibliothèque Nationale; Betzwieser (*Exotismus,* 119) reproduces an excerpt from this with an asymmetry of phrasing to which he plausibly attributes exotic intent. Pierre de Beauchamps refers to publications of ballet verses beginning in 1548; see his *Recherches sur les théâtres de France, depuis l'année onze cens soixante & un, jusques à présent* (Paris, 1735; Geneva: Slatkine, 1968), 3:4 and passim. Texts of the arguments and verses for *ballets de cour* from 1581 to 1652 are published in Paul Lacroix, *Ballets et mascarades de cour de Henri III à Louis XIV,* 6 vols. (Geneva, 1868–70; Geneva: Slatkine, 1968).

16. Ibid. 1:151–52.

17. Ibid. 1:155.

18. Ibid. 3:174.

19. Ibid. 3:155–56, 157. Atahualpa, after fighting his brother for the throne of Cuzco, had only a year or two to enjoy a very local renown before being taken prisoner by Pizarro late in 1532.

20. *The Works of Henry Purcell,* vol. 12, *The Fairy Queen,* rev. ed. by Anthony Lewis (London: Novello, 1968), xxi, 172–73. The verses are obviously based on Davenant's text for a song of Peruvians in his *The Cruelty of the Spaniards in Peru* (1658); see Whaples, "Exoticism," 39–40, 181–82. The non-Shakespearean texts of *The Fairy Queen* are anonymous.

21. See Hodgen, *Early Anthropology,* 230ff., for a survey of this crisis and its bibliography.

22. Ibid., chapter 9.

23. Paquot, *Les étrangers,* 28–29. It is not clear from the sources how many, if any, of the paraded Americans were genuine and how many were impersonated; the fifty actual Tupinambá were augmented by 250 appropriately disguised French sailors (ibid.).

24. William Davenant, *Dramatic Works,* vol. 4 (Edinburgh: William Patterson, 1874), 88, 91. Except for a surviving "Simerons Dance" by Matthew Locke presumed to be from *Drake,* the music for these operas is lost and any other composer(s) unknown. The dance is reproduced in Whaples, "Exoticism," 223.

25. Betzwieser, *Exotismus,* 285.

26. Richard Ligon, *A True & Exact History of the Island of Barbadoes,* 2d ed. (London, 1673; facs. ed., London: Cass, 1970), 55. Ligon's sympathy is suspect: "As for the *Indians,* we have but few, and those fetcht from other Countries; some from the neighboaring Islands, some from the Main, which we make slaves" (54). He does not name the sailor, who is identified in the *Spectator* (no. 11, 13 March 1711) as one Thomas Inkle, who sailed from England on 16 June 1647 on the "Achilles."

27. This confusion may reflect the complex racial situation in the West Indies, but it had, in fact, wider currency. In the frontispiece of the published score of Cesti's festival opera *Il pomo d'oro* (Vienna, 1667), the allegorical figure of America is engraved as a black African in a feathered headdress (reprinted in *Denkmäler der Tonkunst in Österreich,* vol. 6).

28. No comparable taboo operated against a European woman's marrying a Turk. Although the dominant European-Turkish plot is the abduction type, in which the heroine is rescued from the seraglio by her (European) lover, Favart's *Soliman II, ou Les trois sultanes* (music by Paul-César Gibert) has a French heroine, Roxelane, who works her way to the top of the seraglio hierarchy as wife of the sultan. Betzwieser (*Exotismus,* 219ff.) quotes several contemporary reactions, none of which evinces any discomfort with the theme. In a nonmusical play on the same material by Isaac Bickerstaffe in the 1770s, Roxelane is an Englishwoman. In either case she is a voluble spokesperson for liberal European values and outspoken critic of oppressive Turkish ones; Mozart's Blonde is her compatriot and near relation.

29. E. M. Gagey, *Ballad Opera* (New York: Columbia University Press, 1937), 49, 51; and a review of a 1922 London revival of *Polly,* in *The Living Age* 315 (30 December 1922): 787.

30. The principal primary source for the episode is Jean-Baptiste Labat, ed., *Mémoires du Chevalier d'Arvieux* (Paris: Delespine, 1735), 4:125ff. The story, in whole or part, is retold in at least three articles: the first two are Pierre Martino, "La cérémonie turque du 'Bourgeois gentilhomme,'" *Revue d'histoire littéraire de la France* 18 (1911): 37–60; and C. D. Rouillard, "The Background of the Turkish Cere-

mony in Molière's *Le Bourgeois Gentilhomme,*" *University of Toronto Quarterly* 39 (1969–70): 33–52 (an excellent article with a great deal of literary and historical background). The third, with important details and insights but some unfortunate inaccuracies, is a paper by a Turkish scholar of French literature who derives considerable amusement from the episode: Adile Ayda, "Molière et l'envoyé de la Sublime Porte," *Cahiers de l'Association Internationale des Etudes Françaises* 9 (June 1957): 103–13. I am grateful to Richard Sherr for calling this paper to my attention.

31. This is d'Arvieux's spelling (*Mémoires* 4:125); he explains the title as equivalent to gentleman in ordinary to the king. In other accounts it is given as *muta ferraca, mustafaraga,* or (Ayda's) *Muteferrika.*

32. Ibid., 150–51.

33. Ibid., 252–53. By the time he recorded the premiere of the work, which he mistakenly places in September (instead of October) 1670, he was under the impression that the Bourgeois "made himself a Turk so as to marry the daughter of the sultan."

34. Françoise Karro, "L'empire ottoman et l'Europe dans l'opéra français et viennois au temps de Lully," in *Jean-Baptiste Lully: Actes du colloque, Saint-Germain-en-Laye–Heidelberg, 1987,* ed. Jérôme de La Gorce and Herbert Schneider, Neue Heidelberger Studien zur Musikwissenschaft 18 (Laaber: Laaber-Verlag, 1990), 257.

35. Ayda ("Molière," 115) points out, in support of this interpretation, the extraordinary emphasis in the comedy on Jourdain's interest in his new clothes and his dealings with his tailor. The performance dates were 14, 16, 20, and 21 October 1670, at Chambord. A seventeenth-century tradition that is repeated in Grimarest's *Vie de M. de Molière* (Paris, 1705) is that the king appeared so displeased with the piece after its premiere—and Molière's enemies at court therefore felt so encouraged to condemn it—that Molière hid in his room for five days until the second performance. But Georges Mongrédien, in his 1955 edition of Grimarest, corrects the error by giving the actual second date ([Paris]: Michel Brient, 1955, 113, n. 2).

36. Pierre Martino ("La cérémonie turque," 47–49) reprints all of d'Arvieux's descriptions of dervishes and their activities.

37. Ibid., 53–60.

38. The text and music of the "Turkish" scene are analyzed in detail in Whaples, "Exoticism," 98–124.

39. Salomon de Caus, *Institution harmonique* (Frankfurt, 1615), quoted in Thomas Betzwieser, "Die Türkenszenen in 'Le Sicilien' und 'Le Bourgeois Gentilhomme' im Kontext der Türkenoper und des musikalischen Exotismus," in La Gorce and Schneider, *Lully,* 51.

40. Jean-Baptiste du Halde [S.J.], *The General History of China,* 4 vols. (London: J. Watts, 1741), 3:65.

41. Paul Le Jeune [S.J.], "Brieve relation du voyage de la Nouvelle France" (Paris, 1632), in R. G. Thwaites, ed., *The Jesuit Relations and Allied Documents,* 73 vols. (Cleveland: Burrows, 1896–1901), 5:27.

42. Frances Burney, *The Early Diary, 1768–1778,* ed. Annie Raines Ellis, 2 vols. (London: Bell, 1889), 2:133. The date is 14 December 1775. Omai, a native of the

Society Islands who was brought to England by Captain Cook in 1774, cut a successful figure in society during a stay of over two years, until his return to Tahiti in 1777. The best account of the episode is Michael Alexander, *Omai: "Noble Savage"* (London: Collins & Harvill Press, 1970). Fanny Burney was a daughter of the music historian Dr. Charles Burney and a sister of James Burney, who, as one of Captain Cook's officers on both of the voyages that carried Omai as a passenger, was on intimate terms with the visitor.

43. Letter of Mozart to his father, 26 September 1781. *Letters of Mozart and His Family,* trans. Emily Anderson (London: Macmillan, 1938), 3:1144.

44. Whaples, "Exoticism," 101–4.

45. See Richard Hudson, "Chaconne," *New Grove Dictionary of Music and Musicians,* ed. Stanley Sadie (London: Macmillan, 1980), 4:100: "The earliest literary reference to the *chacona* occurs in a poem by Mateo Rosas de Oquendo, describing events in Peru in 1598." There may be an even earlier reference: in 1590 the Jesuit Jose d'Acosta, who had spent the years 1571–87 in Peru, wrote of its people, "There were other dances and maskes, which they called *Guacones,* whose actions were pure representations of the divell" (Jose d'Acosta, *Historia natural y moral de las Indias* [Seville, 1590]; trans. as *The Naturall and Morall Historie of the East and West Indies* [London: E. Blount and W. Aspley, 1604], 492). On its arrival in Spain the *chacona* was a wild and licentious dance.

46. Lacroix, *Ballets* 3:187 ("danseurs de sarabandes, dont la souplesse du corps et la vitesse des pieds estonne les regardans").

47. Beauchamps, *Recherches* 3:55. No music survives.

48. Irene Alm, "Dances from the 'Four Corners of the Earth': Exoticism in Seventeenth-Century Venetian Opera," in *Musica Franca: Essays in Honor of Frank A. D'Accone,* ed. Irene Alm, Alison McLamore, and Colleen Reardon (Stuyvesant, N.Y.: Pendragon Press, 1996), 233–57.

49. Before these, the prologue contains an "Entrée des 4 nations"—French, Spanish, Italian, and Polish. In "Le Turc généreux," an "abduction" story in the first of the four major sections, Provençal color contrasts with Turkish.

50. See Roger Savage, "Rameau's American Dancers," *Early Music* 11, no. 4 (1983): 441–52, and Howard Brofsky, "Rameau and the Indians: The Popularity of *Les Sauvages,*" in *Music in the Classic Period: Essays in Honor of Barry S. Brook* (New York: Pendragon Press, 1985), 43–60.

51. "J'ai caracterisé le chant et la danse des sauvages." Quoted in Savage, "Rameau's American Dancers," 446.

52. Brofsky, "Rameau and the Indians," 52–60.

53. Molière, *Oeuvres complètes,* ed. Maurice Rat ([Paris]: Gallimard, 1956), 2:176.

54. D'Arvieux, *Mémoires* 1:394, quoted in Martino, "La cérémonie turque," 49.

55. Three years earlier, in his *Pastorale comique,* Lully had composed an entry of twelve "Egyptiens" (i.e., Gypsies), four of them playing "gnacares." Thanks to a linguistic ambiguity, these may have been not kettledrums but castanets. An illustration in Filippo Bonanni's *Gabinetto armonico* (Rome, 1723) shows a "Bacchante con Nacchera"; she plays a pair of castanets with each hand (Filippo Bonanni, *The Showcase of Musical Instruments,* introduction and captions by Frank Ll. Harrison and Joan Rimmer [New York: Dover, 1964], plate 93). (For "Egyptians" as a self-

chosen name for Gypsies in the seventeenth century, see Paquot, *Les étrangers,* 93–95.)

56. Betzwieser *(Exotismus,* 127–28) reports that performance materials from later productions of the Mamamouchi scene no longer mention Turkish instruments and deduces that they may have been dropped after the Chambord performances.

57. James Blades, *Percussion Instruments and Their History,* rev. ed. (London: Faber and Faber, 1984), 242–44.

58. Metastasio's *Le Cinesi* (1735, rev. 1751), in which four young Chinese entertain themselves at home with improvised Italian scenes, would also seem to open itself to such "reverse" exoticism. But Gluck at least (the last of three composers to set it) did not take the opportunity to contrast Italian style with musical chinoiserie.

59. The *nagga* was the Tongans' hollow-log drum; *pagges* were not musical instruments but thin paddle-shaped objects, about two and a half feet long, with which Tongan men performed complex dances. The "&c"s may refer to other instruments brought home from the expeditions. Cook is unfailingly complimentary about the music and dancing of the Friendly Islanders, in contrast to his generally unfavorable reports on musical performances in other ports of call. See James Cook, *A Voyage to the Pacific Ocean for Making Discoveries in the Northern Hemisphere,* 3 vols. (London: G. Nicol and T. Cadell, 1785), 1:188, 247–55, and esp. 292–98, which incorporates the fullest description of the instruments, by the Surgeon's Mate William Anderson. All three passages are given in Whaples, "Exoticism," 400–410.

60. Curt Sachs, *Real-Lexikon der Musikinstrumente,* rev. ed. (1913; reprint, New York: Dover, 1964), 5, where it is spelled *Ajacaxtli.*

61. Mozart, *Die Entführung aus dem Serail,* Act 1, no. 2.

62. Lully's is the earliest musical repertoire we have of the French court ballet; one must peruse the title entries in Beauchamps and the texts printed in Lacroix to realize how much music is missing from the history of the exotic entertainment.

63. In an early publication, the texts of three more stanzas and transpositions of the melody into C (for guitar) and G (for German flute) are also included.

64. They are enumerated in a very complete history of the song: John Koegel, "'The Indian Chief' and 'Morality': Eighteenth-Century British Popular Song Transformed into Nineteenth-Century American Shape-Note Hymn," in *Music in Performance and Society: Essays in Honor of Roland Jackson,* ed. Malcolm Cole and John Koegel (Warren, Mich.: Harmonie Park Press, 1997), 437–508. My thanks are due to Professor Koegel for a copy of his article in advance of publication.

65. From Mrs. Hunter's note to the "Death Song" in her 1802 *Poems,* as quoted in F. E. Farley, "The Dying Indian," in *Anniversary Papers by Colleagues and Pupils of George Lyman Kittredge* (Boston: Ginn, 1913), 251–61 (253).

66. *Thraliana: The Diary of Mrs. Hester Lynch Thrale (Later Mrs. Piozzi), 1776–1809,* ed. Katharine C. Balderston, 2d ed. (Oxford: Clarendon Press, 1951), 1:533; italics in the original. All four of Mrs. Hunter's stanzas follow this paragraph, under the title "North American Death Song." Although the two women were the same age and moved in the same circles, they were not intimate: this is the only mention

of Anne Hunter in the almost eleven hundred pages of the *Thraliana.* William Seward was a Fellow of the Royal Society and close friend of the Thrales.

67. Koegel, "The Indian Chief," 461. A comparison with Rameau's "characterization" of North American natives is inevitable.

68. A locus classicus is the gradual process by which Fanny Burney was revealed as the author of her anonymously published novel *Evelina* (1778). See *Diary and Letters of Madame D'Arblay (1778–1840),* ed. Charlotte Barrett (London: Macmillan, 1904), vol. 1, passim. There is, however, no contemporaneous connection between Anne Hunter and the *melody* of the "Death Song."

69. In fact, we know relatively little about her. Her letters have not been published; she left no journal and makes only rare appearances in those of her acquaintances. Almost all contemporaneous references to her are as the wife (or widow) of the eminent surgeon and anatomist Dr. Hunter. During his lifetime she published nothing under her name, and afterward, as a published poet, continued to live in his shadow (or his fame) as "Mrs. John Hunter." We have already noted Mrs. Thrale's somewhat left-handed compliment on someone who was clearly not a favorite. Fanny Burney, an intimate at Streatham herself, met Mrs. Hunter there only once, at the end of 1782. In a second meeting more than seven years later, she suggests that self-effacement may not have been the lady's salient characteristic: "She is a very fine woman, and highly accomplished; but with rather too much glare, both without and within" (*Diary and Letters of Madame D'Arblay* 2:147, 4:375).

"FORREINE CONCEITES AND WANDRING DEVISES"

1. See, for example, Charles Segal, "The Gorgon and the Nightingale: the Voice of Female Lament and Pindar's Twelfth *Pythian Ode,*" in *Embodied Voices: Representing Female Vocality in Western Culture,* ed. Leslie C. Dunn and Nancy A. Jones (Cambridge: Cambridge University Press, 1994), 17–21.

2. Catherine Clément, *Opera, or The Undoing of Women,* trans. Betsy Wing (Minneapolis: University of Minnesota Press, 1988), 58–59, and Susan McClary, "Sexual Politics in Classical Music," in *Feminine Endings: Music, Gender, and Sexuality* (Minneapolis: University of Minnesota Press, 1991), 57–67. For information on more recent subversions of such conventions of vocal gender and power, see Carolyn Abbate, "Opera, or The Envoicing of Women," in *Musicology and Difference: Gender and Sexuality in Music Scholarship,* ed. Ruth Solie (Berkeley and Los Angeles: University of California Press, 1993), 225–58.

3. Edward W. Said, *Culture and Imperialism* (New York: Knopf, 1993), xxv.

4. Sander L. Gilman, *Difference and Pathology: Stereotypes of Sexuality, Race, and Madness* (Ithaca, N.Y.: Cornell University Press, 1985), 17–18.

5. Ibid., 11.

6. Bill Nichols, "The Ethnographer's Tale," in *Visualizing Theory,* ed. Lucien Taylor (New York: Routledge, 1994), 62.

7. See Linda Phyllis Austern, *Music in English Life and Thought, 1550–1650* (forthcoming), and Stephen Greenblatt, *Marvelous Possessions: The Wonder of the New World* (Chicago: University of Chicago Press, 1991), 6.

8. Said, *Culture and Imperialism,* xxv.

9. Greenblatt, *Marvelous Possessions,* 7.

10. See Rana Kabbani, *Europe's Myths of Orient* (Bloomington: Indiana University Press, 1986), 5–6.

11. J[ohn] R[igby] Hale, *England and the Italian Renaissance* (London: Faber and Faber, 1954), 11.

12. See Susan Dwyer Amussen, *An Ordered Society: Gender and Class in Early Modern England* (Oxford: Blackwell, 1988), 2, 155; Joel Hurstfield and Alan G. R. Smith, eds., *Elizabethan People: State and Society* (London: Arnold, 1972), 32–35; L. C. Knights, *Drama and Society in the Age of Jonson* (London: Chatto and Windus, 1937), 141; and Steve Rappaport, *Worlds within Worlds: Structures of Life in Sixteenth-Century London* (Cambridge: Cambridge University Press, 1989), 42–47.

13. See A. J. Hoenselaars, *Images of Englishmen and Foreigners in the Drama of Shakespeare and His Contemporaries* (London: Associated University Presses, 1992), 16–25.

14. Peter Hulme, *Colonial Encounters: Europe and the Native Caribbean, 1492–1797* (London: Methuen, 1986), 109.

15. See Uzoma Esonwanne, "Feminist Theory and the Discourse of Colonialism," in *Reimagining Women: Representations of Women in Culture,* ed. Shirley Newman and Glennis Stephenson (Toronto: University of Toronto Press, 1993), 233.

16. See Simone de Beauvoir, *The Second Sex,* trans. H. M. Parshley (New York: Knopf, 1971), 143.

17. See Kabbani, *Europe's Myths of Orient,* 5–6.

18. See Louis Montrose, "The Work of Gender and Sexuality in the Elizabethan Discourse of Discovery," in *Discourses of Sexuality from Aristotle to AIDS,* ed. Domna C. Stanton (Ann Arbor: University of Michigan Press, 1992), 138–84; and Werner Von Koppenfels, "Dis-covering the Female Body: Erotic Exploration in Elizabethan Poetry," in Marie-Claire Rouyer, ed., *Le corps dans tous ses états* (Bordeaux: Presses Universitaires de Bordeaux, 1995), 255–66. For a brief summary of English attitudes toward travel, exploration, trade, and the wonders of the mapped and unmapped world, see Louis B. Wright, *Middle-Class Culture in Elizabethan England* (Chapel Hill: University of North Carolina Press, 1935), 508–48.

19. John Donne, *Poems* (London: T.N. for Henry Herringman, 1669), 87–89.

20. Ibid., 90.

21. Beauvoir, *The Second Sex,* 141.

22. Esonwanne, "Feminist Theory and the Discourse of Colonialism," 234.

23. Genevieve Lloyd, *The Man of Reason: "Male" and "Female" in Western Philosophy,* 2d ed. (Minneapolis: University of Minnesota Press, 1993), 2. See also Denise Riley, *"Am I That Name?": Feminism and the Category of "Women" in History* (Minneapolis: University of Minnesota Press, 1988), 1–2.

24. See Lloyd, *The Man of Reason,* 10–17.

25. Beauvoir, *The Second Sex,* 139. See also Elena Gianini Belotti, *What Are Little Girls Made Of? The Roots of Feminine Stereotypes* (New York: Shocken Books, 1976), 25–31, and Gilman, *Difference and Pathology,* 19.

26. John Shepherd, *Music as Social Text* (Cambridge: Polity Press, 1991), 154–58.

27. See David Summers, *The Judgement of Sense: Renaissance Naturalism and the Rise of Aesthetics* (Cambridge: Cambridge University Press, 1987), 51.

28. Michel Foucault, *The Order of Things: An Archaeology of the Human Sciences* (New York: Random House, 1970), 39.

29. *The Praise of Musicke* (Oxford: Joseph Barnes, 1586); see also Linda Phyllis Austern, "'No Women Are Indeed': The Boy Actor as Vocal Seductress in Late Sixteenth- and Early Seventeenth-Century English Drama," in *Embodied Voices: Representing Female Vocality in Western Culture,* ed. Leslie C. Dunn and Nancy A. Jones (Cambridge: Cambridge University Press, 1994), 85–102.

30. Thomas Ravenscroft, *A Briefe Discourse of the True (but Neglected) Use of Charact'ring the Degrees* (London: Edward Allde for Thomas Adams, 1614), sig. q^4.

31. Ibid., sigs. q^4–q^{4v}.

32. Gilman, *Difference and Pathology,* 27–28.

33. Helen Haste, *The Sexual Metaphor* (Cambridge, Mass.: Harvard University Press, 1994), 71.

34. See Linda Phyllis Austern, "'Alluring the Auditorie to Effeminacie': Music and the Idea of the Feminine in Early Modern England," *Music and Letters* 74 (1993): 343–54; Thomas McGeary, "Gendering Opera: Italian Opera as the Feminine Other in Britain, 1700–42," *Journal of Musicological Research* 14 (1994): 17–26; and Shepherd, *Music as Social Text,* 157–64.

35. Suzanne G. Cusick, "Gendering Modern Music: Thoughts on the Monteverdi-Artusi Controversy," *Journal of the American Musicological Society* 46 (1993): 1–25. See also Austern, "Alluring the Auditorie to Effeminacie," 343–54, and Susan McClary, "Constructions of Gender in Monteverdi's Dramatic Music," in McClary, *Feminine Endings,* 35–48.

36. See Michel Foucault, *The History of Sexuality,* vol. 1, *An Introduction,* trans. Robert Hurley (New York: Vintage Books, 1990), 157; Jonathan Goldberg, *Sodometries: Renaissance Texts, Modern Sexualities* (Stanford, Calif.: Stanford University Press, 1992), 19; McClary, "Constructions of Gender," 35–52; McGeary, "Gendering Opera," 19–20; Montrose, "The Work of Gender and Sexuality," 138–40; and Joan Wallach Scott, *Gender and the Politics of History* (New York: Columbia University Press, 1988), 42–45. For a summary of the same issue in more recent cultural contexts, see Ruth A. Solie, "Introduction: On Difference," in *Musicology and Difference: Gender and Sexuality in Music Scholarship,* ed. Solie, 1–20.

37. Thomas Laqueur, *Making Sex: Body and Gender from the Greeks to Freud* (Cambridge, Mass.: Harvard University Press, 1990), 61.

38. Robert A. Padgug, "Sexual Matters: On Conceptualizing Sexuality in History," in *Passion and Power: Sexuality in History,* ed. Kathy Peiss and Christina Simmons (Philadelphia: Temple University Press, 1989), 17. See also Foucault, *The History of Sexuality,* 157, and Kathy Peiss and Christina Simmons, "Passion and Power: An Introduction," in *Passion and Power,* ed. Peiss and Simmons, 3.

39. Foucault, *The History of Sexuality,* 17. See also Peiss and Simmons, "Passion and Power: An Introduction," 7.

40. Gilman, *Difference and Pathology,* 37. See also Riley, *Am I That Name?* 18.

41. Laqueur, *Making Sex,* 61–62, 25.

42. See Stephen Greenblatt, "Fiction and Friction," in *Reconstructing Individualism: Autonomy, Individuality, and the Self in Western Thought,* ed. Thomas C. Heller, Morton Sosna, and David Wellbery (Stanford, Calif.: Stanford University Press, 1986), 38, 40; Thomas Laqueur, "Orgasm, Generation, and the Politics of Reproductive Biology," *Representations* 4 (Spring 1986), 4–12; and Stephen Orgel, "Nobody's Perfect, or Why Did the English Stage Take Boys for Women," *South Atlantic Quarterly* 88 (1989): 13.

43. Thomas Gainesford, *The Rich Cabinet* (London, 1615), fols. 163^{v}–64; Laqueur, *Making Sex,* 59–62.

44. See ibid., 57.

45. Joseph Swetnam, *The Arraignment of Lewd, Idle, Froward and Unconstant Women* (London: Richard Meighan, 1620), 38.

46. Gainesford, *The Rich Cabinet,* fol. 164; see also Riley, *Am I That Name?* 1–2, 11.

47. Laqueur, *Making Sex,* 52–53.

48. See Linda Phyllis Austern, *Music in English Children's Drama of the Later Renaissance* (New York: Gordon and Breach, 1992), 12–13; Austern, "No Women Are Indeed," 88–97; Alan Bray, *Homosexuality in Renaissance England* (London: Gay Men's Press, 1982; 2d ed., Boston: Gay Men's Press, 1988), 54–55; Goldberg, *Sodometries,* 17–19; Gordon Lell, "'Ganymede' on the Elizabethan Stage: Homosexual Implications of the Use of Boy Actors," *Aegis* 1 (1973): 7–10; and Orgel, "Nobody's Perfect," 22–26.

49. Goldberg, *Sodometries,* 3, 17–19, 179–222.

50. See Hale, *England and the Italian Renaissance,* 19–21, and A. Lytton Sells, *The Paradise of Travellers: The Italian Influence on Englishmen in the Seventeenth Century* (Bloomington: Indiana University Press, 1964), 42, 133.

51. Roger Ascham, *The Scholemaster* (London: John Day, 1570) fols. 24–24^{v}.

52. Ibid., fol. 26^{v}.

53. *An Italians Dead Bodie, Stucke with English Flowers: Elegies, on the Death of Sir Oratio Pallavicino* (London: Thomas Creede, for Andrew Wise, 1600), sig. B2^{v}.

54. Ascham, *The Scholemaster,* fol. 29.

55. Thomas Coryat, *Coryats Crudities* (London: W.S., 1600), 267.

56. Thomas Dekker and John Webster, *Northward Hoe* (London: G. Eld, 1607), Act 4.

57. See Shepherd, *Music as Social Text,* 156, 164–71.

58. Ravenscroft, *A Briefe Discourse,* sig. A3^{v}.

59. William Prynne, *Histrio-Mastix* (London: Michael Sparke, 1633), 273–77.

60. Charles Butler, *The Principles of Musik, in Singing and Setting* (London: John Haviland, 1636), 2.

61. Thomas Wright, *The Passions of the Minde in Generall* (London: Valentine Simms for Walter Burre, 1604), 159, 166.

62. Thomas Morley, *A Plaine and Easie Introduction to Practicall Musicke* (London: Peter Short, 1597), 172.

63. Butler, *The Principles of Musik,* 4, 96.

64. Prynne, *Histrio-Mastix,* 275.

65. Philip Stubbes, *The Anatomy of Abuses* (London: Richard Jones, 1583), f. 110^{v}.

66. *The Praise of Musicke*, 3.

THE *ALLA TURCA* STYLE

1. One of the most important and best documented of these temporary embassies, that of Mehmet Efendi to Paris in 1720–21, is described in detail in Fatma Müge Goçek, *East Encounters West: France and the Ottoman Empire in the Eighteenth Century* (Oxford: Oxford University Press, 1987).

2. Miriam Karpilow Whaples, "Exoticism in Dramatic Music, 1600–1800" (Ph.D. diss., Indiana University, 1958), appends a useful selection of excerpts of both sorts of writing to the body of her dissertation. Thomas Betzwieser, *Exotismus und Türkenoper in der französischen Musik des Ancien Régime: Studien zu einem ästhetischen Phänomen* (Laaber: Laaber-Verlag, 1993), also includes a number of excerpts; in addition he reproduces in full Charles Fonton's *Essai sur la musique orientale comparée à la musique européenne* (Constantinople, 1751). Mary Rowen Obelkovich, "Turkish Affect in the Land of the Sun King," *Musical Quarterly* 63 (1977): 367–89, includes a variety of French responses to Turkish music, as they found their way into both practice and theory between 1625 and 1700. Among the music theorists of the century who pay significant attention to Turkish music are Johann Georg Sulzer, in both his *Allgemeine Theorie der schönen Künste* (Leipzig, 1771–74) and his *Geschichte des transalpinischen Daciens, das ist, der Walachey, Moldau, und Bessarabiens*, 3 vols. (Vienna, 1781–82; this latter excerpted in Whaples, "Exoticism in Dramatic Music"); Christian Friedrich Daniel Schubart, *Ideen zu einer Ästhetik der Tonkunst* (Vienna, 1806); and Rousseau's *Dictionnaire de musique* (Paris, 1768).

3. "Style" and "topos" for my purposes here are somewhat interchangeable; "topos" normally indicates an inset section of *alla turca* music in a larger piece, whereas "style" normally indicates that a whole piece uses *alla turca* elements. However, I use the terms interchangeably when referring to operatic arias or dance movements in operas.

4. See Rena Kabbani, *Europe's Myths of Orient* (Bloomington: Indiana University Press, 1985); also Suzanne Rodin Pucci, "The Discrete Charms of the Exotic: Fictions of the Harem in Eighteenth-Century France," and Frances Mannsåker, "Elegancy and Wildness: Reflections of the East in the Eighteenth-Century Imagination," both in *Exoticism in the Enlightenment*, ed. G. S. Rousseau and Roy Porter (Manchester: Manchester University Press, 1989), 145–74, 175–96.

5. The brutal images of sultans and other rulers in the tales of the Arabian Nights and their innumerable imitations are the literary background for the terror evoked by the Mozart's Pasha and his colleagues.

6. The notion that Western images of the Orient are constructed to serve Western purposes rather than accurately (or at least complexly) to represent the mores and experiences of other peoples is now commonplace, largely owing to the work of Edward Said in his influential book *Orientalism* (New York: Pantheon Books,

1978). His basic ideas, for example, pervade Rousseau's and Porter's *Exoticism and the Enlightenment.* With respect to "Turkish" music, Whaples ("Exoticism in Dramatic Music") noted as early as 1958 that the *alla turca* style was not closely modeled on actual Turkish music but was, rather, a "wrong-note" version of Western music, altered to replicate the differences between that music and the music with which European composers were familiar.

7. Alain Grosrichard, *Structure du sérail: La fiction du despotisme asiatique dans l'Occident classique* (Paris: Editions du Seuil, 1979), examines the meaning of the Oriental seraglio in European (mostly French) political mythologies from both political and psychoanalytic perspectives.

8. Karl Signell, "Mozart and the Mehter," *Turkish Music Quarterly* 1 (1988): 12. Long used in the West, often with loose rings around the bottom bar, the triangle's jingling may have been intended to replicate that of the Turkish crescent if that was not available.

9. H. G. Farmer and James Blades, "Janissary music," *New Grove Dictionary of Music and Musicians* (London: Macmillan, 1980), 9:497. Many nineteenth-century pictures of British bands show this phenomenon; it seems to have been not unusual for young boys to occupy the role of band "blackamoor," further emphasizing the difference between most band members and the exotic token.

10. This reading is explicitly supported by the text of the Beethoven, but it is also implicit in Haydn's London symphonies, which were written after Haydn is reported (by Dies) to have said that his language could be understood all over the world, and which deploy a dazzling range of topoi, often in striking juxtapositions. See below on a "Turkish" moment in Symphony No. 104. Haydn's remark can be found in H. C. Robbins Landon and David Wyn-Jones, *Haydn: His Life and Music* (Bloomington: Indiana University Press, 1988), 181.

11. Kenneth Mobbs, "Stops and Other Special Effects on the Early Piano," *Early Music* 12 (1984): 471–76.

12. Whaples, "Exoticism in Dramatic Music," 153–66; Jonathan Bellman, *The* Style Hongrois *in the Music of Western Europe* (Boston: Northeastern University Press, 1993), ch. 2, "The Magyars, the Turks, the Siege of Vienna, and the Turkish Style," 25–46.

13. Signell, "Mozart and the Mehter," 10.

14. This approach is dramatically demonstrated in Haydar Sanal, *Mehter Musìkìsì* (Istanbul: Millì Eğìtìm Basimevì, 1961), 121–25, where the few notated examples of pre-1826 janissary music are compared with snippets of Mozart's Rondo "alla turca."

15. Ivano Cavallini, "La musica turca nelle testimonianze dei viaggiatori e nella trattatistica del settecento," *Rivista italiana di musicologia* 21 (1986): 144–69, notes the bewilderment with which many European observers recorded the oral transmission of Turkish music and its consequent lack of sources. Kurt Reinhard, and Ursula Reinhard, *Die Musik der Türkei,* 2 vols. (Wilhelmshaven: Heinrichshofen, 1984), 1:172–76, transmit the three known notated versions of pre-1826 janissary music. (The janissaries were disbanded in 1826.) Thanks to Ralph Locke for pointing out this source. The Hiller quote is from Johann Adam Hiller, *Wöchentliche Nachrichten und Anmerkugen die Musik betreffend* 4:205. Quoted in Betzwieser, *Exotismus und Türkenoper,* 99.

16. Letter to Leopold Mozart, 26 September 1781, in Emily Anderson, trans., *The Letters of Mozart and His Family*, 2d ed. (London: Macmillan, 1966), 769.

17. Whaples, "Exoticism in Dramatic Music," 159.

18. Betzwieser, *Exotismus und Türkenoper*, 88–89, describes Blainville's attempts (in the Turkish chapter of his *Histoire générale, critique et philologique de la musique* of 1767) to explain the microtones of Turkish melody in terms of the European tempered scale, and then to suggest how Turkish melody might be replicated with Western instruments and notation. The attempt to "translate" Turkish music was, then, by no means restricted to composers.

19. Betzwieser, *Exotismus und Türkenoper*, 103–5. The piece also occurs (with variants) in a number of other primary sources.

20. "Mais ce qu'on peut leur reprocher, c'est qu'ignorant les regles de proportion dans l'assortiment des sons, ils n'ont nulle idée de la musique à plusieurs parties, ny du ton divisé en p^{re}. tierce, quinte, et octave, ce qui fait la baze [*sic*] et le fondement de notre musique, et de tout ce qu'on apele [*sic*] contre-point simple, ou figuré. De là vient que dans un concert de musique orientale, l'on n'entend ny basse, ny dessus, ny taille, ny haute-contre &c. Tous les instrumens montés à l'unisson jouent absolument la même chose, et ne paroissent faire qu'un même instrument, tandis que dans la musique europèene la division du ton en quatre, fournit avec les octaves huit parties differentes, dont chaque une sera joué[e] par un instrument, et qui reunies ensemble, ne formeront cependant par le raport et l'analogie qu'il y aura entre elles qu'un tout concordant et harmonique" (Fonton, *Essai*, 48–50, quoted in Betzwieser, *Exotismus und Türkenoper*, 383).

21. Sulzer, *Geschichte des transalpinischen Daciens*, excerpted and translated in Whaples, "Exoticism in Dramatic Music," 320–27.

22. "Les turcs n'ont point de Systême de Musique raisonné, à peine notent-ils leurs airs." Blainville, *Histoire . . . de la musique* (Paris, 1767), quoted in Cavallini, "La musica turca," 160.

23. The opening ritornello divides cleanly into 4 + 4, but both four-measure units are divided 1 + 3, which gives a feeling of irregularity quite missing from the vocal sections.

24. "Malheureuse" follows the D-major opening Scythian chorus with a cross-relation between Iphigenia's solo anacrustic D and the bass D# of the V/ii under her B, while the repetition of the D-major chorus is followed by a first-inversion V/vi (A# in the bass) on Iphigenia's "Dieux."

25. See Cavallini, "La musica turca," 149 (esp. the 1782 *Mémoires* of Baron Tott). The adjectives in my text are from Fonton, *Essai*, quoted in Betzwieser, *Exotismus und Türkenoper*, 83.

26. "La musique des Turcs n'est pas si animée que celle des Bédouins: il y a dans tout ce qu'ils font, un air morne et melancolique" (J.-B. De La Borde, *Essai sur la musique ancienne et moderne* [Paris, 1780], 1:382, quoted in Cavallini, "La musica turca," 167).

27. Lady Mary Wortley Montagu, *Turkish Embassy Letters*, ed. Malcolm Jack (Athens: University of Georgia Press, 1993), 90–91.

28. Said, *Orientalism*, 179–90, suggests that Flaubert's and Nerval's explorations of the feminine Oriental are on the one hand apart from the main thread of Ori-

entalism, and on the other, by no means unique. Lisa Lowe's *Critical Terrains: French and British Orientalisms* (Ithaca, N.Y.: Cornell University Press, 1991) takes up Said's remarks, expanding and nuancing them. More recently, Reina Lewis, *Gendering Orientalism: Race, Femininity and Representation* (London: Routledge, 1996) takes up the question of European women's participation in Orientalist discourse.

29. And Favart's *Les trois sultanes* (1761) quite explicitly feminizes the sultan by having him capitulate to the tricks and wiles of the French slave Roxelane.

30. It is probable that under certain circumstances (the visit of an ambassadorial party, for example) the softer varieties of Turkish music were also heard in Europe, but janissary music was uniquely available.

31. Thomas Betzwieser, "Die Europäer in der Fremde: Die Figurenkonstellation der *Entführung aus dem Serail* und ihre Tradition," in *Mozarts Opernfiguren: Grosse Herren, rasende Weiber, gefährliche Liebschaften,* ed. Dieter Borchmeyer (Bern: Haupt, c.1991), 35–48, describes some ways in which it also differs from its tradition; the chief two are the introduction of Blonde as an Englishwoman, and the plot twist at the end by which the Pasha discovers not that Belmonte is his son (as in the Bretzner libretto on which Stephanie based his), but that he is the son of his former enemy.

32. See Helmut Wirth, "Gluck, Haydn, und Mozart—Drei Entführungsopern," in *Opernstudien: Anna Amalie Abert zum 65. Geburtstag* (Tutzing: Schneider, 1975), 25–35, for a study of the relations between these three operas. Gluck's opera was also translated into German and performed first as *Die unvermuthete Zusammenkunft* (Frankfurt, 1772).

33. This work was the model for Bretzner's libretto *Belmont und Constanze,* set in 1781 by Johann André. Bretzner's libretto was in turn revised by Gottlieb Stephanie for Mozart. See Marita P. McClymonds, "Schiava liberata, La," *New Grove Dictionary of Opera* (London: Macmillan, 1992), 4:217–18.

34. Betzwieser, *Exotismus und Türkenoper,* 215ff. W. Daniel Wilson, *Humanität und Kreuzzugsideologie um 1780* (New York: Peter Lang, 1984), 27–31.

35. Lisa Lowe, *Critical Terrains;* Ralph Locke, "Reflections on Orientalism in Opera and Musical Theatre," *Opera Quarterly* 10, no. 1 (1993): 48–64, and "Constructing the Oriental 'Other': Saint-Saëns's *Samson et Dalila,*" *Cambridge Opera Journal* 3 (1991): 261–302; James Parakilas, "The Soldier and the Exotic: Variations on a Theme of Racial Encounter," *Opera Quarterly* 10, no. 2 (1993–94): 33–56, and no. 3 (1994): 43–70.

36. Wilson, *Humanität und Kreuzzugsideologie,* 27–31.

37. Ibid., 32.

38. Although this character is best known to us from Mozart's *La clemenza di Tito,* the original libretto was written by Metastasio in 1734 and set more than thirty times before Mozart. Among the major pre-Mozart settings of the text are those by Caldara, Hasse (twice), Jommelli, Galuppi, and Gluck.

39. Osmin's loss of perspective here is part of the same comic phenomenon as the end of Figaro's diatribe against women in *Le nozze di Figaro;* both represent the breakdown of controlled rhetoric, the loss of a sense of audience, and an antisocial self-absorption. See John Platoff, "The Buffa Aria in Mozart's Vienna," *Cambridge Opera Journal* 2 (1990): 99–120.

40. Betzwieser, "Die Europäer in der Fremde," 44–45, comments on the unusual integration of Osmin's role in *Die Entführung.*

41. While Betzwieser, "Die Europäer in der Fremde," notes in general that Osmin is integral to the dramaturgy of *Die Entführung,* Thomas Bauman, *W. A. Mozart: Die Entführung aus dem Serail* (Cambridge: Cambridge University Press, 1987), 66–71, describes how Osmin's music blends *alla turca* and other elements to form a complex operatic portrait.

42. Not at all in *Die Entführung,* and only in recitatives and the last ensemble in the two others.

43. Alain Grosrichard, *Structure du sérail,* part 3, "L'ombre du sérail."

44. One might read into this the notion that just as "we" find modified versions of ourselves in "them," so "they" find themselves in "us." Given the sophisticated exoticism of the whole score it is not implausible that Grétry intended this message (see Betzwieser, *Exotismus und Türkenoper,* 317–32 for a detailed discussion of this piece).

45. Cf. Bauman's comments on Stephanie's making the Pasha a renegade European rather than an actual Turk in *Mozart: Die Entführung,* 32–35.

46. Kabbani, *Europe's Myths of Orient,* 22; *Paulys Realencyclopädie der Classischen Alertumswissenschaft,* ed. Georg Wissowa (Stuttgart: Druckenmuller, 1863–1963), s.v. "Dardanidai" and "Dardanos."

47. See, for example, Susan McClary, *Georges Bizet: Carmen* (Cambridge: Cambridge University Press, 1992), 51–58; Locke, "Constructing the Oriental 'Other'"; and Richard Taruskin's essay in this volume.

48. Kabbani, *Europe's Myths of Orient,* 78, 81.

49. The visual record for nonserious opera in the eighteenth century is sketchy at best. However, in a famous painting of an opera production—quite likely of *L'incontro improvviso*—at Haydn's Eszterháza, the eight male characters (four of whom are probably nonsinging servants) are marked as Turkish by turbans and robes over baggy trousers. (The female character—presumably Rezia—wears straightforwardly European garb.) None of the characters is made up to look dark skinned. (Indeed, as Daniel Heartz points out, the heads of the soloists are made of ivory.) Modern productions often add skin color difference to differences in costume. See Daniel Heartz, *Haydn, Mozart, and the Viennese School, 1740–1780* (New York: Norton, 1995), 388, for a discussion of this picture, and p. 293 for a beautiful reproduction of it.

50. Wilson, *Humanität und Kreuzzugsideologie,* 35–36, points out that making the captive both female and European fuses the crusade plot archetype with the escape-from-the-seraglio archetype. My point below is that some of the operatic princesses, and certainly some of their followers, combine aspects of "Europeanness" with a tinge of Orientalism, thus allowing room for the audience both to condemn the injustice of the Islamic seraglio and to enjoy its inmates' exotic allure.

51. Rezia does not demonstrate Konstanze's explicit willingness to endure torture, but she is willing to defy the Pasha, and the heroic tone of the aria lends weight to the latent defiance of the text.

52. The exception is Amine's second air in *La rencontre imprévue,* "J'ai perdu mon étalage," which she sings after Ali has snubbed her. Amine is the third harem

inmate to try and seduce Prince Ali, and the *batterie turque* is particularly evident as she sings "ha ha ha" at the ends of some lines.

53. "Entre l'homme et la femme, la distinction est réelle, tandis qu'entre femmes il n'y aurait que des distinctions numériques" (Grosrichard, *Structure du sérail,* 179).

54. Kabbani, *Europe's Myths of Orient,* 84. Norman Bryson, *Tradition and Desire: From David to Delacroix* (Cambridge: Cambridge University Press, 1984), 156–57, describes the Ingres as a painting "about repetition," by which he means not only the cloned figures within the painting but the reappearance of figures and gestures from his earlier painting.

55. Erica Rand, "Diderot and Girl-Group Erotics," *Eighteenth-Century Studies* 25 (1992): 495–516, describes one instance of the pervasive Enlightenment (male) fear of female collectivity and autonomy; Rand shows how that sense of threat was also associated with the forbidden pleasures of voyeurism.

56. Lisa Lowe, in *Critical Terrains,* 70–72, argues that one function of the homoeroticism of the harem is to suggest a challenge to the patriarchy. I do not disagree with respect to the *Lettres persanes,* but insofar as female homoeroticism is a theme in the operas I am considering, it is, I think, more an erotic than a political issue. Chardin is quoted in Kabbani, *Europe's Myths of Orient,* 26. Malek Alloula, *The Colonial Harem* (Minneapolis: University of Minnesota Press, 1986), 95, is quoted in Lowe, *Critical Terrains,* 72.

57. Gluck's orchestration throughout *La rencontre imprévue* is strikingly lush and unusual, particularly in the arias for Ali and Rezia; one might read this as the seraglio casting its spell even on those who must escape its clutches. Bruce A. Brown has kindly pointed out to me that it also reflects this opera's position as Gluck's "parting shot" in the genre.

58. Helmut Wirth, "Gluck, Haydn und Mozart," describes this trio as one of the high points in the opera, leaving *buffa* characterization behind and entering the world of *opera seria.* Daniel Heartz, *Haydn, Mozart, and the Viennese School,* 386, calls it "the most glorious music in the opera."

59. "Mi sembra un sogno che diletta / la speranza che m'alletta / che mi trae fuor di me. / Sì grata sorte, chi aspettava? / Tal ventura, chi pensava? / Io no certo per mia fè." (I seem to be in a delightful dream [of] hope that charms me and draws me out of myself. Who would have expected such a happy fate? Who would have thought of such an adventure? Certainly not I, indeed.)

60. The only direct comparison is in Martín y Soler's 1786 opera *Una cosa rara,* where the vocal equality of two female peasants and the Queen enacts a pastoral fantasy of a world without social distinction. Mozart's three women in *The Magic Flute*—also an orientalist fantasy in some readings (see Said, *Orientalism,* 118) might also fall into this category, though they have no musical number equivalent in length or expression to the Haydn or Martín numbers.

61. Felicity Nussbaum discusses English ambivalences about the seraglio in *Torrid Zones: Maternity, Sexuality, and Empire in Eighteenth-Century English Narratives* (Baltimore: Johns Hopkins University Press, 1995) ch. 6, "Feminotopias: The Seraglio, the Homoerotic, and the Pleasures of 'Deformity.'" Nussbaum argues here that the concept of the seraglio and its apparent restrictions were used by

women writers as a form of resistance to patriarchal control over English wives' lives. In other words, what might seem like slavery and deformity could serve as covers for female community and self-reliance. My argument coincides with Nussbaum's only to the extent of pointing out that the representation of the seraglio could simultaneously suggest opposing ideas or structures.

62. Said, *Orientalism*, 44–46.

THE HUNGARIAN GYPSIES

1. From a letter to his family, 21 August 1928, as quoted in Barbara B. Heyman, *Samuel Barber: The Composer and His Music* (New York: Oxford University Press, 1992), 57. The "zither" is undoubtedly a cimbalom, with which it is sometimes confused.

2. Johann Georg Kohl, *Austria, Vienna, Prague, Hungary, Bohemia, and the Danube* (London: Chapman and Hall, 1843), 214.

3. See, for example, the dark-skinned, colorfully-garbed old Gypsy fortune-teller in Georges de La Tour's *The Fortune-Teller,* from the first half of the seventeenth century. A recent, readily available reproduction may be found in *Smithsonian* 27, no. 2 (December 1996): 75.

4. See the discussion of the eighteenth-century *Tzigányokról való história* (History of the Gypsies) in Bálint Sárosi, *Gypsy Music* [1971], trans. Fred Macnicol (Budapest: Corvina Press, 1978), 14–15.

5. Roland Hoermann, *Achim von Arnim* (Boston: Twayne, 1984), 94. A more positive version of the relationship between Jesus and the Gypsies is given in the 1978 Frank Pierson film *King of the Gypsies,* where the Gypsy mother Susan Sarandon explains to her child, who is trying to excrete a stolen diamond he ate, that because an old Gypsy stole one of the nails intended for the Crucifixion, Jesus gave the Gypsies permanent license to steal. Whether this story originated in European folklore or a screenwriter's imagination is unclear.

6. Ludwig Achim Freiherr von Arnim, *Arnim's Werke,* ed. Alfred Schier, vol. 2 (Leipzig: Bibliographisches Institut, 1925), 77.

7. Clemens Brentano, *Werke,* vol. 1 (München: Carl Hauser Verlag, 1968), 1213–16.

8. A more thorough treatment of the Gypsies' place in European society and popular culture may be found in chapter 4 of Bellman, *The* Style Hongrois *in the Music of Western Europe* (Boston: Northeastern University Press, 1993).

9. Edward Brown, *A Brief Account of Some Travels in Hungaria, Servia, Bulgaria, Macedonia, Thessaly, Austria, Styria, Carthinia, Carniola, and Friuli* (London: Benjamin Tooke, 1673), 70.

10. *Bilder-Conversations-Lexikon für das deutsche Volk* (Leipzig: F. A. Brockhaus, 1841), 801.

11. *Grosses vollständiges Universal Lexicon aller Wissenschaften und Künste,* vol. 62 [Zen–Zie] (Leipzig: Johann Heinrich Bedler, 1749), col. 523.

12. *Bilder-Conversations-Lexikon,* 801.

13. Rev. Robert Walsh, *Narrative of a Journey from Constantinople to England* (London: Frederick Westley and A. H. Davis, 1828), 324–25.

14. *Bilder-Conversations-Lexikon,* 802.

15. Walsh, *Narrative,* 327–28.

16. *Grosses Lexicon,* cols. 526, 529.

17. *Österreichische National-Encyklopädie,* vol. 6 (Vienna: n.p., 1837), 247.

18. Franz Liszt, *The Gipsy in Music* [French first edition, 1859], trans. Edwin Evans (reprint, London: William Reeves, 1960), 102.

19. Ibid., 13.

20. *Österreichische National-Encyklopädie,* 247.

21. Walsh, *Narrative,* 328–29.

22. Ibid., 356–57.

23. *Bilder-Conversations-Lexikon,* 801. Romani women were thus a convenient analogue to the comely and pliant black slave girl, or for that matter the *mulatrice* described in Jean-Paul Sartre's *Huis Clos*—i.e., husbands and sons are no safer around Gypsies than wives and daughters.

24. *The American Heritage Dictionary of the English Language* (New York: American Heritage, 1969), 1126.

25. Though Béla Bartók found no particular inherent musicality in Romani children (Sárosi, *Gypsy Music,* 61).

26. As quoted in ibid., 23.

27. See ibid., 58–60.

28. Ibid., 153–70.

29. The Jews also had a prominent place in Hungarian music making, although their reputation did not equal that of the Gypsies and, moreover, their assimilation was far more successful, which resulted in eventual access to certain other careers. One illustration of the Jewish presence in Hungarian music was Wagner's insulting reference to the non-Jewish Brahms as a "Jewish tuner-up of Czardas" (Richard Wagner, "On Poetry and Composition" [1879], in *Religion and Art,* trans. William Ashton Ellis [Lincoln: University of Nebraska Press, 1994], 144). The relation between Hungarian Gypsy music and Klezmer music is not all that distant, stylistically. One wonderful illustration of the intersection between the two styles is the CD *The Lost Jewish Music of Transylvania,* by Muzsikás (Hannibal Records, HNCD 1373), wherein pre–World War II Hungarian Jewish music is reconstructed by a Hungarian folk music group with the help of two old Gypsy musicians who had played for Jews, the fiddler Gheorghe Covaci and the cimbalom player Árpád Toni.

30. Mátray, "A magyar zene és a magyar cigányok zenéje" [Hungarian music and the music of the Hungarian Gypsies], in *Magyar és Erdélyország Képekbeni* [Hungary and Transylvania in pictures], vol. 4, ed. Ferenc Kubinyi and Imre Vahot (Pest: 1854), 120, quoted in Sárosi, *Gypsy Music,* 144.

31. 16 August 1859, quoted in Sárosi, *Gypsy Music,* 143.

32. See Sárosi, *Gypsy Music,* 141–50.

33. See Bellman, *The* Style Hongrois, chapter 2.

34. The first movement of Bartók's *Contrasts* (1942) for piano, violin, and clarinet, titled "Verbunkos," is a latter-day evocation of many of the gestures that were most familiar: duple meter, dotted rhythms, florid ornamentation, long decorative triplet passages, accented short-long rhythmic figures.

35. On *hallgató* perfomance style, see Sárosi, *Gypsy Music,* 245–46.

36. On *nóta* songs, see ibid., 151–96.

37. Liszt, *The Gipsy in Music,* 307–8.

38. Although it is striking that Carl Maria von Weber, in writing incidental music for *Preciosa,* an early nineteenth-century play based on Cervantes's *La gitanilla,* a novella about Spanish Gypsies, used both an actual Spanish Gypsy melody he overheard and stock musical figures from the Hungarian Gypsy vocabulary.

39. A wonderfully sympathetic discussion of the whole Gypsy performance equation may be found in Sárosi, *Gypsy Music,* 238–53.

40. Sárosi, *Gypsy Music,* 246–47. *Kuruc* means "crusader" and is pronounced *kurutz.*

41. Bence Szabolcsi, *A Concise History of Hungarian Music* [trans. Sára Karig; trans. revised Florence Knepler] (Budapest: Corvina Press, 1964), 56.

42. Robertson Davies, *The Rebel Angels* (New York: Viking Press, 1982), 132.

43. More detailed treatments of the catalogue of musical gestures that make up the *style hongrois* may be found in chapter 5 of Bellman, *The* Style Hongrois, and in Bellman, "Toward a Lexicon for the *Style Hongrois,*" *Journal of Musicology* 9, no. 2 (spring 1991): 214–37.

44. Sárosi, *Gypsy Music,* 27.

45. This figure dates from the *Kuruc* period, which is that of Imre Thököly, a Hungarian nobleman and patriot who, with his *Kuruc* (crusader) fighters, fought against the Hapsburgs and won a settlement from them in 1673. He declined to be made king by the Turks in 1682, but (as stated above) witheld his support from the Hapsburg forces during the Siege of Vienna. While his power and influence declined toward the end of his life, this epoch is remembered with great patriotic fondness by the Hungarians, and the *kuruc*-fourth evokes the music of that time.

46. Liszt, *The Gipsy in Music,* 332–33.

47. Oszkár Dincsér, *Két csíki hangszer* [Two instruments from Csík] (Budapest, 1943), 4, quoted in Sárosi, *Gypsy Music,* 213.

48. Sámuel Brassai, *Magyar vagy czigány-zene?* [Hungarian or Gypsy music?] (Kolozsvár, 1860), 44, quoted in ibid., 147.

49. See, for example, Sárosi, *Gypsy Music,* 115.

50. Liszt, *The Gipsy in Music,* 333.

51. See Mária Domokos, "Ungarische Verbunkos-Melodie im Gitarrenquartett von Schubert-Matiegka," *Studia Musicologica* 24 (1982): 99–112. For a bibliography of this music, complete with many incipits, see Géza Papp, "Die Quellen der 'Verbunkos-Musik': Ein Bibliographischer Versuch," *Studia Musicologica* 21 (1979): 151–217; 24 (1982): 35–97; 26 (1984): 59–132.

52. Otto Erich Deutsch, *Schubert: Memoirs by His Friends,* trans. Rosamond Ley and John Nowell (London: Adam and Charles Black, 1958), 67.

53. This argument is much more fully developed in Bellman, *The* Style Hongrois, chapter 7.

54. Mária Domokos, "Über die ungarischen Charakteristiken des 'Divertissement à l'hongroise,' D. 818," *Schubert durch die Brille* 2 (1992): 53–64.

55. A more detailed treatment of the book, its complicated authorship questions, and Liszt's relation to the Gypsies and their music in general can be found in Bellman, *The* Style Hongrois, chapter 8.

56. Letter of 13 August 1856 to Carolyne Wittgenstein, from Pest, in Liszt, *Correspondance,* ed. Pierre-Antoine Huré and Claude Knepper ([Paris?]: J. C. Lattès, 1987), 341.

57. Letter of 5 March 1851 to Thaddeus Prileszky, reprinted and translated by Charles Suttoni in "Liszt's Letters: A Travelling Gypsy Troupe," *Newsletter of the American Liszt Society* 16 (1984): 112–14.

58. See Alan Walker, *Franz Liszt: The Weimar Years* (New York: Knopf, 1989), 376.

59. In fairness to Liszt, it is in the anti-Semitic passages that some of the clearest proof of another author may be found. In his own correspondence Liszt was far more moderate when speaking of the Jews, even in such a case where an actual comparison was being made: "All that genius of what is *art,* after all, as embodied in the *Gypsies,* who are its custodians (just as the Israelites are the custodians of the genius of commerce) . . ." (Letter of 5 March 1851, translated by Charles Suttoni in "Liszt's Letters"). He openly praised Solomon Sulzer, cantor of the Prague Synagogue, and taught many Jewish piano students. In fact, one of them (Carl Tausig) was a veritable artistic son; Liszt grieved terribly at his premature death in 1871 and still talked wistfully of him at the end of his life.

60. Liszt, *The Gipsy in Music,* 363.

61. Ibid., 361.

62. Ibid., 363–64.

63. *The Memoirs of Hector Berlioz,* ed. Ernest Newman (New York: Tudor Press, 1932), 391.

64. See Bellman, *The* Style Hongrois, chapter 2.

65. It is also noteworthy that the other Exotics Among Us, the Jews, were never evoked in this way; they assimilated more successfully, got into other areas of endeavor, and many went the mainstream route rather than maintain the old, village-based entertainment patterns.

66. J. A. Westrup, "The Chamber Music," in *Schubert: A Symposium,* ed. Gerald Abraham (London: Oxford University Press, 1952), 66–67, 108.

67. "Husnija J.," quoted in Ute Frings, "'If the World Were Like Us, There Would Be No War': One Quarter of Bosnian Refugees in Berlin Are Romany Gipsies," *Frankfurter Rundschau,* May 1996, provided by the German Newspaper News Service, forwarded to ROMNET, a listserv dealing with Romani issues, on 3 May 1996. I am grateful to Dr. Lawrence Mayer for providing me with a copy of the posting.

CUTTHROATS AND CASBAH DANCERS

A fuller version of the present study is forthcoming in *Nineteenth-Century Music.* It includes, among other things, additional musical examples, more extended discussion of certain works mentioned here (by Boieldieu, Rossini, Weber, Meyerbeer, Bizet, Verdi, Saint-Saëns, and Massenet), as well as further thoughts on the representation of gender/sexuality (especially male homoerotic desire) in Orientalist opera. In two other articles I also discuss in greater detail certain questions broached here: "Constructing the Oriental 'Other': Saint-Saëns's *Samson et Dalila,*" *Cambridge Opera Journal* 3 (1991): 261–302, forthcoming in a revised but much shortened version in *The Work of Opera: Genre, Nationhood, and Sexual Difference,* ed. Richard Dellamora and Daniel Fischlin (New York: Columbia University Press, 1997), 161–84; and "Reflections on Orientalism in Opera and Musical Comedy," *Opera Quarterly* 10, no. 1 (Autumn 1993): 48–64.

1. The Near and Middle Eastern Orient can even at times include Greece and other countries around the Black Sea, and of course Spain during its centuries of Moorish rule. These various southern and eastern European regions, though, are largely excluded from the present study.

2. The problem of distinguishing ancient Egyptian from Arab "Oriental" is treated in Jean-Pierre Bartoli, "À la recherche d'une représentation sonore de l'Égypte antique: L'égyptomanie musicale en France de Rossini à Debussy," in *L'égyptomanie à l'épreuve de l'archéologie,* ed. Jean-Marcel Humbert (Paris: Musée du Louvre, 1996), 479–506. A second article by Bartoli gives close attention to a few of the figures discussed below, notably David, Reyer, Salvador-Daniel, Saint-Saëns, Verdi, and Massenet: "L'évolution des procédés exotiques de Félicien David à Saint-Saëns ou comment s'est *ponctuée* la musique orientale en France au XIXe siècle," forthcoming in the proceedings of the 1992 colloquium *Translations et exotismes des musiques de la Méditerranée* (Lyon). Further on antique color(lessness), see Michael Walter, "Exotik oder Farblosigkeit: Antikebilder in der Oper des 19. Jahrhunderts," *Humanistische Bildung* 19 (1996): 117–55 (with discussions of operas by Spontini, Berlioz, Donizetti, and Boito).

3. *Mercure de France,* cited in Georges Favre, *Boieldieu: Sa vie, son oeuvre,* 2 vols. (Paris: Librairie E. Droz, 1944), 115n.

4. The Middle East, it should be quickly added, had and has its own fascination with the West and with various Western musics. See Bruno Nettl, *The Western Impact on World Music: Change, Adaptation, and Survival* (New York: Schirmer Books, 1985), 44–46, 57–61, 72–83, 121–24, 155–61, 177–79. A recorded anthology of recent popular songs from Egypt, Saudi Arabia, and Iraq, many deeply influenced by Western styles, is *Sif safaa: New Music from the Middle East* (EMI Hemisphere 7243-8-32255-2-1).

5. Said, *Culture and Imperialism* (New York: Knopf, 1993), 186. Confusingly, the word "Orientalism" continues also to be used in its longstanding and more neutral academic sense: the study of Middle Eastern languages, cultures, and politics.

6. Marilyn Butler, "Orientalism," in *The Penguin History of Literature,* vol. 5, *The Romantic Period,* ed. David Pirie (London: Penguin Books, 1994), 395–447, 488–92, citation from 399.

7. Said, *Culture and Imperialism,* 186. Felicity Nussbaum gives some interesting instances of this, e.g., in English lesbian writing about harem women (*Torrid Zones: Maternity, Sexuality, and Empire in Eighteenth-Century English Narratives* [Baltimore: Johns Hopkins Press, 1995], 135–62).

8. See Mike Ashman, "'Lakmé': The Twain Meet," *Opera* 42 (1991–92): 283–86; James Parakilas, "The Soldier and the Exotic: Operatic Variations on a Theme of Racial Encounter," *Opera Quarterly* 10 (1994), no. 2: 33–56 and no. 3: 43–69; and Edward Rothstein, "When Worlds Collide, on the Operatic Stage," *New York Times,* Sunday, 9 October 1994, section H, p. 31. Hugh Macdonald stresses an opposite view—the lack of colonial nastiness in Delibes's English folk—in his "The

outre-manche in 19th-Century French Opera," in *D'un opéra l'autre: Hommage à Jean Mongrédien,* ed. Jean Gribenski, Marie-Claire Mussat, and Herbert Schneider (Paris: Presses de l'Université de Paris-Sorbonne, 1996), 155–62.

9. Said, in *Culture and Imperialism,* repeatedly reminds the reader (especially at the beginnings of chapters) that the imperialist or anti-imperialist thread that he finds in great works of art is not necessarily the work's most important aspect, merely *an* important and neglected one. Further on Said's thinking, see Pegram Harrison, "Music and Imperialism," *repercussions* 4, no. 1 (spring 1995): 53–84. Various critical reproaches to Said (many of them hinging on this question of how important a part of the story the imperialist question is) are summarized in John M. MacKenzie, *Orientalism: History, Theory, and the Arts* (Manchester: Manchester University Press, 1995), 1–42. See also *Edward Said: A Critical Reader,* ed. Michael Sprinker (Oxford: Blackwell, 1992) and, for further bibliography, Locke, "Constructing" (long version), n. 9.

10. Cited in Francis Steegmuller, *Flaubert and Madame Bovary: A Double Portrait* (New York: Viking Press, 1939), as cited in César Graña, *Modernity and Its Discontents: French Society and the French Man of Letters in the Nineteenth Century* (New York: Harper and Row, 1967; first published in 1964 as *Bohemian and Bourgeois*), 132.

11. Graña, *Modernity,* 132–33.

12. Malcolm Warner, "The Question of Faith: Orientalism, Christianity and Islam," in *The Orientalists, Delacroix to Matisse: The Allure of North Africa and the Near East,* ed. MaryAnne Stevens (London: Royal Academy of Art, 1984), 32–39.

13. Chris Bongie, *Exotic Memories: Literature, Colonialism, and the Fin de Siècle* (Stanford, Calif.: Stanford University Press, 1991), 83.

14. *Bayadère* more narrowly referred to a woman of India who did sacred or ritualistic dances; the word derives from the Portuguese *bailadeira* (female dancer).

15. On sages, see Raymond Schwab, *Oriental Renaissance: Europe's Rediscovery of India and the East, 1680–1880,* trans. Gene Patterson Black and Victor Reinking (New York: Columbia University Press, 1984). On languid women, see Nussbaum, *Torrid Zones,* and images in Stevens, *Orientalists,* and other such books (see n. 36).

16. On the limitations of the *alla turca* style (to, primarily, a grotesque and noisy "2/4 racket, suitable for . . . great celebration [e.g., military], fury, or mockery"), see Jonathan Bellman, *The* Style Hongrois *in the Music of Western Europe* (Boston: Northeastern University Press, 1993), 45, 66, 68. His brief account is largely seconded by Anke Schmitt, whose fuller discussion (*Der Exotismus in der deutschen Oper zwischen Mozart und Spohr* [Hamburg: Verlag der Musikalienhandlung Karl Dieter Wagner, 1988], 301–72, esp. 337–64) cites instances in the works of numerous lesser German composers such as Wenzel Müller.

17. The Cherubini is an odd case: the most exotic snippet that he borrows is the well-known Chinese tune cited by Rousseau and used by Weber and, later, Paul Hindemith. (The opera incorporates numbers from an earlier opera by Cherubini that was set in China.) In his setting, though, it does not sound obtrusively Far Eastern.

18. Such at least was the opinion (decades later) of Saint-Saëns, who had heard a good deal of North African music during his winter vacations. See his letter to Camille Bellaigue, 23 January 1897, translated in *Composers on Music: An Anthology*

of Composers' Writings from Palestrina to Copland, ed. Sam Morgenstern (New York: Pantheon Books, 1956), 231.

19. See commentary by Floyd K. Grave in his modern edition of Vogler's *Pièces de clavecin* (1798), *Recent Researches in the Music of the Classical Era,* vol. 24 (Madison: A-R Editions, 1986), ix.

20. Joachim Veit, *Der junge Carl Maria von Weber: Untersuchungen zum Einfluß Franz Danzis und Abbé George Joseph Voglers* (Mainz: Schott, 1990).

21. Reminiscence (dating from 1844–45, recalling an event of forty years earlier) by the poet Franz Grillparzer, in *Beethoven Letters, Journals and Conversations,* ed. Michael Hamburger, 2d ed. (London: Jonathan Cape, 1966), 62–63.

22. The transcriptions and arrangements of Salvador-Daniel are discussed in Bartoli, "L'évolution."

23. Details in Gracian Černušák and Andrew Lamb, "Polka," in *New Grove Dictionary of Music and Musicians* 15:42–44.

24. Victor Hugo, *Les orientales; Les feuilles d'automne,* ed. Pierre Albouy (Paris: Gallimard, Livre de poche, 1964), 23 (from preface to the original edition of 1829).

25. Siegfried Kracauer, *Orpheus in Paris: Offenbach and the Paris of His Time,* trans. Gwenda David and Eric Mosbacher (New York: Knopf, 1938), 22.

26. Janet E. Buerger and David Kwasigroh, "Daguerre: The Artist," *Image: Journal of Photography and Motion Pictures of the International Museum of Photography at George Eastman House* 28, no. 2 (June 1985): 2–20. "Solomon's Temple" was designed by Daguerre and Hippolyte Sébron; "Crucifixion," by the latter alone. Both of these traveled to America.

27. See poster reproduced in Ali Behdad, *Belated Travelers: Orientalism in the Age of Colonial Dissolution* (Durham, N.C.: Duke University Press, 1994), 51.

28. These pieces are recorded by Daniel Blumenthal (Marco Polo 8.223376) and deserve a modern reprint or edition. They are discussed in greater detail in Dorothy V. Hagan, *Félicien David, 1810–1876: A Composer and a Cause* (Syracuse, N.Y.: Syracuse University Press, 1985), 57–65, and in Ralph P. Locke, *Music, Musicians, and the Saint-Simonians* (Chicago: University of Chicago Press, 1986), 185–87, 191, 205, 277.

29. Further on *Le désert,* its origins, music, and wildfire reception, see Hagan, *David,* 67–90; Locke, *Music,* 190–95, 201–11, 276–77; and Ralph P. Locke, "The French Symphony from David, Gounod, and Bizet to Saint-Saëns, Franck, and Their Followers," in D. Kern Holoman, ed., *The Nineteenth-Century Symphony* (New York: Schirmer Books, 1997), 163–94, esp. 166–68.

30. Coached by David, the tenor of the first performances sang the muezzin chant in microtones; David, alas, did not—did not know how to?—notate these nuances in the score.

31. The first page is reproduced and discussed in Ralph P. Locke, "Breezes from the Orient, Airs from the Paris Salon: Félicien David Now on Disc," *Journal of the American Liszt Society* 33 (January–June 1993): 44–49.

32. Théophile Gautier, *Gautier on Dance,* ed. and trans. Ivor Guest (London: Dance Books, 1986), 39–50, 134–37.

33. Indeed, de Meyer had first published it as *Machmudier: Air guerrier des Turques.* See R. Allen Lott, "A Berlioz Premiere in America: Leopold de Meyer and the *Marche d'Isly,*" *Nineteenth-Century Music* 8 (1984–85): 226–30.

34. This tune is in fact still known to all American children, via mocking playground rhymes and cartoon soundtracks. If we sing it in A minor, it begins A–B–C–B–A, A–B–C–E–B–C–A. Some information on the tune's origin and publishing history can be found in James Fuld, *The Book of World-Famous Music,* 3d ed. (New York: Dover, 1985), 276–77.

35. It can be heard, for example, in the selections with *req* (tambourine) on a recent CD rerelease of Egyptian music (*Égypte: Taqâsim & Layali,* Unesco Collection Auvidis D8038), though the player goes on to enrich the rhythm with a dazzling variety of cross-accents.

36. For a brief overview of Orientalist art and its parallels in music and for extensive bibliography, see my "Constructing," long version, 263–65.

37. Complete recording on Capriccio 10 380.

38. Reyer's introductory "Notes" to the piano-vocal score of *Le sélam: Symphonie orientale en quatre parties* (Paris: Bureau Central de Musique, [1850?]; reprint [Paris]: Choudens, n.d.).

39. Further on these and other French biblical oratorios, see Frank Reinisch, *Das französische Oratorium von 1840 bis 1870* (Regensburg: G. Bosse Verlag, 1982), esp. 272–73, 275–92, 312–24, 414–15.

40. To be fair, the tiresome saintliness of the heroine is somewhat relieved by gossamer choruses of *houris* and the like (perhaps based on analogous moments in Weber's *Oberon*).

41. Parakilas, "Soldier," pt. 1, p. 33.

42. One of the tunes, oddly, sounds Chinese-pentatonic.

43. Some of these, one should note, incorporate comic elements, as was increasingly the case in such genres as *opéra lyrique.* (See the discussion below of the *Thaïs* quartet.) An extensive listing of exotic operas from the second half of the century is given in Ragnhild Gulrich, *Exotismus in der Opera und seine szenische Realisation (1850–1910) unter besonderer Berücksichtigung der Münchener Oper* (Anif/Salzburg: Verlag Ursula Müller-Speiser, 1993), 304–8.

44. Locke, "Constructing the Oriental 'Other,'" 271–75.

45. Example 5.6 makes use of a repeated tight turn figure and much pandiatonic harmony. Example 5.7 features melismatic writing in the winds and a fascinatingly shifting modality (both the sixth and seventh degrees can be either flat or natural).

46. Rodney Milnes, "*Hérodiade,*" in *New Grove Dictionary of Opera* 2:702–4 (quotation from p. 704).

47. Gabriele Brandstetter, "*Erodiade,*" in *Pipers Enzyklopädie des Musiktheaters,* 5 vols. to date (1986–), 4:739–42 (citation from p. 740).

48. Joseph Kerman, *Opera as Drama,* rev. ed. (Berkeley and Los Angeles: University of California Press, 1988), 206–7. Paul Robinson says that the Orientalist style conventions "make their historical début in Meyerbeer's *L'africaine,* which took Europe by storm in the 1860s" ("Orientalist Opera?" 137). But, as we have seen, many of these style conventions were established and disseminated long before the premiere of *L'africaine.*

49. Kerman, *Opera,* 206–7. The accusation echoes Wagner's famous complaint about Meyerbeer's "effects without causes."

50. This gives reason to regret the omission of some or all of certain dance

numbers in various commercial recordings, e.g., *Hérodiade* with Plácido Domingo and Renée Fleming (1995) and Rubinstein's *The Demon* (Wexford Festival, 1996). Denizens of neighboring regions include Phoenicians, Babylonians, etc., in *Hérodiade,* Act 4; Persians in *Le roi de Lahore* (1877), beginning of Act 2, and in Mussorgsky, *Khovanshchina* (1872–80), Act 4. On the varieties of national dance earlier in the century and their deployment in theatrical works, see Lisa C. Arkin and Marian Smith, "National Dance in the Romantic Ballet," forthcoming in *Studies in Dance History.*

51. Cf. Carl Dahlhaus, *Nineteenth-Century Music,* trans. J. Bradford Robinson (Berkeley and Los Angeles: University of California Press, 1989), 223 (re.: Moniuszko).

52. This aspect is sensitively explored in Julian Budden, *The Operas of Verdi,* vol. 3 (New York: Oxford University Press, 1981), 203, 206 (the cross-reference should correctly read "Ex. 96"), 209, 236.

53. This finally sympathetic treatment of both women is related to the even-handedness of the politics in *Aida* (regarding which see Locke, "Reflections," 58–61).

54. That is, unless one sees the Philistines as a caricature of the Europeans, and the European audiences, of Saint-Saëns's own day, a quite defensible if incomplete reading. See Locke, "Constructing," 285–89.

55. Kundry, the chief seductress in this scene, is specifically dressed "in somewhat transparent, fantastical garments—approximately of Arabian style." Further on Kundry's, and Klingsor's, desire for Parsifal, see Marc A. Weiner, *Richard Wagner and the Anti-Semitic Imagination* (Lincoln: University of Nebraska Press, 1995), 225–59 (stage direction cited on p. 246, with photo from first production, 1882).

56. Heinrich Schenker went further, espousing frank rejection of non-Western musics: "Arabic, Japanese, and Turkish songs," rather like "the babbling of a child," are "often original [and charming] only because of their imperfections and awkwardness" and therefore can have nothing to contribute to "a more advanced art" such as has been achieved by "the [European] masters" (*Counterpoint: A Translation of "Kontrapunkt,"* ed. John Rothgeb and trans. John Rothgeb and Jürgen Thym, 2 vols. [New York: Schirmer Books, 1982], 1:28–29).

57. Bongie, *Exotic Memories,* 72, 17, cf. 90.

58. On octatonicism and its meanings, see Richard Taruskin, *Stravinsky and the Russian Traditions: A Biography of the Works through "Mavra,"* 2 vols. (Berkeley and Los Angeles: University of California Press, 1996).

59. Simon Trezise, *Debussy: "La mer"* (Cambridge: Cambridge University Press, 1993), 24, 46, 48, 56.

60. Lawrence Kramer carries this thought further, referring to a cult of the beautiful surface (carried out in part through various exotic stylistic devices) in *Daphnis.* Kramer argues that such a work carries out a sublimation in art of energies found more overtly in other aspects of turn-of-the-century French culture, notably consumerism (which likewise depended on imports from the colonies). ("Consuming the Exotic: Ravel's *Daphnis et Chloë,*" in his *Classical Music and Postmodern Knowledge* [Berkeley and Los Angeles: University of California Press, 1995], 201–25.) The absorption of Orientalistic style features into other "non-Oriental"

(and in some cases modernist) works is also touched upon in Bartoli, "L'évolution." Fascinating further instances pop up in Gustav Holst's *The Planets* (1914–16), namely the middle sections of "Venus" and "Mercury."

61. Cited in Norman Del Mar, *Richard Strauss: A Critical Commentary on His Life and Works,* 3 vols., [3d ed.] (Ithaca, N.Y.: Cornell University Press, 1986), 1:243.

62. A contemporary observer, Michel Corday, cited in Kramer, "Consuming," 213.

63. Erno Rapée, ed., *Motion Picture Moods for Piano and Organ: A Rapid-Reference Collection of Selected Pieces Adapted to Fifty-Two Moods and Situations* (New York: G. Schirmer, 1924). The most likely model for such pieces was that feast of augmented seconds, the Bacchanale from Saint-Saëns's *Samson.* On the augmented second in Middle Eastern evocations, see Bartoli, "L'évolution." I call the augmented second reductive in part because it serves as a standardized formula replacing the much richer variety of microtonal inflections in Arab folk and art music. Cf. Locke, "Constructing," 266–67.

64. On evocations of American Indians, see Michael Pisani's essay in this volume.

65. Such postcards form the basis for the ponderings in Malek Alloula, *The Colonial Harem,* trans. Myrna Godzich and Wlad Godzich (Minneapolis: University of Minnesota Press, 1987).

66. These and other *chansons arabes, chansons nègres,* songs relating to the French Foreign Legion (e.g., by Piaf), and of course "Petite tonkinoise" and other bits of *faux*-Asiatica are available on a 2-CD collection (on the French EPM label): *Chansons coloniales et exotiques, 1906–1942,* EPM983312/ADE798. The booklet reproduces travel posters, sheet music covers, and an advertisement for the Exposition Coloniale Internationale (Paris 1931) featuring lesser-known colonies, such as Sudan, and posing the question: "Did you know that France was so big?"

67. This rhythm is used throughout "Sahara" (sung by Nitta-Jo, 1935, with Orchestre M. Cariven), disc 1, band 1 on *Chansons coloniales.*

68. On *Chansons coloniales,* respectively: disc 1, band 7 ("Abd El-Kader," 1930), disc 1, band 2 ("Nuits d'outremer," 1932). Several of these songs toy with the possibility of romance—and even sex and resulting babies—between French people and colonial natives. In the same anthology are parodies of speech and chanting on, among others, disc 1, band 12 ("Ali ben Baba"), disc 1, band 17 ("Le marchand de tapis," a 1931 comic spoken scene by Dominus, ending with a free imitation of a muezzin, or is it of the oboe introduction to Saint-Saëns's Bacchanale?), disc 1, band 24 ("Le Radabi-nacou-naha," 1935), disc 2, band 15 ("Arrouah Sidi!" 1914), and disc 2, bands 7 and 21 ("Butterfly-Tox," 1931, and "À Rabat," 1934, both sung by women and both using "Kradoudja" in the refrain). All four of these also include imitations of *zurna* playing or other instrumental effects, as do various other items on disc 2, e.g, band 1: "Ali Baba," 1933 (sung by the Comedian Harmonists); band 4: "Le caravanier," 1940; band 19: "Le fanion de la légion," 1936; band 23: "Allah oulla," 1931; and band 5: "Estampe marocaine," 1936 (which begins with a brief, marketplace-like mélange of pseudo-Arab chatter and musical sounds).

69. Pierre Boulez, *Orientations: Collected Writings,* ed. Jean-Jacques Nattiez, trans. Martin Cooper (Cambridge, Mass.: Harvard University Press, 1986), 341.

70. Jean-Marcel Humbert, Michael Pantazzi, and Christiane Ziegler, eds., *Egyp-*

tomania: Egypt in Western Art, 1730–1930 (Ottawa: National Gallery of Canada, 1994).

71. Kerman, of course, has done much in other circumstances to reveal and counteract such bias.

72. George Lipsitz invokes organicism in a different way in his critique of recent borrowings and reworkings of Third World musics by Western pop songwriters/composers Paul Simon or David Byrne. Such works as Simon's *Graceland* album are Orientalist (in the broadest sense of the term) and arguably even colonialist in conception, in contrast to the "[mixed and] varied repertoire" of the Texas-raised singer Baldemar Huerta (a.k.a. Freddy Fender), whose "varied repertoire . . . flowed *organically* from his experiences as a worker in a multi-cultural society" (*Dangerous Crossroads: Popular Music, Postmodernism, and the Poetics of Place* [London: Verso, 1994], 49–68, quotations from pp. 64–65, emphasis mine; the term "orientalism" [with a small "o"] recurs throughout the chapter, and "colonize," in regard to Simon, is posited for debate—though not by any means applied as a simple derogatory label—on p. 59).

73. The interpretation proposed in the remainder of this paragraph is offered in the spirit of Marc A. Weiner's recent conclusion, regarding Wagner's works: the cultural impact today of these "documents of a different cultural vocabulary with racist [e.g., anti-Semitic] and exclusionary implications," he notes, is hard to evaluate precisely because certain aspects of that cultural vocabulary—of late nineteenth-century "representations of commonality and difference"—have become dead metaphors, thanks to various shifts in cultural values, whereas others (e.g., "the enigmatically seductive and yet threatening bodily presence of all that is deemed exotic") remain functional and alive (Weiner, *Wagner,* 350–52).

HOW SPAIN GOT A SOUL

For inspiration, advice, and assistance in the preparation of this study, I am grateful to Maribeth Clark, Margaret Cobb, Carol Hess, Mary Hunter, Ralph Locke, Paula Matthews, Clifton Olds, Sharon Saunders, Jennifer Williams Brown, Susan Youens, and the library staffs of Bates College, Bowdoin College, and Harvard University.

1. Artur Schnabel, *Music and the Line of Most Resistance* (Princeton, N.J.: Princeton University Press, 1942; reprint, New York: Da Capo Press, 1969), 87.

2. Sydney Grew, one of those listeners, even credited French and Russian composers with leaving the way "open for native Spaniards to take part in the work." See Grew, "Modern Spanish Music," in *Spain: A Companion to Spanish Studies,* ed. E. Allison Peers, 4th ed. (London: Methuen, 1948), 240.

3. François René de Chateaubriand, "Avertissement" to *Les aventures du dernier Abencérage,* in Chateaubriand, *Oeuvres romanesques et voyages,* ed. Maurice Regard, vol. 2 (Paris: Gallimard, 1969), 1359 (my translation). In an excellent account of the exoticization of Spain in French literature, Léon-François Hoffmann's *Romantique Espagne: L'image de l'Espagne en France entre 1800 et 1850* (Princeton, N.J., and Paris: Princeton University Department of Romance Languages and Presses Universitaires de France, 1961), the chapter "Evolution of the Image: The Influence of Events" begins, like my account, with Napoleon's Spanish campaign.

4. Hoffmann, *Romantique Espagne,* 20.

5. David Charlton, "The Nineteenth Century: France," in *Oxford Illustrated History of Opera,* ed. Roger Parker (Oxford: Oxford University Press, 1994), 140. It is hard to know, however, why Charlton would choose the word *bloodless* to describe either the historical events or their depiction in this opera, famous for its battle scenes.

6. Anselm Gerhard, "Fernand Cortez," in *New Grove Dictionary of Opera* 2:156; Gerald Abraham, "The Best of Spontini," *Music and Letters* 23 (1942): 168; Charlton, in Parker, ed., *Oxford Illustrated History of Opera,* 140.

7. On the influence in France of the Spanish Gallery at the Louvre, opened in 1838 with works plundered from Spanish collections by Baron Taylor, see Alisa Luxenberg, "Over the Pyrenees and through the Looking-Glass: French Culture Reflected in Its Imagery of Spain," in *Spain, Espagne, Spanien: Foreign Artists Discover Spain, 1800–1900,* curated by Suzanne L. Stratton (New York: The Equitable Gallery in association with the Spanish Institute, 1993), 16–19. This entire catalog, with separate essays on the French, British, German, and American traditions, provides an excellent survey of the exotic Spanish theme in nineteenth-century painting. On Spanish influences on Manet, see the catalog *Manet and Spain: Prints and Drawings,* exhibition prepared by Joel Isaacson at the Museum of Art, University of Michigan, Ann Arbor, 1969. See also the catalog of the exhibition *Manet, 1832–1883,* Françoise Cachin and Charles S. Moffett, curators, in collaboration with Michel Melot (New York: Metropolitan Museum of Art and Harry N. Abrams, 1983) for discussion and illustration of Spanish models behind such Manet works as the paintings *The Spanish Singer, Young Woman Reclining, in Spanish Costume, Lola de Valence,* and *The Dead Toreador* and the etching *The Gypsies.*

8. Prosper Mérimée, in his *Lettres d'Espagne* of 1830 (critical ed. by Gérard Chaliand [Paris: Editions Complexe, 1989], 90), writes that in Spain "a bandit generally starts out by being a smuggler." The titles of Mérimée's letters, actually journalistic reports, in themselves spell out the exotic Spanish types: "The Bullfight," "An Execution," "The Bandits," "The Spanish Sorceresses." A more thorough and more modern study of this typology can be found in part 2 of Hoffmann's *Romantique Espagne*: "Analyse de l'image de l'Espagne en France."

9. See the foreword by Juan Manuel Suárez Japón to Manuel García, *Canciones y caprichos liricos,* ed. Celsa Alonso (Madrid: Instituto Complutense de Ciencias Musicales, 1994). "Yo que soy contrabandista" and other songs of García have been recorded by Ernesto Palacio on Almaviva DS 0114.

10. Mérimée, *Lettres d'Espagne,* 89, 81.

11. Christiane Le Bordays, "L'hispanisme musical français," *Revue internationale de musique française* 6 (November 1981): 41–52; see especially 48–51. Similarly, as Rana Kabbani writes in *Europe's Myths of Orient* (Bloomington: Indiana University Press, 1986), 69, "in the Orientalist paintings of the nineteenth century, [the dance] often became a trope for the Orient's abandon."

12. M. Elizabeth C. Bartlet, "Méhul, Etienne-Nicolas," in *New Grove Dictionary of Opera* 3:308.

13. See Hoffmann, *Romantique Espagne,* 112–13. The dance is traditionally said to have been "invented" around 1780, and music to it was certainly in print, in Spain at least, by the beginning of the nineteenth century, in publications such as the *Colección de las mejores coplas de seguidillas, tiranas y polos* (1799) by "Don

Preciso" (Juan Antonio de Iza Zamácola). See Javier Suárez-Pajares, "Bolero," in *Die Musik in Geschichte und Gegenwart,* 2d ed., 2:1–7. The aria in *Le calife de Bagdad* is Késie's "De tous les pays" (Act 1, scene 5).

14. At exactly the same time that Méhul created this effect, Beethoven was building the scherzo (*Allegretto vivace e sempre scherzando*) of his first "Razumovsky" string quartet (op. 59, no. 1) out of another rhythm without a line: the four-measure cello rhythm on a single note that opens that movement.

15. Chateaubriand claimed, perhaps disingenuously, that he delayed the publication because even this story of old Granada would not have been permitted under Napoleon. See Chateaubriand, "Avertissement," 1359.

16. See the present author's "The Soldier and the Exotic: Operatic Variations on a Theme of Racial Encounter," *Opera Quarterly* 10, no. 2 (winter 1993–94): 33–56 and no. 3 (1994): 43–69.

17. Chateaubriand, *Les aventures du dernier Abencérage,* 1373–74 (my translation).

18. The score I have consulted is a vocal score by F. Brissler derived from Spontini's adaptation of the opera in 1828 for Berlin, under the title *Die Abenceragen, oder Das Feldpanier von Granada* (Leipzig: C. F. Peters, [ca. 1873]. The opera is studied from a variety of perspectives in Oliver Heidemann, *Luigi Cherubini: Les Abencérages, ou L'étendard de Grenade: Untersuchungen zur Operngeschichte des französischen Empire* (Münster and New York: Waxmann, 1994). The story, unrelated to Chateaubriand's *Aventures,* is based on legends that had been treated in various sources, most recently in J.-P. C. de Florian's *Gonsalve de Cordoue* (1791).

19. See Spire Pitou, *The Paris Opera: An Encyclopedia of Operas, Ballets, Composers, and Performers,* vol. 2, *Rococo and Romantic, 1715–1815,* (Westport, Conn.: Greenwood Press, 1983–90), 6.

20. Théophile Gautier, *Voyage en Espagne, suivi de España,* ed. Patrick Berthier (Paris: Gallimard, 1981), 43. The collected articles appeared in 1843 under the title *Tra los montes. Voyage en Espagne*; a second edition, called simply *Voyage en Espagne,* appeared in 1845. See the "Notice," pp. 514–16 of Berthier's edition.

21. Luxenberg, in "Over the Pyrenees," places the publication of the first illustrated French guidebook to Spain, Laborde's *Voyage pittoresque et historique de l'Espagne* (1806–20), within a long French tradition of "travels" to Spain.

22. Gautier, *Voyage en Espagne,* 244.

23. Gautier's reviews of Spanish dance in Paris are collected and translated by Ivor Guest in "Théophile Gautier on Spanish Dancing" *Dance Chronicle* 10, no. 1 (1987): 1–104. They are also to be found in Guest's larger collection, *Gautier on Dance,* selected, translated and annotated by Ivor Guest (London: Dance Books, 1986). On Spanish fashions, see especially Gautier's account of his exchange with the tailor Juan Zapata in Granada, in ch. 11 of *Voyage en Espagne* (pp. 261–64 of the Berthier edition).

24. Gautier, "The Spanish Dancers," *La charte de 1830,* 18 April 1837, trans. Guest in "Théophile Gautier on Spanish Dancing," 14, esp. n. 3. There is also a caricature of Fanny Elssler dancing the cachucha with two male Fanny Elssler impersonators, reproduced in Jarmila Weissenbock, *Fanny Elssler: Materialien* (Vienna: Bohlaus, 1984), 39.

25. Gautier, *Voyage en Espagne,* 59.

26. Gautier, "Dolores Serral," *La presse,* 2 October 1837, in Guest, "Gautier on Spanish Dancing," 22.

27. See Guest, "Gautier on Spanish Dancing," 4. On the *escuela bolera,* see the bibliography in Suárez-Pajares, "Bolero," in *MGG2,* 2:6–7.

28. Gautier, "The Spanish Dancers," in Guest, "Gautier on Spanish Dancing," 8.

29. Hugo wrote "Guitare," in 1837 and published it in his collection *Les rayons et les ombres* in 1840. Louis-James-Alfred Lefébure-Wély, *Boléro de concert,* op. 166, ed. Ewald Kooiman in *Incognita organo,* vol. 30 (Hilversum: Harmonia, 1984). Pauline Viardot, "Madrid" (Paris: Heugel, n.d.) reprinted in Pauline Duchambge, Loïsa Puget, Pauline Viardot, and Jane Vieu, *Anthology of Songs,* intro. Susan C. Cook and Judy S. Tsou (New York: Da Capo Press, 1988); publication information on p. 201 of A. Rozanov, *Polina Viardot-Garcia* (Leningrad: Muzyka, 1973), the only work yet on Viardot-Garcia to give attention to her achievement as a composer.

30. A typical description is Willi Kahl's in the article "Bolero" in *New Grove Dictionary of Music and Musicians* 2:871: "Chopin's *Boléro* op. 19 more nearly resembles a polonaise, at least in the *allegro vivace* parts." Suárez-Pajares ("Bolero" in *MGG2,* 2:6) likewise calls it "really a bolero-polonaise."

31. The controlled trill in the third measure of this example can be found, for instance, in the songs of Manuel García. A collection of those songs (*Caprichos liricos españoles*) had recently been published in Paris, in 1830 (reprint, Geneva: Minkoff, 1993).

32. On the influence of French culture, including French musical culture, on Verdi, see Marcello Conati, "Verdi et la culture parisienne des années 1830" in *Music in Paris in the Eighteen-Thirties,* ed. Peter Bloom (Stuyvesant, N.Y.: Pendragon Press, 1987), 209–27. On Verdi's adaptations of musical genres from French opera, see two articles by James Hepokoski: "Genre and Content in Mid-century Verdi: 'Addio, del passato' (*La traviata,* Act III)," *Cambridge Opera Journal* 1, no. 3 (November 1989): 249–76, and "*Ottocento* Opera as Cultural Drama: Generic Mixtures in *Il trovatore,*" to appear in the proceedings of the Belfast Verdi conference, ed. Martin Chusid.

33. The libretto of *Don Carlos* was, moreover, in part the work of Camille Du Locle, who, given his roles in the creation of *Carmen, Aida,* and Reyer's *Salammbô,* can be considered one of the most important purveyors of operatic exoticism in nineteenth-century Paris.

34. Roger Parker, "*Traviata, La,*" in *New Grove Dictionary of Opera* 4:801.

35. Alexandra Orlova, *Glinka's Life in Music: A Chronicle,* trans. Richard Hoops (Ann Arbor, Mich.: UMI Research Press, 1988), 448 (20 May/1 June 1845), 474 (4/16 July 1846).

36. Ibid., 450 (7/19 June 1845), 473 (11/23 June 1846).

37. Ibid., 467 (not later than the second half of January 1846), 464 (28 December 1845/9 January 1846).

38. Ibid., 457 (the manuscript score is dated Madrid, 24 September 1845), 467 (not later than the second half of January 1846).

39. Nevertheless, Glinka may have learned the melody in an ethnographic way. On 22 June/4 July 1845 he wrote: "Among our acquaintances, the son of a merchant here by the name of Felix Castilla plays the guitar very lively, especially the *jota*

aragonesa, which I have committed to memory along with his variations" (Orlova, *Glinka's Life,* 451).

40. Ibid., 453 (3/15 August 1845).

41. Glinka, Bolero for piano, critical edition in the complete works (M. I. Glinka, *Polnoe sobranie sochinenij,* ed. V. Ja. Shebalin et al. [Moscow: Gosudarstvennoe Muzykal'noe Izdatel'stvo, 1955–69]), 6:208–16. He created the piece from the melody of his song "O, deva chudnaja moja."

42. In that sense, Glinka's work in Spain can be considered comparable to Dvořák's composition of works on American subjects during his time in the United States.

43. Orlova, *Glinka's Life,* 459 (from the second half of October 1845).

44. Ibid., 473 (beginning of June 1846).

45. See Robert Stevenson, "Liszt at Madrid and Lisbon: 1844–45," *Musical Quarterly* 65, no. 4 (1979): 493–512, and Derek Watson, *Liszt* (New York: Schirmer Books, 1989), 73. *Grosse Konzertfantasie über spanische Weisen* (Leipzig: Fr. Kistner, 1887) was conceived in Lisbon in 1845.

46. At the time this essay is being written, the *Rondeau fantastique sur un thème espagnol (El contrabandista),* op. 5 (Leipzig: Fr. Hofmeister, 1837), is to be reissued, in the New Liszt Edition, for the first time since the original edition. The polo Bizet imitated was García's "Cuerpo bueno, alma divina," which had then just reappeared in an arrangement by P. Lacome and J. Puig y Alsubide in their collection *Echos d'Espagne: Chansons et danses populaires,* with French texts by P. Lacome and J. de Lau-Lusignan (Paris: Durand, Schoenewerk, 1872).

47. Liszt letter of about 1 September 1845 to Felix von Lichnowsky, in *Bayreuther Blätter: Deutsche Zeitschrift im Geiste Richard Wagners* 30, nos. 1–3 (1907): 35; cited in Stevenson, "Liszt at Madrid," 493, n. 2. The *Rhapsodie espagnole* (Leipzig: C. F. W. Siegal, 1867) was written in Rome about 1863.

48. As an American musician arriving at a time of conflict between Spain and the United States, Gottschalk was advised to portray himself as a Frenchman. Instead, he constructed a favorable political identity for himself as a non-Frenchman by giving the Spanish public a "monster" concert piece such as no French musician would have composed: *El sitio de Zaragoza* for ten pianos, using the *jota aragonesa* among other Spanish themes to celebrate a famous Spanish stand against the French in the Napoleonic Wars. See Clyde W. Brockett, "Gottschalk in Madrid: A Tale of Ten Pianos," *Musical Quarterly* 75, no. 2 (summer 1991): 279–315.

49. The *jota aragonesa* figures in the *Capricho español* (Madrid: C. Monier, 1852), *El sitio de Zaragoza* for ten pianos (performed in Madrid on 13 June 1852; original version lost; solo piano version in autograph in the New York Public Library for the Performing Arts, Gottschalk Family Collection, item 108), and, naturally enough, *La jota aragonesa: Caprice espagnol* (New York: William Hall, 1855). The *Chanson du gitano* was first published in *The Little Book of Louis Moreau Gottschalk: Seven Previously Unpublished Piano Pieces,* transcribed and ed. Richard Jackson and Neil Ratliff (New York: New York Public Library and Continuo Music Press, 1976); see also the editors' commentary on the piece, 18–19. *Manchega: Etude de concert* is reproduced from an original edition, along with three other "Spanish" pieces, in *Piano Music of Louis Moreau Gottschalk,* ed. Richard Jackson (New York:

Dover, 1973). Near the end of his stay in Spain, Glinka reported attending dancing parties "where during the dances the best native singers there poured forth in an oriental style, while the dancers adroitly executed their steps; it seemed that one could hear three different rhythms." Glinka, *Memoirs* (winter 1846–47), quoted in Orlova, *Glinka's Life*, 484.

50. Carl Loewe, "Der Sturm von Alhama," op. 54, and the *Drei Balladen von Freiligrath*, op. 97, for instance; Robert Schumann, *Spanisches Liederspiel* for vocal quartet with piano, op. 74, and *Spanische Liebeslieder* for vocal quartet with piano, four hands, op. 138.

51. In Schumann's *Spanisches Liederspiel*, op. 74, the most striking reference to Spanish music, in fact the closest approach to exoticism, comes in the added-on song "Der Contrabandiste," which takes a translation of García's song "Yo que soy contrabandista" for its text, but refers only indirectly to García's music.

52. See Hugh Macdonald, "Lalo, Edouard," in *New Grove Dictionary of Music and Musicians* 10:387–89. Sarasate, *Zigeunerweisen*, op. 20 (Leipzig, 1878); *Spanische Tänze* (Berlin: Simrock, 1878).

53. See Boris Schwartz, "Sarasate, Pablo de," in *New Grove Dictionary of Music and Musicians* 16:496, where that portrait is reproduced.

54. Teresa Berganza, letter to Peter Diamond for the program of the 1977 Edinburgh Festival production of *Carmen*, reproduced in the booklet of the recording of that production (Deutsche Grammophon 2709 083), English trans. Lionel Salter, 9.

55. Hoffmann, in an appendix to *Romantique Espagne*, 167–78, gives an invaluable list of works on Spanish themes (including operas and ballets) presented in Paris theaters in the first half of the nineteenth century—as many as fifteen new ones in a single year, and the list is not without omissions. I am unaware of any comparable list for the years after 1850.

56. See Mina Curtiss, *Bizet and His World* (New York: Vienna House, 1974; originally published 1958), 391. This work also provides a rich portrait of Galli-Marié and her role in the creation of the opera.

57. Yradier, *El arreglito: Canción habanera*. The first two pages of the original Madrid edition of 1840 are reproduced in the entry "Habanera" by Arno Fuchs in *MGG1*, 5:1188. It had been published in Paris (in a volume entitled *Fleurs d'Espagne* issued by Heugel in 1864) by the time Bizet learned it. The excerpt given here, in Example 6.10, is from an Heugel republication of the 1880s entitled *Chansons espagnoles del Maëstro Yradier*, with texts translated by Paul Bernard and D. Tagliafico. For a complete account of Bizet's borrowings from Spanish sources in the whole of *Carmen* (not a long list), see Winton Dean, *Georges Bizet: His Life and Work* (London: Dent, 1965), 227–31.

58. It was, not surprisingly, this bass rhythm that I heard when I tried out the "Carmen" button on an electronic keyboard instrument in a store recently—almost the only "classical music" rhythm that the instrument offered. But then, the habanera/tango (not the bolero) is the longest-surviving of Spanish dance rhythms in Western popular music and dance.

59. See Curtiss, *Bizet and His World*, 383.

60. See Parakilas, "The Soldier and the Exotic," part 1.

61. Letter to Charles Lamoureux, 25 October 1882, in Emmanuel Chabrier, *Cor-*

respondance, ed. Roger Delage and Frans Durif with Thierry Bodin (n.p.: Klincksieck, 1994), 168, 169.

62. Letter to Wilhelm Enoch and Georges Costallat, 21 October 1882, in Chabrier, *Correspondance,* 166–67.

63. See Martin Cunningham, "Spain, II, 8: History of folk music collection," in *New Grove Dictionary of Music and Musicians* 17:804. Rimsky-Korsakov used the first volume of Inzenga's *Cantos y bailes populares de España* (Madrid: A. Romero, 1874), which presented music from Galicia and Asturias. Inzenga published two other volumes in the series, presenting music of Murcia and Valencia, in 1888.

64. Bourgault-Ducoudray in *Le ménestrel,* 18 November 1883, quoted in Yvonne Tienot, *Chabrier: Par lui-même et par ses intimes* (Paris: Lemoine, 1965), 40. See Marion Papenbrok, "History of Flamenco," especially the section "The 'Golden Age' of Flamenco," in *Flamenco: Gypsy Dance and Music from Andalusia,* ed. Claus Schreiner, trans. Mollie Comerford Peters (Portland, Ore.: Amadeus Press, 1990). A thought-provoking analysis of the controversies surrounding the origins of flamenco music and dance can be found in Timothy Mitchell, *Flamenco Deep Song* (New Haven, Conn.: Yale University Press, 1994).

65. Chabrier, letter to Enoch and Costallat, 21 October 1882, in *Correspondance,* 166; 169, n. 2; letter to Edouard Moullé, 4 November 1882, in *Correspondance,* 174.

66. See Anna Ivanova, *The Dance in Spain* (New York: Praeger, 1970), 148–49.

67. It is established that Ravel heard Rimsky conduct the *Capriccio on Spanish Themes* at the Exposition concert in 1889; see G. W. Hopkins, "Maurice Ravel," in *New Grove Twentieth-Century French Masters* (New York: Norton, 1986), 186. Ravel scholars have regularly pointed to the *Capriccio* as one of the crucial influences on Ravel's orchestration; see, for example, Arbie Orenstein, *Ravel: Man and Musician* (New York: Columbia University Press, 1975), 136. Debussy seems not only to have heard the *Capriccio* in 1889 but also to have performed a piano duet arrangement of it with René Chansarel in 1894; see Edward Lockspeiser, *Debussy: His Life and Mind,* vol. 1, *1862–1902* (London: Cassell, 1962), 52, n. 1. As to the music performed by Spanish Gypsies at the exposition, see François Lesure, "Debussy et le syndrome de Grenade," *Revue de musicologie* 68, nos. 1–2 (1982): 102.

68. Noël Lee rehearses the evidence of Debussy's borrowing from the Ravel Habanera in the notes to *Lindaraja* in his edition of the *Oeuvres pour deux pianos* in the *Oeuvres complètes de Claude Debussy* (Paris: Durand-Costallat, 1986), xvii–xix. Debussy's "Spanish" songs include "Madrid, princesse des Espagnes" of about 1879 (on the same Musset text set by Viardot-Garcia); "Séguidille" of about 1881 (Gautier); and "Chanson espagnole" of 1883 (Musset—Delibes's "Les filles de Cadix" of 1872 is a more famous setting of the same poem). The cantata was *Zuleima,* on a text derived from Heine's *Almansor*; the opera was *Rodrigue et Chimène,* to a libretto by Catulle Mendès. On the nature and fate of these two projects, see Lockspeiser, *Debussy* 1:66–67, 74–75, 97–99.

69. The Chabrier is the Habanera for piano of 1885. Among other habaneras that Ravel could have known and that exhibit the same features are several in Paul Lacome's *Album national espagnol: Danses et chansons populaires* for piano, published in the Collection Litolff (Brunswick: Henry Litolff, n.d.).

70. Lesure, "Debussy et le syndrome de Grenade," 106.

71. Washington Irving, *The Alhambra,* ed. William T. Lenehan and Andrew B. Myers, vol. 14 of *The Complete Works of Washington Irving,* Richard Dilworth Rust, general ed. (Boston: Twayne Publishers, 1983), 60–62. The first French translation of *The Alhambra* appeared in 1832, the same year that it was published in the original. In 1886—Debussy's day—a new French translation was published.

72. Manuel de Falla, "Claude Debussy and Spain" (1920), reprinted in Falla, *On Music and Musicians,* ed. Federico Sopeña, trans. David Urman and J. M. Thomson (London: Marion Boyars, 1979), 42. Claude Debussy, letter of 11 February 1901 to Paul Dukas, in *Debussy Letters,* ed. François Lesure and Roger Nichols, trans. Roger Nichols (Cambridge, Mass.: Harvard University Press, 1987; French ed. Paris, 1980), 118. His only surviving comment on his "Soirée dans Grenade" is in the same vein: "if this isn't exactly the music they play in Granada, so much the worse for Granada" (letter of July 1903 to Pierre Louÿs, in *Debussy Letters,* 107).

73. This and the previous sentence quoted from Falla both come from "Claude Debussy and Spain," 42.

74. Lockspeiser cites several letters of Debussy, from the early stages of his work on *Ibéria* and its companion pieces, in which he describes them as *Images* for two pianos; that would not mean, of course, that he wasn't also thinking of orchestrating them. See Lockspeiser, *Debussy: His Life and Mind,* vol. 2, *1902–1918* (New York: Macmillan, 1965), 29, n. 2.

75. Debussy, letter of 10 August 1908 to Jacques Durand, cited in Lesure, "Debussy et le syndrome de Grenade," 106–7.

76. Debussy, letter of 26 February 1910 to André Caplet, in *Debussy Letters,* 217.

77. See the foreword to Debussy, *Préludes,* ed. Roy Howat with Claude Helffer, series 1, vol. 5 of *Oeuvres complètes de Claude Debussy,* xvii. Debussy wrote in a review that "few pieces of music are as good as *El Albaicín* . . . where one finds . . . the muffled sound of the guitar lamentingly playing to the night, with its sudden upsurges and nervous somersaults" (review of 1 December 1913 in bulletin of SIM, reprinted in *Debussy on Music,* ed. François Lesure, trans. and ed. Richard Langham Smith [New York: Knopf, 1977], 301), from which the quotation on Albéniz's sense of humor is taken.

78. See notes by Joan Brown to the Epic recording (SC 6058) of Albéniz, *Iberia* and *Navarra,* by Alicia de Larrocha.

79. The postcard is reproduced in François Lesure, *Claude Debussy,* vol. 4 of *Iconographie musicale* (Geneva: Minkoff, 1975), 180.

80. Debussy, letter of 14 July 1915 to Jacques Durand, in *Debussy Letters,* 297, letter of 4 February 1916 to Robert Golet, in *Debussy Letters,* 314.

81. Falla, "Notes on Maurice Ravel," *ISLA,* September 1939, reprinted in Falla, *On Music and Musicians,* 94. Maurice Ravel, interviewed by André Révész in *ABC de Madrid,* 1 May 1924; trans. in *A Ravel Reader: Correspondence, Articles, Interviews,* trans. and ed. Arbie Orenstein (New York: Columbia University Press, 1989), 431.

82. Laurence Davies, *Ravel: Orchestral Music* (Seattle: University of Washington Press, 1971), 12.

83. Debussy, for instance, wrote of Spain's folk and popular music, and even its Renaissance church music: "There is no reason why these traditions should have changed" (review of 1 December 1913, in *Debussy on Music,* 301).

84. I derive these attributions from Roger Nichols, *Ravel* (London: Dent, 1977), 147–48.

85. Ravel, interviewed by R. Bizet in *L'intransigeant,* 17 May 1911, reprinted in Orenstein, ed., *A Ravel Reader,* 412, 411.

86. According to Vladimir Jankélévitch, "*L'heure espagnole* . . . is rather Italian, with its *vocalises* and ornaments." See his *Ravel,* trans. Margaret Crosland (New York: Grove Press, 1959), 127.

87. By contrast, Debussy, after his youthful songs, never touched the bolero rhythm.

88. See Hans Heinz Stuckenschmidt, *Ravel: Variations on His Life and Work,* trans. Samuel R. Rosenbaum (Philadelphia: Chilton Books, 1968; original German ed., 1966), 230. On the phenomenon called *nacionalflamenquismo,* see William Washabaugh, "The Politics of Passion: Flamenco, Power, and the Body," *Journal of Musicological Research* 15, nos. 1–2 (1995): 95.

89. See Nichols, *Ravel,* 137.

90. Gautier, review of Rosa Espert and Joaquina Segura, August 1851, in "Gautier on Spanish Dancing," 65.

91. Falla, "Claude Debussy and Spain," in *On Music and Musicians,* 45.

92. On Falla's love of France and his hostility to Germany for its Protestantism, see Ramón Barce, "Profilo ideologico di Manuel de Falla," *Musica/Realtà* 42 (1993): esp. 41–45.

93. Burnett James, *Manuel de Falla and the Spanish Musical Renaissance* (London: Gollancz, 1979), 94.

94. Tomás Marco, *Spanish Music in the Twentieth Century,* trans. Cola Franzen (Cambridge, Mass.: Harvard University Press, 1993), 25.

95. Falla, *Mazurka,* ed. Antonio Gallego (Madrid: Manuel de Falla Ediciónes, 1992). In later works, the unfinished opera *Fuego fatuo* (1918–19) and the choral *Balada de Mallorca* (1933), he would take a different step, yoking Chopin's music to Spain.

96. Falla, "Igor Stravinsky, the Great Musician of Our Time," *La tribuna,* 5 June 1916, trans. in Falla, *On Music and Musicians,* 11. James considers the relationship of *El retablo* to Stravinsky in *Manuel de Falla,* 104–10.

97. He wrote of "La soirée dans Grenade": "Here we are actually given Andalusia, the truth without the authenticity, as it were" (Falla, "Claude Debussy and Spain," 42).

98. At the same time, Falla relied on his studies of music from other Mediterranean cultures and even from distant Asian ones in constructing the "Spanish" sound world of his music. This reliance was explored by Michael Christoforidis in a talk, "From the Gardens of the Alhambra to the Temples of Java: Oriental Perceptions and Appropriations in the Works of Manuel de Falla," given at the 1996 annual meeting of the American Musicological Society, Baltimore.

99. See, for example, Carol Hess, "Manuel de Falla's *The Three-Cornered Hat* and the Right-Wing Press in Pre–Civil War Spain," *Journal of Musicological Research* 15, nos. 1–2 (1995): 55–84.

100. Miles Davis, *Sketches of Spain,* arranged and conducted by Gil Evans, Columbia Records CS 8271. See Gunther Schuller's essay in this volume on European music as an exotic object to American Jazz musicians.

101. José Saramago, *The Stone Raft,* trans. Giovanni Pontiero (New York: Harcourt Brace, 1995; original ed., Lisbon: Caminho, 1986).

"ENTOILING THE FALCONET"

This essay originated as a contribution to a symposium, organized by the Dallas Opera and Southern Methodist University around the Opera's production of Borodin's *Prince Igor,* in November 1990. This chapter is a combined version of two pieces: "'Entoiling the Falconet': Russian Musical Orientalism in Context," *Cambridge Opera Journal* 4, no. 3 (1992): 253–80 and "Russian Musical Orientalism: A Postscript," *Cambridge Opera Journal* 6, no. 1 (1994): 81–84.

1. The genre had a quaint eighteenth-century forerunner in *Fevey* (1786), a *Singspiel* by Vasiliy Pashkevich to a libretto by Catherine the Great, which sports a chorus of "Kalmyk" (Mongolian) kumiss-drinkers.

2. "Dvadtsat' pyat' let russkogo iskusstvo: Nasha muzïka" (six installments; *Vestnik Yevropï,* 1882–83), rpt. in V. V. Stasov, *Izbrannïye sochineniya* (Moscow: Iskusstvo, 1952), 2:522–68; the discussion of the four points is on pp. 525–29. For a translation, see Piero Weiss and Richard Taruskin, *Music in the Western World: A History in Documents* (New York: Schirmer Books, 1984), 390–94.

3. *The Song of Igor's Campaign,* trans. Vladimir Nabokov (New York: Random House, 1960), 70.

4. For the complete list see Georgiy Ivanov, *Russkaya poèziya v otchestvennoy muzïke,* vol. 1 (Moscow: Muzïka, 1966), 288.

5. Mikhail Ivanovich Glinka, *Memoirs,* trans. Richard B. Mudge (Norman: University of Oklahoma Press, 1963), 47.

6. Side 3, bands 5 ("Machkal," duduks instrumental) and 6 (Shirak Folk Dance with Tara).

7. Hermann Laroche (German Larosh), "'Der Thurm zu Babel' Rubinshteyna," in Larosh, *Muzïkal'no-kriticheskiye stat'i* (St. Petersburg: Bessel, 1894), 117.

8. "Might seem," since on deeper reflection it might also seem a manifestation of a characteristic ambivalence that Russian composers (unlike French or German ones) felt toward "the Eastern theme." Russia was a contiguous empire in which Europeans, living side by side with "Orientals," identified (and intermarried) with them far more than in the case of the other colonial powers; and, as we have already learned from Stasov, Oriental coloration was one of the ways by which the composers of the "New Russian School" strove to distinguish themselves from those of Western Europe. It was simultaneously and ambiguously a Self-constructing and an Other-constructing trait. This irony will find an echo later in the present essay.

9. See Nabokov's commentary in Aleksandr Pushkin, *Eugene Onegin: A Novel in Verse,* trans. Vladimir Nabokov (New York: Pantheon Books, 1964), 2:186, where Nabokov speaks of the word's "emphasis on otiose euphoria and associations with softness, luxuriousness [and] tenderness." As an alternative he proposes "dulcitude."

10. Edward W. Said, *Orientalism* (New York: Pantheon Books, 1978), 196.

11. David Brown, *Mikhail Glinka: A Biographical and Critical Study* (London: Oxford University Press, 1974), 223.

12. *Eugene Onegin* 2:186.

13. Sergey Lyapunov, ed., *Perepiska M. A. Balakireva s P. I. Chaikovskim* (St. Petersburg: Zimmerman, 1912), 49–50.

14. N. I. Kompaneysky, "K novïm beregam: Modest Petrovich Musorgskiy" (originally published in the *Russkaya muzïkal'naya gazeta* in 1906), in E. M. Gordeyeva, ed., *M. P. Musorgskiy v vospominaniyakh sovremennikov* (Moscow: Muzïka, 1989), 126.

"I'M AN INDIAN TOO"

This article is a result of research undertaken for a Ph.D. dissertation, "Exotic Sounds in the Native Land: Portrayals of North American Indians in Western Music" (Eastman School of Music, University of Rochester, 1996), in which many of these issues are discussed in greater detail. I am grateful to Ralph P. Locke for his many insightful comments on this encapsulated version.

1. The associations of this figure with horse riding will be discussed later in the chapter.

2. Mick Gidley, "'The Vanishing Race' in Sight and Sound: Edward S. Curtis's Musicale of North American Indian Life," in *Prospects: An Annual of American Cultural Studies,* vol. 12 (Cambridge: Cambridge University Press, 1987), 60.

3. These plays have been surveyed separately as literature, drama, and cultural phenomenon. See Albert Keiser, *The Indian in American Literature* (New York: Oxford University Press, 1933), 65–100; David Grimsted, *Melodrama Unveiled: American Theater and Culture, 1800–1850* (Chicago: University of Chicago Press, 1968), 215–18; and Roy Pearce, *The Savages of America: A Study of the Indian and the Idea of Civilization,* rev. ed. (Baltimore: Johns Hopkins Press, 1965), 176–78.

4. Michael Castro, *Interpreting the Indian: Twentieth-Century Poets and the Native American* (Albuquerque: University of New Mexico Press, 1983), xvi.

5. Jon W. Finson, *The Voices That Are Gone: Themes in Nineteenth-Century American Popular Song* (New York: Oxford University Press, 1994), 246–55. On the *bel canto* tradition in popular song, see Charles Hamm, *Yesterdays: Popular Song in America* (New York: Norton, 1979), 62–88.

6. Many of Heinrich's works are either unpublished or found in original editions in special collections. The score of *Manitou Mysteries, or The Voice of the Great Spirit: Gran Sinfonia Misteriosa Indiana* has been edited by Sam Dennison in the series *The Symphony, 1720–1840,* ser. F, vol. 8 (New York: Garland, 1984).

7. Cecil Jones, "Policies and Practices of Wallack's Theatre, 1852–1888" (Ph.D. diss., University of Michigan, 1959), 90. For a discussion of the music of Brougham's parody, see William Brooks, "*Pocahontas*: Her Life and Times," *American Music* 2 (winter 1984): 19–48.

8. Castro, *Interpreting the Indian,* xvi.

9. See Roger Savage, "Rameau's American Dancers," *Early Music* 11, no. 4 (October 1983): 441–52.

10. Much of Lumbye's music, including the ballet, was lost in a fire. Orchestral musicians, apparently out of love for the composer, reconstructed some of the most popular works from surviving parts and "from memory." See liner notes by

Svend Erik Sorenson to "Hans Christian Lumbye: More Galops, Marches, and Dances" (Unicorn-Kanchara DKP-CD 9143).

11. According to Richard Storrs Willis in the (New York) *Musical World* 21, no. 4 (1859), 52.

12. Entry dated 8 January 1859 from *Life of Henry Wadsworth Longfellow, with Extracts from his Journals and Correspondence,* vol. 2, ed. Samuel Longfellow (Boston: Houghton Mifflin, 1851), [368].

13. Michael Pisani, "Robert Stoepel: A Musical Life in the Nineteenth-Century Theatre" (unpublished manuscript).

14. Unsigned review, "Dramatic Feuilleton" in the (New York) *Saturday Press,* 26 February 1859.

15. Robert Stevenson, "Written Sources for Indian Music until 1882," *Ethnomusicology* 17 (1973): 25.

16. Henry Wadsworth Longfellow to his father, 29 October 1837, letter at the Houghton Library, Harvard University.

17. Karl Krueger inverted the last two movements for the 1967 American Musical Heritage recording.

18. Further elaboration of these ideas may be found in Pisani, "Exotic Sounds," 99–100 and 116–19.

19. For an overview of the latter dance (apparently derived from the "sauvages des îles Canaries") and its rhythm as cited by Thoinot Arbeau (1589), see Willi Apel, *Harvard Dictionary of Music,* 2d ed. (Cambridge, Mass.: Belknap Press, 1972).

20. See Jonathan Bellman, *The* Style Hongrois *in the Music of Western Europe* (Boston: Northeastern University Press, 1993), 93–130, or for a brief treatment, section V of his essay in the present volume.

21. See Roger Fiske, *Scotland in Music: A European Enthusiasm* (Cambridge: Cambridge University Press, 1983).

22. Ralph L. Baldwin, *Wanita, or The Indian Maiden's Mission* (Boston: Miles and Thompson, 1892), esp. the Overture and Finale.

23. Philip Hale on "MacDowell's Suite and 'Indian Tunes,'" *Musical Courier* 32, no. 6 (5 February 1896): 23. Revised from a previous review in the *Boston Journal.*

24. John Philip Sousa, "The Red Man," from *Dwellers in the Western World* (1910; Cincinnati: John Church, 1916).

25. Theodore Baker, *Über die Musik der nordamerikanischen Wilden* (Leipzig, 1882), trans. Ann Buckley, *On the Music of the North American Indians* (New York: Da Capo Press, 1977).

26. William Tortolano, *Samuel Coleridge-Taylor: Anglo-Black Composer, 1875–1912* (Metuchen, N.J.: Scarecrow Press, 1977), 31.

27. Review by "H.F.," (London) *Musical Times,* 1 June 1924, 551.

28. Colin Taylor, "The Indian Hobbyist Movement in Europe," *History of Indian-White Relations,* vol. 4 of *Handbook of North American Indians* (Washington: Smithsonian Institution, 1988), 563.

29. See, for example, John Clapham, "Dvořák and the American Indian," *Musical Times* 107 (1966): 863–67, reprint in *Dvořák in America: 1892–1895,* ed. John C. Tibbetts (Portland, Ore.: Amadeus Press, 1993), 113–22, and Michael Beckerman's three articles: "Dvořák's 'New World' Largo and *The Song of Hia-*

watha," *Nineteenth-Century Music* 16 (1992): 35–48; "Henry Krehbiel, Antonín Dvořák, and the Symphony 'From the New World,'" *Notes* (December 1992): 447–73; and "The Dance of Pau-Puk-Keewis, the Song of Chibiabos, and the Story of Iagoo: Reflections on Dvořák's 'New World' Scherzo," in Tibbetts, ed., *Dvořák in America,* 210–27. The evidence that "Hiawatha's Wooing" (canto 10) and "Hiawatha's Wedding-Feast" (canto 11) musically shaped the second and third movements of the Ninth Symphony seems to me incontrovertible. The associations in the scherzo have been most convincingly presented. For the *largo,* even Beckerman's well-argued suggestions—as well as those of James Hepokoski, who proposes a different scenario—remain largely speculative. See Hepokoski, "Culture Clash," *Musical Times* (December 1993): 685–88. Most of these articles, and exhaustive documentation on this symphony, can be found in Robert Winter's interactive CD-ROM *Antonín Dvořák, Symphony in E Minor* (Irvington, N.Y.: Voyager, 1994).

30. See Beckerman's chart that correlates Longfellow's text with parallel passages in Dvořák's music in "Dance of Pau-Puk-Keewis," 214–15.

31. Horace Greeley, "The Plains: As I Crossed Them Ten Years Ago," in *Harper's Magazine* (1869), excerpted in *Harper's: An American Perspective, 1850–1984,* ed. Ann Marie Cunningham (New York: Harper's, 1985), 92.

32. Joan Mark, *A Stranger in Her Native Land: Alice Fletcher and the American Indians* (Lincoln: University of Nebraska Press, 1988), 16–17.

33. We can find this device in popular use as recently as Billy Joel's "Ballad of Billy the Kid" (1973).

34. See Pisani, "The Indian Music Debate and 'American' Music in the Progressive Era" *College Music Symposium* 37 (Fall 1997) for a more detailed explanation of the connection between Fletcher, Fillmore, and Dvořák.

35. As a footnote to the published piano vocal score of his cantata *Hiawatha* (1898), Burton writes, "the theme of this number, comprised in the first nine measures, is a song of the Kwakiutl Indians. I am indebted for it to Mr. H. E. Krehbiel who took it down in the course of observing one of the tribal ceremonies." See also Krehbiel, "Folk-Music in Chicago, II: Cannibal Songs of the Indians," *New York Tribune,* Sunday, 6 August 1893, 2:14. The Kwakiutl "Hamatsa" may in fact be one of four such Hamatsas recorded at the fair on cylinder by Benjamin Ives Gilman. See Dorothy Sara Lee, *The Federal Cylinder Project,* vol. 8 (Washington, D.C.: American Folklife Center of the Library of Congress, 1984), 33–34.

Burton wrote in his posthumously published *American Primitive Music* (New York: Moffat, Yard, 1909), 190: "The 'Dance of Pau-Puk-Keewis' . . . was written years before I had become an enthusiast in our primitive music. For the limited purpose it was designed to serve, the Indian theme was decidedly useful, and development was spontaneous." Burton does not give many dates, so it is difficult to pinpoint exactly when he "had become an enthusiast." He does mention, in conjunction with his study of Miss Fletcher's Omaha publication, that "I was then at work on the composition of 'Hiawatha,' and that I wished to give the music a distinctively American color" (19).

36. Though the Library of Congress catalog dates Burton's manuscript orchestral score of this work as 1882, the actual score of the movement is not dated, nor is there a library deposit stamp. It could not have been composed before 1893.

37. Alice Fletcher, *Indian Story and Song from North America* (Boston: Small, Maynard, 1900; rpt., New York: AMS Press, 1970), vii.

38. Ibid., viii, ix.

39. Nina Marchetti Archabal, "Frances Densmore: Pioneer in the Study of American Indian Music," in *Women of Minnesota: Selected Biographical Essays* (St. Paul: Minnesota Historical Society Press, 1977), 98.

40. Willard Rhodes, "On the Warpath, 1942," *Modern Music* 20, no. 3 (March–April 1943): 160.

41. Boris Asafiev, *Musical Form as a Process* (Leningrad, 1963), cited in Carl Dahlhaus, *Nineteenth-Century Music* (1980), trans. J. Bradford Robinson (Berkeley and Los Angeles: University of California Press, 1989), 38.

42. "Navajo War Dance," from *From Mesa and Plain: Indian, Cowboy, and Negro Sketches,* five pieces for piano (Wa-Wan Press 4, no. 28, 1905) was actually the second such-titled work Farwell wrote. An earlier unpublished *Navajo War Dance* (1904) was edited by John Kirkpatrick in 1940 and later published as *Navajo War Dance No. 2* (Music Press, 1947).

43. Harvey W. Loomis, "Around the Wigwam" and "Chattering Squaw" from *Lyrics of the Red Man,* the former from book 1 (Newton Center, Mass.: Wa-Wan Press, 1903), the latter from book 2 (Newton Center, Mass.: Wa-Wan Press, 1904). Both are reprinted, ed. Vera Brodsky Lawrence (New York: Arno Press, 1970). Angelo Read, the Canadian composer and conductor, illustrated melodic similarities between "Indian music" and "Asiatic music" in a *Musical America* article of 13 July 1907. The idea of Native American descent from Asiatic tribes, expressed elsewhere during this period, were aligned with those of Francis E. Leupp, Theodore Roosevelt's Commissioner of Indian Affairs, and other race fusionists.

44. Brian W. Dippie, *The Vanishing American: White Attitudes and American Indian Policy in the Nineteenth Century* (Middletown, Conn.: Wesleyan University Press, 1982), 250.

45. See Farwell's ideological writings in *The Wa-Wan Press,* ed. Vera Brodsky Lawrence (New York: Arno Press, 1970) as well as Edward N. Waters's critical discussion "The Wa-Wan Press: An Adventure in Musical Idealism," in *A Birthday Offering to Carl Engel,* ed. Gustave Reese (New York: Schirmer, 1943), esp. 220–24.

46. The most inclusive study of the operas is Harold Briggs, "The North American Indian as Depicted in Musical Compositions, Culminating with American 'Indianist' Operas of the Early Twentieth Century, 1900–1930" (masters thesis, Indiana University, 1977).

47. Herbert's *Natoma* set the stage for dozens of other operas on Indian subjects, though only one of these, Cadman's *Shanewis,* first given at the New York Metropolitan in 1918, had proved a legitimate rival in the number of subsequent performances.

48. *Hiawatha,* dir. Carl Laemmle (1909), filmed on locale in Minnesota, and *Hiawatha,* dir. F. E. Moore (1913), with a musical score arranged from Ojibwa Indian music by John Braham.

49. *Boston Advocate* (December 1916) as quoted in Robert Joseph Garofalo, "The Life and Works of Frederick Shepherd Converse" (Ph.D. diss., Catholic University of America, 1969), 79; revised and published as *Frederick Shepherd Converse (1871–1940): His Life and Music* (Metuchen, N.J.: Scarecrow Press, 1995).

50. "Music of Frederick S. Converse," *Christian Science Monitor,* 15 January 1910, quoted in Nicholas E. Tawa, *Mainstream Music of Early Twentieth-Century America: The Composers, Their Times, and Their Works* (Westport, Conn.: Greenwood Press, 1992), 24.

51. Converse would later turn to the Hopi legend of creation in "Bright Angel Trail" from his orchestral *American Sketches* (1928).

52. The use of a borrowed tune serves less as allusion (since the melody would not likely be recognizable by a non-Cheyenne audience) than as the representation of a narrator, signifying the composer's authorial "voice" each time it reappears.

53. *The Indians' Book,* recorded and edited by Natalie Curtis (1st ed. 1907), 2d ed. (New York: Harper, 1923; rpt., New York: Dover, 1958), 153.

54. Ibid., 319.

55. Curtis, "Busoni's Indian Fantasy," *Southern Workman* 44 (1915), 540.

56. I use the term "American West" here in the sense of a construct. Clearly, the musical feature of the rising 5 to 6 over a tonic major and a submediant minor have been used in European music as well, notably by Edvard Grieg in the "Morning" music from *Peer Gynt.*

57. From the notebooks of Martha Graham. Cited by Marta Robertson, "Scores of Evidence: Martha Graham's Musical Collaborations," unpublished paper read at the Sonneck Society Conference in Madison, Wisconsin, April 1995.

58. An entirely separate semiotic use of open fifths, a result of nineteenth-century historical interest in medieval and Renaissance music, can be seen, for example, in some works of Paul Hindemith. This usage also penetrated art music in the United States in the 1930s and 1940s in the music of Roy Harris, Samuel Barber, and others.

59. Charles Wakefield Cadman, "The American Indian's Music Idealized," *Etude* 38, no. 10 (October 1920): 659–60.

60. Laurie Anderson, "Hiawatha," from *Strange Angels,* Warner Brothers CD 25900 (1989).

"THE EAST IN THE WEST"

1. Henry Cowell, "Current Chronicle," *Musical Quarterly* 34 (July 1948): 412.

2. Edward Lockspeiser, *Debussy: His Life and Mind,* 2d ed. (Cambridge: Cambridge University Press, 1978), 1:208.

3. Photographs of dances witnessed by Debussy are reproduced in Anik Devries, "Les musiques d'Extrême-Orient à l'Exposition Universelle de 1889," *Cahiers Debussy,* n.s., 1 (1977): 25–37.

4. Neil Sorrell, *A Guide to the Gamelan* (London: Faber and Faber, 1990), 2.

5. Richard Mueller, "Javanese Influence on Debussy's *Fantaisie* and Beyond," *Nineteenth-Century Music* 10, no. 2 (fall 1986): 158; Julien Tiersot, *Musiques pittoresques: Promenades musicales à l'Exposition de 1889* (Paris: Librairie Fischbacher, 1889); Louis Bénédictus, *Les musiques bizarres à l'Exposition* (Paris: G. Hartmann, 1889).

6. The full text of the letter is to be found in *Debussy Letters,* ed. François Lesure and Roger Nichols (Cambridge, Mass.: Harvard University Press, 1987), 76.

7. Lockspeiser, *Debussy* 1:115. Lockspeiser's comments on the gamelan appear-

ances at the 1889 and 1900 Expositions are not entirely reliable: he reports that the ensemble attending the 1900 festivities was "apparently the Solo gamelan from Bali." Solo (synonymous with Surakarta) is, of course, in Java.

8. Robert Orledge, *Debussy in the Theatre* (Cambridge: Cambridge University Press, 1982), 190.

9. Mueller, "Javanese Influence," 162–73. See also Roy Howat's dismissal of Mueller's claim in his article "Debussy and the Orient" in *Recovering the Orient: Artists, Scholars, Appropriations,* ed. Andrew Gerstle and Anthony Milner (London: Harwood, 1995), 48, n. 10. For further discussion of the Javanese influence on Debussy, see Jürgen Arndt, *Der Einfluß der javanischen Gamelan-Musik auf Kompositionen von Claude Debussy* (Frankfurt: P. Lang, 1993).

10. Quoted in Roger Nichols, *Debussy* (Oxford: Oxford University Press, 1972), 7. Even the conservative Saint-Saëns had borrowed the Arab *hijāz* mode (with its augmented second between second and third scale degrees) for exotic tonal coloring in *Samson et Dalila* two years before making this remark: see Ralph P. Locke, "Constructing the Oriental 'Other,'" *Cambridge Opera Journal* 3, no. 3 (1991): 266–68.

11. According to Léon Pillaut's article "Le gamelan Javanais" in the 3 July 1887 issue of *Le ménestrel,* the two lowest punctuating gongs in the Paris Conservatoire's gamelan were tuned to pitches approximating to F♯ and B.

12. For further examples, see Howat, "Debussy and the Orient," 54–56.

13. E. J. Dent, "The Pianoforte and Its Influence on Modern Music," *Musical Quarterly* 2 (1916): 271–94.

14. Quoted in Roger Nichols, ed., *Debussy Remembered* (Portland, Ore.: Amadeus Press, 1992), 171.

15. Malcolm Gillies, ed., *Bartók Remembered* (New York: Norton, 1990), 118.

16. Carol Oja, *Colin McPhee: Composer in Two Worlds* (Washington, D.C.: Smithsonian Institution Press, 1990), 153, 179.

17. Letter dated 1 October 1932; see Sidney Buckland, ed., *Francis Poulenc, "Echo and Source": Selected Correspondence, 1915–1963* (London: Gollancz, 1991), 97.

18. Ibid., 236.

19. The system in question here (Javanese *pelog,* Balinese *saih pitu*) is in fact heptatonic in theory, but often pentatonic in practice.

20. Francis Poulenc, "Hommage à Benjamin Britten," in *A Tribute to Benjamin Britten on his Sixtieth Birthday,* ed. Anthony Gishford (London: Faber and Faber, 1963), 3.

21. See Teresa Balough, *A Complete Catalogue of the Works of Percy Grainger* (Nedlands: University of Western Australia Press, 1975), 91.

22. Teresa Balough, *A Musical Genius from Australia* (Nedlands: University of Western Australia, Department of Music, 1982), 78.

23. Quoted in Wilfrid Mellers, *Percy Grainger* (Oxford: Oxford University Press, 1992), 142.

24. The full texts of all twelve lectures are to be found in John Blacking, *"A Commonsense View of All Music": Reflections on Percy Grainger's Contribution to Ethnomusicology and Music Education* (Cambridge: Cambridge University Press, 1987), appendix A.

25. Balough, *A Complete Catalogue,* 234.

26. McPhee's time on the island is vividly chronicled in his book *A House in Bali* (New York: John Day, 1947).

27. Colin McPhee, *Tabuh-Tabuhan* (1936; New York: Associated Music Publishers, 1960), 3.

28. McPhee, *A House in Bali,* 203.

29. The recording made by Britten and McPhee contains five pieces for two pianos, along with two transcriptions for flute and piano (one of which, "Lagu Ardja," had formed the melodic basis for the slow movement of McPhee's *Tabuh-tabuhan).* In addition to the three movements of the *Balinese Ceremonial Music* ("Pemoengkah," "Gambangan," and "Taboeh Teloe"), Britten and McPhee recorded two unpublished numbers ("Rebong" and "Lagu Delem"). It appears that Schirmer originally planned to publish a second set of transcriptions (advertized in McPhee, *A House in Bali,* 214), but this projected volume failed to materialize.

30. Although gamelan instruments were known in the United Kingdom during the nineteenth century and their tuning systems studied as early as 1885, the first instance of a specific allusion to the gamelan in the work of an English composer appears to date from the late 1930s, shortly before Britten's first involvement with Indonesian music. The work in question is Michael Tippett's Piano Sonata No. 1 (1936–38), which contains in the fifth variation of its first movement a fleeting reference to the same Balinese tuning system as that imitated by Poulenc (example 9.1c). Tippett had been lent a recorded anthology of ethnic musics by Aubrey Russ, and in borrowing material from a gramophone record he anticipated the later work of Grainger and Britten. It was not until 1978, however, that Tippett found the opportunity to visit Indonesia for himself, on which occasion the experience of live gamelan performances left its mark on his Triple Concerto. In the following year a gamelan first made an appearance at the BBC Promenade Concerts.

31. Prince Ludwig of Hesse, *Ausflug Ost* (Darmstadt: privately printed, 1956). Brief extracts from the diary were published in English translation in Gishford, ed., *A Tribute to Benjamin Britten,* 56–65. A detailed account of Britten's activities in Indonesia is to be found in Mervyn Cooke, *Britten and the Far East,* Aldeburgh Studies in Music no. 4 (Woodbridge: Boydell and Brewer, 1997), chapter 3.

32. Unpublished letter from Britten to Imogen Holst, 17 January 1956. © The Britten-Pears Foundation.

33. *Ausflug Ost,* 65. Prince Ludwig notes that three further pieces were recorded that same afternoon in his absence.

34. For further discussion of this topic, see Mervyn Cooke, "Britten and the Gamelan: Balinese Influences in *Death in Venice,*" *Benjamin Britten: "Death in Venice,"* ed. Donald Mitchell (Cambridge: Cambridge University Press, 1987), 115–28.

35. Mueller, "Javanese Influence," 177–78.

36. Oja, *Colin McPhee,* 93.

37. *Modern Music* 23 (1946): 111–15.

38. *Musical Quarterly* 35 (April 1949): 250–81; Oja, *Colin McPhee,* 166.

39. Steve Reich, "Postscript to a Brief Study of Balinese and African Music, 1973," in *Writings about Music* (Halifax: Press of the the Nova Scotia College of Art and Design, 1974), 38.

40. *Ô Bali: Colin McPhee and His Legacy* (MVCD 1057, 1993). Composers represented are Jose Evangelista, Mark Duggan, Jon Siddall, and Andrew Timar.

41. Henry Cowell, "Towards Neo-Primitivism," *Modern Music* 10 (1933): 150–51.

42. Personal communication from Britten's librettist, the late Mrs. Myfanwy Piper.

43. Philip Brett, "Eros and Orientalism in Britten's Operas," in *Queering the Pitch: The New Gay and Lesbian Musicology,* ed. Philip Brett, Elizabeth Wood, and Gary Thomas (New York: Routledge, 1994), 235–56.

44. Sorrell, *A Guide to the Gamelan,* 3.

45. Donald Mitchell, "An Afterword on Britten's *Pagodas*: The Balinese Sources," *Tempo* 152 (March 1985): 9, n. 4.

JAZZ AND MUSICAL EXOTICISM

1. See Gunther Schuller, *Early Jazz* (New York: Oxford University Press, 1968), appendix, 359–72.

2. While Joplin's piano rolls give little indication of any kind of swing, that is most likely due to the medium; piano rolls were uniformly incapable reproducing anything even close to swing. The Welte recordings in the 1920s would have been able to catch some of touch, articulation, swing—but they never "recorded" any Ragtime or Jazz musicians. The Armstrong variety of swing was in fact an updating, of a decade or so later, of what the Ragtimers were doing, that is, *how* they were phrasing the syncopations. The "earlier sedate form" of swing as practiced by the ragtimers was slightly stiffer, still more dependent on "classical" syncopations, than Armstrong's later version, which had a looser, more spontaneous feeling, more energy, and thus much more swing.

3. For more on the development of Ragtime (and Jazz) syncopation and its African derivation, see Schuller, *Early Jazz,* 18–26.

4. Aaron Copland, *The New Music, 1900–1960* (originally *Our New Music,* 1941; rev. ed., New York: Norton, 1968), 63–64.

5. As for example in the *Musical Digest* 13, no. 3 (1928): 49, 51; included in Arbie Orenstein, *A Ravel Reader* (New York: Columbia University Press, 1990), 390.

6. In an unsigned article from 1929 in the Bern, Switzerland, newspaper *Der Bund,* Ravel is quoted as follows on the relationship of Jazz to the machine age: "But technology, machinery, and industry, in their contemporary incarnation, can also be interpreted by artistic means, and for that purpose we certainly don't need the deafening noise of jazz. It would be unfortunate if only the ultramoderns were right: jazz might serve many of us as entertainment, *but it has nothing in common with art*" (quoted ibid., 466; emphasis added). With regard to its supposed decreasing importance, he said in a 1931 Paris interview, "But jazz influence is waning. Gypsy music has returned to Paris, together with the whirling waltz, which I have often paid homage to" (quoted ibid., 473).

7. Stravinsky, also in America around the same time—invited as well by Stokowski—did not get introduced to real Jazz; whether for lack of interest on his part or lack of opportunity, it is hard to say.

8. Ernest Ansermet, "Bechet and Jazz Visit Europe, 1919," in Ralph de Toledano, *Frontiers of Jazz* ([New York]: Oliver Durrell, 1947), 121–22.

INDIAN RESONANCES IN THE BRITISH INVASION

This study was read (in abbreviated form) at the national meeting of the U.S. chapter of the International Society for the Study of Popular Music in Denver, Colorado, on 4 October 1996. It has also previously appeared in somewhat longer form in the *Journal of Musicology* 15, no. 1 (winter 1997). I am indebted to Joel Bellman, F. Susan Fast, Ralph Locke, and D. MacLaughlan for their comments and suggestions, and to the first of those individuals in particular for crucial research assistance.

1. This "American Indianist" Rock strain is not to be confused with the later Native American "nationalist" work, such as Jim Pepper's "Witchi-tai-to" and the music of the band Redbone (although Redbone was not composed only of Native Americans). The Shadows were a British group, having formerly backed the "UK Elvis," Cliff Richard.

2. This song, a textless version of which had been a hit for the Weavers in the early 1950s, was widely covered later on, by artists as diverse as the New Christy Minstrels (a somewhat kitschy early-60s folk-pop treatment), Robert John (a slick, bubble-gum version), Brian Eno (all instrumental accompaniment was synthesized), the Nylons (an expert a capella treatment), and Ladysmith Black Mambazo (wherein this low-to-middlebrow Western pop tune is given a dignified rendition by traditional African singers).

3. Issue of 22 August 1964, cited in Jon Savage, *The Kinks: The Official Biography* (London: Faber and Faber, 1984), 58.

4. John Platt, Chris Dreja, and Jim McCarty, *Yardbirds* (London: Sidgwick and Jackson, 1983), 50.

5. The phrase "Raga Rock" was apparently the invention of a publicist, who was characterizing the Byrds' (an American group) single "Eight Miles High" (March 1966), which supposedly made use of a sitar. This catchphrase eventually came to describe any Rock song that evoked an Indian or generally Oriental mood, whether by use of sitar or another instrument imitating it (Lillian Roxon, *Lillian Roxon's Rock Encyclopedia* [New York: Tempo Books, 1971], 398).

The Byrds' lead singer, Roger McGuinn, offered an interesting insight on the band's exposure to Indian music when interviewed for the 1995 PBS television documentary *Rock and Roll.* He explained that in the early days (1964–65) the band had been recording at World Pacific Studios, house studio of World Pacific Records. Their producer at the time, Jim Dickson, introduced them to some of the world music that the label also featured, including Ravi Shankar. It is hard to tell exactly what came first at this point, since (as will be seen) other Indian-influenced pop songs had already been released by the time "Eight Miles High" was recorded, in December 1965 and January 1966. Another "Indian" aspect of "Eight Miles High," incidentally, is the four-note guitar figure that functions as transition from the opening harmonic background to the song proper: it is lifted from John Coltrane's "India" (Robert Palmer, *Rock & Roll: An Unruly History* [New York: Harmony Books, 1995], 165).

6. Although these songs were released as album tracks and single B-sides by the Beatles, the involvement of John Lennon, Paul McCartney, and Ringo Starr in Harrison's Indian-influenced songs ranged from slight to nonexistent.

7. There are recent examples of this familiar oversight. The 1995 PBS *Rock and Roll* documentary mentioned only Harrison and Shankar in the context of Indian influences on English musicians in the mid-1960s. In *The Beatle Anthology,* another much-publicized TV documentary of the same year, Harrison wearily rehearsed a somewhat shorter version of the story that appeared in the Timothy White interview, cited immediately below; contemporaries went unmentioned.

8. Timothy White, "A Portrait of the Artist," *Billboard* (5 December 1992), 23.

9. Ibid.

10. Ibid.

11. Harrison played guitar and sang, Anil Bhagwat played tabla, and although it has been assumed that Harrison also played sitar, recently discovered notes from the recording session seem to indicate that another member of the Asian Music Circle played it. See Mark Lewisohn, *The Complete Beatles Chronicle* (New York: Harmony Books, 1992), 217.

12. Wilfrid Mellers also remarks on this unadventurous use of the sitar in *The Music of the Beatles: Twilight of the Gods* (New York: Schirmer Books, 1973), 59–60.

13. A large proportion of Rock songs are based on three chords, and some songs on two, but to use *one* is highly atypical. It can also happen in Funk music, but Funk is a very different style.

14. Bonnie C. Wade, *Music in India: The Classical Traditions* (Englewood Cliffs, N.J.: Prentice-Hall, 1979), 240.

15. Savage, *The Kinks,* 57–58. For dating of the trip to India, see p. 46.

16. John Mendelssohn, *The Kink Kronikles: An Unauthorized—and Uncensored—History of the Second Longest-Lived Group in Rock* (New York: Quill, 1985), 59.

17. Savage, *The Kinks,* 58.

18. Ibid., 58.

19. Ray Davies, in his "unauthorized autobiography" *X-Ray* (1994; London: Penguin Books, 1995), a fictionalized treatment of the early years of the Kinks, speaks very highly of Fantoni and mentions his early proximity to and friendship with him. This particular incident is not mentioned. In any case, Davies himself, oddly, does not seem to care much about pioneering the Raga Rock genre. He discusses the songs, sometimes in detail ("See My Friends" on pp. 204–5 and 275–76 and "Fancy" on pp. 40 and 274), but betrays no interest in the later development of the genre. This is particularly interesting because it is obvious from the book that a sense of competition with the Beatles was keenly felt.

20. Ibid., 173; Paul Gambaccini, Tim Rice, and Jonathan Rice, eds., *British Hit Singles,* 8th ed. (New York: Billboard, 1991), 153; Dave McAleer, compiler, *The All Music Book of Hit Singles: Top 20 Charts from 1954 to the Present Day* (San Francisco: Miller Foreman Books, 1994), 110.

21. Savage, *The Kinks,* 173.

22. A postcolonialist critic might point out that such a beat is more reminiscent of traditional evocations of the Arab world, not India, and that this kind of pan-Eastern exoticism, lumping together only barely related gestures in one exotic whole, represents a kind of us-versus-everybody else colonialism. Such a critic would be right but, rightly or wrongly, it does not matter; the addition of that

evocative beat in a Western pop song provides an exotic center off which the other exotic gestures can play.

23. Savage, *The Kinks,* 174, 80.

24. Hunter Davies, *The Beatles* [revision of 1968 authorized biography] (New York: McGraw-Hill, 1978), 357; John Mendelssohn, liner notes to *Kink Kronikles,* a 1972 Warner Brothers double album anthology of the Kinks' music.

25. Lewisohn, *Complete Beatles Chronicle,* 217.

26. McAleer, *The All Music Book of Hit Singles,* 110.

27. Platt et al., *Yardbirds,* 55.

28. This version is available on the Yardbirds, *Greatest Hits,* vol. 2: *Blues, Backtracks, and Shapes of Things to Come.* CD. Legacy Records 48658.

29. Felix Aeppli, *Heart of Stone: The Definitive Rolling Stones Discography, 1962–1983* (Ann Arbor, Mich.: Pierian Press, 1985), 81–82. On the other hand, a kind of residual Indian feel is acknowledged by the silly caricature of five Indians that graced the sleeve of the single version released in Spain, May 1966, which is shown in Aeppli, 88.

30. Nonetheless, Ray Davies's *X-Ray* gives no impression of friendship between the Kinks and the Beatles, just a sense of competitiveness and distrust.

31. Krishna Singh, "How Does Meditation Work?" in *Maharishi: The Guru,* ed. Martin Ebon (New York: Signet Books, 1968), 33.

32. Bill Harry, ed., *The Ultimate Beatles Encyclopedia* (New York: Hyperion, 1992), 427–28.

33. Richard Poirier, "Learning from the Beatles," *Partisan Review* 34, no. 4 (fall 1967): 534.

34. Ibid., 541.

35. Ebon, be it said, was last sighted as a "historian of Santa Claus" on a *Biography* episode on the Arts & Entertainment cable TV channel.

36. Singh, "How Does Meditation Work?" in Ebon, ed., *Maharishi,* 35–36.

37. Chester Butterworth, "The Beatles Without Mask," in Ebon, ed., *Maharishi,* 56.

38. Don McNeill, "'He Turned Us On!'" in Ebon, ed., *Maharishi,* 94.

39. James Crenshaw, "Beyond 'Pot' and LSD," in Ebon, ed., *Maharishi,* 100.

40. This song's light touch shows the same music hall influences found in Paul McCartney's work.

41. The methods by which this *accelerando* takes place are discussed in Wade, *Music in India,* 121. For purposes of comparison, the corresponding increase in rhythmic density without an actual *accelerando* that characterizes Karnatic (South Indian) performances is discussed on 126–27.

42. Ray Davies, interview with Maureen Cleave, quoted in Savage, *The Kinks,* 60. Davies offers a longer and somewhat more vague discussion of "See My Friends" in *X-Ray,* 275–76.

43. Savage, *The Kinks,* 80.

44. Ibid., 60.

45. John Lennon's one truly exotic work is, however, both an LSD song and a religious song, and it excited nowhere near the interest Harrison's songs did. This is "Tomorrow Never Knows," from the 1966 album *Revolver,* a song for which

Lennon requested some kind of apparatus that would make him sound like the Dalai Lama singing from a hilltop. The strategy involved recording his voice through a revolving Leslie speaker, then adding many overdubs, tape loops, tracks of Paul McCartney and Ringo Starr playing bass and drums in rhythmic unison, one organ note played continuously, two guitar solos (one also put through a Leslie speaker and the other distorted), and a honky-tonk piano (Lewisohn, *Complete Beatles Chronicle*, 70–71). Lennon supposedly wrote this on LSD (Paul called it "an LSD song, probably the only one"), and for his lyrics used material from Timothy Leary's version of the Tibetan *Book of the Dead.* The words were thus far closer to the real thing than anything Harrison or the others had done. The music was totally uncommercial, however, and thus it was not the song to start or continue a trend.

46. The guitarist Ry Cooder's CDs *Talkin' Timbuktu* (Hannibal 1381, with Ali Farka Toure) and *A Meeting by the River* (Water Lily Acoustics 29, with Vishwa Mohan Bhatt) illustrate this more subtle approach.

CONTRIBUTORS

LINDA PHYLLIS AUSTERN is currently Visiting Associate Professor in the School of Music at the University of Iowa. She has published extensively on sixteenth- and seventeenth-century musical topics including gender theory and cultural criticism in such journals as the *Journal of the American Musicological Society, Renaissance Quarterly,* the *Journal of the Royal Musical Association, Music and Letters,* and the *Journal of Musicology.* Her book *Music in English Children's Drama of the Later Renaissance* appeared with the Gordon and Breach Monographs in Musicology series, and she is currently completing a two-volume study of music in sixteenth- and seventeenth-century English intellectual culture. She has been awarded fellowships from the American Council of Learned Societies, the British Academy, the Mary Ingraham Bunting Institute of Radcliffe College, the Andrew Mellon Foundation, the National Endowment for the Humanities, and the Newberry Library of Chicago.

JONATHAN BELLMAN is Associate Professor of Music at the University of Northern Colorado. His book on the Hungarian Gypsy style, *The* Style Hongrois *in the Music of Western Europe,* was published by Northeastern University Press in 1993, and he is currently writing a college text, *A Short Guide to Writing about Music.* He has published articles on Chopin, nineteenth-century piano performance practices, and nineteenth-century musical style in such publications as the *Journal of Musicology, Historical Performance,* and *Piano and Keyboard.* A pianist as well as musicologist, he continues to perform occasionally and has recorded two CDs of his own compositions for use in ballet studios.

MERVYN COOKE studied at the Royal Academy of Music, London, and as a Scholar at King's College, Cambridge, where he completed a doctoral thesis on the Oriental influences on Benjamin Britten. He was for six years Research Fellow and Director of Music at Fitzwilliam College, Cambridge, before being appointed Lecturer in Music at the University of Nottingham in 1993. His recent publications include books on Britten's *Billy Budd* and *War Requiem* (both for Cambridge University Press), a monograph *Britten and the Far East* (Boydell and Brewer) and two volumes on Jazz (Thames and Hudson); he is currently editing *The Cambridge Companion to Britten* and co-editing the third volume of Britten's letters. He is also active as a pianist and composer; his compositions have been broadcast on BBC Radio 3 and Radio France and performed at London's South Bank.

MARY HUNTER is Chair of the Music Department at Bowdoin College. She has written a number of essays on late eighteenth-century opera, has co-edited, with James Webster, *Opera Buffa in Mozart's Vienna* (Cambridge, 1997), and is the author of *The Poetics of Entertainment: Comedy, Convention, Class, and Gender in Vienna's Opera Buffa* (Princeton University Press, forthcoming).

RALPH P. LOCKE is Professor of Musicology at the University of Rochester's Eastman School of Music. He is an editorial board member of the *Journal of Musicological Research* and senior editor of Eastman Studies in Music, a series of the University of Rochester Press. His writings include *Music, Musicians, and the Saint-Simonians* (University of Chicago Press, 1986), now available also in French translation. Three of his articles on music and society received the ASCAP–Deems Taylor Award in 1992 and 1996. His current research interests include the portrayal of the non-Western world in European and American opera and instrumental music, and the nature and funding of America's musical institutions. He has co-edited with Cyrilla Barr (and contributed several essays to) a forthcoming collective volume, *Cultivating Music in America: Women Patrons and Activists since 1860* (University of California Press, 1977).

JAMES PARAKILAS is Professor of Music and Chair of the Humanities Division at Bates College. Trained as a musicologist at Cornell University, he is the author of *Ballads Without Words: Chopin and the Tradition of the Instrumental Ballade* (Amadeus Press, 1992) and the editor of the anthology *The 19th-Century Piano Ballade* (A-R Editions, 1990); he has also published articles on nineteenth-century opera and piano music and on uses of the musical canon. Currently he is at work on a study of religious themes in nineteenth-century opera, is co-editor of the *Journal of Musicological Research,* and is one of the directors planning Piano 300, a nationwide project marking the three-hundredth anniversary of the invention of the piano.

MICHAEL V. PISANI is Assistant Professor of Music at Vassar College. He has written articles on Prokofiev and several American composers and is also writing a book on music and melodrama in the nineteenth-century theater. A pianist and conductor as well as musicologist, he has conducted and coached for a number of American and European opera houses, among them the Houston Grand Opera, the Seattle Opera, and the Opera Company of Boston. As a pianist, he played under Leonard Bernstein, who invited him to prepare the casts for the European productions of his opera *A Quiet Place* at La Scala and the Vienna State Opera.

GUNTHER SCHULLER is a composer, conductor, teacher, Jazz historian, and author who was a horn prodigy before he gave up playing to become a full-time composer. Winner of a MacArthur Fellowship in 1991 and the Pulitzer Prize in 1994, he has composed over two hundred works in many idioms, coining the term "Third Stream" along the way. He has conducted many of the world's major ensembles and was head of the Berkshire Music Center at Tanglewood for twenty years. Schuller is the author of five books, including the renowned Jazz histories *Early Jazz* and *The Swing Era.*

RICHARD TARUSKIN is Professor of Music at the University of California, Berkeley. His most recent books include *Musorgsky: Eight Essays and an Epilogue* (Princeton University Press, 1993), *Text and Act* (Oxford University Press, 1995), and *Stravinsky and the Russian Traditions* (University of California Press, 1996). His articles have appeared in the *New York Times*, the *New Republic*, and many scholarly journals.

MIRIAM K. WHAPLES is Professor of Musicology at the University of Massachusetts, Amherst. Her dissertation, "Exoticism in Dramatic Music, 1600–1800," was the first systematic study of musical exoticism. She has published an edition of songs from the medieval *Carmina burana*, the *Bach Aria Index*, and articles on Schubert, Mahler, Bach, and Ockeghem.

INDEX OF NAMES AND WORKS

Page numbers in italic indicate musical examples.